An Islamic Perspective on Governance

NEW HORIZONS IN MONEY AND FINANCE

Series Editor: Mervyn K. Lewis, *University of South Australia*

This important series is designed to make a significant contribution to the shaping and development of thinking in finance .The series will provide an invaluable forum for the publication of high quality works of scholarship on a breadth of topics ranging from financial markets and financial systems to monetary policy and banking reform, and will show the diversity of theory, issues and practices.

The focus of the series is on the development and application of new original ideas in finance. Rigorous and often path-breaking in its approach, it will pay particular attention to the international and comparative dimension of finance and will include innovative theoretical and empirical work from both well-established authors and the new generation of scholars.

Titles in the series include:

Banking Reforms in South-East Europe
Edited by Zeljko Sevic

Russian Banking
Evolution, Problems and Prospects
Edited by David Lane

Currency Crises
A Theoretical and Empirical Perspective
André Fourçans and Raphaël Franck

East Asia's Monetary Future
Integration in the Global Economy
Suthiphand Chirathivat, Emil-Maria Claassen and Jürgen Schroeder

Reforming China's State-Owned Enterprises and Banks
Becky Chiu and Mervyn K. Lewis

Financial Innovation in Retail and Corporate Banking
Edited by Luisa Anderloni, David T. Llewellyn and Reinhard H. Schmidt

An Islamic Perspective on Governance
Zafar Iqbal and Mervyn K. Lewis

An Islamic Perspective on Governance

Zafar Iqbal

Professor of Finance, National University of Computer and Emerging Sciences, Pakistan

Mervyn K. Lewis

Professor of Banking and Finance, University of South Australia and Fellow, Academy of the Social Sciences in Australia

NEW HORIZONS IN MONEY AND FINANCE

Edward Elgar

Cheltenham, UK • Northampton, MA, USA

Published by
Edward Elgar Publishing Limited
The Lypiatts
15 Lansdown Road
Cheltenham
Glos GL50 2JA
UK

Edward Elgar Publishing, Inc.
William Pratt House
9 Dewey Court
Northampton
Massachusetts 01060
USA

A catalogue record for this book
is available from the British Library

Library of Congress Control Number: 2009922753

PEFC/16-33-111
CATG-PEFC-052
www.pefc.org

ISBN 978 1 84720 138 6

Printed and bound by MPG Books Group, UK

Contents

Figures and boxes

FIGURES

BOXES

Tables

Abbreviations

AH	*anno Hegirae* (from the year of the *hijra*)
ANWT	Annual net worth tax
CE	Common Era dates (AD)
CSV	costly state verification
ET	equitable taxation
FE	fiscal exchange
MENA	countries and territories of the Middle East and North Africa region
OT	optimal taxation
(pbuh)	peace be unto him (follows text references to Muhammad)
PLS	profit-and-loss sharing
SHS	Schanz–Haig–Simons concept of comprehensive income
SWF	social welfare function

Glossary

This section explains Arabic words and terms used in this book.

Abd is servant. Also refers to mankind. *Abd Allah* means servant of God.
Adl means justice, impartiality, and fairness.
Allah is Arabic for God.
Amana is trust; the contract of *amana* gives rise to fiduciary relationships and duties.
Aqidah (pl. *aqa'id*) is article of faith, tenet or doctrine.
Asabiyyah is the basis for group solidarity or national consciousness. It means *esprit de corps*.
Ayah (pl. *ayat*) means symbol or the sign. Refers to a verse of the Holy Qur'an.

Bai bi-thamin ajil is deferred payment sale by instalments.
Bai'muajjal is deferred-payment sale.
Bai'salam is pre-paid purchase.
Bay (bai) is a comprehensive term that applies to sale transactions, exchange.
Bay'ah is the contractual relationship among the ruler and the ruled and is circumscribed by *shari'ah*.
Bayt al-mal means house of wealth. It is a medieval financial institution aimed at managing the monetary activities of the 'Islamic state' and can be regarded as a public treasury.
Bida refers to innovation, deviation from Islamic tradition.
Birr is piety, righteousness.

Dhimmi is a non-Muslim citizen of a Muslim state who enjoys freedom and protection in return for fulfilling tax obligations.
Diya is the blood money paid by the murderer to the legal heirs of the murdered in return for exemption from the death penalty.

Falah means welfare, success, prosperity, thriving.
Fasad means iniquity, immorality, corruption, viciousness.
Fatawa (sing. *fatwa)* are legal decisions or opinions rendered by a qualified religious leader *(mufti)*.
Fard-e-kifaya is a community obligation in Islam. If some members

discharge it, others are exonerated. If none discharges it, the whole community is culpable in the eyes of God.

Fiqh is Islamic jurisprudence, the science of religious law, which is the interpretation of the Sacred Law, *shari'ah*.

Fuqaha (sing. *faqih*) are Muslim jurisprudents who have religious authority.

Fuqara are poor, needy, lacking basic wherewithal for honourable living.

Ghanima are spoils of war.

Gharar is uncertainty, speculation.

Hadd (pl. *hudud)* is a punishment fixed in the Holy Qur'an and *hadith* for crimes considered to be against the rights of God.

Hadith (pl. *ahadith*) is the technical term for the source related to the *Sunnah;* the sayings – and doings – of the Prophet (pbuh), his traditions.

Hajj is pilgrimage to Makkah.

Hakimiyya means sovereignty, judgeship, domination, jurisdiction over making rules.

Halal means permitted according to the *shari'ah.*

Haram means forbidden according to the *shari'ah.*

Hiba means gift, present, donation, grant.

Hijra marks the emigration of the Prophet Muhammad from Makkah to Madinah in 622 CE.

Hisba is prudential supervision/regulation of markets and transactions.

Hila (pl. *hiyal)* are 'permissions' or legal manipulations, evasions.

Ibada (pl. *ibadat*) is worship, adoration, religious observance.

Ihsan is benevolence, beneficence.

Ihtisab means accountability.

Ijarah contract is a leasing contract.

Ijarah wa iqtina is a lease-purchase contract, whereby the client has the option of purchasing the item.

Ijma means consensus among jurists based on the Holy Qur'an and *sunnah,* and one of the four sources of law in Sunni Islam.

Ijtihad means the act of independent reasoning by a qualified jurist in order to reach new legal rules.

Ijtihadi is a practice permitted through the application of *ijtihad.*

Iman means faith.

Imam is commonly used as a title for significant religious leaders.

Infaq is spending on charitable cause, in excess of need.

Insan means human being, human race.

Islam is submission or surrender to the will of God. Religion of Muslims (those who submit).

Isnad is ascription of a *hadith* or an Islamic tradition, the uninterrupted chain of authorities on which a tradition is based.
Israf is extravagance and as such condemned in Islam.
Istislah is public interest.
Istisnaa is a contract to manufacture.
Iztirar means compulsion, coercion, exigency, plight, predicament.

Jihad is struggle or battle against inner or outer impediments against implementing *shari'a* as the law of the land.
Jizya is poll tax levied on a *dhimmi* otherwise exempt from *zakah*.
Ju'alah is the stipulated price (commission) for performing any service.

Khalifa (caliph) means successor or 'deputy'. Ruler of the community of Islam (to the Prophet Muhammad's (pbuh) political position, but not to his prophethood).
Kharaj is land tax.
Kharajite were a dissident religious sect in Islam that demanded equitable treatment among Arab and non-Arab Muslims.
Khums is one fifth of treasure trove due to an Islamic state.

Madinah Medina, capital of the Al Madinah Province of Saudi Arabia and the second holiest city in Islam.
Mafasid (sing. *mafsada*) means malicious acts, chicaneries, causes of evil and corruption.
Makkah Mecca, capital of the Makkah Province of Saudi Arabia, which is the holiest city in Islam and the destination of the *Hajj*.
Maqasid (sing. *maqsid*) means goals, aims, objectives, ends, designs, intentions.
Masakin (sing. *miskin*) are the poor, miserable, beggars, humble.
Masalih (sing. *maslaha*) are those acts or matters which promote welfare.
Masjid is the place where Muslim prayers are conducted (that is, a mosque).
Maysir means gambling, from a pre-Islamic game of hazard.
Mu'amala (pl. *mu'amalat*) is conduct toward others in social intercourse, including business.
Mudarabah contract is a trustee financing contract, where one party, the financier, entrusts funds to the other party, the entrepreneur, for undertaking an activity.
Mudarib means an entrepreneur or a manager of a *mudaraba* project.
Mufti is a jurist who is authorized to issue a *fatwa* or legal decision on a religious matter.
Muhtasib is the ombudsman's office.

Mujtahid is the one qualified for undertaking *ijtihad*, primarily in the *shi'ite* tradition.
Murabahah is resale with a stated profit, for example the bank purchases a certain asset and sells it to the client on the basis of a cost plus mark-up profit principle.
Musharakah contract is an equity participation contract, whereby two or more partners contribute with funds to carry out an investment.
Muslim is one who professes the faith of lslam or is born to a Muslim family.

Nisab is the minimum acceptable standard of living.

Qard hasan is a benevolent (interest free) loan.
Qisas is requital, retaliation; punishment, castigation, chastisement.
Qist is fairness, justice, equitableness.
Qiyas means analogical deduction.
Qur'an is the Holy Book, the revealed word of God, followed by all Muslims.

Rabb al-mal refers to the owner of capital or financier in a *mudarabah* partnership agreement (also called *sahib al-mal)*.
Rahn is pawning, mortgaging, pledging.
Rashwa is bribery, dishonesty, corruption.
Riba is literally 'excess' or 'increase', and covers both interest and usury.

Sadaqa is alms, charitable gift; almsgiving, charity, freewill offering.
Salam is soundness, peacefulness, unimpairedness, well-being; peace, safety, security.
Shari'ah is Islamic religious law derived from the Holy Qur'an and the *sunnah*.
Sheikh is head of a tribe; elder, chief; master of an order (Sufism).
Shia is a *Shi'ite* Muslim, whose members comprise about 10 per cent of the world population of Muslims.
Shirkah (or *sharika*) is a society or partnership.
Shi'ite comes from the religio-political party championing the claims of 'Ali ibn abi Talib and his heirs to the rightful leadership of the community and to their status as Imams. Since the beginning of the sixteenth century, *Shi'ism* has been the official state religion of Iran and most of its followers live there.
Shura is consultation, deliberation, taking counsel.
Sukuk are bonds legitimized by contemporary *fiqh* experts.
Sukuk-al-ijarah is the most popular form of *sukuk* in which the underlying asset pool comprises physical assets that are leased at pre-specified rentals.

Sunnah (pl. *sunan*) is habitual practice, customary procedure, or action, norm, usage sanctioned by tradition. In Islam, it refers to the sayings and practices of the Prophet Muhammad (pbuh), established as legally binding precedents in addition to the Law established by the Holy Qur'an.

Sunnis are orthodox Muslims and constitute the majority form of Islam, those who follow the *sunnah* (thus being called the *ahl al-sunnah*), of the Prophet Muhammad (phuh) and his companions.

Sura (pl. *surat*) is a chapter of the Holy Qur'an. There are 114 *suras* of varying length and in all references to the Holy Qur'an (for example 30:39) the first number refers to the *sura* and the second to the *aya*, or verse.

Takaful refers to mutual support which is the basis of the concept of insurance or solidarity among Muslims.

Taqwa is devoutness, godliness, piety.

Tawhid is the belief that God is one, unique and incomparable.

Ulama are the learned class, especially those learned in religious matters.

Umma means a nation or community, which shares a belief system; the body of Muslims.

Umrah is the 'minor' or 'lesser' pilgrimage to Makkah which can be made at any time of the year.

Ushr is tenth part; tithe due to an Islamic state on agricultural crops.

Ushur are custom duties.

Usul-ul-fiqh are the principles of jurisprudence in Islam.

Waqf is a trust or pious foundation.

Zakah is a religious levy or almsgiving as required in the Holy Qur'an and is one of Islam's five pillars.

Zulm is the opposite of justice. It is oppression.

Preface

There is now a substantial Western literature on governance in its many dimensions, but there are few studies that examine governance issues from the perspective of Islamic economics and fewer still that compare the Islamic and Western viewpoints on the topic. In writing this volume we sought to correct these omissions by providing a systematic analysis of certain key areas of governance from an Islamic standpoint, drawing on classical Islam and contemporary sources, to produce a framework that is then contrasted with the Western position.

The volume seeks to make a distinctive contribution in a number of ways. First, as we have said, it develops an Islamic perspective on matters widely acknowledged as being under-researched in the Islamic discipline. Second, it (hopefully) brings a fresh and contemporary perspective on these issues by drawing insights from modern theory and practice, combining them with classical and modern Muslim interpretations. There is thus an attempt to integrate East and West and merge the normative as well as the positive. Third, in order to provide a different reference point, there is abstraction from traditional terminology and a focus on the spirit of Islam. That becomes explicit in the approach to the topics on taxation and the financing of public sector organizations. Fourth, the analysis explicitly acknowledges the self-interested behaviour of major economic actors, both local and international. This adds a public choice dimension to appreciating the limitations as well as the workability of any governance arrangements.

The study has its origins in the PhD dissertation, 'An Islamic perspective on public finance', completed by the first-named author under the supervision of the second. Not only did the dissertation win the World Business Institute Best Doctoral Thesis Award for 2005, but both examiners (eminent Islamic scholars) were adamant that it should be published, and we thank Edward Elgar Publishers for agreeing with them. For this purpose, all original chapters have been thoroughly revised and rewritten and much new material added especially on governance principles generally, *sukuk* and other recently developed methods of government financing, and issues of accountability.

It would be most remiss of us to conclude these comments without thanking our wives (one of whom, Kay Lewis, did much of the typing) for their patience and forbearance during the many hours that were spent working on the manuscript. We hope that they feel that it was all worthwhile.

1. Perspectives on governance

INTRODUCTION

The need for good governance has become almost a mantra in analyses of the problems of developing economies. Governance has been used in a number of different contexts, such as 'monetary governance' (the making of monetary policy), 'economic governance' (ensuring the smooth workings of a market economy), 'public governance' (the efficient running of the nation state and the public sector), and of course 'corporate governance' (the effective functioning of market and state-owned enterprises). The concept of governance has also been used for defining the interests of international economic institutions like the OECD and World Bank in programmes of social and economic development and structural adjustment in developing countries.

Interestingly, despite the fact that some of the poorest countries in the world are Muslim nations, issues of governance are invariably discussed solely from a Western perspective, ignoring the contribution of Islamic economics – a branch of knowledge that aims at analysing, interpreting, and resolving economic problems with reference to the methodology of Islam. This volume consequently examines, from an Islamic perspective, some of the central issues in public governance, economic governance, and corporate governance. An appropriate starting point is to ask specifically what we mean by these terms and, in general, by the expression 'governance'.

MEANINGS OF GOVERNANCE

There is not as yet a unified expression in Arabic to represent the meaning of governance in its various manifestations, although there has been work in this area by the Egyptian Linguistic Department (Sourial, 2004). Perhaps the closest concept to 'governance' in Arabic is *al-hakimiya*, which in its connotations goes beyond the procedural view of governance to identify the blueprint of a higher moral social order to which all decision-making structures or 'authority' ought to submit, if they believed that peace in its outer and inner manifestations could be achieved only by surrendering one's will to the Will of God (Bahlul, 2000). This is an illustration that some of the most commonly used categories in conventional social sciences are somehow changed and transformed when applied to societies and cultures in which they did not originate (Mumtaz Ahmad, 1986, p. 2).

By contrast, the English terminology has clear origins in terms of procedural arrangements. *The Macquarie Encyclopedic Dictionary*, 1990, traces the etymological roots of the word 'governance' from the Greek *kybernan* to the Latin *gubernare* and to the Old French *governer*. *Kybernan* means to 'steer', 'guide' or 'govern'. At its broadest, governance – the act of governing – refers to the relationship between the governors and the governed, such as that between the government and the people, and has at its basis the decision-making powers ceded by individuals to those in authority so that the common interests of society can be served. The ship of state needs a good captain and crew to guide it but it also has to have a clear idea of where it is, where it is going, and how well it is progressing. Governance mechanisms are designed for these ends.

In the prologue to his book *The Mechanisms of Governance*, Oliver Williamson provides two definitions of governance. One, based on the concept of eunomics, is 'good order and workable arrangements' (Williamson, 1996, p. 11). The other, based on John R. Commons (1932), is 'the means by which *order* is accomplished in a relation in which potential *conflict* threatens to undo or upset opportunities to realise *mutual* gains' (Williamson, 1996, p. A2). These definitions make clear that the concept can be applied to a variety of organizations and institutions, and is thus not limited to economic activities, and can be expressed in a variety of political and social arrangements.

Public Governance

This would appear to be the concept of governance employed by the World Bank and the OECD. For example, World Bank documents have used the concept of governance to 'capture and define the interest of both the World Bank and other international institutions in the political and institutional factors affecting structural adjustment' (Frischtak and Atiyas, 1996). As another example, the Development Assistance Committee of the OECD defined governance from the particular viewpoint of donor institutions as denoting the 'use of political authority and exercise of control in a society in relation to the management of its resources for social and economic development' (OECD, 1993). In this respect, three specific aspects of governance are identified: the form of political regime, the processes by which authority is exercised in the management of a country's economic and social resources, and the capacity of government to formulate and implement policies and discharge its functions. In these respects, governance of this type corresponds to what Apreda (2003) calls 'public governance'. As he puts it, 'governance in the public sector of any country points to the running of the State, taking into account the mechanisms by which the government should work well' (p. 12). Public governance is defined as 'the governance of organizations in representative democracies' (p. 13).

Public governance operates where economics, political science and law overlap and relates to the exercise of political, economic and administrative authority to manage a nation's affairs. Box 1.1 sets out the three dimensions that constitute the World Bank's approach to public

BOX 1.1 THE WORLD BANK'S APPROACH TO PUBLIC GOVERNANCE ISSUES

1. The process of selecting, monitoring and replacing governments

Associated measurable concepts:
- (a) Voice and external accountability through citizens' feedback, democratic institutions and a competitive press
- (b) Political stability and lack of violence, crime and terrorism.

2. The capacity to formulate and implement sound policies, and deliver public services

Associated measurable concepts:
- (a) Government effectiveness (including quality at policy-making, bureaucracy, and public service delivery)
- (b) Lack of regulatory burden.

3. The respect of citizens and the state for the institutions that govern economic and social interactions among them

Associated measurable concepts:
- (a) Rule of law (protection of property rights, judiciary independence)
- (b) Control of corruption.

Source: Fremond and Capaul (2002)

governance issues. Other relevant issues are: the founding Charter and Bill of Rights; the tradition and institutions by which the authority in a country is exercised; institutional design, division of powers and bureaucracy to run the government; rent-seeking and 'state-capture' by entrenched interests; the role of civic groups, non-profit organizations and the media.

Economic Governance

From the particular perspective of developing and emerging market economies, a more tightly focused set of issues and outcomes has been suggested. Dhonte and Kapur (1997) argue that a secure economic environment is essential to sustained growth in a market economy. This is brought about from the assurance that the return on enterprise and investment will accrue to the entrepreneur and the investor; as such, it is a critical requirement for sustained growth. The provision of such an environment seems particularly important for the development of private initiatives in a market economy, in contrast to government investment (or investment by an enterprise in a command economy) which is less dependent on the certainty of expected returns and where the government is in a better position to influence the outcome. Their suggestion is that such a secure environment requires the existence of effective laws and institutions, including the government, which must ensure that there is freedom of entry into the market, access to relevant information, and the security of contracts. Accordingly, good governance in their view promotes the creation and maintenance of these conditions in a rules-based system. This is the basis of what they term 'economic governance' where 'good' or 'bad' is assessed from the capacity to support the effective functioning of a market economy.

Monetary Governance

Yet Dohnte and Kapur recognize that markets cannot operate effectively without 'reasonable macroeconomic and political stability'. The risk for the private investor is that the business environment, as shaped by government behaviour and policies at a point in time, may be adversely affected by shifts in government policy, resulting in harm to the conduct of business. Some would put the point stronger. Buiter *et al.* (1997, p. 3) argue that the 'first priority for a government interested in promoting the welfare of its citizens must be macroeconomic control'. Because lack of macroeconomic control is an important cause of poor enterprise performance, provision of macroeconomic stability is a pure public good. And since high inflation is the most obvious manifestation of a lack of macroeconomic control, this places a premium on 'monetary governance'. Kzrak and Schubert (1997, p. 28) define monetary governance as 'the combination of the legal framework, the strategy and the operational framework of monetary policymaking in a particular country'. At issue are matters such as central bank independence, monetary policy targeting, the instruments of monetary policy, and the interdependence of monetary and exchange rate policy.

Corporate Governance

Public governance, economic governance and monetary governance, as defined above, can be regarded as establishing the preconditions for the workings of a market economy, but will the right set of outcomes emerge? Arguably what is also needed is a culture of business. The system of corporate governance interacts with a number of other factors that shape the business environment and thus influence business outcomes.

Any organized society engaged in productive activities needs to establish some conditions or rules relating to business organization, viz:

1. Conditions for entry and establishment, that is, how and in what form are business enterprises to be formed?
2. Conditions for ownership, that is, who should own firms and under what conditions?
3. Conditions for financing, that is, how should enterprises be financed?
4. Conditions of operation, that is, how are firms organized and run?
5. Conditions for exit and closure, that is, how are business enterprises closed down?

Corporate governance, that is, the institutional arrangements and relationships through which companies and institutions are 'directed and controlled' (Cadbury Committee, 1992), bears most directly upon the fourth aspect, but is obviously affected by the others. How well firms are run will be influenced by whether foreign participation is allowed or whether companies must be domestically chartered and owned, whether shares are closely held or widely-owned, whether and how easily ownership can be transferred, whether banks and other financiers can own shares in companies in which they lend, and whether creditor rights or debtor rights are reflected in insolvency laws.

An important conditioning factor upon governance is the nature of ownership. Shareholders need to ensure that the managers engaged in the day-to-day running of the organization are marshalling the enterprise's resources for the shareholders' benefit. Without some checks and balances on managerial behaviour, there can be no guarantee that the interests of those owning shares will be furthered. Much the same delegation problems arise with public officials elected to make decisions on voters' and taxpayers' behalf.

This control problem is normally couched in terms of agency theory: shareholders/voters must ensure that the managers/officials, who are their agent/representatives, are monitored, motivated and disciplined to act to the best advantage of the organization/society at large. Consequently, a major part of corporate governance, indeed governance in general, is concerned with the design of checks and balances.

A TAXONOMY OF GOVERNANCE

These examples bring out the point that governance incorporates a number of overlapping elements. First, just as governance of the nation state is informed by a theoretical model of the ideal state and the proper way to run a country (in Plato's *Republic* the choices are between monarchy, democracy, oligarchy), so too governance in all of its facets needs to be rooted in an appropriate conceptual framework. This is the idea of 'governance as a discipline'. Second, governance almost invariably involves a delegation of some, and most often many, important decision-making powers. This process of delegation gives rise to the need for checks and balances on decision-making authority and reliance on a system of 'gatekeepers'. Hence the notion of 'governance as a system of checks and balances'. Third, governance is about decision-making. What are being delegated are decision-making powers, and a system of governance needs to be concerned with the effectiveness of the decisions that are being made. This is the basis of 'governance as decision-making'. Box 1.2 provides a guide to the discussion.

Governance as a Discipline

Apreda (2003) argues that governance needs to be seen as if not quite a discipline then certainly as a field of learning and practice. As such, the aim is to provide a conceptual framework that is broad enough to encompass the different types of governance (for example, public, economic, monetary and corporate governance) and the different levels or 'arenas' (Ostrom, 1999) at which governance may apply (for example, the individual enterprise, a specific industry or economic sector, a region or community, the nation state or multilateral bodies).

The conceptual framework that Apreda suggests be applied to governance issues is based around goals, principles and processes. Thus the main elements of a system of governance are:

BOX 1.2 A TAXONOMY OF GOVERNANCE

Governance as a discipline

A conceptual framework

- Goals
- Principles
- Processes

Action levels of governance

- Constitutive
- Directive
- Operational

Arenas of governance

- International
- National-level
- Regional-level
- Sector or industry
- Organization or enterprise

Governance as checks and balances

Modes of governance

- State authority
- Markets and market structure
- Hierarchies (public and private)
- Networks, associations and communities

Constraints

- Constitution/charter or conventions
- Political philosophy/theories of justice
- Regime of governance and behaviour
- Culture and religion

Gatekeepers

- External disciplines/audit
- Internal disciplines/audit

Governance as decision-making

Dimensions of decisions

- For whom
- By whom
- To whom and with what resources

Positive/normative aspects

- Normative
- Positive
  - Outcomes
  - Processes

Applications

- Public governance
- Economic governance
- Monetary governance
- Corporate governance

- the setting of goals and objectives stemming from the charter of the organization or bodies (the 'goals');
- the development of principles, rules and good practices that allow the organization to be efficiently run and managed (the 'principles'); and
- the design of mechanisms of representation, legitimate ways of exercising power, enforcement of rules and procedures, accountability, controls, incentives and standards of performance to be applied to organizations (the 'processes').

These three elements provide a common thread running through corporate, public and global governance.

In broad terms, a similar classification is employed by Hupe and Hill (2006) who, in their 'three action levels of governance', distinguish 'constitutive governance' (the framing of rules), 'directive governance' (collective choice about desired outcomes) and 'operational governance' (the managing of the realization process). These sets of activities are described respectively as structure-oriented, content-oriented and process-oriented. Thus, at the system-wide level (corresponding to what we would term public and economic governance), constitutive governance involves 'institutional design', directive governance relates to 'general rule setting', while operational governance is concerned with 'managing trajectories' (p. 23).

Governance as Checks and Balances

As a consequence of the process of delegation or representation in decision-making powers, and the potential for agency problems to arise, most systems of governance encapsulate checks and balances. The classic example comes from those built in to the governance of a nation state. For instance, under the American system of government, as fashioned by James Madison, there are three basic arms, equal but separated, in a system designed to constrain the expansion and over-use of government powers. Madison's conception divided government into three different branches which would check and balance one another: a two-house legislature, an independent executive, and an independent judiciary. Each would have specific functions and would see to it that the others did not overstep their bounds (Blum *et al.*, 1963).

These checks and balances are often articulated and enacted in terms of constitutions and bills of rights. In this way, the concept of constitutive governance in terms of the framing of rules (Hupe and Hill) or the development of principles (Apreda) extends to political philosophy or theories of justice. In the words of Uhr (2006):

> Think of constitutions as laws about laws: they are the articles of association for political communities, establishing the rules to determine who governs and how they govern. Constitutions are meant to bring stability to an organization and are therefore often designed to withstand pressure for easy change by those in power. Constitutions are prior to governments which must work within the limits of their constitutional powers. Typically, constitutions allocate governing powers among the core institutions of state, frequently arranged according to a separation of powers among legislative, executive and judicial branches of government. Constitutions often specify a range of basic rights enjoyed by citizens which governments may not curtail.
>
> In many democratic regimes (for example, the United States), the constitution is a formal written document deriving from a founding period of nation-building. Some democracies however (for example, the United Kingdom), have a variety of traditional core legal documents, some old (such as the Bill of Rights of 1689) but others quite new (such as the European Convention on Human Rights), that serve constitutional purposes. Rights come in all shapes and sizes. (p. 171)

In economic governance, checks and balances come from the different 'modes' of governance (Bell, 2002). Institutions and authority structures that allocate resources and coordinate economic activity take a variety of forms: state, market, hierarchies, networks, associations and communities. While the state will inevitably have a major role in any mode of governance, its control powers will be curtailed by the other participants. Regulation that is too heavy-handed will see economic activity stultified or market participants migrate to other less regulated locales. Nor does the government have a monopoly upon regulation. Self-regulation through networks and associations often co-exists with state control, allowing government to be at one remove from direct interference in market activity.[1]

Bell suggests that the specific modes of economic governance will be shaped by what he terms a wider 'regime' of governance. The particular mix of state, market and other modes of economic governance in a particular 'arena' will be conditioned by the specific 'interests, norms, power distributions, and institutional complexes that tend to dominate in particular historical settings' (2002, p. 14). At the same time, 'incentive structures, roles, obligations, notions of "appropriate" behaviour, and specific discourses of institutional life are said to inevitably shape the ideas, preferences, and decisions of actors, be they in state, associations, or corporations' (p. 15). It is in such a context that religion can directly influence economic behaviour, because religion is a part of a society's overall culture, which in turn moulds many other formal and informal institutions and networks that have an effect upon economic life (Lewer, 2007). This theme is one that we will return to below when we consider Islamic governance norms.

Finally, checks and balances also feature prominently in corporate governance. The corporate structure in Anglo-Saxon countries is often referred to as a system of 'shareholder democracy', but the reality in most English-speaking countries is that the CEO has considerable latitude to run the company as the leader of the senior executive team. Management's fiduciary duty is to serve shareholders, but the shareholders' control has often to be exercised indirectly through the market for corporate control via takeovers and mergers and acquisitions, much like citizens ultimately control their representatives via the ballot box. There are also various checks and balances upon managerial control. Some of these checks and balances may be internal to the enterprise, for example, the internal audit process, while others are external, for example, the external auditors. The latter are one of a number of 'gatekeepers' or 'reputational intermediaries' that underpin accountability mechanisms. In corporate governance, their numbers include independent directors, investment bankers, rating agencies, public regulators and the financial press. For public governance, the main gatekeepers are civic groups, political action groups, unions, religious bodies, non-profit organizations and the media.

Governance as Decision-making

Many of the ideas for corporate governance reform in the West are predicated on the assumption that managers have too much power, and that the secret to better corporate performance is to return power to shareholders and directors. Examples of power-shifting reforms are to separate the roles of CEO and chairman of the board, limit the number of executive directors, restrict the tenure of the CEO, have outside, independent directors evaluate the CEO annually, and so on. However, these moves may be misplaced if the fundamental problems of corporate governance do not stem from imbalances of power but from failures in corporate decision-making procedures. In this case, power-based reforms are not the key to correcting the problem.

This, at least, is the view of John Pound. He contends that most corporate failures are not the result of power imbalances. Instead, failures usually result from a few well-intentioned but flawed management decisions that are not challenged in an efficient, effective manner. Corporate failures occur because of subtle failures in the decision-making process – in how boards and managers make decisions and monitor corporate progress (Pound, [1995] 2000, p. 81).

Too often, Pound argues, the focus is on who is in charge rather than on how decisions are made in the organization. A takeover may change the ownership structure and shift control, but it is not axiomatic that it will bring about improved decision-making. According to Pound, governance failures do not stem solely from bad managers and bad incentives, that is, from factors that can be changed readily, but emanate also from the culture, behaviour, personalities, politics and motivation within the organization.

Just as corporations survive according to whether they make good decisions, so too governments fall or are re-elected on whether they make good decisions (for example, the Vietnam War, the invasion of Iraq). However, changing the government may not improve matters if the problems lie in the structure of government, the workings of the public service, and the quality of advice provided and available to those involved in making decisions. Again, decision-making rules and procedures are paramount. Hupe and Hill (2006) make clear that constitutive governance concerns 'decisions about decision rules', while directive governance involves 'the formulation of and decision making about collectively desired outcomes' (p. 22).

From this alternative perspective, whether considering corporations or government bodies, governance is essentially about decision-making. In this respect, the pertinent issues are threefold: for whom, by whom, and with what resources ('to whom'). These three dimensions of decision-making apply irrespective of whether we are governing a nation or governing an organization such as a business enterprise. 'For whom' decisions are made is stipulated by the underlying constitution or charter. 'By whom' decisions are made depends on the decision-making structure developed. 'With what resources' determines 'to whom' accountability is due for the usage made of them.[2]

A governance agenda for decision-making would focus on:

- the distribution of decision-making responsibilities among different participants in the organization;
- rules and procedures for making decisions;
- the degree of involvement in decisions;
- the structure through which the goals and objectives are set;
- the means of attaining those objectives; and
- review and monitoring performance.

In general, the aim would be to develop internal and external supports to 'better' decision-making.

But how do we judge what is 'better' or 'worse'? As with any issue of public policy, matters can be evaluated through alternative prisms: positive and normative. In terms of corporative governance, for example, one can ask how firms are directed and controlled (positive) or one can ask how firms should be directed and controlled (normative). The positive can be further divided into 'outcomes' and 'processes'. With corporate governance the normative question is: how should firms be governed? From the positive perspective, an outcomes-based approach would focus on the performance of firms, while a process-based approach would examine the mechanisms by which firms are directed and controlled. In terms of public governance, the normative approach would ask a question such as: what is the desirable system of revenue-raising? The positive approach in relation to outcomes would consider how effective is the associated provision of public goods and how efficient is revenue-raising. For processes, the positivist aspect would focus on the political processes and institutional mechanisms that generate the outcomes. As we shall see, the normative/positive distinction is of considerable relevance when we explore Islamic governance.

AN ISLAMIC PERSPECTIVE

This book considers a number of key issues in public, economic and corporate governance. The four areas chosen for examination are, first, the theory of justice, second, taxation, third, government budget deficits and public sector financing, and fourth, accountability, governance and corruption. The study of these topics is carried out explicitly with reference to the value framework of Islam. The aim is to develop a contemporary Islamic standpoint on these issues, which both complements and contrasts with conventional economic analysis, using the basic building blocks of Islamic economics.

What is Islamic Economics?

Islamic economics is a branch of knowledge that aims at analysing, interpreting, and resolving economic problems with reference to the methodology of Islam. The word Islam means the 'tranquillity' and inner 'peace' (*salam)* that can be attained by submitting, surrendering, or giving oneself up to the Will of God as manifest in the revealed law. The revelation (the Holy Qur'an) conceives human beings as the trustees of God on earth and bound by a covenant that is endorsed by voluntarily observing a compact (*shari'ah*) regulating life. Such compact makes no distinction between the sacred and the profane.

Islamic economics remained primarily an integral part of the unified social and moral philosophy of Islam until after World War II. It only assumed the shape of an independent discipline in the second half of the twentieth century as intellectuals in rnany lands with majority Muslim populations began to reflect on alternative modes of post-colonial social organization. Neither of the then prevailing secular models of economic organization, namely, communism and capitalism, fitted well with the Islamic ethos. The new research programme that developed distinguished itself from the conventional paradigm in many ways. Citing Chapra (2000):

> The Islamic paradigm . . . gives primary importance to moral values, human brotherhood, and socio-economic justice and, unlike its Marxist or capitalist counterparts, does not primarily rely on either the state or the market for realizing its vision. It rather relies on the integrated role of values and institutions, market, families, society, and the state to ensure *falah* or the well-being of all. It places great emphasis on social change through a reform of the individual and his society, without which the market and the state could both perpetuate inequities. (p. 57)

These differences between the Islamic and the Western positions are understandable. Islam is a norm-based way of life seeking spiritual fulfilment in public as well as in private life whereas conventional economics has developed into a predominantly secular discipline insisting on maintaining a difference between the positive and normative. It can be argued, however, that these differences hide a degree of unity at the roots: issues of governance and public policy in the West are implicitly informed by social values that have religious (in particular, Christian) origins while the decision-making framework of the Islamic *shari'ah* explicitly recognizes the role of reason in the contextual application of religious precepts.

Against this backdrop, Islamic economic theorists appreciate the fact that conventional economics has made valuable analytical contributions and greatly enhanced human understanding about economic phenomena in general. It is not the aim of the Islamic economic discipline to eschew such achievements, but rather to build upon them and give a characteristic human face to economics. How does Islamic economics purport to do that? Khurshid Ahmad (Abu-Rabi, 1995), an eminent Islamic revivalist, explains in broader terms:

> Islamic resurgence has drawn attention to the idea that Western culture, Western thought, and Western values must be looked upon again with an openness, not with a closed mind. A lot of positive developments, which have become a part of the permanent legacy of mankind, have taken place in the modem Western world, in my view, Muslims must not deny this out of any prejudice, yet they should be sincere and loyal to their own value framework. The criterion by which Muslims decide what must be accepted and assimilated and what must be avoided or rejected is their value framework. Muslims must be in a position to preserve and protect the moral, ethical, and intellectual fibre of Islam. They must consciously avoid what is at variance with their Islamic understanding. (p. 69)

Consequently a contribution to Islamic economics requires that the conventional body of knowledge in the chosen field be understood thoroughly and then evaluated in the light of the human purpose and goals, and the corresponding values depicted by the Holy Qur'an and the *sunnah*. If it is compatible with them, it is accepted; if it is not, then an alternative should be proposed.

It is in this vein that this study compares the Western and Islamic perspectives on justice and social organization, taxation, government borrowing, and accountability, governance and corruption. Together these topics are widely recognized as having a significant bearing not only on the overall level of a society's achievements but also on how the fruits of such endeavours are distributed across its members. In other words, they condition the goals, principles and processes of public governance.

The Islamic Heritage on Public Finance

All four of the areas selected for study involve aspects of government fiscal organization. As well as standard economics, this volume draws extensively on the Islamic canonical resources and the past scholarly works in the area. It therefore seems appropriate to provide a brief sketch of the

Islamic heritage on public finance. Historically, public finance had been one of the pioneering independent subject areas (apart from the traditional disciplines built around the Holy Qur'an and *hadith*) that attracted the attention of Muslim scholars. This interest grew out of the unprecedented expansion of the Islamic state in its first century,[3] and the need to standardize and harmonize varying taxation arrangements and land policies in these territories. Twenty-seven titles on public finance appeared from around the end of the second to the tenth *Hijra* centuries (Sharfuddin, 1995). Many do not appear to have survived the Mongol invasion and destruction of Baghdad. Nevertheless, six are still in existence, the most prominent being that of Abu Yusuf's (d.182 AH/798 CE) *Kitab al-Kharaj* [1392] (1969), which has become a classic. It contains advice on matters of governance, an analysis of state revenues, and comments on public expenditure, all subsumed within a primary concern for public welfare and rendering justice. Al-Dawudi's (d.402 AH/1012 CE) *Kitab al-Amwal* (1995) also sheds light on the same issues, albeit with somewhat lesser sophistication. Among recent noteworthy contributions are Islahi (1988), which includes a condensation of (Imam) Ibn Taymiyyah's (1263–1328 CE) views on public finance, while recent translations of Ibn Taymiyyah ([1976] 1982) expand upon public duties in Islam, in particular, the regulation of individual and business conduct in market transactions through the institution of *hisba*[4] (regulator of the market) in order to secure a just and efficient market economy. As we shall see, this institution is one of the major planks of the Islamic system of governance.

Another institutional development of significance in the classical period was the formation of the *bayt al-mal.* Under Prophet Muhammad (pbuh)[5] and Abu Bakr, the first Caliph, revenue receipts were disbursed to the needy forthwith. The second Caliph, Umar, organized such disbursements on more professional lines and in the wake of vast increases in public receipts, he reluctantly agreed to follow the Byzantine precedent of setting up a central treasury (*bayt al-mal*). The Arabic word *bayt al-mal* literally means 'the house of (public) property', that is, the premises where property is stored, However, as Levy ([1957] 1979) explains:

> the term had no reference to any particular building or locality, but was applied to that part of the Caliph's activities concerned with such wealth, either in specie or in kind, as belonged to the community of Islam as a whole and which passed through the hands of the *'amils*, the agents or tax-gatherers of the community. (p. 308)

The *bayt al-mal* financed government activities, disbursed stipends and pensions to the needy and the military personnel in accordance with a register, and performed some of the tasks undertaken by a modern central bank. Borrowing and lending without interest was permissible. However, the oversight of financial intermediation and the issuance of currency lay beyond its jurisdiction. The *bayt al-mal* also did not engage in deficit finance (Ghaffari, 1989, pp. 46–7; Ra'ana, 1991, pp. 104–6; Hasanuz Zaman, 1991).

Along with the classic Islamic treatises on public finance, there are scores of classical works on exegesis, jurisprudence, ethics, history, sociology, and state-craft that each devote a chapter or two to the area of public finance. In this category, Ibn Khaldun (1332–1406 CE) (1967), stands out.[6] He examines patterns and revenues of taxation within the broader politico-economic context and links them on the one hand with the spending norms exhibited by a dynasty during different stages of its rule and on the other hand with the taxpayers' incentive to work, discovering regularities that are akin to the Laffer curve and political business cycle theory. These insights seem well ahead of their time.

A renewed interest in the classical Islamic scheme was evident early in the twentieth century roughly coinciding with the introduction of income taxation in the United States. In 1916, Columbia University published *Mohammedan Theories of Finance* based on the PhD thesis of Nicolas P. Aghnides. The work explains the classical scheme with a special emphasis on the dialectical and legalistic (*fiqhi*) bases of different opinions. No elaborate attempt, however, was made to relate the overall system or individual opinions to the deeper moral philosophy of Islam or to the then prevailing material conditions. This gap was filled by Hasanuz Zaman (1991) who provided a record of the fiscal norms as well as practices in the classical period and their relationship with the broader moral foundations of the Islamic economic system.[7]

There, it would seem, matters have largely stood. While conventional analysis of public finance has expanded from a study of taxation and government borrowing to an examination of all government economic policy in the form of 'public sector economics', studies in the Islamic economic tradition by comparison are still in their infancy. In taking stock of the contemporary literature on public finance in the Islamic tradition, Chapra (2000, pp. 330–42) found that the analysis of taxation, expenditure, budgetary deficit, money creation, and public debt has hardly progressed beyond that written in classical times. He offered suggestions and guidelines for further studies. On taxation, he advocated an expansion beyond the classical scheme to examine modern means of taxation – income, corporate, property, value-added, wealth and inheritance taxes – with reference to realizing the Islamic goals (*maqasid*). On public expenditure, he proposed the development of a rational and consistent theory of state expenditure based on legal maxims of Islamic jurisprudence that arbitrate among conflicting goals of fiscal policy. Chapra admits the possibility of a state ending up in deficit in spite of attempts to expanding revenues and reducing wasteful spending. How is such a deficit to be financed from an Islamic perspective? The area remains largely unexplored. Finally, he identified another gap in the literature:

> There is hardly any worthwhile study indicating the extent of corruption in Muslim countries . . . The economist may not be able to perform his task of analysis unless the relevant data are available and he feels free to say what he considers to be right, without fear of losing his job, being put in jail, or being penalized in other ways. (pp. 339–40)

These issues, and the gaps in the literature they represent, essentially frame the content of this book.

AN OUTLINE OF THE BOOK

It is apparent from the previous section that a whole range of subject-matter that falls under standard public sector economics remains largely unexplored from an Islamic perspective. In seeking to redress this imbalance in this volume, there is the question of where to draw the line, balancing a detailed treatment of one area, *vis-à-vis* leaving others out. Such considerations led us to lean to the former and to the choice of four areas to consider. These are: (1) the theory of justice, (2) taxation, (3) budget deficits and government finance, and (4) accountability, governance and corruption.

It is appropriately with Islam that we commence. Chapter 2 outlines the nature of Islam and Islamic law, and compares the methodology of Islamic economics with that of conventional positive economics. Chapter 3 then traces the origins of the theory of justice and examines the distinctive Islamic position on state–citizen relationships and welfare obligations. Together, these two chapters provide a broader basis for understanding the similarities and differences between different approaches to organizing society and government.

The next two chapters take up the question of taxation. Chapter 4 develops the classical and contemporary Islamic position on taxation, tax bases and fairness in taxation, integrating history, the theory of justice, earlier works on this topic and modern economic analysis. From these perspectives, Chapter 5 looks at the realities of taxation in Muslim countries, and the difficulties of implementing the Islamic approach to taxation in contemporary Muslim societies.

Issues involved in budget deficits and government financing in Islam are explored in Chapters 6 and 7. Chapter 6 examines Islamic attitudes to deficit financing in terms of inter-generational equity and political economy issues. Islam has very strict rules about financing, and Chapter 7 consider the implications of these precepts for government financing. This is an area in which there has been a tremendous amount of financial innovation in recent years with the development of *sukuk* financing structures that draw on the techniques of conventional structured finance. It is thus an opportune time to review the new developments in the light of the underlying principles of Islamic financing.

Chapters 8 and 9 focus on accountability, governance and corruption. Accountability is central to governance under Islam, and Chapter 8 develops the basic principles of Islamic governance whether applied to public governance or to issues of corporate governance. In terms of our earlier discussion of the nature of governance and the different frameworks, Islamic methodology has a distinctive stance on governance issues. In particular, it is found that Islam has very clear views on the goals of a society, principles for governing it, and the processes employed (in Apreda's taxonomy) or about the framing of rules, choice over desired outcomes, and management of processes (in the classification of Hupe and Hill). Islam also has a strong position on the nature of decision-making and the questions of 'by whom', 'for whom' and 'to whom'. It also envisages an important role for 'gatekeepers' in ensuring accountability appropriate for an Islamic society. Chapter 9 then looks at governance and corruption. The chapter considers the economic effects of corruption and outlines a framework to improve governance. It also presents an Islamic approach to these issues and compares and contrasts it with the standard approach against the backdrop of third-party qualitative survey ratings of corruption and governance around the globe.

Finally, Chapter 10 sums up the conclusions reached and outlines a reform agenda for governance and fiscal management for Muslim countries.

NOTES

1. Regulation of the Australian stock market, for example, is shared. The privately listed Australian Stock Exchange supervises stockbrokers and disclosure requirements, while the government body Australian Securities and Investments Commission licenses participants and is responsible for legal enforcement.
2. Those who have studied economics will recognize that these dimensions parallel the three fundamental problems of economic society, as articulated in classics such as Samuelson's *Economics*, namely:

1. 'What' commodities shall be produced?
2. 'How' shall they be produced, that is, 'by whom' and 'with what resources'?
3. 'For whom' are goods produced?

Substituting decision-making into this triplet, 'by whom', 'with what resources' and 'for whom' decisions are made are identified in our classification. That leaves 'what decisions' are made and they relate to public governance, economic governance and corporate governance and the issues encompassed within them, that is to the applications of decision-making.

3. The first year of the Muslim calendar (AH *anno Hegirae*) is from the year of the *hijra* (Prophet Muhammad's (pbuh) migration from Makkah to Madinah in the face of persecution) in 622 CE. The calendar is a lunar calendar, containing 12 months (some of 29 days and others 30 days), based on the motion of the moon. Year 1 of the Islamic calendar corresponds to 622 in the Gregorian calendar (which is based on the motion of the sun). The Islamic year is therefore shorter than the Gregorian year, so that there is no exact equivalence between Islamic and Gregorian year numbering, and in successive years, Islamic months and festivals occur at different dates in the Gregorian calendar. Unless explicitly stated, we will use Common Era (CE) datings.
4. Historical records depict regulators laying down guidelines for transactions free of *riba* (interest); depicting forms of permissible barter, cash, and credit agreements in *shariáh*; and overseeing the honouring of credit transactions (Khan, 1982).
5. When Muslims mention the Prophet Muhammad in speech or print, they usually follow the name with an expression in Arabic which can be translated, 'May the peace and blessings of Allah be upon him', sometimes written as 'pbuh', short for 'peace be upon him'. This is not dissimilar to those Christians in earlier times who, when referring to a revered forebear, would say 'may his or her soul rest in peace'.
6. Ernest Gellner (1981, pp. 16–48) provides a comprehensive discussion of Ibn Khaldun's sociological and economic theories, and their influence on and relationship with modern Western thought.
7. Other noteworthy titles on the classical scheme include Osman (1976), Qureshi (1978), Al-Sayed (1982), Ghaffari (1989), and Ra'ana (1991).

2. The methodology of Islamic economics

INTRODUCTION

In the last chapter it was noted that the closest concept to 'governance' in Arabic is *al-hakimiya* which stems from *hukm* meaning judgement, opinion, decision, rule and administration of justice. In fact, for many traditional Islamic thinkers such as Mawdudi (1998), the only valid starting point for any analysis of the concept of governance in Islam is the notion that rulership or sovereignty belongs to God (that is, *al-hakimiya lillah*). Such a view implies that there exists a revealed set of guidelines on social organization, which stands independently of and prior to any mechanisms for governance. In a Muslim society these standards alone ought to become the basis for all subsequent delegation and exercise of power and authority. In other words, any decision, no matter how fair from a procedural point of view does not carry moral validity to a Muslim if it contravenes or fails to conform with the revealed blueprint of social order.

However, the divine guidance does not come in the form of codified laws ready to be implemented. It has to be mediated by human reason to bring it to the stage of legislation. Who is to perform this task and by what rules and procedures? What are the implications of this additional step for conceptualizing governance in Muslim societies? How does this paradigm compare with the conventional Western views on the methodology of social sciences? This chapter offers an overview and comparison of these two 'disciplinary matrices' so as to delineate the methodology of this volume, for the Islamic perspective on governance and its differences from Western approaches cannot be appreciated without understanding the basic tenets, the philosophy of knowledge and the legal tradition of Islam. Together these constituents define the Islamic approach to social enquiry.

THE METHODOLOGY OF ISLAM

Islam commands authority over the totality of a Muslim's being, not accepting any distinction between the sacred and the secular. Economics, politics, religious and social affairs all fall under the jurisdiction of the divine law of Islam – the *shari'ah* (formally *shari'ah Islami'iah* but generally abbreviated to *shari'ah* or *shari'a*). The literal meaning of the Arabic word *shari'ah* is 'the way to the source of life' and, in a technical sense, it is now used to refer to a legal system in keeping with the code of behaviour called for by the Holy Qur'an and the *hadith* (the authentic tradition). Muslims cannot, in good faith, compartmentalize their behaviour into religious and secular dimensions, and their actions are always bound by the *shari'ah*. Belief in the sovereignty of God is the centrepiece of the Islamic faith, in that it is focused around the worship of God (in Arabic *Allah*) and divine revelations as given in the Holy Qur'an, revealed between 610 and 632 CE to the Prophet Muhammad ibn 'Abd Allah'. The Holy Qur'an is for Muslims, in the most literal sense, the word of God, and Islamic law flows directly from it and is wholly inspired by it. Every act of believers must conform to Islamic law and observe ethical standards derived from Islamic principles. These ethical principles define what is true, fair and just, the nature of individual and corporate responsibilities, and the priorities to society.

Basically, the concept of trusteeship provides the *raison d'être* of good governance in Islam. To a Muslim, all resources are God-given, and ownership of wealth belongs to God. Individuals are only trustees and are accountable to God for their actions. Embedded in the notion of trusteeship is a call for conduct based on a code of personal ethics and a blueprint of justice. Together these canons establish rights and obligations across a network of relationships – familial, social, economic, political and environmental – and regulate both inter- and intra-community affairs. At the intra-community level, Muslims are organized around the fundamental articles and duties of the Islamic faith as contained in the Six Beliefs (in God (Allah), the angels, the prophets, the revealed holy books, the day of judgement, and predestination and the decree of God) and the Five Duties (testimony/affirmation of God and Muhammad (pbuh) as his messenger, prayers (*salat*) five times a day, almsgiving (*zakah*), fasting during the month of Ramadan and pilgrimage (*hajj*) to Makkah (Mecca), which every Muslim must uphold or perform once in life, means permitting). At another level, emphasis is laid on facilitating peaceful interaction among a large number of communities, internally organized around their own sets of beliefs and ways of life different at least in some respects from one another. While the modes of intra-community governance may differ, inter-community relations need regulation too in the spirit of common interests of mankind. Islam proffers broad guidance on all these issues as part and parcel of an ethical framework that constitutes the inner core or 'the soul of governance'.

Based on Mawdudi (1998) and other sources, the basic principles or 'inner core' around which the Islamic theory of governance is built can be summarized in the following terms. First, the concept of *tawhid* overrides all other considerations, in that sovereignty is due to God alone and there is commitment to the life-giver as the only source of value. Second, individuals are trustees ('vicegerents') on Earth for what they are given by God and must account to God in all matters pertaining to human behaviour. Third, the will of God to the viceregents on Earth has been revealed through a succession of Old and New Testament prophets (such as Abraham, Moses, Jacob, Joseph, David, Solomon through to Jesus), the last messenger of God being the Prophet Muhammad (pbuh), the 'seal of the prophets'. Fourth, the exercise of political authority is through the successor of the Prophet (political leader or *Khalifa* (Caliph)) or by the Muslim community (*umma*) in the form of popular viceregency. Fifth, popular representation in the political system is through the institution of *shura* (mutual consultation). The *Shura* (Consultative Council) is a fundamental institutional support of the *Khalifa* in political decisions, while the process of mutual consultation underpins all decision-making and governance matters. Sixth, all aspects of life and political authority must be regulated by *shari'ah*. Seventh, the *bay'ah* (offering of allegiance) to the *Khalifa* is conditional and rests on *shari'ah* being followed as the basis for the legitimate exercise of political authority.

Nevertheless, it is recognized that no ethical code can provide solutions for all possible situations that may arise in future. This creates scope for the role of reason in three respects. First, there is need for a methodology that can relate the revealed guidelines to a given context on a consistent basis. Second, revealed principles need to be actualized through institutional arrangements which define the 'outer core of governance' in Islam. To the extent that such institutions are not given, reason ought to be exercised to arrive at the best temporal solutions. And third, there are other matters on which revelation is silent giving humanity wider scope for the application of rationality.

Traditionally, such processes have fallen in the domain of jurisprudence. This is because in Islam the place of theology is taken by laws and jurisprudence. Those who deal with the intellectual aspects of the religion are jurists or *fuqaha* and not theologians, and at the centre of higher education is jurisprudence and not theology. Since Islam takes personal life and social living in a holistic perspective, Islamic jurisprudence covers all areas of life and not simply those that are of interest to a secular state or society. It is not limited to questions of belief and religious practice, but also deals with criminal and constitution matters, as well as many other fields which in other societies would be regarded either as the province of the secular authorities or none of their business. For instance, strict food laws forbid pork, blood, carrion, specify the method of preparing animals, ban the drinking of any alcoholic beverages and prohibit intoxicants. Also prohibited is the representation of animals or the human figure in art, as a precaution against any lapse into idolatry. The other areas covered by Islamic law are considerable, and include *inter alia,* marriage, divorce, sexual relations, care of children, adoption, maintenance, commercial transactions, and so on. Hussain (1999) provides a survey, while Brown (1997) examines how traditional *shari'ah* law has been adapted in a variety of ways to meet current social needs in Egypt and some of the Gulf States.

Boxes 2.1 and 2.2 provide background to this chapter and, indeed, to the book as a whole. Box 2.1 lists the key dates in Islamic history, beginning with the significant events in the life of the Prophet Muhammad (pbuh) through to the four 'rightly-guided' Caliphs to subsequent dynasties. Box 2.2 gives some brief details of leading Islamic scholars who have contributed to the development of Islamic doctrine, Islamic law and philosophy, including contributions to governance and public finance. Notable among the scholars are those who were instrumental in founding the four major Sunni schools of jurisprudence (Abu Hanifah, Malik, al-Shafi'i and Hanbal).

BOX 2.1 SELECTED DATES IN ISLAMIC HISTORY UNTIL THE SECOND WORLD WAR (COMMON ERA DATES)

Muhammad (pbuh)	*c.* 570–632
Beginning of revelation (recitation)	610
Hijra (emigration to Madinah, 'flight') Year zero of Islamic calendar	622
Announcement of the Constitution of Madinah	623
Battle of Badr. First Muslim victory over Makkans	624
Muslims occupy Makkah	630
Rule of *Rashidun* (rightly-guided) Caliphs	632–61
Caliphate of Abu Bakr (until death)	632–4

Caliphate of Umar ibn al-Khattab (until assassination at dawn prayer). Defeat of Sassanian and Byzantine armies as Islam expands across Arabia, Egypt and Persia	634–44
Caliphate of Uthman ibn Affan (until assassination by insurgents)	644–56
Caliphate of Ali ibn Abi Talib (until assassinated by a Kharijite while praying). First civil war over *qisas* for Uthman	656–61
Caliphate of Mu'awiya, military governor of Syria	661–80
Umayyad rule First 'secular' (non-sanctified) kingdom. Damascus replaces Madinah as Muslim centre	661–750
Mu'awiya dies. Nominates his son, Yazid, as successor	680
Second civil war over succession (murder of Ali's son, Hussain, at the battle of Karbela)	680–92
Caliphate of 'Abd al-Malik	685–705
Arabs conquer Seville	712
Reign of Umar II, conciliatory Umayyad Caliph	717–20
Battle of Poitiers ends Muslim expansion in France	732
Third civil war (Shi'ite uprising. Revolt in support of the descendants of Abbas, the Prophet's uncle, sees Abu al-Abbas of Abbasid house placed on the throne)	744–50
Abbasid dynasty rules most of the Middle East	750–1258
Foundation of Baghdad as new capital of Abbasids	762–3
Caliphate of Harun al-Rashid, zenith of Abbasid culture	786–809
Caliphate of al-Ma'mun	813–33
Buyid dynasty of Daylamite nomads rules Persia and most of central Middle East from Baghdad	945–1055

Seljuks rule Persia and central Middle East from Baghdad	1055–1118
Berber Almoravid (Moors) dynasty rules Morocco, expands into Africa and Spain	1056–1147
First Crusade. Franks invade Syria and Anatolia	1096
Saladin takes Jerusalem from the Crusaders	1187
Age of Mongol domination	1220–1369
Mongols devastate Baghdad, ending the Caliphate	1258
Osman, first Sultan of the Ottomans, leads expansion into Anatolia	1290–1326
Crusaders expelled from Syria	1291
Constantinople captured by Mehmed for the Ottomans and renamed Istanbul, city of Islam	1453
Ottoman Empire rules Anatolia, central Middle East and North Africa, and expands into east and central Europe	1453–1924
Fall of Granada. Arabs expelled from Spain	1492
Muslim dynasties establish rule in Sumatra and eastern Java	1507–22
Rule of Mustafa Kemal (Ataturk) in Turkey. Caliphate abolished. Civil court replaces *shari'ah*	1924–38
Ibn Saud, leader of Wahhabi movement, establishes the Kingdom of Saudi Arabia	1932

Source: Based on information in Lindholm (1996)

Islamic jurisprudence grew after the death of the Prophet Muhammad (pbuh) as many informal groups tried to fill the vacuum on advising the interpretation of the rules of the Holy Qur'an. These groups gradually developed into more organized schools, and produced jurists variously known as '*fuqaha*' and '*ulama*'. Eventually four slightly different schools of thought came to be recognized in Sunnism. The four orthodox schools are the Hanafi, the Maliki, the Hanbali and the Shafi'i. The differences of

BOX 2.2 SOME LEADING ISLAMIC SCHOLARS OF THE EIGHTH TO FIFTEENTH CENTURIES (COMMON ERA DATES)

Abu Hanifah al-Numan b. Thabit (700–767) The founder of the Hanafi school of jurisprudence was born in Kufah and died in Baghdad.
Malik b. Anas (716–95) Founder of the Maliki school of jurisprudence, born and died in Madinah, he gave customary usages of Madinah (*'amal ahl al-Madinah*) great importance in the derivation of rules. His work *al-Muwatta* is the earliest collection of *hadith.*
Yaqub b. Ibrahim Abu Yusuf (731–98) He was the student of Abu Hanifah and one of the co-founders of the Hanafi school of jurisprudence and became chief justice during Harun al-Rashid's era (786–809), the Abbasid Caliph, on whose request he authored *Kitab al-Kharaj* (the Book on Taxation), one of the earliest works on the Islamic system of taxation. Its text was first printed in Cairo in 1885. E. J. Brill published Shemesh's English translation as *Taxation in Islam*, vol. 3, in 1969.
Abu Zakariyya Yahya b. Adam al-Qurashi (752–818) He was a reliable transmitter of traditions. His *Kitab al-Kharaj* was first published by Juynboll in 1896. E.J. Brill published Shemesh's English translation as *Taxation in Islam*, vol. 1, in 1958, Leiden.
Muhammad b. Idris al-Shafi'i (767–820) The author of the famous work *Kitab al-Umm*, he was the architect of systematic Islamic Law. He did not himself found a school of jurisprudence; this was done by his disciples.
Ahmad b. Hanbal (780–855) The originator of the Hanbali school of jurisprudence, he studied in Baghdad and received instructions from the great legal theoretician Iman al-Shafi'i. He is also the compiler of a large collection of *ahadith*.
Abu Ja'far Ahmad b. Nasr al-Dawudi (d. 1012) His *Kitab al-Amwal* was studied and edited by Najib Abdul Wahhab al-Fili. Al-Dawudi's work is important in that it is the only work on the subject of public finance from al-Maghrib. It makes use of earlier, now lost, Malikite and non-Malikite studies of the topic.
Ali b. Muhammad al-Mawardi (974–1058) Born in Baghdad, his work *al-Ahkam al-Sultaniyyah* (the Ordinances of Government, tr. by Wahba, H. Wafa and published by Garnet Publishing, Reading, 1996).

Abu Hamid Muhammad b. Muhammad al-Ghazali (1058–1111) Most of his economic ideas are found in *Ihya 'Ulum al-Din* and *al-Tibr al-Masbuk fi Nasihat al-Muluk* that contain a wide range of subjects including market supervision, taxation and economic role of government.
Fakhr al-Din al-Razi (1149–1209) Judge, theologian (*mutakallim*) and historian, his commentary on the Holy Qur'an, *Mafatih al-Ghayb*, is characterized by philosophical exposition.
Yahya b. Sharaf al-Nawawi (1233–77) Born at Nawa in Syria, and brought up in Damascus he was a great scholar of *hadith* and jurisprudence. He asked the Mamluk sultan to free people from the war taxes imposed upon them. He is author of *Minhaj al-Talibin* (Cairo, 1296 AH) in Shafi'i *fiqh*, commentary on *Sahih Muslim* (Cairo, 1283 AH) and many other important works.
Taqi al-Din Ahmad bin Abd al-Halim Ibn Taymiyyah (1263–1328) His two works *al-Siyasah al-Shar'iyyah* (English translation by Farrukh Omar, 1966) and *al-Hisbah fi'l-Islam* (translated by Muhtar Holland, 1980) present great insights on economic matters. The collection of his *Fatawa* (35 volumes) has a wealth of materials on socio-economic and religious issues.
Abu Is'haq Ibrahim b. Musa al-Shatibi (d. 1388) Born and died at Granada, he was an expert of the principles of jurisprudence. In his *Fatawa*, he accepts social change and application of *al-masalik al-mursalah* (welfare consideration for which there is no specific text). For this reason he allowed certain taxes not mentioned in the *Shari'ah* but made necessary by the economic difficulties of the Nasirid Kingdom in Granada.
Abd al-Rahman Ibn Khaldun (1332–1406). He was born in Tunis and died in Egypt. His work *Kitab al-'Ibar* is a principal source of reference to the history of Arab and non-Arab nations until his time. His *Muqaddimah* (An Introduction to the History), is considered the intellectual achievement of the Middle Ages.

Source: Based on Islahi (2005)

emphasis between individual scholars and schools led to some concern lest Islamic law disintegrate in a plethora of private opinions. In order to counter this risk, al-Shafi'i, who died in 820 CE, produced a doctrine of the four 'roots' of' Islamic law, which was to provide jurists with a fixed and common method of finding law. The first 'root' of Islamic law is naturally the Holy Qur'an. The second 'root' is the *sunnah,* the sum total of inspired practice of the Prophet (pbuh), so important for interpreting and clarifying the rules of the Holy Qur'an. The third 'root' is the *ijma,* the consensus reached by the learned in the Islamic community. The fourth and last 'root' is analogy (*qiyas*), that is, the application to new and similar cases of rules established by the Holy Qur'an, the *sunnah*, or *ijma.* As Zweigert and Kotz (1998, p. 308) note, this classical system of the four 'roots' of Islamic law comprises very different things, namely: two sources – the Holy Qur'an and the *sunnah;* a method – the use of analogy (*qiyas*); and a judgement – that of *ijma*.

Strictly speaking, a distinction can be made between *shari'ah,* the Arabic term referring to the canons that come directly from the original sources, and *fiqh*, the code that is derived from these sources through the exercise of the principles of jurisprudence (*usul-ul-fiqh*). *Shari'ah* is considered as immutable while *fiqh* is subject to revisions. However, in common usage, Muslims continue to take *shari'ah* in a wider sense so as to include both the revealed rules as well as the rules derived through the exercise of logic. The four schools give different emphasis to the methods of jurisprudence, but all are unanimous in requiring that Islamic law be God-given and not man created. As such, the Holy Qur'an and the *sunnah* are fully binding; the other sources of authority are in one way or another justified by reference to these two basic sources.

The most important sectarian division in Islam is the one that separates Sunni and Shia believers, which arose in 661 CE on the question of the rightful leadership of the community. Shi'ism, which has various subsects, is predominant in Iran, and has significant numbers of followers in Iraq, India and many of the Gulf States. There are considerable doctrinal differences between the Shia and the four Sunni schools of Islamic law, in terms of who is permitted to interpret *shari'ah* law. Shi'ites believe that living religious scholars, known as *mujtahids,* have an equal right to interpret Divine Law as eminent jurists of the past, and their judgements replace the Sunni source of deduction by analogy. Consequently, there is in Shi'ism no great body of laws and legal thinking comparable to that found in Sunnism. In spite of such differences the mainstream Shi'ite position on many matters comes within a hair's breadth of Shafi'i understanding. This may ultimately be attributed to the singularity of source material especially the Holy Qur'an among both Shi'ites and Sunnis.

Thus the sources of *shari'ah* are the Holy Qur'an and the *sunnah* (the primary sources) and the interpretations and opinions of the learned jurists (the secondary sources). A brief outline is given below.

PRIMARY SOURCES OF ISLAMIC JURISPRUDENCE

Holy Qur'an

By far the most important source is the Holy Qur'an, the collection of the revelations. The Holy Qur'an is organized into 114 chapters – called *surahs* – of unequal length. Together they contain more than 6200 verses, called *ayah(s)*. The Arabic word '*ayah*' means symbol or the sign of God emphasizing the significance of the revealed word (41:53). The chapters and verses are not arranged in a chronological order implicitly asserting that the guidance is free from the bounds of time and space and has universality. In view of the fact that there are a number of English translations in existence, it should be noted that we have used the 'King Fahd version', namely the English translation of the meanings and commentary as revised and edited by The Presidency of Islamic Researchers, completed at The Custodian of The Two Holy Mosques King Fahd Complex for the Printing of the Holy Qur'an, Madinah under the auspices of The Ministry of Hajj and Endowments, Saudi Arabia.

As Kamali (1998, p. 19) suggests, altogether, there are close to 350 verses in the Holy Qur'an with a legal import. Most repeal customs such as infanticide, usury, gambling and unlimited polygamy. Others laid down penalties to enforce these reforms. There are an estimated 140 verses on devotional matters, another 70 pertaining to rules surrounding marriage, inheritance and bequest. Rules concerning commercial transactions such as sale, lease, loan and mortgage, are indicated in another 70 verses. There are about 30 verses on crimes and penalties. Another 30 verses speak of justice, equality, evidence, consultation and the rights and obligations of citizens. Finally, there are about ten verses relating to other economic matters such as regulating relations between the poor and the rich, workers' rights and so on. Together all these ordinances encompass instruction on three critical areas: faith (*aqidah*), worship (*ibadat*) and social transactions (*mu'amalat*) requiring substantial ideological and social transformation. However, even if only three prohibitions of benefiting from fixed interest (*riba*), speculative exchange (*maysir*) and asymmetric information (*gharar*) were to be taken seriously, it would require re-engineering of the entire financial system with deep implications for the economic system as a whole.

Abdur Rahman i Doi (1989, pp. 38–9) has classified verses with legal import in the Holy Qur'an under four headings:

1. The concise injunctions – these are precise commandments but the Holy Qur'an does not give detailed rules about how they are to be

carried out. Examples of these are prayer, fasting, and payment of *zakah* (alms).

2. The concise and detailed injunctions – these are commandments about which some details are given in the Holy Qur'an, but further information may be discovered from the *hadith* and other recognized sources. Examples are the rules about relations with non-Muslims.
3. The detailed injunctions – the Holy Qur'an gives complete details about these commandments and nothing further is required or may be sought, for example the punishments for specific crimes and also rules about inheritance.
4. Fundamental principles of guidance – these principles do not have clear-cut definitions and the way to put them into effect must be determined through *ijtihad* (use of personal reasoning) in every age.

It is generally agreed that the injunctions contained in the Holy Qur'an must not be altered, but the legal consequences, if any, which attach to their disregard are at times not specified.

The Sunnah

Next in importance after the Holy Qur'an as a source of guidance is the *sunnah* of the Prophet Muhammad (pbuh). The literal meaning of the Arabic word *sunnah* is habit, practice, customary procedure, or action, norm and usage sanctioned by tradition. This was the sense in which the term *sunnah* was customarily applied in early Islam not only to the sayings and normative actions of the Prophet Muhammad (pbuh), but also to the sayings of the companions and the customs and mores of the Muslims in general. However, in the legal thought in Islam, *sunnah* evolved to denote the sayings, actions, and the normative behaviour of the Prophet Muhammad (pbuh). Thus understood, the Holy Qur'an contains general principles of social order couched mostly in ethical rather than legal terminology while *sunnah* demonstrates the application of these principles in the life of individuals, a community, and a state, all under the auspices of the Prophet Muhammad (pbuh).

The legal validity of this source is referred back to the Holy Qur'an which declares that in the life of Muhammad (pbuh) there is an excellent model for humanity to follow and that his extra Qur'anic judgements are binding upon the Muslim community (3:31,132; 4:65,81; 7:157; 16:44; 33:36; 59:7). However, a distinction is usually made between non-legislative *sunnah* and legislative *sunnah*. The former refers to Prophet Muhammad's acts in person that are peripheral to his Prophetic mission, peculiar to him, or not binding on his followers while the latter incorporates the normative rules and principles of *shari'ah* that the Prophet laid down in his capacity as a messenger of God, as the head of state, or as an adjudicator (Kamali, 1998, pp. 44–85). In this respect *sunnah* serves primarily as complementary to the Holy Qur'an clarifying its speculative (*zanni*) verses or specifying and qualifying the general and the absolute contents of the Holy Qur'an. For example, *sunnah* provides essential details for the obligatory redistribution scheme (*zakah*), and also makes the Qur'anic principles on the sanctity of property and general taxation explicit by elaborating their contextual application.

The *sunnah* is extracted from the reports called *hadith* (plural: *ahadith*) that record the Prophet's sayings (*qawli*), actions (*fi'li*), and tacitly approved acts (*taqriri*). In contrast to the Holy Qur'an that was formally recorded by the official scribes, learnt by heart by many, and recited in prayers five times a day and in full in the month of fasting, *ahadith* were in general preserved through committing to memory and communicating through study circles spread from Madinah to Iraq, Egypt, Palestine and North Africa. The first state-sponsored collection of *ahadith* was undertaken during the period of Caliph Umar bin Abdul Aziz (d. 101 AH/719 CE) against the backdrop of the last of the companions of the Prophet Muhammad (pbuh) passing away in the closing decade of the first Hijra century. This collection was, however, not sorted out by topics. The one with well-arranged topics was compiled by Imam Malik bin Anas (95–179 AH) in his private capacity under the name of *Al Muatta*/*Muwatta*. Malik had become prominent in Madinah in issuing religious rulings (*fatawa*). Madinah being the cradle of Islam, Malik obviously had access to a large number of Prophetic traditions. *Muwatta* remains today, a highly trusted source of *ahadith* (DeLorenzo and Al Shaikh-Ali, 1990).

Against the rise of *Shi'ite–Sunni* differences, historically a great effort has been expended on developing a meticulous science of *hadith* evaluation. In general, a *hadith* is divided into two parts: the *matn* (text) and the *isnad* (chain of reporters). To examine *isnad*, a new branch of knowledge called '*asma-ur-rijaal*' (biographies including habits, biases, and inclinations – in brief, integrity – of *hadith* narrators) was invented that devised methods to scrutinize the character and the conduct of hundreds of thousands of people who were part of the chains of narration of *ahadith* from the Prophet. Further scrutiny was based on continuity of the chain, ascertaining that a meeting between the successive narrators did take place, on textual characteristics of the reported words of the Prophet, and on concordance with the Qur'anic message (Karim, 1969, pp. 21–4). On this basis, six collections of *ahadith* have attained a canonical status in Sunni jurisprudence. Named after their compilers, these are, Sahih Bukhari (810–70 CE), Sahih Muslim (817–74 CE), Nasa'i (d. 915 CE), Abu Dawood

(817–88 CE), Tirmizi/Tirmidhi (821–92 CE), and Ibn Majah (824–86 CE). Sahih Bukhari is considered as the most authentic after the Holy Qur'an and contains close to 3000 *ahadith*.[1]

In short, Holy Qur'an and *sunnah* go hand in hand in providing source material for deducing regulations. Following Kamali (1998, 366–8), based on text and *hadith* veracity, the legislative material in these sources is classified as:

1. Evidence that is authentic and clear (that is, definite) in meaning;
2. Evidence that is authentic yet imprecise (that is, speculative) in meaning;
3. Evidence that is less than authentic (for example, a *hadith* with a defect in its chain of narrators) but definitive in meaning;
4. Evidence that is speculative both in respect of authenticity and meaning.

Items 1 and 2 above apply to both sources while 3 and 4 apply to *hadith* literature only.

SECONDARY SOURCES

Ijtihad

Methods of Islamic jurisprudence consist of the rules of linguistic and textual interpretation, and guidelines on modes of reasoning (such as *qiyas*, *istihsan*, *istishab*, etc.) and reaching consensus (*ijma*) in order to facilitate and inform law-creation. In essence, all such modes fall under the broad category of *ijtihad* (Kamali, 1998, pp. 1–5). The term '*ijtihad*' literally means 'exertion of one's abilities'. Shah Wali Allah (Ahmad, 1993, p. 346) defines *ijtihad* as exhausting one's intellectual effort in arriving at legal rulings in matters over which there is no explicit statement in the Holy Qur'an or the *hadith*, and it is a communal obligation until the end of time. A number of Qur'anic verses (for example, 29:69), *ahadith*, historical instances, and rational arguments can be cited in support of the validity of *ijtihad*. The most frequently cited *hadith* records a conversation that took place between the Prophet Muhammad (pbuh) and Mu'adh ibn Jabal on the occasion of Mu'adh's appointment as governor of Yemen:

> How will you adjudicate in matters that will be put before you? He replied: I shall judge in accordance with Allah's Book (Holy Qur'an). The Prophet asked: (What will you do) if you do not find any guidance in Allah's Book? He replied:

(I shall act) in accordance with the *sunnah* of the Apostle of Allah (peace be upon him). The Prophet asked: (What will you do) if you do not find any guidance in the *sunnah* of the Apostle of Allah (peace be upon him)? He replied: I shall do my best to form an opinion and I shall spare no effort to arrive at the right decision. The Apostle of Allah (peace be upon him) then patted him on the breast and said: Praise be to Allah Who has guided the messenger of the Apostle of Allah to find what pleases Allah and the Apostle of Allah. (Sunan Abu Dawood, *Hadith*, 3585)

Clearly, the essence of *ijtihad* lies in discovering the broader goals of *shari'ah*, the rationale behind its individual provisions, and the link between the two.[2]

Qiyas or analogy

The starting point for *ijtihad* is '*qiyas*' or analogy. Lambton (1981, p. 9) explains two methods. First, the solution to a problem can be arrived at by discovering a similarity between its external features and those of a case already decided in the Holy Qur'an or *sunnah*. Second, the solution can be based on an investigation of the rationale behind a certain *shari'ah* provision and the application of that rationale to the case under consideration. For example, analogical reasoning extends the ban on alcohol to narcotics.

Istihsan or juristic equity

Istihsan as a principle of *ijtihad* was originally developed by the *Hanafi* school of legal thought and its purpose was to set aside the results of analogy if it was likely to cause undue inconvenience or hardship to people, was not in the interest of the public good, was against the broader rules of justice, or a common-sense solution appeared more equitable than analogy. An example comes from the Prophetic saying that one who purchases cereal should not on-sell it before taking delivery (Al-Muwatta (*Hadith*, 31.49)). Ibn Abbas extended this provision to all other things using analogy. However, some jurists do not agree with such extension because of the undue hardship it imposes on business and the fact that not extending this ruling to all things does not contravene any Qur'anic or *hadith* commandment.

Istislah or public good

Istislah is somewhat similar to *istihsan* but the prime consideration here is to the conditions which secure benefit or prevent harm. Examples come from decisions of Caliphs in issuing currency, establishing prisons, and imposing taxes on agricultural lands, and so on. Obviously, given that the explicit and definitive principles and commandments of *shari'ah* themselves are based on the objective of attaining public good and welfare, *istihsan* and *istislah* cannot override *shari'ah* (Kamali, 1998, p. 267).

General guidance, commutation and preference

There is an established principle in *shari'ah* that compelling circumstances – rigour or harm – justify commutation (2:185; 22:78). The Prophet Muhammad (pbuh) once said, 'Religion is very easy and whoever overburdens himself in religion, will not be able to continue' (Sahih Bukhari (*Hadith*, 1.38)). Such commandments have led *fuqaha* to lay out certain general principles for guidance, commutation and preference. First, whatever leads to a forbidden act is also forbidden. Second, choose the easier of the two equally valid alternatives. Third, do not force on people what is preferable but not obligatory if it causes hardship. Fourth, commutation must correspond with the degree of compulsion and lapse with the removal of hardship. Fifth, under compulsion, choose the lesser of two evils. Sixth, warding off bad has a priority over doing good. This means *shari'ah* is more liberal with easing the rigour of dos than relaxing the don'ts. Seventh, it is unlawful to repel a bad when it is expected to result in a bad with equal or greater magnitude (Mawdudi, 1994, pp. 306–7).

Miscellaneous sources

Among other recognized sources of *ijtihad* are: customary law or practice which is akin to consensus (silent *ijma*) and mostly overrides analogy; revealed laws prior to Islam but not abrogated by Islam; guiding propositions such as what was not prohibited could be considered valid; and thoughtful, weighed, and rational opinion that does not contradict primary sources.

Consensus (*ijma*)

The word *ijma* is derived from the Arabic word '*ajma'a*' that means 'unanimous agreement'. In the Islamic legal terminology, the word *ijma* signifies unanimous agreement of competent *fuqaha* on any matter after the Prophet Muhammad (pbuh) expired. This definition precludes from the ambit of *ijma* the agreement of those not competent in *shari'ah* (Kamali, 1998). In theory, *ijma* can also represent agreement of all the scholars in a particular locality that binds the community in that locality to that decision while a universal *ijma* binds the entire Muslim community on that issue. However, while local *ijma* is easier to establish, the universal *ijma* is operationally difficult to achieve. The term *ijma* is also interpreted sometimes within the confines of an established legal school. The support for *ijma* comes from the Holy Qur'an (for example, 42:38) and *ahadith. Ijma* has played a pivotal role in the development and advancement of the body of Islamic law. In fact, a major portion of the Islamic law consists of the consensus of jurists' opinions (which is the case in the finance area).

The *ijtihad–ijma* process

The essence of the *ijtihad–ijma* process lies in the natural growth of ideas and expansion of knowledge in the life of a community. As Kamali (1998, p. 171) explains, it begins with the personal *ijtihad* of a competent Muslim advancing an opinion on a particular issue not explicitly addressed in the Holy Qur'an and the *sunnah*. The opinion is evaluated by other jurists and a debate on the issue is initiated. Differences of opinion are tolerated and there is no scope for the imposition of one opinion on the whole community. Over time, a greater acceptance of one opinion over others thrusts the dialogue towards some sort of consensus or defines the range within which opinions on a matter diverge.

The *ijtihad–ijma* process ends up in classifying conduct into five categories: prescribed (obligatory), recommended (preferable/meritorious), permissible (allowed), disliked, and the unlawful (*haram* or prohibited). The obligatory acts again have two aspects: those obligatory in person and those obligatory upon the community so that if some fulfil these acts, others are exonerated. This latter category is called *fard-e-kifaya*.

The status of *ijtihadi* law

Although *ijtihad* is meant to be a corollary of the Holy Qur'an or *hadith*, its product is considered to be a weak source of law and its authority is ranked lower than the text of the Holy Qur'an and *hadith* or that of *ijma*. This is because the law created through *ijtihad* cannot be expected to escape in full, the limitations of time, space, and socio-economic circumstances within which the interpretation of speculative text is undertaken. Also, there is scope for inadvertent mistakes in undertaking *ijtihad* even though Prophet Muhammad (pbuh) has made it clear that such efforts in good intention are spiritually rewarding (Sahih Bukhari (*Hadith*, 9.450). On this basis, on matters where there is no clear revelation, none of the schools of *fiqhi* thought has an exclusive claim to truth. Rather, these schools offer a range of choices among equally valid alternatives. These choices can always be put to the test of *shari'ah* evidence, reasoning, and practicality and the most suitable alternative can be chosen. Moreover, the 'gates' to *ijtihad* are not closed.[3] Given sound rationale, there is always scope for revision as long as the revised understanding is in keeping with the updated understanding of *shari'ah*.

A CRITIQUE OF ISLAMIC METHODOLOGY

There is potential for scrutinizing Islamic methodology primarily on the basis of the validity and integrity of metaphysics as a source *per se* of knowledge let alone of deriving precepts for social organization. As we shall see later in this chapter, the theory of positivistic basis for knowledge has been at the forefront of such critique. Once we go beyond this point, other issues emerge as part of a broader Western evaluation of Islam. In particular, there are reservations about the claims of Muhammad (pbuh) as the Prophet of God, of the Holy Qur'an as the Divine revelation, of *ahadith* as authentic and as a trustworthy and substantive record of *sunnah*, of *sunnah* as a source of law, and of *ijma* as a formally recognized source of law in early Islam. Such critiques surface against the backdrop of there being hardly any source material existing on early Islam that is independent of the Islamic tradition itself. A detailed analysis of such critique lies outside the scope of this book. Readers interested in these issues may like to read Bennett (1998) and Ali (1997) for a broader review and response to such criticism.

A related issue is the implementation of the Islamic methodology. Three points are noteworthy. First, unless one is well versed in the sum total of *shari'ah* commandments on any given issue, there is a possibility of selectively picking and choosing some pieces giving rise to a distorted view of Islam on a particular issue. Second, one may be well-versed on all of the *shari'ah* commandments on a particular issue but still fall short of understanding the broader goals and the spirit of *shari'ah* and how objectives in a specific area relate to the broader goals. The result may be no different. Third, there is a danger that one may emphasize methodology at the cost of the spirit of *shari'ah*, ending up in suppressing rather than bringing out the best in Islam. According to Kamali (1998), Islamic legal thought has, on the whole, been preoccupied with ensuring conformity with the letter of the Divine text, and the legal science of *usul-al-fiqh* has facilitated this pursuit (p. 400). As we shall see later, this is an important issue surrounding judicial issues on the legality of Islamic financial instruments.

Arguably, one major reason for this state of affairs is the education system in many Muslim countries that produces graduates familiar with the modern social sciences but having little awareness of the distinctive methodology of Islam. In contrast to this are the products of the private religious school system familiar with Islam but with little appreciation of modern social scientific knowledge. The result is that those who know Islam find it difficult to actualize its principles through institutional means that have evolved within a Western context; and the ones familiar with the Western concepts find a compulsion to drag whatever they know about Islam towards the framework with which they are familiar. How to get these two streams to begin to interact in the spirit of discovering the truth, and actualizing it, is a major challenge for Muslim countries.

THE WESTERN PERSPECTIVE

The roots of the modern Western scholarship on social sciences stretch back to Greek thought and its emphasis among other things on the study of being or existence (ontology), knowing (epistemology), and acting as a person (ethics). Interest in these divisions of philosophy was reignited in the fifteenth and sixteenth centuries when increased dynamism in trade and commerce undermined a hierarchical feudal-cum-religious order and gradually transformed Europe into a society with a more individualistic and secular outlook. A key intellectual enquiry of the times focused on finding a rational basis for organizing society. Scientific discoveries over the seventeenth and eighteenth centuries, in particular the explanation by Newton (1642–1727 CE) of the movement of heavenly bodies in terms of universal laws of gravitation, led to the question of whether the humanities too could discover the laws underlying social phenomena if only researchers would follow the same logical structure of inquiry as in hard sciences (for example, physics). The objective was to systematically explain, predict, and control social phenomena based on factual evidence rather than religion. That paradigm has since lived on. It is no wonder then that most books on methodology of economics begin with the philosophy of science.

The scientific method

Descartes (1596–1650) is generally regarded as the founder of modern philosophy due to his commitment to the scientific method. It was with the intention of extending mathematical method to all fields of human knowledge that he developed his methodology or method of 'Cartesian doubt' as it has come to be called (Bertrand Russell, 1961). In the *Discourse on Method* (1637) and *Meditations* (1642), Descartes discards the authoritarian system of the scholastics and begins with universal doubt. But there is one thing that cannot be doubted: doubt itself. This is the kernel of truth expressed in the phrase, *Cognito, ergo sum* ('I think, therefore I am'). What is important in this doctrine is the method of critical doubt. Cartesian philosophy, by emphasizing thoughts as the indubitable starting points, has influenced European philosophy ever since, both in the rationalist and the empirical camp.

Rationalism sees knowledge as metaphysical, existing independently of the physical reality, and discoverable through the use of reason. It trusts the capacity of the mind to know things even without experience (Descartes, Spinoza, Leibniz). Empiricism, on the other hand, is the belief that experience – sense perception – is the source of knowledge (Locke, Berkeley, Hume). The dominant paradigm at present can be described as empirical realism or logical empiricism.

Three propositions mark logical empiricism. First, reality (the ultimate object of scientific investigation) exists for the most part quite independent of or at least prior to the observer and the way in which it is investigated. Second, what can be known (knowledge) about reality is grounded in sense experience or impression. In fact, anything not given in sense experience is not to be counted as reality (positivism). Third, the human mind (knower) while fantasizing or thinking spontaneously is guided gently by 'resemblance', by temporal and spatial 'contiguity' and by 'causation'. However, while making inferences, it is guided, rather less gently, by causation (David Hume's (1711–76) analysis of causality). Causation is the conjunction of two events that happen to be contiguous in time and space: the one that is prior in time is labelled the cause while the one that happens later is the effect. There need not be any necessary connection (intervening mechanism) between the cause and effect. Nevertheless, the object of scientific effort is to search, explain, and predict such causation (Blaug, 1980; Lawson, 1997). Is there a standard methodology to execute this task?

Methodological debates

Inductive inference was considered to play a major role in scientific investigation in the nineteenth century. Inquiry began with the unprejudiced observation of facts leading, through inductive inference, to the formulation of a general law about these facts, and by further induction, to statements of even more generality, called theories. Both laws and theories were tested for their truth content by confronting the empirical predictions derived from them with all available observations (Blaug, 1980, p. 2). However, there was a problem recognized since the days of David Hume: there was no form of logical argument that justified the truth of anyone's claims to empirical knowledge of the form of a general statement (for example all hitherto unobserved emeralds are green), which could be a law of economics or the criterion for choosing between competing explanations, based on the truth of any number of singular observation reports (for example every emerald observed so far has been green). Such inferences occurred all the time but the argument was that the premises did not logically imply the conclusions. Thus, in the above example, it is not inconsistent with the observation (premise) that the general conclusion drawn is false (Boland, [1982] 1998).

In the twentieth century, the methodology was given a new turn by the 'verifiable principle of meaning' advanced by the Vienna Circle ('logical positivism'). The Vienna Circle was formed around Moritz Schlick when he was professor of philosophy at the University of Vienna in the 1920s.[4] The movement considered philosophy an analytical, rather than a speculative enquiry, and sought to introduce to it the methodology of the natural sciences. Knowledge, it was argued, was grounded in experience and verifiable by observation and experiment, resulting in a formal link between sense experience (empirical evidence) and the ideas and theories that constitute our understanding of the world. Those propositions for which it was not possible to establish such a correspondence were considered as meaningless. The implication was that there was a clear demarcation between logically/empirically verifiable disciplines, such as science on the one hand and empirically non-verifiable areas, such as metaphysics (and by extension, philosophy), religion and ethics, on the other hand. Scientific (that is, rational) statements were either analytic statements, true by virtue of the definition of their own terms (tautologies), or synthetic statements, true by virtue of practical experience and, in principle, empirically verifiable. The latter were seen as the ultimate criterion of truth and rational belief as part of a cultural agenda to rid social disciplines of any metaphysical foundations and re-establish them on scientific lines geared to predicting the future based on analysing past or present regularities (Blaug, 1980; Redman, 1991).

On closer scrutiny, it became clear that the propositions advanced by the Vienna circle could not overcome the problem of induction but rather complicated it even further. Karl Popper (1959), for example, demonstrated that verification was a logical fallacy equivalent to induction. Every explanation involved assumptions of a strictly universal nature (for example, 'all swans are white') that could never be verified with empirical observations. However, it was possible to refute such propositions based on a single observation (for example, 'Today, I saw a black swan in the zoo'). Besides, the criterion of verifiability excluded non-observable entities such as electrons in particle physics, and natural selection in the theory

Table 2.1 A comparison of the positions of Popper and the Vienna Circle

Popper	Vienna Circle
1. Science starts with a problem 2. Popper radically rejects induction 3. Against verifiability 4. Advocates demarcation between pseudoscience and science 5. Perceives his work as philosophy; critical of traditional philosophy	1. Science starts with observation 2. Assume Hume's proof of the logical invalidity of induction but still find induction useful 3. For verifiability 4. Advocate demarcation between meaningful and meaningless statements 5. Most members reject philosophy

Source: Redman, 1991, p. 58.

of evolution. This provoked Popper's famous comment that positivists, in their anxiety to destroy metaphysics, destroyed natural sciences along with it. To overcome these objections, logical positivists advanced confirmability as an alternative but it turned out to be too weak to exclude all statements that did not make sense. Popper's criterion of falsifiability became hard to bypass (Redman, 1991).

A question arises: if the scientific process consists in endless refutation of existing hypotheses, from where do the hypotheses emanate? Whereas logical positivists saw sense experience as the source of primary hypotheses, Popper entertained a wide array of sources including conjecture, value judgement, or even a myth rooted in personal or historical experience. The chief differences between Popper and the Vienna Circle are summarized in Table 2.1.

In turn, Popper's view of falsification has not gone unchallenged. Redman (1991, pp. 32–5), for example, gives five reasons why falsification fails. First, the problem of induction resurfaces, as a number of theories may explain the available facts. That requires some choice criteria for which induction resurfaces. Second, theories unlike simple statements ('all swans are white') are a complex web of assumptions, laws, and conditions. Falsification may point to a problem with the assumptions rather than with the theory *per se*. Third, application of the falsification criteria to the history of science indicates that some of the best theories would have been rejected. Theories are not necessarily rejected when observations conflict with them. Fourth, Popper overestimates the objectivity of the scientific enterprise. Theories can be immunized against refutation through tactics or stratagems. Fifth, as Popper himself argues, the empirical basis of science itself is fallible. The acceptance or rejection of basic statements in science is an outcome of a decision-making process akin to trial by jury and there is nothing 'absolute' or 'definite' about it.

Post-war views

As a consequence of such critiques, a more moderate view of science has emerged after the Second World War. It is argued that all truly scientific explanations have a common logical structure: they consist of 'explanans' or premises (at least one universal law plus a statement of relevant initial or boundary conditions) from which 'explanandum' (a statement of some event for which explanation is sought) is derived through the rules of deductive logic. Laws express regularities of the form 'whenever event x then event y' (note the implicit Humean view of causation) whereas 'event x' can be a composite of many events and the proposed relationship between events can be probabilistic or deterministic. In practice, such laws are assessed (confirmed, corroborated, falsified, tested) by their instances. This view has become the received view about the scientific method and is variously known as 'logical empiricism', a 'hypothetico-deductive' model, Popper–Hempel theory, covering law, or deductive–nomological (D–N) model of scientific explanation (Lawson, 1997).

It was initially thought that explanation and prediction involved logical inferences of the same kind. The symmetry thesis, as it became known, was subsequently contested and rejected. Prediction, it was argued, only requires a correlation whereas explanation requires an intervening mechanism that connects cause with effect. Note, however, that causal mechanism may after all be a metaphysical concept, for example, gravity in Newton's theory of gravitation. Thus in the words of Blaug, it is perfectly possible to predict well without explaining anything. Conversely, Darwin's theory explains how species may have evolved in the past but cannot predict the path of their future evolution (Blaug, 1980).

Logical empiricism has been criticized on the basis of its mismatch with the history of science, and alternative philosophies have been offered, for instance, by Feyerabend (1965), Kuhn (1962, 1974), Toulmin (1961), Berger and Luckmann (1966) and others. The general thrust of such argument is that:

1. The distinction between fact and value is mistaken. Language, the basic forms of human society, and theory formulation are intimately involved in the acknowledgement of any situation as a 'fact'. Facts are not given prior to any theoretical presumptions. Rather, faced with conflicting evidence it is usually possible to keep the theory and revise the facts, as well as to keep the facts and revise the theory. Nor is there

any hard line between fact and convention, between the analytic and the synthetic (Sheehan, 1995, p. 9).

2. Research is conceived, undertaken and analysed within a conceptual framework, world view or disciplinary 'matrix'. It is this disciplinary matrix that determines the formulation of questions, methods of enquiry, criterion of fact finding, and significance attached to these facts. Researchers with different world views may see very different things in the same phenomenon. In other words, research is inherently subjective because observations and facts are theory-laden and all knowledge is socially constructed (Burgess-Limerick *et al.*, 1994).
3. It is hard to characterize science by its subject matter. Rather, science is distinguished by its method of formulating and testing propositions. The demarcation criterion should be taken as describing a more or less continuous spectrum of knowledge, with natural sciences such as physics at one end, poetry, the arts and literary criticism at the other, and with history and the social sciences in between, hopefully nearer to the former (Blaug, 1980, pp. 12–13).
4. It is inappropriate to equate science with certain knowledge. As Popper (1959) says:

   > There is no criterion of truth at our disposal, and this fact supports pessimism. But, we do possess criteria which, if we are lucky, may allow us to recognize error and falsity. Clarity and distinctness are not criteria of truth, but such things as obscurity or confusion may indicate error. . . . Neither observation nor reason is an authority. Intellectual intuition and imagination are most important, but they are not reliable: they may show us things very clearly, and yet they may mislead us. They are indispensable as the main sources of our theories; but most of our theories are false anyway. (p. 28)

   > I believe that it would be worth trying to learn something about the world even if in trying to do so we should merely learn that we do not know much. This state of learned ignorance might be a help in many of our troubles. It might be well for all of us to remember that, while differing widely in the various little bits we know, in our infinite ignorance we are all equal. (p. 29)

5. Emphasis on one standard methodology should be viewed with suspicion. The evolution of science indicates that scientific advances do not depend on adherence to methodological rules.

THE METHODOLOGY OF CONVENTIONAL ECONOMICS

Hume's views on causality proved influential in the search for grounding social sciences, in some form of utility or features of human nature.

Individualism became a key tenet of the science of economics. In general, economics has followed in the footsteps of the philosophy of science in making the hypothetico-deductive model of scientific enquiry its ideal. Econometrics and economic theory both reflect this understanding. Nevertheless, three formal views on the methodology of economics – conventionalism, instrumentalism and apriorism – warrant consideration. These are examined below after a study of the principles of methodological individualism and welfarism.

Individualism and welfarism

In modern-day economics, groups do not have identifiable existence distinct from individuals. Societies therefore have no ends apart from those of its individuals. Individuals alone have means, values, plans and ends. Individuals alone are the best judges of their self-interest and welfare. Individual subjective perceptions of a social state are the only allowable basis for evaluating the well being of society. Paternalism (Mrs Thatcher's 'the nanny state') is ruled out since parties external to those directly concerned are not allowed to impose their views and values on others. According to Boland ([1982] 1998, p. 41), the methodological essence of this proposition is that it provides the 'atoms' or minimal facts from which one is to induce laws of economics. In effect, the only allowable exogenous variables in any theory are the psychological states of individuals and natural givens.

The psychological states of individuals are entailed in the concept of utility, a theoretical measure equated with happiness, desire fulfilment, or satisfaction of preferences. It is assumed that human beings are independent, rational, self-seeking individuals embedded in a network of exchange, maximizing utility through interaction with others. However, since utility by definition is a state of mind, it is unobservable. It has to be inferred from revealed preferences – actual choices made, say, in buying and selling of goods and services in the market. This change in focus from subjective preferences to actual choices brings a corresponding shift in viewing social arrangements in terms of end-states or outcomes to the processes under which these outcomes are generated. If there is 'freedom to choose', whatever emerges from this process is acceptable in line with classical liberal thought.

Free markets facilitate consumers to choose the bundle of goods that maximizes their utility and allows producers to choose the input–output combination that maximizes their productive profits. A market, however, cannot operate in a vacuum. Property rights must be assigned and protected, and contracts respected and implemented. Besides, market participation is not the only goal. There are common goals (social goals) that a group of individuals may wish to pursue in addition to private goals, hence the institution of government. If the market by and large is a spontaneous order, the government is quite the opposite. It is an institution by design, and as such poses a challenge to the postulate of individualism: what criteria should the government follow to make a choice among alternative actions? The objective is to identify social preferences (social choice criteria) from the preferences of individuals, that is, individual rankings of alternative social states. This task has traditionally been assigned to welfare economics.

Pigovian welfare economics considerably simplified the problem of aggregation by assuming interpersonal utility comparisons. This allowed for studying distributional issues in addition to the traditional efficiency concerns. As Lionel Robbins (1935) argued, however, such comparison is tantamount to a value judgement. How then to aggregate individual preferences if these are ordinal and non-comparable? The answer in terms of the Pareto principle – that is, a group of individuals increases its welfare in moving from social state a to b if at least one individual is better off in b and no individual is worse off – was not only unrealistic, but ignored other important aspects of social states, *viz.* liberty, rights and distribution of goods (Acocella, 1998).

Attempts to overcome these shortcomings with a set of widely accepted axioms (for example by Arrow, [1951] 1963) indicate that a complete ranking of social states is not possible without accepting the preferences of one individual (that is, dictatorial choices). Alternatively, interpersonal utility comparisons (value judgements) have to be admitted to obtain a non-dictatorial social ordering. There is the need to supplement the Pareto criteria with a principle that enables us to evaluate all possible alternative situations, especially in the realistic case where an improvement in one person's situation comes at the cost of another. The search for such principles brings welfare economics full circle back to theories of distributive justice that have been the concern of philosophers since the times of Aristotle. It is from these disciplines that economics, in its applied or policy persona, borrows the criteria of social choice.

Conventionalism

Conventionalism can be stated as follows. Given that the truth of any theory cannot be established with reference to the facts, the most one can achieve is a logically valid, that is, consistent, deductive proof based on the 'prior' acceptance of a set of conventions. Thus the classic problem of induction is redefined to one of choosing the 'best' theory among several competitors. In other words, a theory can be 'better' or 'worse' than some other competing theory (subject to conditions) but a 'better' one or even the 'best' so obtained may not necessarily equate with the 'true' theory. The emphasis here is twofold, first on improving the empirical support for a theory (that is, to maximize the quantity of facts or improve their quality) and, second, on providing some criterion, such as 'generality' as a substitute for truth (Boland, [1982] 1998).

Instrumentalism

Instrumentalism deals with the problem of induction in economics by separating the 'truth status' of a theory from its success in generating useful predictions or conclusions for practical policies. Based on Friedman (1953), the only relevant test of the validity of a hypothesis is comparison of its predictions with experience. The hypothesis is rejected if its predictions are contradicted ('frequently' or more often than predictions from an alternative hypothesis), accepted if its predictions are not contradicted, and great confidence is attached to it if has survived many opportunities for contradiction. On this criterion, the realism of assumptions does not matter and the choice among alternative hypotheses equally consistent with the available facts is rather arbitrarily based on a priori criteria such as simplicity, fruitfulness and generality.

The difference between instrumentalism and conventionalism is quite subtle. Both agree that there is no direct solution to the problem of induction, they only disagree about what should be done. While conventionalism looks for some criterion to provide a truth substitute, instrumentalism seeks short-run criteria that promise immediate success regardless of their truth status. The classic choice is between 'generality' and 'simplicity'. Conventionalists favour generality while instrumentalists favour simplicity. Generality fits well with the conventionalist view that a theory is a filing cabinet for systematically storing and describing available facts, hence the more that can be stored, the better (Boland, [1982] 1998, pp. 146–7).

Apriorism

Apriorism, most characteristically associated with von Mises (for example, [1949] 1996) is based on strict insistence on the aprioristic nature of theoretical knowledge in economics, and, for that matter, of all human action. The proposition is that the human mind is not a *tabula rasa* on which the external events write their own history but rather equipped with an a priori set of tools to grasp reality, namely the logical structure of human ideas (based on certain fundamental logical relations) and principles of causality and teleology. It is through pure deduction from a series of postulates derived a priori from inner experience – not open to external verification – that the system of economics is derived. Given that an argument begins with an a priori true statement and the logical steps for deduction are sound, the conclusions reached would be philosophically sound, that is, beyond doubt. The approach is criticized on many accounts, for example, how can the (ideal-type) claim that someone has discovered a unique set of a priori true axioms be established? Von Mises' position was that one either likes it or not. Certainly many renowned economists, who followed in the tradition of the Austrian school, were to a lesser or greater degree apriorists (Boettke, 1999).

A critique of the methodology of economics

Boland ([1982] 1998) argues that the focus of conventionalism on resolving the 'irresolvable' problem of induction is misplaced. The philosophy of science contends that one can never prove that one is correct, even if one is. Rather, the most one can know is that one's understanding is false – if it actually happens to be false. But what does falsifiability achieve? It precludes tautologies but does not preclude metaphysics. Metaphysics instead becomes a matter of choice. In fact:

> The most important assumptions in neoclassical economics, such as the maximization hypothesis or the assumption of the variability of all factors, are unfalsifiable. . . . Similarly, the most important assumptions in Marxist theory are unfalsifiable. . . . If we believe in a Conventionalist implementation of falsifiability criterion, there would virtually be no acceptable social theory, since all explanatory theories involve at least one key assumption which is put beyond refutation. (p. 173)

Yet, metaphysics does not stop there. As we noted in the discussion on the philosophy of science, the very distinction between fact and value is open to questioning. Against this backdrop, Boland (p. 17) reminds us that the oft-repeated distinction in economics textbooks, between the positive and the normative, is just a relic of the late nineteenth century attempts to save inductivism.

Where does it all lead in terms of methodology? Boland appears to be arguing that a far humbler view of the neoclassical paradigm ought to prevail. It is possible that additional bits of information that 'confirm' accepted theories over time simultaneously increase the chances of their refutation. It is possible that conventionalism's criteria for theory-choice are totally inappropriate in terms of the 'realism', that is the 'truth' or 'falsity' of economic models. After all, if many theories can fit available data, what motivates the introduction of certain theory-choice criteria? Once certain conventions and formats are widely adopted as standards of acceptability for published research, only already accepted positions on many issues are perpetuated and the scope for research and dialogue on alternative possibilities diminishes. What is required then is to assimilate the lesson from the philosophy of science that there does not exist any rational process which yields guaranteed true knowledge. Therefore every contribution to economics should be welcomed, considered conjectural but potentially valid, and criticized (refuted) on merit without having regard to it conforming with a given (for example, neoclassical) paradigm. This also means accepting the fact that there is no universal, all-purpose methodology but instead many possible methodologies, each appropriate for a particular set of problems. With this thought in mind, we now return to the Islamic paradigm.

COMPARING THE TWO METHODOLOGIES

Nearly one thousand years ago, there was a debate among Muslim philosophers about the cause-and-effect relationship in physical phenomena. Two representative views, then considered as poles apart, were canvassed. Ibn Sina (aka Avicenna (980–1037 CE)) thought that objects in the universe were real, existed independently of one another, and were driven by their inherent nature. Accordingly, what appeared as cause-and-effect, too, was real and there was a logical impossibility of a departure from the natural course of events in the physical world. In contrast to this, Ghazali (1058–1111 CE) thought that the existence of universe was a manifestation of God's power to create and sustain, which meant that God was intimately involved with His creation through its continuous re-creation. In this larger context, regularities in nature were the result not of the inherent properties of objects (cause-and-effect) but rather of God's custom and choice to recreate (35:41). Human minds, however, interpret things differently:

> when something . . . is repeated over and over again (so as to form the Norm), its pursuance of a uniform course in accordance with the Norm in the past is indelibly impressed upon our minds. (Al-Ghazali, 1958, p. 189)

Nevertheless, God, the Almighty, is not bound by how human beings interpret His ways. He could cease to re-create anything at any moment, cause an unexpected event as He causes expected ones, or bring anything into existence afresh anytime.

Note that Ghazali is not denying the impression of cause-and-effect recorded on the human mind, for, assertion of anything contrary to that, that is of a 'regular irregularity' in nature would make human beings schizophrenic. Rather, his concern appears to be to save science from self-aggrandisement or redeem belief from rendering God irrelevant. This he does by emphasizing the importance of the First Cause and the nature of its involvement every moment with the creation. His position reconciles the possibilities of knowledge about the nature of the created manifest reality with that of religion and is in harmony with the revelation of the Holy Qur'an.

Examining the views of both Ibn Sina and Al-Ghazali on this issue, Harding (1993) points out that they respectively pre-empt the modern Newtonian and Quantum models of the universe. Clearly then, insofar as physics is concerned, there is no difference between the Islamic and the Western positions on methods. In this respect, it is interesting to note the views of Schumpeter (1954) on Newton and other scientists of the time:

> For any worker whose philosophy includes Christian belief, research is research into the works of God. For him, the dignity of his vocation flows from the conviction that his work is revealing a part, however small, of the Divine order of things. Thus, Newton expressed Christian beliefs in a purely scientific work. Leibniz went readily from matters of pure physics and mathematics to matters of theology – he evidently saw no difference of methodological principle between the two, and theological aspects suggested themselves to his mind with the utmost ease. Leonhard Euler (1707–83) argued for his 'method for finding curves that enjoy certain extremal properties' on the ground that the world is the work of the most perfect Creator and hence must be amenable to description in terms of maximum and minimum propositions. (p. 31)

Nevertheless, Schumpeter puts his own interpretation on their beliefs:

> nobody doubts that there was no influence of this kind, that is, (a) that the scientific work of the . . . authors mentioned was not deflected from its course by their theological convictions; (b) that it is compatible with any philosophical positions; and (c) that there would be no point in trying to explain its methods or results by their philosophical positions. They simply co-ordinated their methods and results with their live Christian belief as they would co-ordinate with it everything else they did. They put their scientific work in a theological garb. But, so far as the content of this work is concerned, the garb was removable.
>
> I hold that the garb of philosophy is removable also in the case of economics: economic analysis has not been shaped at any time by the philosophical opinions that economists happened to have, though it has frequently been vitiated by their political attitudes. (pp. 30–1)

To a degree, there is some agreement also between Islamic and Western positions on the inability of human beings to generate knowledge about the nature of the First Cause and other entities that exist beyond their sense perception. But in this realm, there is a major difference too. A Muslim would accept revelation as a source of knowledge on metaphysical issues as well as on ethics and justice. By contrast, the whole evolution of economic methodology has been in the direction of getting rid of values and ethical theory. In particular, economics construes a person (effectively *Homo economicus*) as a collection of preferences (attitudes, tastes, actions, and laws) that adjust to the changes in the costs and benefits of adapting such preferences. By comparison, Islam considers a human being as a servant and vicegerent of God on earth. In that capacity, adherents ought to struggle on an ongoing basis to adjust their behaviour so as to bring it closer to the model laid out in *shari'ah* whatever the cost.

This difference between the two models of human behaviour might be explained with the help of an example given by Jensen (1998, p. 23). Extramarital sex and cohabitation of unmarried couples was morally unacceptable in the East and the West some decades ago (even though both were undoubtedly practised). However, the advent of birth control techniques has, according to Jensen, reduced the cost associated with sexual intercourse causing a shift in the sexual behaviour as envisaged on the basis of *Homo economicus*. The result, he argues, is a wider acceptance of extramarital sex and cohabitation. Once extramarital cohabitation is explained in this manner, however, it can be asked how is economic methodology to assist in the next step to public policy, that is, legislation on taxation, redistribution, inheritance, separation and responsibility for child rearing traditionally borne by a family unit. If as per economic methodology, social preferences are to be derived from individual preferences alone the answer would probably not be far from ethical naturalism, that is, 'what ought to be' is to be derived from 'what is'. It is in taking this step that Islam would part company with standard economics. From an Islamic perspective, to the extent 'what ought to be' is clearly spelled out in *shari'ah*, it cannot be derived from 'what is' regardless of whether this derivation is tantamount to a logical fallacy or not.

In fact, there is one more aspect of this problem on which Islam would take a rather different stand. This pertains to analysis *per se* of the observed facts. In the example given, the question at stake is whether changes in the 'risk-and-reward' of sexual activity alone are responsible for the acceptability of extramarital sex. Here, Islam would examine the process of preference formation rather than take preferences as given. This is in line with the statement of the Prophet that every child is born with a good nature but the immediate environment corrupts it. Thus the process of social-shaping of preferences needs a greater focus. Some contemporary sociologists and communitarians appear to agree. Leming (2002), for example, explains that as individuals grow, they locate themselves within a socially created order – *nomos* or culture or tradition – by sharing collectively produced behavioural expectations, roles, identities, aspirations, and by implication, economic preferences. This process serves the function of ordering of experience: a meaningful normative order, or *nomos*, is imposed upon lives of individuals and their discrete experiences providing a shield against instability. Although once produced, a culture cannot be wished away, people are by no means inert, passive participants in this socially created 'reality'. They are active participants both in adapting to it as well as shaping it.

This possibility of change, however, may not come with ease if we bring to bear the Qur'anic insights of a public choice nature on this model of social reality. In particular, the historical examples and parables given in the Holy Qur'an (for example, 6:123; 33:67; 10:75–78, 83) depict that some human interests and instruments are wedded with reproducing 'what is' and engineering and legitimizing a social order that is removed from the innate nature of human beings. Thus, to Muslims (and many Christians) 'what is' has false attractions, and there are influential groups that seek to keep it removed from the 'revealed'. Within every community, their deeds seem fair (6:108). It is for this reason that 'conjecture' alone may be a poor basis for obtaining knowledge about the longer run consequences of a given social order. 'What ought to be' therefore cannot be derived from 'what is' without some transcendental guidance on social reality. It is from this perspective that Islam lays a great stress on keeping one eye on the material and another on the spiritual.

There are other parallels in Western thought to the Islamic critique of the methodology of economics. For instance, Etzioni (1988) takes economics to task for its stance on methodological individualism. He argues that the assumption that the preferences of individuals are given may insulate manipulation of individual liberty by social forces, but overlooks the role that education, persuasion (including advertising), and leadership play in preference formation. After all, individuals are not born in their mid-twenties, complete with their preferences. Preferences are at least partly socially shaped. Failure to acknowledge this process obviates the need to analyse the historical, cultural, economic, political and other societal forces that create the social context within which individuals operate (pp. 5, 10).

A related question is the moral dimension of individual preferences. The issue at stake here is that:

> The neoclassical paradigm does not merely ignore the moral dimension but actively opposes its inclusion. Thus, it is stressed that various individuals may have different rankings of preferences over a field of choice, but none can be

> deemed to be better. Indeed, Crouch (cited by Winrich, 1984, p. 994) adds that 'Unwillingness to accept this conclusion has been and still is a source of much mischief in the world.' Winrich (1984, p. 994) responds: 'And how lucky we are that such mischief abounds; complete relativism justifies all choices no matter how distorted, perverse or destructive.' Other neoclassicists . . . belittle the role of values, or see them as but one source of 'tastes' among many others. (Etzioni, 1988, p. 12)

The mono-utility paradigm of rational choice in mainstream economics thus undermines of the role of values in socio-economic dialogue. One of the consequences of this stand is that the whole dimension of achieving certain policy goals through appealing to people's moral resources is ignored and there is an overemphasis on pecuniary incentives, as becomes clear when we look at the issue of corruption.

Lawson (1997) too in some respects echoes the Islamic disposition to a deeper analysis of the social phenomenon. He argues that the philosophy of logical empiricism by focusing on event conjunctions undermines not only a deeper analysis of social events but also constrains the potential for highlighting opportunities for improvement. Human beings, he argues, are not passive sensors of atomistic events or recorders of their conjunctions. Rather, there is an agency aspect to their being and an institutional context within which they operate. To incorporate this aspect of being into economics, there is need for a richer concept of causality in human action. This is possible, he argues, by replacing logical realism with transcendental realism. Only by illuminating such structures and mechanisms can economists focus on policies that can replace those structures that constrain the spread of empowerment and equitable opportunities for all humanity. Only by so doing, can economists tap into the potential of human agents to change for the better and obtain real freedom of choice.

Since Robbins (1935) dismantled the idea of interpersonal comparisons and Arrow ([1951] 1963) revived interest in the subject of social choice, it has become clear that it is not possible to derive collective choice from individual preferences without admitting values. The one alternative that is advanced is the Pareto criteria. However, it cannot rank all possible social states, and is a very imperfect criterion upon which to base an entire social order. Some theory or conception of justice is needed as a supplement, even under conventional articulation (Acocella, 1998).

Once such issues are countenanced, the scope for a dialogue between Islam and standard economics becomes possible. Islam generally encourages trade and free markets, and an analysis of the behaviour of market participants to pecuniary incentives is also fully admitted. Where Islam differs is in the issue of legitimizing such behaviour over all spheres of human activity. Islam takes the institution of the market neither as a benchmark nor as a reference point for a reflection on organizing other spheres of human interaction. Instead, market behaviour, considered as only one kind of interaction among many that constitute social organization, finds its role and rules determined by reference to the Islamic theory of justice. It is this theory of justice that holds sway over all spheres of human interaction. In fact, so much is this so that the famous Muslim scholar Ibn Sina (Avicenna) once said that justice (*adl*) maintained by Law is indispensable for sustaining the life of the human species on earth (Smirnov, 1996). Such is the emphasis on governance in Islam. In this larger context, the state enters the picture as a carrier, interpreter, and implementer of justice through law. Consequently, an analysis of the state's fiscal role begins with an examination of the theories of justice rather than from a study of what markets can or cannot do, and feedback from the latter area illuminates how one part of the Islamic theory of justice knits with its other parts.

For its turn, once standard economics also admits the need for a theory of justice as a starting point to tackle governance issues, there is scope again that Islam and the West can strike a common cord on some issues. There is room as well for mutual learning on how best to actualize some principles of justice. This indeed is what has happened in the past. Greek, Roman, Christian and Islamic civilizations have borrowed, learned, and enriched each other, sometimes through peaceful coexistence, and at others times through conquest. In such a broader context, the scope for mutual exchange and learning about managing human affairs is evident in the following saying attributed to the Prophet Muhammad (pbuh):

> Allah's Messenger (peace be upon him) said, The word of wisdom is to a wise man like the lost property is to its owner who has a better right to it (than any one else) wherever he finds it. (Transmitted by Tirmidhi (*Hadith*, 216))

TWO APPROACHES TO ISLAMIC ECONOMICS

Where does the above debate lead us in terms of the methodology of Islamic economics and finance? If we begin with the Islamic claim that revelation alone provides certainty amidst conjecture then we come back to the traditional Islamic position that the scope for rationality lies in undertaking *ijtihad*. A well known scholar of the twentieth century, Mawdudi (1994), proposes how to conduct it in the field of economics and finance. The starting point for him is the premise that:

> The principles of *shari'ah* are unalterable, but the laws deduced from them by human agency are subject to modification and revision. The reason is that the former are God given, the latter are man-made. The principles of *shari'ah* are

> applicable to all ages, places, affairs and needs, but the laws are deduced from these principles to deal with particular circumstances and cases. (p. 298)

As to the circumstances, he admits freely that since the codification of laws took place in early centuries of Islam, a radical change has occurred in the cultural, economic, and technological conditions of the world. This requires fresh *ijtihad* and recodification of laws relating *shari'ah* principles to the new environment. Such recodification, he clarifies, is not aimed at legitimizing an empire of business magnates, bankers and industrialists who accumulate wealth by any means (that is through means prohibited in *shari'ah*), but rather to reassert the economic norms of Islam, the aim of which is to promote need fulfilment and mutual growth through co-operation, broad participation, and sympathetic accord. If wealth does get accumulated through following these norms, there should be no qualms about accepting that it is a bounty from God to be spent in accordance with the guidelines revealed on the matter.

He then lays down the procedure for undertaking *ijtihad* on matters economic and financial. These steps are, first, a deep and extensive study of the Holy Qur'an and *sunnah* should be made to grasp its spirit, goals and objectives, and, how *shari'ah* establishes a balance among different objectives. Second, the religious injunctions pertaining to a particular field of enquiry should be reviewed in order to comprehend the overall scheme of things and its relationship with the broader objectives of the *shari'ah*. Once an insight has been gained, one may come across situations where sticking to the letter of the law may contravene the spirit of the law. Under these circumstances, he advises one to set aside the text and reflect on a course of action that fulfils the spirit of *shari'ah*. The third step is concerned with the lowest rung, that is, that of individual laws and their interrelationship. His suggestion is to reflect on the characteristics of each commandment, and its role *vis-à-vis* other related commands in terms of providing for human nature, yet establishing balance and equity.[5] Fourth and finally, he recommends an assessment of the changing socio-economic environment. The objective is to gain an insight on (a) the nature of forces operating behind these changes, for example, in case of finance, the theory, principles, and methods of modern exchange and finance, (b) the features of human nature that such changes bear upon or bring out, (c) the viewpoint of Islam on these changes, and (d) the changes required in law to actualize the goals of *shari'ah* in the light of changed circumstances. He divides the changes in material circumstances into two broad categories, those due to the natural advancement of human intellect inventing improved means of communication and technology for resource exploitation, and those which are due to economic ideologies that are inherently in conflict with the revealed norms. The former are construed as real changes while the latter are only artificial from the standpoint of Islam. For the real changes, a fresh codification of laws is required. For artificial changes, a restatement of Islamic norms is warranted.

Mawdudi's differentiation between the real and artificial changes brings to fore a central question facing Muslims, namely, how should the Western heritage be viewed? On this issue, the Islamic position has been very clear throughout the centuries. The Islamic claim to truth is not exclusive but only to the safeguarding of such truth. Truth, the Holy Qur'an says, was revealed across time and space. The Holy Qur'an teaches that God sent a series of messengers and prophets. Jesus is accepted as a prophet, as are Moses (Musa), Abraham (Ibrahim), Jacob (Yakub) and so on. The Prophet Muhammad (pbuh) completed their message and is seen as the last (the 'seal') of the prophets. The three great monotheistic religions – Islam, Christianity and Judaism – are interlinked because all three are, in reality, worshipping the same One God. To the extent that developments in other religions (or cultures and civilizations) reflect the essence of the revealed truth, they are openly acceptable in Islam – in fact, they are Islam. This is why when Muhammad (pbuh) came as the Prophet of God, he did not re-engineer the society from scratch. He enunciated a set of principles and demonstrated their reach by accentuating those prevailing modes of moral, economic, and financial interaction that preserved and sustained justice, peace, and equilibrium on earth (57:25), and curbing those which undermined these goals. It is this method that can serve as a model for evaluating prevailing policies, and modes of business and finance. Among modern writers, Khurshid Ahmad (Abu-Rabi, 1995), Chapra (1985, 1992, 2000) and Siddiqi (1996) promote this line of thinking.

This stand, when seen in the light of developments in the philosophy of science, opens up a complementary second route to the methodology of economics and finance in Islam. It can be argued, for example, that once economics acknowledges the problem of induction, it becomes possible to accept religious premises as the basis of initial theory (see Popper's position above). As Chapra (2000, pp. 127, 139) argues, given Islam's position on a rational relationship between its norms and human wellbeing, there should be no qualms in taking the next step and testing the hypothesis and its predictions against available (current or historical) empirical evidence. The idea is to understand 'what is' – the prevalent behaviour and its social, economic, political and institutional context – in order to suggest a workable strategy for socio-economic and political change ('what ought to be') in conformity with the humanitarian goals sponsored by *shari'ah*. It can be seen from this formulation that Chapra admits empirical testing not in the sense of falsification since the basic commandments of *shari'ah* and human goals implicit in them remain unchallenged in spite of such testing. This stand, in its external form, is arguably a parallel to apriorism associated with von Mises ([1949] 1996) who, as we discussed above, begins by admitting the truth of certain a priori axioms derived from inner experience.

THE APPROACH IN THIS BOOK

This book in fact essentially adopts a third route to resolving the challenge faced by Muslim people in assessing the developments in knowledge and institutions since they effectively handed over the torch to the West in the Middle Ages. The method is implicit in the way we defined the scope of this study in Chapter 1. Our analysis, we said, critically examines, from an Islamic perspective, selected topics in the theory and practice of government economic organization as envisaged by conventional economics.

To this end, we visualize the contemporary knowledge in conventional economics and finance as being organized within various compartments in a filing cabinet, with each folder having an identifier corresponding to a subfield in economics.[6] Each folder is opened up and an examination of its contents is undertaken. Subsequently, Islamic theory and practice on that subfield is surveyed with special reference to analysing and bringing out the underlying values and objectives that it carries. A comparison of the two is then undertaken with the view to identifying and selecting those 'rationalities' that do not contradict with the Islamic position. The idea is to evolve a contemporary Islamic perspective on the issue at hand.

In a way, this methodology selects out of all the available 'ratio-based' theories those which are closest to the Islamic spirit and then builds upon them. In other words, Islamic principles and practice provide the theory-choice criteria in the case of our analysis. These principles are set out in the next chapter on theories of justice. This justice-based approach is then strengthened later with an ethics-based approach for the subject of corruption, and a principal–agent-based approach for a number of issues that revolve around governance matters.

By way of justification, it can be argued that, given that Islamic economics is still a nascent discipline, there is a merit in our approach to sift the range of research already conducted within standard and alternative economics and apply the Islamic value premises to it as the theory-choice criteria. The theories selected in this way can then be used as a basis upon which to build further. One critique of this method could be that it legitimizes the Islamic stand in a circular fashion. This criticism, in our view, carries little weight. For, if there is any lesson in the literature on the methodology of social sciences – in particular on finding the solution to the problem of induction – it is that legitimacy in many cases is a step prior to rationality. Social scientists would admit it, however, only in a roundabout manner. Patinkin (quoted in Redman, 1991) is an example:

> What generates in me a great deal of skepticism about the state of our discipline is the high positive correlation between the policy views of a researcher (or, what is worse, of his thesis director), and his empirical findings. (p. 133)[7]

At another level, one may ask the critics, what then is the methodology that can be used to segregate a 'true' theory out of a myriad on the same issue? In the case of Islam, at least, the answer is straightforward. A theory is required to understand revelation itself more deeply and open it up for a challenge from rationality.

Admittedly, it may be the case that any existing theory on a given issue is in harmony with *shari'ah* or the goals implicit in *shari'ah*. This raises the question whether there could be multiple variants of institutional arrangements in say, the financial, fiscal or monetary areas that meet *shari'ah* commandments. The answer to this query is in the affirmative. Alternatively, one may find none of the existing theories meeting the standards set by *shari'ah*. In that case, one has to make a fresh start by reverting to the methods outlined above by Mawdudi (1994) and Chapra (2000).

CONCLUSION

In this chapter, we have argued that, in the light of the problem of induction and its unsatisfactory resolution through the theory-choice criteria, there is a need to admit the fallibility of many received economic theories and, as a corollary, welcome alternative perspectives on economic issues. Also required is a deeper examination of what is termed the 'reductionist axioms of choice' and the role that they may have been playing in positioning much economic analysis so as to legitimize 'wants' instead of 'human needs' and 'what is' at the cost of 'what ought to be'. From the perspective of Islam, reintroducing moral commitments, altruism, and justice back into the economic agenda is considered as one way of checking that trend.[8] So, also, is analysing economic problems in terms of the dynamics of underlying social, economic, political and international institutions and power structures that are shaping the governance context within which such problems arise.

Some developments outlined earlier in the philosophy of science may be interpreted as endorsing the Islamic position that rationality alone has a limited capacity to lead to certainty of 'truth' in the forest of 'conjecture'.

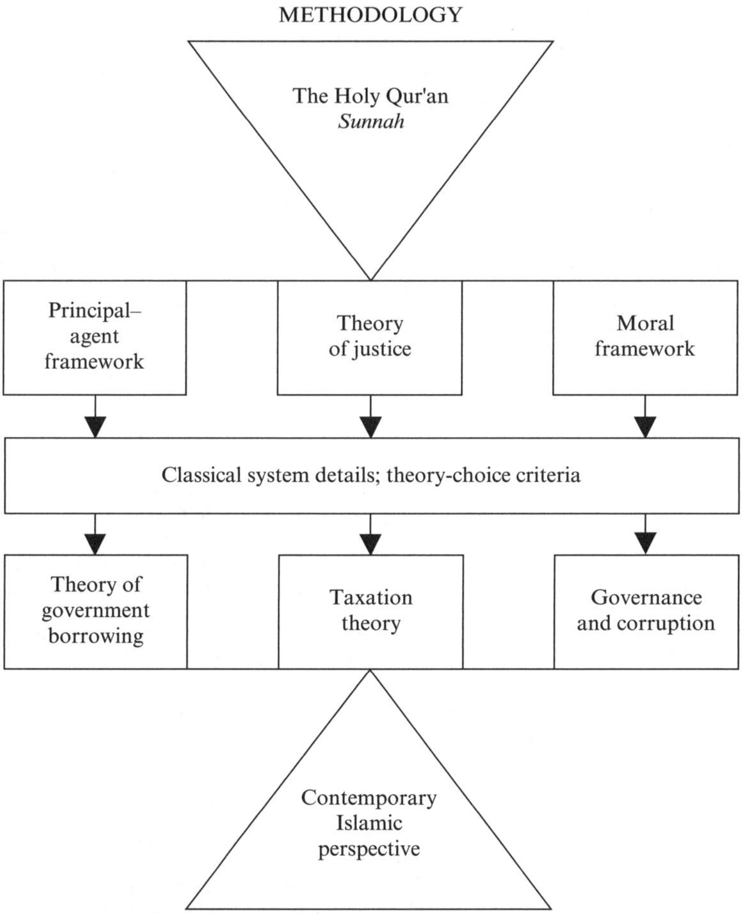

Figure 2.1 Framework of Islamic methodology

In particular it can be argued that the problem of induction, bounded rationality, self-seeking, public choice considerations, and immersion in a role within a *nomos*, render psyche alone inadequate to reach the truth about a social order that is in harmony with all known entities and the unknowns that respond to it. What is required from an Islamic viewpoint is that people put their trust in the revealed code of ethics and justice, and use it to mediate among conflicting signals. It is this stance (summarized in Figure 2.1) that serves as the methodological framework elucidating the Islamic position and illuminating the solution to the problems that we have chosen for examination.

In brief, we source principles of justice and the ethical framework from the Holy Qur'an and *sunnah* and consider the God–human trustee relationship within the context of the broader principal–agent framework contained in *shari'ah*. These principles are then employed to illuminate system design in many governance situations. The classical era of Islam provides a time-bound example of an application of the revealed canons. To arrive at a contemporary Islamic standpoint on public governance, we use compatibility with *shari'ah* as the criteria to choose among alternative Western social-scientific theories on taxation, government finance (borrowing) and accountability and governance. We then build further upon the selected theories to come to 'an Islamic perspective on governance'.

NOTES

1. Most *hadith* quoted in this book are taken from the relevant books stored in *The Alim for Windows Release 4.5* (1986) Software Corporation, USA and Canada.
2. Iqbal ([1928] 1996) and Kamali (1998) treat this subject in a greater detail.
3. In the early tenth century (CE) it came to be held that the gates of *ijtihad* had been closed. In the nineteenth and twentieth centuries, when many new problems arose, the gates were reopened.
4. Other luminaries were Friedrich Waismann, Otto Neurath, Rudolf Carnap, Herbert Feigl, Victor Kraft and Karl Menger. The Circle disintegrated after the Nazis took control of Austria in 1938.
5. He provides an example of the poll tax that the Holy Qur'an levies on people of the Book in lieu of *zakah* (see section on taxation 'The eternal and finite in the classical scheme', p. 106, for further details). Following the spirit of this command, it was extended to followers of other religions also such as to Magians of Persia and to Hindus of India.
6. Note that this description resembles Friedman's (1953, p. 7) articulation of the role of a theory in positive economics as 'to serve as a filing system for organizing empirical material and facilitating our understanding of it; and the criteria by which it is to be judged are those appropriate to a filing system. Are the categories clearly and precisely defined? Are they exhaustive? Do we know where to file each individual item, or is there considerable ambiguity? Is the system of headings and subheadings so designed that we can quickly find an item we want, or must we hunt from place to place?'
7. In this respect, recall the last phrase in the earlier quotation from Schumpeter (p. 48).
8. We say 'reintroducing' because such values occupied a central position in the attitudes of Greek philosophers such as Aristotle and medieval philosophers such as St Thomas Aquinas to matters of economics and finance. For their view on usury, for example, see Lewis (2007).

3. Justice: the inner core of governance

INTRODUCTION

Chapter 1 examined various perspectives on governance and developed its taxonomy. It was argued that governance is a complex phenomenon and many of its facets converge with economics, politics and law. This observation leads us to choose political economy as the starting point of our investigation. Briefly, in its origin, political economy is the social science developed by Adam Smith, John Stuart Mill and Karl Marx to give broad visions of the social system based on a conception of justice (Clark, 1998, p. ix; Schmoller, 1893). It discusses what, why and how certain social arrangements would be considered as 'good order and workable arrangements'. In the process, it elucidates collectively desired goals and means for constitutive and directive governance (Hupe and Hill, 2006). The closest parallel in Islam (that obviously originated prior to the splintering of political economy from ethics, and of politics and economics from political economy) would be a theory of justice extracted from Islam's fundamental tenets. Such a derivation is the task undertaken in this chapter. A comparison of the Western and the Islamic approaches then brings out key similarities and differences yielding valuable axioms for our research on different aspects of governance.

WESTERN PERSPECTIVE

The idea that the primary object of government is to secure justice is well known in history. '*Remota justitia, quid sint regna nisi magna latrocinia*' (Removed from justice, what be rulers if not large-scale robbers), St Augustine remarked in the fifth century CE. But, what exactly is justice and what are its demands? According to Miller (1991), the best general definition comes from the Byzantine emperor, Justinian (482–565 CE), namely that justice is the constant and perpetual will to render to everyone his due. As to what is a due share, we take Aristotle's argument that the emphasis ought to be on equality apart from any other considerations that matter, as the starting point of our discussion. To elaborate:

> since the equal is a mean, the just must also be a mean. Now equality cannot be stated in less than two terms. From this certain consequences naturally flow. *First*, the just is both a mean and an equal. *Second*, in its character as mean it must have extremes between which it lies. *Third*, in its character of equal its equality must be expressed in two equal parts of what is shared. *Fourth*, in its character of just there must be certain persons to whom it is just. Here then is a minimum of four terms in which justice finds expression – two *persons* and two *shares*. And the equality of the second pair will be reflected in the equality of the first. The ratio will be the same in the one case as in other, because, if the persons are not equal, their shares will not be equal. As a matter of fact when quarrels and complaints arise, it is when people who are equal have not got equal shares, or *vice versa*. (*The Ethics of Aristotle*, Thomson, 1953, pp. 145–6)

Aristotle then divides justice into three branches: distributive justice is concerned with the distribution of honour or money or the other divisible assets of the community (social benefits and burdens) among its members; justice in exchange stands for equality between whatever goods are exchanged; and corrective justice means establishing equality between punishment and the crime.

Aristotle sees these demands of justice being met in a state ruled by a political constitution and impersonal laws, laws that are geared to realizing the conception of good imbued in the *telos* of mankind. Although all men are considered equal before the law, they are not necessarily equal in status and therefore, a hierarchical social structure is envisaged wherein citizenship is reserved only for those who are economically self-sufficient. Slaves, craftsmen and traders are excluded. There is little room for pursuing commerce and wealth for its own sake; and trading and usury are considered to pose threats to the moral wellbeing of a person. In short, community is given an upper hand over an individual and the state itself is taken as the highest form of community pursuing the highest form of moral good. Thus individuals are subordinated to the state and the state to an ethical purpose (Bowle, 1961, pp. 40–2; Harmon, 1964, pp. 29–52; Muller, 1993, p. 41).

Clearly, state and community are the dominant modes of governance in Aristotelian thought. The scope for employing the market as a tool for regulating transactions among citizens is considered very limited. In general, this intellectual revulsion to money based market exchange prevailed in Europe for over a thousand years after the fall of the Roman Empire particularly under the influence of the teachings of the Church that, as expressed by St Augustine and other clerical philosophers, were not dissimilar to those of Aristotle.[1]

However, these concepts came under close scrutiny between the fourteenth and eighteenth centuries amidst increasing opportunities for commerce and industry. As the economic power started shifting to the merchant class, a parallel political dynamic began to emerge reinforcing the hand of first the monarch and then parliament *vis-à-vis* the Church and the feudal lords (Tawney, 1926). By the time the modern nation state was born the intellectual tide under Protestantism had already turned in favour of admitting the market *pari passu* with the state and society as one of the three key modes of governance. Gone in particular was the disapprobation against commerce and usury. Free market exchange began to be seen as a legitimate mechanism to achieve individual freedom and wealth. As Kolm (1996, p. 59) says, this tradition, called in its fully evolved form as libertarianism/liberalism/full-process freedom is the historically original, founding, and central theory of modernity.

Libertarianism

Libertarianism stands for the type of social arrangements that guarantee each person the greatest amount of liberty commensurate with the same liberty for all (Sterba, 1992). As such, libertarians define liberty as autonomy of individual choices and immunity from interference by others. The crucial issue is whether choices are being made by the person concerned rather than by other individuals and institutions on his behalf. In this respect, the emphasis usually is on 'negative freedoms', that is, the absence of obstacles external to a person – coercion and legal prohibitions – that prevent wilful action. This libertarian stress on negative freedoms then translates into a number of rights to life, liberty and property (which includes protection against theft, fraud and breach of contract), the right to defend against violations of these rights, and the right to restrain or punish those trespassing on those rights. Justice is considered as done when each person respects every other person's rights (Haslett, 1994, p. 55).

Market exchange then becomes the cardinal mechanism of governance in the libertarian conception of a social order. However, since the distributional consequences of market arrangements depend on the existing allocation of property rights, the starting point for resource distribution has to be justified in some normative sense. This is done largely through the principles of self-ownership and just acquisition, which consists of appropriating un-owned resources (Hausman and McPherson, 1996, pp. 126–7). The rectification of past unjust acquisitions is usually limited to living generations only (although not in the case of native title and indigenous peoples in Australia, Canada, the United States and Scandinavian countries).

Given initial property rights and a procedure for further entitlements, protection from theft, fraud and coercion cannot be left as everybody's business. A government or communal structure must be established to protect individual property rights and 'enforce compliance with the rules' (Friedman, 1962, p. 25). Persons join in, on their own accord, as free and equals. Financing of such a 'night-watchman state' is on a *quid pro quo* basis. Provision of public goods and taxation for purposes other than for a 'minimal' state, is viewed as 'forced labour' (Nozick, 1974). Some libertarians (notably Adam Smith) do however entrust government with a limited mandate for undertaking works of a 'public good' nature.

In summary, libertarianism as a political philosophy of 'equal liberty for all' has championed the cause of *laissez-faire* capitalism and limited the role of government to one of the protection of property rights. The most common critique of this view is that the ideal of how much one is allowed to do needs to be distinguished from the ideal of how much one is able to do, a distinction first noted by John Stuart Mill ([1869] 1999) and later illustrated by Isaiah Berlin (2002). In other words, while free markets are important, they may not necessarily produce results that are compatible with liberty. No one whose claim to property is legitimate is morally bound by this view to use it in ways that satisfy equality of opportunity or outcomes. There may result 'a degree (and/or kind) of inequality which is distinctly evil or unlovely' (Simons, 1938, pp. 18–19). Poverty and hunger can exist precisely because people have 'negative freedoms' but no right to nourishment which is a precondition for appreciating freedom. The implication would appear to be that libertarianism is indifferent to achieving substantive liberty as an end, raising the question why the status of economic needs, which can be a matter of life and death, should be lower than that of personal liberties (Sen, 1999, pp. 64–7). Certainly, libertarians such as Milton Friedman (1962) have accepted the need for some redistribution via a negative income tax, but not the socialist ideal of a welfare state.

Socialist Justice

On a strict interpretation, social arrangements based on a guarantee of negative freedoms are largely indifferent to the distribution of social product and the opportunity aspect of freedom. The practice of *laissez-faire* capitalism in the eighteenth and nineteenth century England illustrated what can happen under these circumstances. A sixteen-hour working day, child labour, and struggle to make ends meet in spite of such effort were 'all too illustrative of a social climate in which the practices of most callous inhumanity were accepted as the natural order of events and even more important, as nobody's business' (Heilbroner, 1967, pp. 96–7). There was the ideal of private altruism, as reflected in the writings of Charles Dickens.

Nevertheless, utopian socialist and Marxist thought was chiefly a product of that age. Karl Marx (1818–83 CE), in particular, questioned whether the supply of wage labour by propertyless workers was really free or forced? To him, workers paid only subsistence wages were forced to work at that price because the alternative was starvation. This, he thought, was akin to slavery and implied a contradiction to the libertarian principle that a person was entitled to the full marginal product of their labour. In fact, he argued, it was in this phenomenon of compensating labour with less than what was due to them together with past accumulation by war, looting, or slavery wherein lied the source of exploitative capital accumulation. The proposed solution was the abolition of private property (nationalization of the means of production) and the pursuit of the ultimate vision, 'from each according to his ability, to each according to his need'. This goal is reminiscent of Rousseau's (1712–78 CE) egalitarian ideal, 'No one should have either so little as to have to sell himself or so much as to be able to buy someone else' (Kolm, 1996, pp. 237–41). This intellectual heritage of public ownership retains a strong hold over public opinion in terms of much resistance to privatization. Nevertheless, some contemporary socialists recommend a less radical route of spreading the ownership of the means of production through a wider share ownership (especially of privatized enterprises) or worker share participation schemes.

Welfare Liberal Justice

The welfare liberal tradition takes a middle path between liberalism and Marxism, combining both liberty and equality into a political conception that derives from a fair social contract. Rawls (1971) has been the most influential contemporary philosopher in this tradition. Of course, many prior to him, in particular, utilitarian economists, have justified redistributive philosophy based on 'maximum utility' (Musgrave, 1985; Sterba, 1992). We examine each alternative in turn.

Justice as Fairness

Rawls (1971) considers justice to be as much a virtue of social institutions as truth is of systems of thought. He derives the principles of justice for the basic structure of a society by abstracting people from the knowledge of their current and future position in the society, as reflected in endowments and natural abilities, degree of risk aversion, and other circumstances such as race, sex, political and economic situation. This is achieved by putting them behind a 'veil of ignorance'. The veil also simulates the likelihood that post-contract one may end up having any combination of natural endowments and social status so bringing home the consideration that the good of every one else is one's own. Rawls argues that behind such a veil of ignorance, rational people would opt for minimizing the risk of ending up in the worse socio-economic circumstances. Thus they choose the following principles of justice:

1. Each person is to have an equal right to the most extensive total system of equal basic liberties compatible with a similar system of liberty for all.
2. Social and economic inequalities are to satisfy two conditions: first, they must attach to offices and positions open to all under conditions of fair equality of opportunity; and second, they must be to the greatest benefit of the least advantaged members of society.

The first of these principles calls for right to political liberties, that is, the right to vote, to be eligible for public office, freedom of speech and assembly, freedom of thought, liberty of conscience, freedom from arbitrary arrest and confiscation, and the right to hold property. The second of these (termed the difference principle) challenges the notion that only morally arbitrary inequalities, that is, race, sex and social background need equalizing on the grounds that no one 'deserves' to be born with exceptional talents anymore than they 'deserve' to be born in socially advantaged or disadvantaged households. Both circumstances are beyond one's control and arbitrary in nature. With reference to this premise and its negative implications for the argument for self-ownership, then, the difference principle is justified in admitting the distributional inequality of any kind only if it is to the benefit of those who are disadvantaged in any manner (pp. 219–22).

What are the implications of this view for the institutional structure of an economy? To quote Rawls:

> Since under socialism the means of production and natural resources are publicly owned, the distributive function is greatly restricted, whereas a private-property system uses prices in varying degrees for both purposes. Which of these systems and the many intermediate forms most fully answers to the requirements of justice cannot, I think, be determined in advance. . . . it depends in large part upon the traditions, institutions, and social forces of each country, and its particular historical circumstances. . . . The political judgement in any given case will then turn on which variation is most likely to work out best in practice. (1971, pp. 273–4)

Nevertheless, the social system is to be designed so that the resulting distribution is just, however things turn out. That implies some view of human good implicit in the principles of justice to be realized through the design of institutions. The call therefore is to consider a blend of moral, political, and economic criteria in designing institutions that actualize principles of justice as fairness (pp. 259–60). Efficiency, in this scheme, provides too narrow a basis for such design. Building on Musgrave's (1959) original conception of the government's fiscal department being divided into different 'branches', it is envisaged by Rawls that the government should balance different claims by having (a) an allocation branch, (b) stabilization branch, (c) transfer branch, and (d) distribution branch. The allocation branch promotes competitive markets that are necessary for preserving incentives to create wealth, while the stabilization branch aims at achieving full employment. However, since markets give little consideration to needs and the appropriate standard of life, they are therefore supplemented with distribution of 'suitable minima' through the transfer branch. Finally, the distribution branch aims at gradually correcting wealth distribution with the view that its concentration does not reach the level that threatens the very institutions that are to insure 'fair value' of political liberties and equality of opportunity.

Rawls' position that all inequalities are morally arbitrary is in direct conflict with the libertarian argument of self-ownership, that is, that individuals have unfettered right to the usufruct of themselves. However, Rawls' articulation has been criticized on many accounts. Among others that there is a need to differentiate among inequalities that result from people's choices from those that result from people's circumstances (Dworkin, 1981). In practice, however, it is not easy to identify such differences. There is also perceived to be a duty of care for dependents harmed by others' 'inappropriate' choices that, in most Western societies at least, extend to within the family unit.[2]

Utilitarian Justice

Utilitarianism has dominated moral and political philosophy, economics, and public policy for more than a century. It stands for the type of social arrangements that maximize aggregate utility, whereas utility, in its Benthamite interpretation, depicts the tendency of an action/law/institutional arrangement to augment happiness. Although pleasure and happiness are essentially mental characteristics that defy precise measurement, it is not considered absurd to relate them to maximizing some observable economic characteristic, for example, income, which is a means to achieving many aims. The idea is to shift the foundations of public action from religion and natural laws to some secular and scientific basis. Utility is central to that notion because it is committed neither to an a priori conception of human nature nor to a specific role of government.

Sen (1999, pp. 58–9) has split the informational content of utilitarian justice into three components: consequentialism, welfarism, and sum-ranking. Consequentialism requires that all choices among alternative courses of action – including rules, institutions, policies – be made on the basis of the goodness of the states of affairs that they generate. This rules out actions based on norms of righteousness that disregard consequences. Welfarism stands for evaluating the goodness of a state of affairs on the basis of the corresponding utility information. Finally, sum-ranking requires that the utilities of different people in a group or society simply be added together to arrive at the total utility – social utility – corresponding to a state of affairs. This requirement is indifferent to the distribution of individual utilities. The net result of the three components is that every choice is to be judged by the sum total of utilities generated through that choice. Thus the principle of greatest happiness for the greatest number does not commit utilitarians either to *laissez-faire* capitalism or to equal distribution of wealth but rather to a substantial role for legitimate government activities (Musgrave, 1985).

The concept of market failure has played a key role in the utilitarian recommendations for government interventions in the economy. For example, J.S. Mill in his *Principles of Political Economy* published in 1848 argues for expanding the role of government to natural monopolies, public goods (education, caring for neglected children, and provision for the poor and mentally handicapped), and promotion of speculative knowledge. He also makes an important departure from the classical economics of Ricardo and Malthus by differentiating between production and distribution. For production, he considers *laissez-faire* as probably the best but for distribution, a socialist-type approach appears more convincing. Mill's concern is that:

> no rational person will maintain it to be abstractly just, that a small minority of mankind should be born to the enjoyment of all the external advantages which life can give . . . while the immense majority are condemned from their birth to a life of never-ending, never intermitting toil, requitted by a bare, and in general a precarious subsistence. (cited in Fusfeld, 1999, p. 53)

The solution that he recommended was workers' co-operatives and profit-sharing schemes. Henry Sidgwick (1838–1900) and A.C. Pigou (1928) followed in his footsteps identifying other market failures and arguments for government intervention. Pigou, for instance, argues for what have become known as Pigovian taxes (subsidies) to obtain an efficient allocation in the face of externalities. He also demonstrated that because of its failure to assess social costs, the market mechanism tends to misallocate resources between increasing-cost and decreasing-cost industries. His most controversial contribution, however, was in seeking to justify income redistribution on the grounds of diminishing marginal utility of income, so that redistributing income from the rich (with low marginal utility) to the poor (with high marginal utility) will raise overall utility. This position was demolished by Lionel Robbins' (1935) argument that interpersonal comparisons of utilities are tantamount to ethical judgements that have no role in economic policy. As a result, the information base of utilitarianism was ultimately reduced to Pareto criteria, that is, raising one person's utility while not reducing anyone else's.

In short, in the search for attaining the greatest happiness for the greatest number and under the influence of socialist thinking, utilitarianism pushed public economics away from the classical liberal notion of limited government. While a commitment to private property remained sacrosanct, redistribution became accepted and an expanded role of government was envisaged under varying degrees of market failure. In this way the role of the state began to be favoured again over market as a mechanism for governance.

This at least was the position for the first two-thirds of the twentieth century. Since then there has been a marked revival of faith in the power of free market outcomes. At an intellectual level, libertarian views have been revived, or more correctly restated, by Hayek (1944) and Friedman (1962), reinforced by George Stigler (1971) and his analysis of the 'capture theory' of regulation, and of Tullock (1965) and Buchanan (1980) of 'rent-seeking' behaviour. These analyses, along with the pressure of think tanks such as the American Enterprise Institute, the Cato Institute, the Hoover Institute and the Institute for Economic Affairs, provided the theoretical backing for the institution of 'Thatcherism' and 'Reaganomics' which presided over privatization and the roll-back of some of the welfare state at the micro level, along with deregulation and market reforms at the macro level.

At first confined to a number of developed countries, the 'return to the market' accelerated with the collapse of Communism, and with its Marxist ideology, in Eastern Europe and the institution of market reforms both in those countries and in countries such as China and Vietnam which retained ostensibly Communist systems. Interestingly, the swing back towards libertarianism has probably made least headway in many Muslim countries. In the Gulf region, for example, what can best be described as a 'sheikhocracy' continues to operate, based around oil revenues, extensive public works and a welfare system involving generous social security (but for nationals only). This present-day reality provides a backdrop to our analysis of the Islamic position on the theory of justice in society.

THE ISLAMIC THEORY OF JUSTICE

Background

The Arabia into which the Prophet Muhammad (pbuh) was born in 570 CE had no central authority akin to a state. The vacuum was filled to some extent by clans or tribes who prized their independence. A tribe was headed by a senior person known as *sheikh*. A *sheikh* would resolve intra-tribal matters through a mix of mutual consultation, custom and moral persuasion. He usually had no enforcement mechanisms *per se* at his disposal; the virtual subsistence level economy in the desert levelled all differences among people. In this sense, a desert Arab (*Bedouin*) was a born democrat (Hitti, 1970). However, the situation in commercial towns such as Makkah was different. Here markets operated freely and great differences in wealth left the poor, orphans and women at the receiving end of exploitation and injustice (Esposito, 1995, pp. 28–9).

Given the absence of central authority and the proximity to the 'state of nature', inter-tribal conflicts were commonplace. Against this backdrop, the most common notion of fairness known among Arabs, which was tantamount to retributive justice, consisted in taking revenge. A peaceful alternative thereto, *diya* or blood money was also admitted depending on needs of survival and strength in bargaining. The following quotation from El-Awa (1983) is self-explanatory:

> It was by no means rare for small disputes to turn into an actual war between two tribes; for example, the war between the tribes of Banu Bakr and Banu Taghlib lasted for forty years because one of the Bani Taghlib killed a female camel belonging to a women of the Bani Bakr. An attempt at a peace settlement was made after the son of a distinguished Arab, Shas b. Zuhayr b. Judhaymah, was killed, but the father asked the representative of the killer's tribe to do one of three things in order to stop him from taking revenge for his son: to return his son to life, to fill his garment (*rida*) with the stars, or to hand over to him all the members of the killer's tribe to be killed. 'Still,' the father added, 'I will not be compensated for my son'. (p. 70)

It can be argued from the above picture that in pre-Islamic Arabia, individuals keenly defended negative freedoms of their own and their tribesmen but respected little of the same for others. The Holy Qur'an attributes this state of affairs to corruption of reason, lack of faith, moral ignorance, and pride in ancestry, strength and riches, a condition frequently present in the history of mankind (91: 7–10; 17:49–51; 34:31–6; 48:26; 9:69). Not surprisingly, the remedy suggested is to establish the rule of law in accordance with a blueprint of justice revealed through the Holy Qur'an and *sunnah* (5:49; 57:25).

Meaning

In general, the Holy Qur'an brings three terms, *adl* (justice), *qist* (equity/fairness), and *meezan* (balance/scale) to signify justice and equity. Among the meanings of these words are: to straighten, setting in order, and fixing in the right place; to balance, counterbalance or establish equilibrium; to be equal or equivalent or to match; fairness, impartiality, absence of discrimination; and, honesty, straightforwardness, uprightness, righteousness, and correctness. The antonym of *adl* is *zulm* which is used in the Holy Qur'an (2:124; 4:148) to mean indulgence in wrong, evil, iniquity, injustice, oppression and unfairness that eventuates in corruption (11:85) and disruption of peace, in fact sheer destruction (21:11). It also means darkness that beclouds and overshadows the truth (24:40; 57:9). Finally, the Holy Qur'an (16:90; 3:134; 9:100, 120; 55:60; 5:93; 7:56; 2:195) stresses that *adl* be complemented with *ihsan* or benevolence.

The Holy Qur'an (4:58, 105, 135; 5:8, 44–5, 48–50, 6:152; 7:29; 11:85; 16:90; 55:7–9; 57:25; 60:8) and *sunnah* elucidate all these different dimensions of *adl*, *qist* and *meezan* with reference to the Divine attributes, the standards of conduct required of individuals, and the characteristics of systems of governance put in place to rule a people. As al-Ghazali (translated by Bagley, 1964, p. 55) illustrates, the paramount duty of government in Islam has been historically understood as to bring development and prosperity to the world through justice and equitable rule. The idea is to provide persons the necessary security and patronage so that they can develop their full potential as free individuals and procure the needs and demands of their body and soul without violating the liberty of others (Mawdudi 1994).

In fact, Al-Ghazali (1937: 139–44) and Al-Shatibi (n.d.: 8–25, 176–86)[3] see the whole structure and content of *shari'ah* geared to achieving human welfare through the demarcation of spheres of liberties-and-violations associated with the pursuit of diverse ends in life in particular, the goals of *din* (religion), *nafs* (life), *aql* (intellect or reason), *nasl* (family), and *mal* (property). The concept of limits (*hudud*: 9:12) set by God on individual freedoms in these areas is critical. These limits are set so as to promote *masalih* (social utilities or welfare), that is, all activities or things that help achieving these goals equitably and prohibit *mafasid* (disutilities) which detract from (justly) obtaining these goals. In case there is a conflict of interest, there are rules of precedence to help resolve such conflicts, with the key objective remaining *muslaha al deen wa al-dunya*, 'goodness of this life and the Hereafter' (Al-Ghazali, n.d. *Ihya*, 2:109).

This brings us to the second perspective on the issue of understanding *adl* in Islam which is elaborated by Tahir-ul-Qadri (1995, p. 86). He

Table 3.1 Adl *(justice) and* Ihsan *(benevolence)*

Adl (Justice, equity)	*Ihsan* (Benevolence, kindness)
Equity is to give as much as is due, to take as much as is due*.	Benevolence is to give more than is due and to take less than is due on one's own accord.
Equity is that one should enjoy oneself and let others enjoy themselves as well.	Benevolence is that one should sacrifice his sense of personal enjoyment for the enjoyment of others.
It is equity that one should live for himself as well as for others.	It is benevolence that one should live only for others (for example, Prophets of God mentioned in the Holy Qur'an, Ch. 28).
Equity is equality and the condition of faith.	Benevolence is unconditional sacrifice and the perfection of faith.

Note * This point is referred further to Imam Raghib's *Al-Mufradat*.

views the Qur'anic stress on *adl* in human conduct in light of the condition of faith mentioned in the Prophet's saying: 'I swear by the Lord who controls my life that a person is not a true believer unless he likes for his brother what he likes for himself' (Sahih Bukhari, *Hadith*, 1.12). Thus justice consists of those principles which one would like to apply to one's ownself if in a similar situation. Qadri then contrasts *adl* with *ihsan* in detail. We summarize the discussion in Table 3.1 which distinguishes *adl* from *ihsan*.

Clearly, as Yusuf Ali argues in his commentary on the Holy Qur'an (p. 760), while justice is a comprehensive term, and may include all the virtues of cold philosophy, religion asks for benevolence which is something warmer and more humane. It calls for the doing of good deeds even where perhaps they are not strictly demanded by justice. This requirement means returning good for ill, obliging those who in worldly language 'have no claim' on you, and of course a fortiori, the fulfilling of the claims of those whose claims are recognized in social life. Similarly the opposites are to be avoided, in particular, the deeds described in the Holy Qur'an (16:90) as shameful and unjust, and any inward rebellion against Allah's Law or our own conscience in its most sensitive form.

It can be argued from Table 3.1 and discussion that at least in its external form, this understanding of justice comes very close to the Golden Rule to which the Western Kantian or welfare liberal conceptions of justice refer. Widely attributed to Jesus (pbuh) this principle of 'reciprocity' was enunciated earlier by Confucius (*c*. 551–479 BCE) and can be traced back to the

Torah (the Hebrew name for the Law of Moses or the Pentateuch, the first five books of the Old Testament) in Leviticus (*c.* 1440 BCE):

- 'Do unto others as you would have them do unto you' – Jesus in the Gospels, Matthew 7:12, Matthew 22:39, Luke 6:31, Luke 10:27.
- 'Zigong asked: 'Is there any single word that could guide one's entire life?' The Master said: 'Should it not be *reciprocity*? What you do not wish for yourself, do not do to others'' – Confucius in the Analects 15:24 (Leys, 1997).
- 'Thou shalt not avenge, nor bear any grudge against the children of thy people, but thou shalt love thy neighbour as thyself: I am the lord' – Leviticus 19:18.
- 'When an alien lives with you in your land, do not mistreat him. The alien living with you must be treated as one of your native-born. Love him as yourself, for you were aliens in Egypt. I am the lord your God' – Leviticus 19:33–4.

As noted above, much the same rule was stated by the Prophet Muhammad (pbuh) as reported (in slightly different words) in the following *hadith*:

- 'None of you truly believe until he loves for his brother what he loves for himself' – Muhammad, *Hadith* 13 of al-Nawawi's Forty *Hadith*.

Nevertheless, in comparison with the others, there is some ambiguity as to the meaning of 'brother' in this context and whether the 'law of general beneficence' in Islam extends to non-believers with the full force that it does to adherents.

Note, however, as Musgrave (1985) observes, the Golden Rule as an exclusive basis for deriving a theory of justice results in an asking for an equal division of the cake. That, under normal circumstances, would come under benevolence from an Islamic perspective rather than justice. The balancing act is another saying by the Prophet Muhammad (pbuh): 'Gabriel kept on commending the neighbour to me so that I thought he would make an heir?' (Abu Dawood, *Hadith*, 5133). Nevertheless, it was not done. Also, the blueprint of justice is as such specified in *shari'ah* rather than left for human reason to speculate about from a single principle or two.

The third perspective on *adl* is presented by Smirnov (1996). He argues that *adl* equated with the straight path (*sirat al mustaqim*) of the Holy Qur'an[4] can be understood as the middle path between two extremes where both get the best chance to display their spirit, the opposition between the two is neutralized, and harmony and unity emerge. Thus justice suffers when exactness of 'preserving the middle' is lost through a twist one way or the other. This interpretation is supported by a saying of the Prophet Muhammad (pbuh), '*Khayr al-umur awsatu-ha*: the middle path (in things/commands/matters) is the best.' We may add that this principle can be deduced directly from the Holy Qur'an (2:143) that refers to the community of [practising] Muslims as 'the middle (justly balanced) nation' and therefore the 'best nation' (3:110). Seen from this angle, there is a common chord with the Aristotelian interpretation of justice mentioned above, that is, justice is a modal path between the two extremes.

Finally, there is a fourth perspective too, presented in Smirnov (1996). He argues that, in keeping all the different dimensions that the concepts of *adl*, *qist*, and *meezan* imbue, Muslim scholars throughout history have emphasized that justice in the secular definition of 'giving what is due,' assumes in Islam, the character of establishing the right (*haqq*) in its due place (*makan*), that is to give back the really necessary to the one to whom it should belong, having taken it away from the usurper. This interpretation, appiied, for example, to the system of holding power and exercising rule, focuses not merely on the 'right' of a single person, group, community or ruling person – regarded as separate units – but instead on *al-haqq*, that is, both the rights and obligations that make sense only within the overall network of linkages that knit the whole system into unity. Such unity under Islam comes by submitting to the certainty that flows from the absolute knowledge of the Divine Law-Giver.

Content

Under the conception of Al-Ghazali and Al-Shatibi, the structure of Islamic *shari'ah* focuses on protecting the foundations of good life through specifying a rights–obligations framework in relation to religion, life, intellect, family and property. Rather than elaborating all of the different dimensions of this blueprint, we limit ourselves to four aspects of the Islamic theory of justice that have important bearing on the economic role of the state and its institutional architecture. These are, first, the concept of equality, second, the state–citizen relationship, third, economic and property rights, and fourth, welfare rights and obligations.

Equality, Brotherhood, and the Mission of Muslims

A study of the Holy Qur'an and *sunnah* makes it clear that human equality is the fundamental tenet of Islam. Consider, for example, the following verses from the Holy Qur'an:

> O mankind! Lo! We have created you male and female, and have made you nations and tribes that ye may know one another. Lo! the noblest of you, in the sight of Allah, is the best in conduct. Lo! Allah is Knower, Aware. (49:13). O mankind! Be careful of your duty to your Lord Who created you from a single soul and from it created its mate and from them twain hath spread abroad a multitude of men and women. Be careful of your duty toward Allah in Whom ye claim (your rights) of one another, and toward the wombs (that bore you). Lo! Allah hath been a Watcher over you. (4:1)

Islam thus stresses that the apparent diversity in race, colour, languages and even religion veils a much deeper basis for co-operation among mankind, namely that all are part of a single brotherhood by virtue of common origin. This brotherhood is reasserted from many different angles. Three are worthy of note. First, external forms of rituals apart, the ideational aspect – core beliefs and values – of all religion is one (22:67). Accordingly, religion *per se* ought not to be the basis for disunity but rather for unity in competing for actualizing the good in life (2:140). Second, in conformity with this philosophy of equality and brotherhood, arrogance and defamation of fellow human beings – consisting in suspicion, spoken or written offensive individual or group titles, nicknames and false propaganda – is prohibited (49:11–13). Third, there is consequently an emphasis on holding the hands of all those seeking peace through abiding by a contract against mutual hatred, aggression, and deceit (25:63; 4:90; 8:61). The objective is to establish a just and equitable world order based on principles of mutual respect, tolerance, and justice. The community of Muslims is required to play a special role in bringing about such order through another level of brotherhood (among Muslims) based on common belief, values, symbols, and mission. In his farewell pilgrimage the Prophet Muhammad (pbuh) emphasized:

> Behold! all practices of paganism and ignorance are now under my feet. The blood-revenge of the Days of Ignorance (pre-Islamic time) is abolished . . . Usury is forbidden . . . Fear Allah concerning women! Verily you have taken them on the security of Allah . . . O people! beware! Your God is one, no Arab has any superiority over a non-Arab, and no non-Arab any superiority over an Arab, and no white one has any superiority over a black one, and no black one has any superiority over a white one, except on the basis of *taqwa* (fear / love of Allah or piety).[5]

The purpose of Islamic brotherhood is to exemplify Islam by presenting a living picture to the world of the concepts of *tawhid*, justice, and benevolence (3:110; 2:143; 49:10). Bhutto (1976) is most perceptive in reminding the political significance of such teachings:

> our vocation as Muslims is not to harbour hostility against other human communities, East or West, North or South, but to conduct ourselves that we can

help build bridges of communication and sympathy between one set of nations and another. We draw our inspiration from the Holy Qur'an and I quote:

> Say: To Allah belong both East and West: He guideth whom He will to a straight path. Thus We have appointed you a midmost nation that you might be witnesses over the nations and the Apostle a witness over yourselves. [2:142–43]

> In being called the midmost nation or the People of the Middle, we are charged with the mission of mediating conflicts, spurning the doctrines of bigotry and hate, trampling underfoot the myths of racial or cultural superiority and translating into social terms the concepts of mercy and beneficence which constitute the core of our faith.
>
> The concept of the People of the Middle is suggestive also of a new synthesis. Through a conventional opposition, the East has been contemplative and the West, materialistic and pragmatic. Islam rejects such dichotomies. The Muslim accepts both worlds, the spiritual and the material. What he tries to do is to find the reserves of spirituality, the respect for human personality and the sense of what is sacred in all cultural traditions, which could serve to fashion a new type of man. His aim is more than the mere mastery of Nature. If he is a true Muslim, he is at once Eastern and Western, materialistic and spiritual, a man of enterprise as well as of grace. (pp. 50–1)

How is the Islamic basis for equality and universal brotherhood to be actualized in a political context? This is the issue to which we turn.

State–Citizen Relationship

As we saw above, the core of law in Islam is sacred, that is, beyond the tampering of the religious or temporal authorities and not always in line with the temper of the times. There is a detailed *shari'ah* structure in place to protect the five foundations of good life: faith, intellect, life, family, and property. This means that even the state cannot encroach upon the freedoms and protections given in these areas (Chapra, 1992, p. 208). Bernard Lewis (1993) accepts that the relationship between an Islamic state and its citizens is contractual in nature and subject to maintaining *shari'ah* as the law of the land. This principle of the supremacy of *shari'ah*, we may recall, flows directly from the Holy Qur'an and *sunnah* and on it, throughout history, there has been an *ijma* (consensus) of Muslim scholars. The following advice by Prophet Muhammad (pbuh) on the occasion of the farewell pilgrimage is typical:

> If a slave with dark complexion and deformed limbs is appointed to govern over you and he conducts your affairs according to the Book of Allah, listen to him and obey his orders. (Sahih Muslim, *Hadith*, 2977)

What are the citizens' rights implicit in the Book of Allah in return for the obligation to support the *shari'ah*-abiding state/ruler in thick and thin? Iqbal (1986) illustrates with an example from history:

> It is reported that one night while crossing a street of Madinah, Caliph Umar heard sounds of debauchery coming from inside a house. He lost his temper and tried to enter the house, but no one answered his knock at the door. He climbed upon the roof and from it shouted down to the owner who was present in his lawn: 'Why are you breaking the law and allowing such behavior in your house?' The man replied: 'No Muslim has the right to speak to another in that manner. Maybe I have committed a wrong, but think how many wrongs you have committed. For instance: (1) spying – despite Allah's command "thou shalt not spy"; (2) breaking and entering – you came in over the roof despite the command of Allah, "enter a house by the door"; (3) entering without the owner's permission – in defiance of Allah's command: "enter no house without the owner's permission"; (4) omitting the *salam* – though Allah has commanded "enter no house without indicating that you are a friend and calling peace (*salam*) on those within".' Umar felt very embarrassed and withdrew saying: 'Well, I forgive your wrong.' The owner retorted: 'That is your fifth infringement; for if you claim to be an executor of Islamic law, then how can you say that you forgive what Allah has condemned as a wrong?' (p. 49). [6]

Thus Islam allows no interference or intrusion into the personal or family affairs of anyone. Also, spying is forbidden in normal times even if there is a strong probability that something wrong is going on in someone's house. Having guaranteed freedom of action in the private space, the public space is then protected from the exhibition of preferences that contradict *shari'ah* and could influence or undermine decent family values.

Note also that one aspect of human freedom is that, on certain specific matters pertaining to law, and public finances, non-Muslims of an Islamic state are differently placed *vis-à-vis* Muslims. In particular, the Holy Qur'an refers to Jews and Christians as *ahl al-kitab*, the People of the Book, because they belong to 'revealed religions' (Stork, 1999, p. 16). Although in one of the verses in the Holy Qur'an they are reserved Allah's curse for stubbornly rejecting Faith (2:159), generally they are offered forgiveness (4:153), praise for devotion to learning (5:82) and placed in the ranks of the righteous (3:113–114). Under Islamic law, People of the Book are accorded the status of *dhimmis* (non-Muslims protected by a treaty of surrender), a position which, like the Arabic word itself, means 'protected' or 'guilty'. They are protected because they have been recipients of genuine revelations (the Book) and share common religious beliefs with Muslims such as God, Angels and the Last Day. On these grounds, they received the status of 'protected minorities' (*ahl adh-dhimma*). At the same time, People of the Book are guilty of not accepting Prophet Muhammad (pbuh) as a prophet, and as having misinterpreted (or distorted) the revelations that they did receive (al-Mawardi, [1405 AH] 1985). There are differences, for example, on the Oneness of God, the Prophets, Revealed Books, lawful food, inheritance, etc., that pose difficulties for marriage between Muslims and non-Muslims and for the bringing up of children.

As *dhimmis*, Jews and Christians may live in Muslim states and practise their religions, but under certain conditions and not quite as equals with Muslims. On the interpretation of this framework given by Schacht (1964):

> a treaty of surrender is concluded which forms the legal basis for the treatment of the non-Muslims to whom it applies. It is often called *dhimma*, 'engagement', 'obligation', 'responsibility', because the Muslims by it undertake to safeguard the life and property of the non-Muslims in question, who are called *dhimmis*. This treaty necessarily provides for the surrender of the non-Muslims with all duties deriving from it, in particular the payment of tribute, that is, the fixed poll-tax (*jizya*) and the land-tax (*kharaj*), the amount of which is determined from case to case. . .
>
> they are excluded from the specifically Muslim privileges, but on the other hand they are exempt from the specifically Muslim duties. (pp. 130–1)

Nevertheless, on the position of *dhimmis vis-à-vis* Muslims, we need to consider the following advice of Umar bin Khattab, the second Caliph, in his last moments (on his deathbed):

> I warn you concerning those given protection by Allah and His Apostle (that is, *dhimmis*): fulfil their contracts; fight for them; and do not burden them with what is beyond their ability. (Sahih Bukhari (*Hadith*, 4.287))

Traditionally, this treatment has meant freedom of belief, religious rites, worshipping places, the following of family laws, and maintaining culture. On these matters, *dhimmis* are not obliged to follow the Islamic law but, under the treaty of protection, are instead guaranteed freedom to follow their own ways (5:47).

Of course, no set of laws is ever enforced with uniform enthusiasm and diligence, and an interesting commentary on how this legal framework worked out in practice is provided in a recent volume *People of the Book. The Forgotten History of Islam and the West* (Karabell, 2007), from which we quote at some length.

> From the beginning of Islam, Muslims viewed Jews and Christians as distant, slightly errant, relatives. In honor of the fact that they worshiped the same God and had been given the same revelation as Muhammad, they were called *abl al-kitab*, the People of the Book. Muslims were expected to treat them honourably. (p. 4)

> Today, the notion that a Muslim ruler and a Muslim state might tolerate and even welcome other faiths is alien, not only to people in the Judeo-Christian West but to hundreds of millions of Muslims as well. The early-twenty-first-century world is polarized by the conflict between Muslims, Christians, and Jews. Many Americans and Europeans see Islam as a religion of violence, especially toward those who do not share the faith, and millions of Muslims understand the history of Islam to be one of conquest and victory over non-believers, followed by defeat and setbacks. On all sides, this lens distorts the past, constricts our present, and endangers our future. (p. 5)
>
> Christians, Jews, and Muslims have lived constructively with one another. They have taught one another and they have learned from one another. Judaism was central to the formation of Islam, and for a millennium and a half until the end of World War II, Jews under Muslim rule enjoyed more safety, freedom, and autonomy than they ever did under Christian rule. Muslim states over the course of fourteen centuries have allowed for religious diversity and not insisted on trying to convert those who follow a different creed. From the beginning of Islam, Christian and Muslim states traded with one another. . .
>
> . . .Focusing only on conflict is like skipping every other page while reading a book. It isn't just incomplete; it is misleading to the point of incoherence. At the same time, it is important to avoid the opposite temptation and not replace one distorted reading of the past with another. Too often, those who attempt to rectify the imbalance provide the missing pages but delete the others. The result is just as skewed. The tolerance of Muslim society is praised and moments of concord are highlighted, but the violence and animosity are downplayed. Coexistence is treated as the norm and conflict as the anomaly, when in truth, both are threaded through the past and our present. (p. 8)

Economic and Property Rights and Obligations

Islam preserves an individual's right to acquire and have property (4:29). However, the test lies in seeking property through means that are not unjust to fellow beings. To elaborate, Islam preserves the Judaeo-Christian ban on interest (or predetermined returns) without distinction among any (2:275–9). Fixed interest is equated with *zulm* which as we mentioned above, is the converse of justice, that is, oppression. In contrast, trade with mutual consent is made legitimate (2:275), writing and witnessing of trade contracts is encouraged (2:282), and the fulfilment of promises is mandatory (2:177). Nevertheless, transactions containing *gharar*, that is, elements of uncertainty as regards the possession, quality, quantity, price or delivery date of the goods being transacted are prohibited and so is outright gambling (5:90). Also, hoarding is disallowed; trading in pork and intoxicants is prohibited for Muslims (2:173, 219, 5:90); and deceit, bribery, pornography and prostitution (83:1–3; 17:32–9; 24:2) are considered as various manifestations of corruption that distort socio-economic equilibrium. Subject to these far-reaching reforms, the Islamic economic philosophy accepts the profit motive, protects lawfully gained private property, prohibits intervention in real-supply-and-demand driven market prices, and admits the market economy in general.

Against this larger context, earning one's livelihood and engaging in economic activity is considered obligatory and next only to devotional worship.[7] Work is thus equated with seeking the bounties of Allah (16:14). Through it, human beings can test their potentialities, suffice their earthly requirements, and fulfil their obligations. Asceticism is discouraged[8] and begging is frowned upon unless one is desperate (57:27). Income through one's own labour is considered a means to befriending God[9] and trading within the Islamic ethical framework earns the Almighty's choicest blessings.[10] Naturally, such an all-embracing concept of worship does not prohibit engaging in business on the Islamic holy day, Friday, before and after the congregational prayer (62:10).

Welfare Rights and Obligations

Two concepts – that of the trusteeship of humankind and the brotherhood of all – are most relevant in elaborating the Islamic position on welfare rights and obligations (although they are by no means unique to Islam). Trusteeship means that the ownership of all the physical and mental resources belongs in an absolute sense to God (19:40, 80). Anything produced too by the use of these resources therefore belongs to God. Another way of looking at this issue is that granted for a moment the ownership of human beings to their usufruct, the share in that usufruct of the forces of nature is far too great compared to what comes from people themselves. As a result, the Holy Qur'an reminds that people's claims that 'We have been given it only on account of knowledge or effort or entitlement' are not tenable in an absolute sense (28:78–82; 18:32–44; 67:30; 17:66–9; 68:19–33; 27:60–66). The reality is that God enlarges the livelihood for whom He will and restricts it for whom He will (17:30; 30:37–9; 34:35–7; 34:39; 42:12). In that distribution there is a test for mankind.[11] Consider, for example, the following *hadith*:

> Allah's Apostle (peace be upon him) said, verily, Allah, the Exalted and Glorious, will say on the day of resurrection: O son of Adam, I was sick but you did not visit Me. He will say: O my Lord, how could I visit Thee when Thou art the Lord of the worlds? Thereupon He will say: Didn't you know that a certain servant of Mine was sick but you did not visit him, and were you not aware that if you had visited him, you would have found Me by him? O son of Adam, I asked you for food but you did not feed Me. He will say: My Lord, how could I feed Thee when Thou art the Lord of the worlds? He will say: Didn't you know

> that a certain servant of Mine asked you for food but you did not feed him, and were you not aware that if you had fed him you would have found him by My side? (The Lord will again say:) O son of Adam, I asked you for something to drink but you did not provide Me with any. He will say: My Lord, how could I provide Thee with something to drink when Thou art the Lord of the worlds? Thereupon He will say: A certain servant of Mine asked you for a drink but you did not provide him with one, and had you provided him with a drink you would have found him near Me. (Sahih Muslim, *Hadith*, 6232)

Thus the test of the trusteeship of humankind lies in seeking the bounty of God (4:32; 43:32) and spending from it as ordained by God (17:26–7; 4:36 8; 2:177; 51:19).

The actualizing of the second concept, that of the universal brotherhood of humankind (most certainly shared with Christianity), is most manifest in a *hadith* narrated in Sahih Muslim (2219) by Jarir which depicts Prophet Muhammad's (pbuh) great unease (the colour of his face changed) on coming across a people stricken with poverty. He then called the people of Madinah reciting Holy Qur'an (4:1) exhorting them to give freely until two heaps of eatables and clothes were piled and the face of the Messenger (peace be upon him) began to glisten like gold (on account of joy).

Some may argue that the precedent set by the Prophet was a requirement of *ihsan* (benevolence) and *birr* (virtue) rather than justice. Insofar as justice is concerned, the relevant question is that if after all that is said above about obligation to earn, protection of property rights, and moral exhortation to spend voluntarily on the poor, a person fails to attain basic needs, does Islam offer a positive right to minimal subsistence through redistribution? The short answer to this question is, yes. Society is obliged to fulfil the basic needs of its members, the basic needs being interpreted in the socio-economic context of a society on this issue. Chapra (1992) and Siddiqi (1996) note that prominent jurists of the past centuries and of the present age have full agreement. However, there are other sources to turn to in case of need. Family, neighbourhood,[12] and state provide successively higher levels of resources to draw upon. In the case of family, for example, children, parents, and near relatives have rights and obligations upon each other (31:14; 2:83, 180, 215; 4:7, 11, 33, 36, 135; 6:151; 17:23). Nevertheless, in respect to one aspect of these obligations, Ashtor (1976, p. 112) acknowledges that the Muslim law of (obligatory) inheritance most likely resulted in frittering away the big properties and probably impeded the accumulation of capital in rich merchant families during the Middle Ages. As far as the responsibility of the state is concerned, needs are to be fulfilled through an obligatory religious due called *zakah* levied on income and wealth. Details are provided in Chapter 5. If *zakah* does not suffice, additional taxes may be levied on the rich subject to the state itself not indulging in profligate expenditure. Referring to such obligations, Ali, the fourth Caliph after the Prophet Muhammad (pbuh) is reported to have said:

> Allah has levied upon the rich among Muslims, in their wealth, an amount that would suffice for the poor among them. If the poor starve or go unclad it is because of what their rich are doing. Beware, Allah the mighty and the exalted will take a tough account from them and punish them with a painful torment. (Siddiqi (1996, p. 9) refers it further to Al-Tabarani's Al-Mu'jam al-Saghir and Abu Ubayd's Kitab al-Amwal)

This position is compatible with many verses in the Holy Qur'an which count charity as a part of faith and righteousness. Consider, for example, the Holy Qur'an (Al-Balad, 90: 1–20):

> I swear by this city (Makkah);
> And you are a freeman of this city;
> And by the begetter (that is, Adam) and that which he begot (that is, his progeny);
> Verily We have created Man (*insan*) into toil and struggle;
> Thinketh he that none hath power over him?
> He says (boastfully): 'Wealth have I squandered in abundance!'
> Thinketh he that none beholdeth him?
> Have We not made for him two eyes?
> And a tongue and two lips?
> And shown him the two highways (good and evil/justice and injustice)?
> But he hath made no attempt to walk on the highway that is steep (that is, that leads to goodness and success);
> And what will make you know the path that is steep?
> (It is:) freeing a neck (slave/bondsman);
> Or the giving of food in a day of privation;
> To an orphan near of kin;
> Or to a poor in misery;
> (Only) then will you be of those who believe and enjoin patience (constancy and self-restraint) and do deeds of kindness and compassion.
> Such are the Companions of the Right Hand.
>
> But those who reject Our Signs they are the (unhappy) companions of the Left Hand.
> On them will be fire vaulted over (that is, wrath of God (see 6:65)).

In brief, wealth acquired through legitimate means ('entitlement') is not an end in itself in Islam but a means to moral and spiritual enrichment. This happens when it is spent voluntarily (and in this way purified) in fulfilling the needs of fellow human beings. Only then are human beings released from miserliness, greed, and pride.

Summary

To summarize, Islam views justice as the precondition for preserving peace, equilibrium, and harmony on earth, characteristics which are essential in their own right as well as to enable humankind to understand the demands of their position as the trustees of God on earth. Justice must be understood as a set of pairs of individual freedoms-and-limits, rights-and-obligations, and *masalih*-and-*mafasid* (social utilities and disutilities) elucidated by God (16:116) through His Prophets (7:157) so that human beings honour the rights of their fellow beings and do not exploit them. Justice also has to be complemented with benevolence so that in the words of Mawdudi (1994), the former removes conflict and bitterness from a society while the latter imparts grace and excellence to it by filling it with 'pleasant' harmony and 'sweet' accord. To implement justice, the state assumes a central role. First, it subjugates itself to the demands of justice by establishing an institutional framework based on the principles of equality of all, respect for privacy, freedom of faith, constraints on arbitrary state action, and consultation (*shura*) in state affairs. Second, it establishes a *shari'ah* framework for entitlement to income and wealth, and guarantees the resulting economic and property rights. Third, it implements the redistributive system of Islam (*zakah*) to guarantee minimal subsistence. Explaining the relationship between justice so perceived and the role of the state in implementing it, a renowned scholar of Islam, Ibn Taymiyyah once said, 'God upholds the just state even if it is unbelieving, but does not uphold the unjust state even if it is believing,' and that, 'the world can survive with justice and unbelief, but not with injustice and Islam.' Chapra (1992, p. 209) elaborates this point clearly: injustice and Islam are at variance with each other and by their very nature, one of these has to uproot or weaken the other in order to survive and remain strong. How does this conception compare with the different traditions within the Western thought? This is the question to which we now turn.

ISLAM AND THE WEST ON JUSTICE: A COMPARISON

When comparing the Islamic approach to justice with the different Western positions, the first thing to be said is that our focus throughout this chapter has been on the normative and not the positive, or, more accurately, on principles and not practice. This focus shall continue for the time being. It is only when we examine topics such as taxation, accountability, and governance and corruption later in the volume that the transition is made to 'what is' and the divergence between theory and practice.

Second, the next thing to be said is that, to the extent that Aristotelian thought focuses on the essential nature or *telos* of humankind – which is equated with moral rationality – while elucidating the terms of participation in a political community, it strikes a measure of harmony with Islam. In particular, if *telos* is unchanging, the basic rules of justice or social order too ought to remain constant. Truth in this sense is that which remains consistent amidst the flow of things changing, although Western thinking would draw a sharper distinction between principles and their exemplification. The principles of justice may remain unchanged, but most Westerners would expect that the process of putting these principles into practice would not be unchanging. That is, while the Holy Books contain the word of God and embody universal truths, they were given to particular peoples facing particular problems at particular times and cannot be used in their strict literal form for all times. Thus the translation of the essential truths into practice would not stand still in the face of changes in social mores about, for example, the role of women in society.

Nevertheless, the common heritage and commonality on the nature of humankind leads to some similarities in the profile of conduct required of individuals while dealing with others. On this account, one must regard Christianity as close to Islamic thinking (and hardly surprising in view of the origins of the two religions). In fact, this was clearly the case on matters of justice in exchange (that is, ban on usury) when the Church was in power (Lewis, 2007). But since the renaissance and the rise of Protestantism the emphasis has been on the much quoted answer by Jesus on the question of taxes. Consider Matthew 22: v. 15–21 (Phillips edition):

> The Pharisees went off and discussed how they could trap him in argument. Eventually they sent their disciples with some of the Herod-party to say this, 'Master, we know that you are an honest man who teaches the way of God faithfully and that you are not swayed by men's opinion of you. Obviously you don't care for human approval. Now tell us – Is it right to pay taxes to Caesar or not?'
>
> But Jesus knowing their evil intention said, 'Why try this trick on me, you frauds? Show me the money you pay the tax with.' They handed him a coin, and he said to them, 'Whose face is this and whose name is in the inscription?'
>
> 'Caesar's,' they said.
>
> 'Then give to Caesar,' he replied, 'what belongs to Caesar and to God what belongs to God!'

Focus on this Biblical injunction has encouraged a divergence in the West between the sacred and secular. As Noonan (1993) observes, after the Middle Ages, even the Church's teachings on issues such as usury, marriage, and religious freedom have undergone substantial change approaching dominant secular trends of the epoch. Under Islam, however, any separation between the realms of God and Caesar is an anathema. In fact, the Holy Qur'an (5:46–7) goes a step further than that and interprets the mission of Jesus Christ (pbuh) (5:46–7) in no less equal terms. Why have these two civilizations diverged so on the basic principles of running a society?

Islam would answer that basic truths have been upheld. The Christian Church would argue that the essential aims (for example, preventing exploitation by usury) have not changed, but have been reinterpreted in the light of different circumstances (for example, the rise of a modern competitive international financial system). In fact, as we shall see, in terms of reality rather than rhetoric, Islamic practices on the question of interest or usury are much closer to those in the West than is commonly known. Indeed, we will show that the prohibited practice of *riba* has become the norm in the Islamic world at the same time as the principle of prohibition continues to be proclaimed by the very bankers who breach it.

This brings us to the third observation on the differences between the two world-views which stem from the different paths of their historical evolution. As Gellner (1981, p. 2) observes, Christianity initially flourished among the politically disinherited and did not assume the role of Caesar for a considerable time. Jesus was a revolutionary but not a political one, and this potential for political modesty has thus underpinned the intellectual base of Christianity ever since. In comparison, Islam, unlike Christianity, was not born within an empire. On the contrary, it was born outside the two empires of its time and created an empire of its own which found legitimization in faith. Seen from a Muslim viewpoint then, Islam acts as the blueprint as well the social cement of a civilization. To Muslims, all the good of that civilization can be attributed to motivation by faith and the bad to a deviation from the model set forth by the Prophet and his immediate successors during what is seen as the 'Golden Age'.

Fourth, and again alluding to the different paths of evolution of the two civilizations, the Christianity that was absorbed into the remnants of the Roman empire some two centuries prior to the rise of Islam, faced the trappings of a feudal system that albeit, not of its own making, was legitimized by it through resources outside the teachings of Christ (pbuh). In the feudal society, most exchange was in kind and, in line with Aristotelian ideas, Christianity retained for a considerable time, an aversion to trading and market exchange. In contrast, Islam had to deal with the problems associated with monetized free market exchange from its inception. Trading, as such, was extolled. What was needed was to elucidate which forms of exchange were unjust. On that account there is a detailed framework which prohibits usury, gambling and *gharar*, and even condemns unequal barter exchange encouraging instead monetized trade to avoid potential for uncertainty of value.

This brings us to the fifth point, the difference between the modern Western views of justice and Islam. Apart from the socialist conception of justice, other secular views are silent on the issue of just exchange. The Marxist (Soviet style) and libertarian views, for example, define two opposing poles. The former, a planned economy, has nothing akin to a market as we know of it, that is, unhindered exchange of supply and demand signals through the price mechanism. In contrast to this situation is the libertarian view which not only embraces the market in full but, in fact, takes the principles of 'negative freedoms' and 'Pareto optimality' that underlie a market exchange as benchmarks for measuring the achievements of the entire public sphere of a social order. Welfare liberalism, that attempts to strike a middle ground between these positions by enforcing fair competition rules and consumer protection regimes, does not go far enough from an Islamic perspective. Its focus remains on 'external', that is, state-sponsored correction of market outcomes through taxation, redistribution and competition policy. To some extent this environment is complemented by an appreciation of the significance of workers' equity participation, but this dimension has yet to be raised on the political agenda to the level *pari passu* with a stress on protecting the welfare system.

The Islamic stand on these matters is that 'external' correction is needed to maintain the dignity of a 'fallen' human being, but on its own its reach could be too limited. It does not strike at the root of those mechanisms or exchanges 'internal' to the market that enable accumulation through means that are unfair and keep alive the possibility of *zulm* (oppression) on people by their own kind. Consequently, while the market itself is retained, the aim is to reform it 'internally' and organize it on a more dignified footing. It is perhaps with such possibilities in mind that Musgrave (1985) was prompted to remind us that the equality of earnings from labour and capital was never taken for granted by some renowned thinkers of the past, although contemporary libertarians tend to accept it without questioning. In fact, one can build further on this point and argue that there are grounds on the basis of fair exchange, in particular from behind the Rawlsian veil of ignorance, to prefer a profit-and-loss (PLS) sharing contract over a fixed interest contract as a more just form of exchange. Interestingly, while PLS investment vehicles are identified with (the principles if not always the practice of) Islamic financing, there is some evidence to suggest that they were utilized by medieval bankers under the Christian ban on usury (Lewis, 2007), although it is not known how widespread the practice was.

Sixth, excepting modern libertarians,[13] there is a consensus among Christianity, Islam, socialist and welfare liberal conceptions of justice on the need for redistribution. For instance, Rawls' contention that all differences among people are arbitrary from a moral perspective is in accord with Islam. Where Islam differs is on the solution. It first lays a prime emphasis on the responsibility of individuals to fulfil their obligations to support themselves, parents, family, neighbours, near relatives, and others. The idea is to keep those institutions and bonds intact which constitute the building blocks of a society, yet make the state responsible to step in for assistance in circumstances out of an individual's control. Thus the obligatory dues for redistribution – *zakah* – may appear modest by any modern measure of spending on the welfare state. But its dedicated expenditure directions make it difficult to fall prey to the 'public choice' trappings of redirecting distribution away from the poor toward the well-off 'pressure groups' and lobbies. Also, such redistribution is complemented by the desire to reform market exchanges *per se* by banning usury and speculation.

Combining the above elements into a vision for the role of the state in an economy, we find that insofar as Islam is concerned, the state enters into human life as a carrier and implementer of justice. Nowhere does Islam make it explicit that the market is the natural order that ought to serve as the benchmark for reflecting on or organizing other spheres of human interaction. Instead, market behaviour stands shoulder to shoulder with all other human interactions (that constitute socio-economic and political organization) ready to be examined and corrected with reference to the simple and complex goals of human life incorporated in the precepts of justice. Thus if freedom ought to be the goal, then processes as well as outcomes need to be geared toward this objective. When this consistency check – that is, compatibility of goals versus process-cum-outcomes – is applied to the market, then Islam finds it necessary to prohibit certain forms of exchange and partially correct outcomes.

By comparison, the dominant Western philosophy (or, at least, standard economics based on it) takes the market as the point of departure for defining the role of the state. A case for government intervention exists in circumstances of market failure, that is, imperfect competition, incomplete markets, and failure to reach competitive equilibrium. There may be scope for regulating externalities (for example, pollution), providing public goods (for example, defence), alleviating moral hazard (through institutional means and legal enforcement), creating missing markets (for example, compulsory third-party insurance, student loans, etc.), fulfilling needs (redistribution), and satisfying merit wants (for example, schooling). Desirably, in this scenario, the intervention should be through the market by creating new property rights (the Coase theorem), such as carbon emissions trading, water entitlements, vouchers for education, etc. Also, the argument against entrusting some or many of these tasks to the public

Table 3.2 Philosophical commitment and size of the public sector

Political standpoint	Percentage of GNP
Neo-libertarians	0
Classical libertarians	Low, decentralized, and diffused
Minimal state (Locke–Nozick)	1 or 2 (plus army)
Hayek	About 5 (plus army)
Friedman	About 8 (plus army)
Welfarist public economics	For example, 30
Administrative socialism	For instance, 80

Source: Adapted from Kolm (1996, p. 381)

sector is based either on entitlement (that is, libertarian case against redistribution) or on an inability of the public sector to improve upon market outcomes. In other words, parallel to market failure is government failure. Therefore, the former does not necessarily call for government action, and may be worsened by it.

Once there is an acceptance of the claim that markets might be subjected to the tenets of justice, then the Islamic and the standard economic approaches to the role of the state are not necessarily mutually exclusive. There is potential for both to learn from one another. How do these similarities and differences translate into the size of the public sector? Here, we introduce Table 3.2, based on Kolm (1996).

What is the Islamic position? Naturally, it would vary from country to country depending on economic conditions. As a guess, if *zakah* is estimated at some 5–7 per cent of GNP, and on top of that one adds, say 8 per cent plus army, then anything between 20–30 per cent of GDP would seem a reasonable estimate provided that reforms internal to market exchange are actually carried out in accordance with the Islamic position on usury, gambling, and *gharar*. In the absence of such reforms, some greater wealth concentration may continue and some greater allocations for redistribution 'external' to the market may be required on a continuous basis.

This brings us to our last point regarding the differences in the political conception of the Islamic and the Western theories of justice. Seen from one angle, the Islamic protection of the private space, its guarantee of not only the religious rites but also the personal laws of minorities, and its insistence on *shari'ah* law for the rest would seem to be broadly equivalent to the Rawlsian position that there is a common political conception of the good but insofar as the private sphere of life, individuals are free to follow whatever conception they prefer.[14] However, there is one caveat. The Islamic permission to safeguard the personal law of each community (although not granting *dhimmis* equal status with Muslims) is in essence aimed at keeping the metaphysical, through whatever tradition it is perceived, at the forefront of a person's life. In contrast, the modern secular visions of justice, by in certain cases restricting the freedom for individual traditions to observe different personal laws where they conflict with the prevailing laws, might be thought by some to undermine the importance of the metaphysical in individual life as reflected in those different practices.[15] For example,

> many of the undoubted virtues of pluralism – respect for the individual and a belief in the essential equality of all human beings, to cite just two – have strong roots in the union of the spiritual and the political achieved in the vision of Christianity. The question that secularists have to answer is whether these values can survive without these particular roots. In short, can we be good without God? (Tinder, 1989, p. 2)[16]

Someone who regards themselves as being a humanist or rationalist would baulk at this suggestion. To many of this ilk, the religious impulse is seen as an inability 'to contemplate man as man', responsible to himself and uncosseted by a higher power.[17] Lutz (2001) might be taken to imply how difficult it could become employing the tools of rationality alone to justify even the fundamental tenet of an equitable social order – the equality of all human beings. Yet, as we have seen, the Golden Rule or principle of reciprocity or law of general beneficence is not restricted to the three great monotheistic faiths. Ghandi famously remarked that one could agree with the teachings of Jesus (pbuh) without being a Christian. Certainly, C.S. Lewis in *The Abolition of Man* (1947) traced the reciprocity ethic to Confucius' *Analects*, Virgil's *Aeneid* and other non-religious sources. Religion casts the general beneficence principle in terms of the universal brotherhood of humankind with no real cause for a race for superiority and shedding the blood of one another, although there are question marks about the scope of brotherhood (whether it extends to non-Jews in Judaism and on what terms it applies to non-Muslim believers and unbelievers in Islam). For sure, people of religion have faltered in understanding the full demands of the universality principle, but that reflects on them not on the principle *per se*.

CONCLUSIONS

We began this chapter by exploring the question: what is justice? Our initial answer was: equality across some spheres of human action. If anything, contemporary libertarians are the closest in thought to this interpretation of the meaning of justice. To them, equity means preservation of negative freedoms (full stop).[18] Beyond that, a positive call for the support of 'fallen' human beings is perceived as a requirement of charity (preferably private) but not of justice. This is because human beings are said to have the 'right' to own the usufruct of themselves. In challenging this right, many rival views on justice are at one, the Islamic conception being one of them, Christianity another, and in total agreement with the modern Rawlsian liberal welfare conception that all human inequalities are arbitrary from a moral standpoint. Yet, 'money makes the mare to go', and the role of incentives cannot be ignored. The various insights meet in admitting the market mechanism but supplementing its outcomes with state-sponsored support for the needy in order to protect human life and dignity.

There are some differences between the welfare liberal and the Islamic visions. First, whereas the modern day welfare liberal would appeal to humanist principles or documents such as the Universal Declaration of Human Rights, the Islamic position is rooted in the metaphysical and the responsibilities of adherents as the trustees of God on earth. The nature of these responsibilities means that the challenge lies not in freeing oneself for what Aristotle calls as the pursuit of the highest good – contemplation of unchanging truths *per se* – but rather in using such soul-searching as a means to internalizing universal moral truths so as to undermine inhibitions within people (for example, pride, greed) that compel them to indulge in injustice and miserliness. With a reformed frame of mind, justice and benevolence flow naturally and so does socio-political action to universalize these attributes.

Second, while encouraging redistribution, there is considerable emphasis in Islam on preserving the social structure, in particular that of family. Thus justice and charity begin from home. Of course, no religion or ethic can claim a monopoly on such matters. Notably, 'charity begins at home', 'duties to parents, elders and ancestors' and 'duties to children and posterity' are among the principles of natural law that C.S. Lewis (1947) identified as held by people in a wide variety of cultures and civilizations. In the particular case of Islam, there are mutual rights and obligations among parents, children and near kin, and there is the obligatory distribution of inheritance among extended family. Also, through the concept of '*fard-e-kifaya*', that is, communal obligation there are rights and obligations of individuals over community and vice versa. Furthermore, there are elaborate mechanisms to institutionalize philanthropy (Hasan, 2007). Together these provisions cultivate and reinforce social capital and create a large space for informal societal and communal modes of governance.

Finally, Islam calls for reforming those market exchanges – constituting the basis of entitlement to earnings – that it considers inherently oppressive, that is, usury, speculation, and *gharar*. In this respect, there are parallels not only with other religions in the past (Judaism, Christianity, Hinduism), but also with the present day 'ethical investment' movement in the West that began with the application of Christian religious principles to investment and now embraces, under a decidedly secular banner, a variety of humanist, environmental and social responsibility concerns. Insofar as the Islamic investment rules are concerned, we will explore in later chapters how they impinge upon what used to be called the 'principles of public finance.'

NOTES

1. See Lewis (2007) for a comparison of Augustine and Aristotlian views on usury.
2. Thus in Australia, for example, some children 'at harm' are removed into foster care, and young adults who wish to leave home because of family problems may be provided with support to do so.
3. Zarqa (1980) and Ghazanfar and Islahi (1990, 1997), Siddiqi (1996) and Islahi (2005) examine the works of these scholars.
4. See, for example, (6:151–53; 16:76).
5. The last sermon of the Prophet Muhammad (pbuh) is available in books of *hadith*, *sirah* (that is,, the life of Muhammad) and also on some internet sites. This excerpt is compiled from Sahih Muslim (*Hadith*, 2803.1) and from the internet site: http://www.usc.edu/dept/MSA/fundamentals/prophet/lastsermon.html, 26 June, 2000.
6. See, for example, Holy Qur'an (49:12, 2:189, 24:27, 61).
7. *Hadith* from Suyuti, Al-Jami al-Sghir, quoted in Chapra (1992).
8. 'Umar . . . passed by a group of Qur'an-readers who were sitting with their heads bent down. He was told that they were *mutawakkilun* (resigned to fate). Thereupon he exclaimed: No. Rather they are *muta'akkilun*, that is, parasites who consumed other people's money. The true *mutawakkil* is one who sows the seed and depends on Allah for its germination' (Yusuf, 1988, p. 17).
9. 'The Prophet Muhammad (pbuh) said: 'Nobody has ever eaten a better meal than that which one has earned by working with one's own hands. The Prophet of Allah, David, used to eat from the earnings of his manual labour' (Sahih Bukhari, (*Hadith*, 3286)).
10. 'The truthful and honest merchant shall be with the Prophets, with the standard bearers of truth and with the martyrs' (Tirmidhi (*Hadith*, 2796)).
11. He it is who hath placed you as viceroys of the earth and hath exalted some of you in rank above others, that He may try you by (the test of) that which He hath given you. Lo! Thy Lord is swift in prosecution, and lo! He is Forgiving, Merciful (6:165).
12. Mujahid said that Abdullah ibn Amr slaughtered a sheep and said: 'Have you presented a gift from it to my neighbour (who was a Jew), for I heard the Apostle of Allah (peace be upon him) saying: "Gabriel kept on commending the neighbour to me so that I thought he would make an heir?"' (Abu Dawood (*Hadith*, 5133)).
13. John Locke is an exception. Consider, the following excerpt from his book: 'The right to the product of one's own labour does not permit one to let another person starve: God "has given no one of his children such a property, in his peculiar portion of the things of this world, but that he has given his needy brother a right to the surplusage of his goods; so that it cannot justly be denied him, when his pressing wants call for it." (book 1, ch. 4, p. 205). This third proviso seems to be a necessary consequence of Locke's basic idea that everyone must seek to preserve human life' (cited in Sugden, 1992, p. 280).
14. Surely, Islam has many rules applicable to the private spheres for example, marriage,

separation, inheritance, food, prayers, festivals, etc. but these rules are applicable only to those who profess Islam.

15. Of course, we are talking about very different circumstances. Islam had to develop rules for Jews, Christians and others in the lands they conquered as we explained earlier in this chapter when discussing the status of 'People of the Book' and *dhimmis*. Most Muslims today living in nominally Christian societies have voluntarily chosen (or their forebears chose) to live in societies that are predominantly secular.
16. Page numbers refer to the internet copy taken from: http://theatlantic.com/election/connection/religion/goodgod.htm 21 January 1999.
17. Amis (2008, p. 26) attibutes this viewpoint to Sir Vidiadhar Naipaul, the British writer of Indo-Trinidadian descent who was awarded the Nobel Prize for Literature in 2001.
18. In taking this stand, they are at one with the concept of justice that prevailed in pre-Islamic Arabia.

4. An Islamic perspective on taxation

GOVERNANCE AND TAXATION

So far we have considered governance in the abstract. At its broadest, public governance is about the use of social norms, rules, institutions and decision-making structures of the state to allocate, coordinate or control activity in a society (Bell, 2002). As such, the concept embraces both the normative (for example, what is the desirable provision of collective goods and services and system of revenue raising) and the positive (what institutional and political processes generate an efficient provision of public goods and revenues). We also saw that, in line with conceptions of justice, there may be different forms of an 'inner core' of governance resulting from the socio-political and moral framework within which a society operates (Dhonte and Kapur, 1997).

In this chapter, we bring to bear these insights to investigate the Western and Islamic perspectives on taxation. The importance of taxation for governance is obvious enough. Public governance depends on taxation revenues for financial resources when providing collective goods and services. At the same time, how governments tax does matter for society (Moore, 2007). This chapter is concerned with the normative, with the issues of implementation left to the next. To this end, we begin by examining how the three Western academic approaches, namely, equity in taxation, optimal taxation, and fiscal exchange approach the question of what constitutes a good tax system. Then the traditional Islamic schema of taxation is examined both with respect to its standing in light of *shari'ah* and also with respect to the findings of economic theory. The objective is to comprehend the Islamic approach by separating the eternal rules from the finite and by gauging how Islam and traditional jurists actualized principles of justice in taxation. Finally, the scope for synthesizing the Western and Islamic approaches is explored.

WESTERN PERSPECTIVES

Serious analysis of taxation in the West did not begin until after the decline of the feudal system and with the rise of trade and commerce, especially following the discovery of the Americas and the New World. The emerging centralized state needed vast amounts of money if only to pay for armies of mercenaries and adventurers, along with the navies and armaments that were replacing men and materials provided by feudal lords to support the monarchs. Measures were put in place to expand the revenue base, including providing encouragement to nobles to engage in industry and commerce through supplying part of the capital, and granting of charters and monopoly rights. Profits from these ventures were then taxed to increase state revenue. Bodin ([1576] 1955) described revenue streams as:

> There are, generally speaking, seven sources of revenues. . . . The first is the public domain, the second the profits of conquests, the third gifts from friends, the fourth tribute from allies, the fifth the profits of trading ventures, the sixth customs on exports and imports, and the seventh taxes on the subjects. (Book VI, Chapter 2, opening para: www.constitution.org/bodin/bodin_6.txt)

He saw the last item on the list as least preferred, to be levied with public consent, regarded as a temporary measure of last resort, and applied without arbitrariness, that is, in proportion to ability to pay – a recommendation made against the backdrop of the privileged being virtually immune from taxation (Seligman, 1931, p. 8).

This theme was taken up by the natural law philosophers, Hugo Grotius (1583–1645), Thomas Hobbes (1588–1679), Samuel von Pufendorf (1632–94), Baruch Spinoza (1632–77) and John Locke (1632–1704)[1] who argued that arbitrariness of any kind in the state–citizen relationship was unjustified. To them, society had to be organized around two concepts: equality of all in a commonwealth and the universality of reason. Fairness in taxation was admittedly only one, albeit a very important dimension, in this call for a constitutional government. Nevertheless, it gave a tangible expression to defining the relationship between state and the individual.

On this point, however, broad philosophical differences exist, as we saw in Chapter 3. At one end of the scale there is John Locke's proposition – in his *Two Treatises of Government* (published in 1690) grounded in the philosophy of natural law – that one is entitled to the fruit of one's labour and that the state must not interfere with it in the name of redistributive justice (Locke, 1690). Accordingly, no confiscation by taxation is allowed. Only permitted are those taxes that follow the benefit rule, providing a *quid pro quo* to the payee (the entitlement principle). Nozick (1974) in his later extension of the Lockean doctrine even likens redistributive taxation to slavery since the payee is forced to work for the recipient. On the other end of the scale there is the proposition argued by Rawls (1971) that the accident of birth, with its differential endowment of talent, wealth and position, does not establish a legitimate claim to deserved reward. Any fruits of superior talent are subject to communal claim and not to personal entitlement. Redistribution and the supply of merit goods are not only admissible, but seen as a social necessity to be funded through taxation.

Caught between such abstract notions of political philosophy, on the one hand, and the search by political leaders to raise public finances through the least politically costly means, on the other, economists have elaborated certain dimensions of the taxation problem. To them, fairness in taxation has two dimensions. First, the ends to which government measures such as taxation are designed should be just, and, second, the costs in pursuing such ends should not be distributed on an arbitrary basis (Brunner, 1989, pp. 1–6). The former leads to the theory of public expenditure while the latter branches into the normative principles of horizontal and vertical equity in taxation, and thence to welfare economics.

Of course, it might be argued that taxation revenues do not need to accompany spending *pari passu* because government expenditure can be funded in two other ways: by printing money, and by borrowing. However, a moment's reflection is sufficient to appreciate that these are not really alternatives at all. If money is printed faster than it is demanded, then it will generate inflation and inflation is simply a different form of tax – essentially a tax on money balances (Friedman, 1963).[2] If, on the other hand, cash is created in line with demand, then it represents borrowing by means of government debt, but in this case at a zero rate of interest via seigniorage. Moreover, if we accept the argument of Buchanan (1958), borrowing (for example, by government bond issue) is simply a way of deferring and transferring the tax burden to future generations. In the end, it all comes down to taxation in one form or another, and the issues need to be addressed within the broader framework of public and economic governance.

Ever since Musgrave (1959) developed his conception of the Allocation Branch, Distribution Branch, and Stabilization Branch of public finance, it has been recognized that the aims of taxation relate to three parallel goals of economic policy: resource allocation, distribution and economic stabilization. Increasingly, nowadays, the economic stablilization function of taxation has been downplayed (although not entirely shelved) due to time lags in instituting taxation changes through the legislatures, and monetary policy has taken on the role of the first-to-be-employed 'swing instrument' in economic policy. At the macro level, taxation policies are aimed more at longer-term development goals (Tanzi and Zee, 2000). This leaves the allocation and distribution roles, and in traditional analysis, taxation assists in these goals without losing sight of its primary revenue-raising purpose. Standard theory then divides into positive or normative approaches to the issues, the former dealing with the allocational and distributional consequences of different tax regimes, while the normative examines the ethical criteria governing whether such consequences are 'good' or 'bad' or 'acceptable' or 'unacceptable'. It is the normative dimension which is of immediate interest to us and the issues involved can be classified under three broad categories: equitable taxation, optimal taxation, and fiscal exchange.

Equitable Taxation (ET)

ET's objective is to promote fairness in the application of the tax process among people in similar economic circumstances in terms of horizontal equity, for example, people in equal positions should be treated equally for tax purposes, and vertical equity, for example, people in unequal positions should pay tax that bears a meaningful relationship to the differences in their position (Hettich, 1979).

The roots of ET go back to the faculty theory or the ability-to-pay principle which holds that individuals should contribute to the public purse in accordance with their means or ability to pay. The focus is on the tax side and the benefits that people derive from public expenditure are ignored. 'Faculty' was originally identified with property but was later equated with income. The rise in popularity of this principle came in the latter half of the nineteenth century when 'it had become obvious that an unfettered market system (especially if superimposed on aristocratic foundations, as in England) was producing a social system that many, including many economists, considered unjust' (Kiesling, 1992, pp. 56–7). Natural law principles would baulk at the compulsory taking of income from those whose claims to it may be strong under the rules of the marketplace. But if the original distribution of income is found to be less than fair, and 'undeserved', claims to it may be weakened.

When correcting inequalities, taxation deals with consequences, not causes. It might be thought better to go to the root of the matter, and tackle the causes themselves – by equalizing opportunity through access to education, by control of monopolies, and by removing conditions which make possible 'undeserved' profits. Others argue that the solution is to provide people with equal opportunities to develop talents and resources, and that this goal can be achieved only through progressive taxes combined with a greater public expenditure on social goods.

Such a prescription raises, first, the question of the degree of progression, for progression can come about either by the application of graduated tax scales (of rates to be determined) or by a general exemption for those at the bottom of the income scale coupled with a flat rate of tax, producing, as a matter of arithmetic, progression in effective rates. At a second level, there is the question of what is meant by 'means' in this context.

Here, the problems posed from a governance perspective are quite complex. Over the late nineteenth and twentieth centuries, the concept of 'income' was fiercely debated and Kaldor, Hicks and Fisher all advanced their definitions (see Parker and Harcourt, 1969). Nevertheless, the Schanz–Haig–Simons (SHS) concept of comprehensive income gained wide acceptance, with Simons (1938) providing the most systematic articulation of SHS income, defined as the money value of the net accretion to one's economic power during an accounting period. It equals 'the algebraic sum of (1) the market value of rights exercised in consumption and (2) the change in the value of the store of property rights between the beginning and end of the period in question' (p. 50).

Yet, the devil lies in the details, and researchers in the ET tradition subsequent to Simons (Musgrave, Vickrey, Pechman, Shoup, Goode and others) have sought to adapt the wealth accretion concept to real world complexities. Musgrave (1976) suggests the following normative rules: (1) capital gains should be treated as ordinary income, whether realized or not, with allowance for averaging and loss offset; (2) gifts and bequests should be treated similarly; (3) corporate income should be integrated into the individual income tax base, whether or not distribution occurs, with no separate corporate tax; (4) household wealth calls for the taxation of imputed rent, combined with deduction of depreciation and mortgage interest; and (5) income should be defined in real terms, after inflation adjustment.

Seen through the framework of governance developed earlier, it is not easy to make these concepts operational and therefore, ET has been criticized on a number of grounds. First, ET is said to be driven by horizontal equity and provides little guidance on vertical equity (Musgrave, 1976). Simons (1938) himself saw that the case for progression rested 'on the ethical or aesthetic judgement that the prevailing distribution of wealth or income reveals a degree (and/or kind) of inequality which is distinctly evil or unlovely' (p. 18). Second, ET does not integrate efficiency objectives into tax analysis in any systematic way. Third, difficult (that is, controversial and legally contestable) procedures may be required for valuing asset (wealth) accretion (Goode, 1977). Fourth, inflation adjustment is administratively cumbersome (Sandford, 2000, p. 39). Fifth, J. S. Mill and many others since have argued that income tax imposes double taxation on savings, once by reducing the amount that can be saved and then by taxing the returns to savings. In lifetime models, a Kaldor-style personal expenditure tax could offer a fairer, and less distorting, basis. Sixth, as Atkinson and Stiglitz (1980, p. 261) argue, SHS income bears little relationship to 'ability to pay' defined in terms of opportunity; people with the same endowments and market opportunities may end up with different incomes because of labour–leisure preferences, and other lifestyle choices. Following through this line of thought, some have been led to wonder whether income should include the imputed value of leisure.

Optimal Taxation (OT)

ET seeks to avoid utility theory. This is not the case with OT theory which evolved from the fair sacrifice doctrine, which holds that justice in taxation means 'equality of taxation' which in turn means 'equality of sacrifice'. It seems possible that an extra dollar has less 'value' to a person with \$1 000 000 of income than for a person with only \$10 000 of income per year. A fair tax would take more, perhaps proportionately more, from the wealthier if it is to result in 'equality of sacrifice'. In turn, equality of sacrifice has a number of meanings. *Equal absolute sacrifice* imposes taxes such that each individual experiences the same loss in total utility. *Equal proportional sacrifice* requires that the ratio of the utility lost to total utility for each individual should be the same. Finally, *equal marginal sacrifice* necessitates that taxpayers' marginal sacrifices, measured in utility terms, be equal.

Sacrifice doctrine makes assumptions about the reactions that people have in common to money, specifically that a person's 'taste' for money declines as the amount of money that they have increases. In short, there is envisaged a general utility curve for money which has a downward slope. There are a number of problems with this idea. Even if we go along with this assumption, it is by no means axiomatic that sacrifice principles lead unambiguously to a progressive tax, and it is even more difficult to determine a just scale of progressive rates (Blum and Kalven, 1963). In broad terms, assuming declining marginal utility of income, equal absolute and proportional sacrifice result in mild progression for a range of commonly depicted income–utility schedules, but outside of that range, little can be said. By contrast, the principle of equi-marginal sacrifice yields unambiguous support for progressive taxation: the top income is to be confiscated until it is reduced to the next highest, and so on until the required revenue is obtained. Given that each unit of income taxed has lower utility than the next one, aggregate sacrifice too is minimized through equal marginal sacrifice. In the words of Pigou, the system would necessitate 'lopping off the tops of all incomes above the minimum amount and leaving everybody, after taxation, with equal incomes' (Pigou, 1951, p. 57).

The only escape from such 100 per cent rates in this case would come from the impairment-to-incentives argument and the damage to society from lower productivity. Even the strongest advocates of progression have accepted the lessening of economic productivity as a counterbalancing consideration. This is why Kaldor (1955) proposed a progressive tax on expenditure (in order to avoid the double-taxation of savings and the disincentives to risk-bearing due to income taxes).

A final point concerns the idea of interpersonal comparisons of utility. To fit the requirements of sacrifice theory, the utility curve for money must apply not for a particular person but for people in general. Examining the way in which each person satisfies their wants does not provide the basis for interpersonal comparisons. In the words of Lionel Robbins (1935):

> it is one thing to assume that scales can be drawn up showing the order in which an individual will prefer a series of alternatives, and to compare the arrangements of one such individual scale with another. It is quite a different thing to assume that behind such arrangements lie magnitudes which themselves can be compared. . . . There is no means of testing the magnitude of A's satisfaction as compared with B's. (pp. 138 – 140)

Of course, this is an old dilemma, for people have long speculated on whether the person in the palace is happier than the one in the cottage. In the end, satisfaction or happiness defies precise quantification and, in the face of this difficulty, the possibility of using sacrifice theory as a guide to taxation policy evaporates. Direct interpersonal comparisons of utility are no longer believed necessary in the new welfare economics (Mishan, 1969). This is how the sacrifice principle makes way for the optimal taxation theory.

OT uses the new welfare economics (relying on Pareto improvements) based on a generalized notion of utility that opens up possibilities for introducing variables such as 'leisure' into tax analysis. A variety of tax bases – labour income, capital income, consumption, leisure, hourly wage rates, etc. – and rate structures can be examined within an explicitly normative framework. The emphasis is on minimizing welfare losses.

From the second fundamental theorem of welfare economics, policymakers can achieve a desired Pareto (first best) allocation as a competitive equilibrium if lump sum taxes and transfers are undertaken such that each individual is able to purchase the consumption bundle implicit in that allocation for him (Myles, 1995, p. 48). In practice, as Mrs Thatcher discovered, lump sum (poll) taxes can play only a limited role. For this reason, the theory of optimal taxation aims at discovering principles of raising a given amount of revenue when lump sum transfers are ruled out, and the tax structure reflects a society's preferred trade-off between distributional equity and allocative efficiency goals. Such goals are incorporated in a social welfare function (SWF) that depends not only on the total but also on the distribution of individual utilities. The optimal tax structure crucially depends on the articulation of such function. The approach as such has its origins in the works of Edgeworth (1925), Ramsay (1927) and Pigou (1928) while Mirrlees (1971), Atkinson and Stiglitz (1976), Stern (1987), Stiglitz (1987, 1988) and others have extended it further adding a range of policy choices that take account of the twin goals of minimizing efficiency losses for a given set of distributional preferences.

One key focus of such analysis has been the examination of the degree of income tax progressivity. For linear tax schedules, Stern (1976) estimated that optimal flat-rate tax was 19 per cent for a 'utilitarian' SWF compared to 80 per cent for a 'Rawlsian' SWF assuming government expended 20 per cent of national income on goods and services, excluding transfer payments. For non-linear tax schedules, based on the UK data, the optimal tax schedule was approximately linear with an exemption level below which transfers applied and the marginal tax rates were rather low. Income tax appeared much less effective than transfers for reducing inequalities (Mirrlees, 1971).

To these results may be added insights from the information theoretic analysis of optimal taxation by Stiglitz (1987, 1988), Boadway and Keen (1993) and several others. These insights are, first, that the higher the productivity of a group, the lower the marginal tax rate. Second, the higher the labour supply response, the lower the marginal tax rate. Third, the larger the fraction of population at a particular income level, the lower the marginal tax paid; otherwise high marginal rates applied to so many could create large distortions. Some of these results conflict with some prevailing ideas about income tax.

Obviously, the OT analytical framework is highly stylized: it depends crucially on an extensive set of assumptions on the structure of preferences, differences between households, and value judgements on a society's equity and efficiency goals. It can be of help in directive governance, that is, on general rule setting but it ignores important considerations on institutional design and operational costs leaving little guidance on constitutive and operational governance issues.

Fiscal Exchange (FE)

FE is the historically evolved form of the benefit theory or *quid pro quo* principle, which holds that individuals should be taxed according to the benefits each would receive from expenditure programmes financed by tax revenue. John Locke's entitlement theory mentioned earlier is a case in point. The relationship between the state and an individual is construed on a give-and-take basis akin to transactions in the marketplace. The state provides protection, and individuals effectively purchase it in relation to the benefits that they receive from such protection. Since protection consists in guarding life and property, entitlement theory calls for a mixture of a poll tax, a proportionate tax on property, and user charges for public services.

A modern attempt to reinterpret the benefit principle, undertaken by Wicksell (1896), Lindahl (1919), Samuelson (1954, 1955) and Musgrave (1981), focuses on the nature of public goods and the processes through which they are determined. Pure public goods are non-rival in consumption. Unlike private goods, individuals cannot be excluded from receiving benefits from such goods. Also, each consumer shares the same quantity although marginal evaluations differ. Ideally, the taxation (price) for such goods is explicitly linked to the outlays (costs) by the efficiency condition that the marginal cost equates to the sum of the marginal evaluations (utilities) by all beneficiaries. However, this is not what happens. Typically, expenditure decisions are made independently of tax votes, or are related only vaguely to them. As a result, expenditure votes are not cost-conscious, nor are revenue votes benefit-conscious. Consequently, the composition of the tax structure is determined without reference to the expenditure pattern and new expenditures are voted without specifying who pays. Common sense would suggest that for efficient decisions to be made, tax and expenditure issues ought to be decided jointly. As Musgrave (1981) asks, how can a person decide whether to vote for or against a particular expenditure project without knowing what it will cost him? This linkage was recognized by Wicksell, who first addressed this problem over one hundred years ago. He suggested that tax and expenditure decisions be made jointly, so that voters can decide whether any particular project is worth the tax price that they are asked to pay, allowing expenditure to be linked to matching revenue votes when made initially.

In this schema, benefit-based taxation emerges as a mechanism by which taxpayers are forced to eschew behaving as 'freeriders' (that is deliberately understating their true evaluation of social goods) and instead are induced to reveal their true preferences. Linking both sides of the budget equation means that revenues needed to finance public services have to be drawn from taxpayers in line with benefits received. Such taxes might be expected to rise with income as higher-income earners will likely value a common level of public services, for example, for protection and security, more highly than low-income earners. But whether the tax would rise less, or more rapidly than income depends on the price and income elasticity of demand for public goods, not on income redistribution policy, for the benefit tax is distributionally neutral in the sense that it reflects (rather than adjusts) the prevailing state of income distribution (Musgrave, 1981).

If it is argued – as Wicksell did – that benefit taxation can be considered just and equitable only if imposed on a just and equitable distribution of income, then a benefit approach to the financing of public services is in no way incompatible with being supplemented by a distinct set of tax-transfer measures designed to alter the prevailing income distribution. In this setting, the distribution of earnings which results in the market has to be adjusted to meet the standard of fairness, so that some degree of redistribution is required. Benefit taxes can still retain a place in the finance of social goods, but the benefit principle itself ceases to rule as the universal maxim of tax equity.

One closely related concern has been the potential for political irresponsibility with taxation policy (Buchanan, 1967). The classic argument on this point (for example, Friedman, 1962; Blum and Kalven, 1963) is that a system in which the majority (low income earners) have the voting power to set the tax rate paid by the minority (wealthy individuals) through legislating progressivity is one that is open to abuse. Whether taxpayers have ever indulged in such a naked exercise of political power is questionable, although very high marginal tax rates (even up to 98 per cent) were enacted by socialist governments in Western Europe after the Second World War. Of course, there are some limits. As the extent of redistribution rises, so does the number of losers relative to that of gainers, so that the majority available for further action falls. Low-income voters who aspire to move up the income scale will hesitate to lower their prospects, and demands for redistribution will be dampened by concern for adverse productivity effects (and the migration of the wealthy to lower tax regimes!).

Thus another counterbalance is the incentive to tax avoidance. High graduated rates have often been accompanied by big holes in the tax base. Musgrave observes that, short of compulsory labour, ultimately the wealthy can substitute leisure for income, and since only income can be transferred but not leisure, redistribution in the last resort is conditioned by consent. Society, as he paraphrases Karl Marx, may choose to give according to need; but it cannot ensure contribution according to ability. Many years ago, Milton Friedman argued that 'a much lower set of nominal rates, plus a more comprehensive base, through more equal taxation of all sources of income, could be both more progressive in average incidence, more equitable in detail, and less wasteful of resources' (Friedman, 1962, p. 173).

Finally, a large body of research addressing public choice concerns has emerged from, for example, Brennan and Buchanan (1980) who argue for limiting government's power to tax through a tax constitution that would restrict legislators to narrowly defined elastic bases providing opportunity for taxpayers to escape into non-taxed alternatives if the public sector grows excessively. In the same spirit, Buchanan and Flowers (1980) examine the role of constitutional rules such as budget balancing, capping government outlays or growth therein as a percentage of national income, and assignment of different tax bases and functions to different levels of government. Again, this tradition of addressing fairness in taxation through making rules on collective-choice rules goes back to Wicksell who recommended reform of electoral rules on fiscal decisions toward simultaneous voting on taxing and expenditure, and unanimous decision-making or at minimum consent of a qualified majority of some five-sixth of the members of a legislature to approve of a budget proposal.

While FE does not primarily concern itself with the study of tax rates and tax structures, its focus on the process and context of fiscal decisions – collective choice mechanisms – provides food for thought for enacting the constitutive layer of governance in the fiscal arena as well as designing checks and balances to mitigate possibilities of government's misuse of power to tax.

ISLAMIC PERSPECTIVES ON TAXATION

In the previous section, we examined the context and the product of deliberations in the West on establishing taxation on a just footing. In comparison, the progress of Islamic thought on this issue has been rather sporadic since many researchers continue to take the classical Islamic scheme and its revenue sources as sacrosanct. Taxation was a major theme in the classical era. Ben Shemesh (1967) identifies 21 works on taxation written during the early centuries of Islam (some of which feature in Box 2.2). The problem with some modern analyses that follow in this tradition is that the socioeconomic and political context in which the classical scheme evolved is forgotten. So too are the more generally accepted normative principles outlined in earlier chapters upon which Islam stands. Before we take a fresh look at the question of taxation in Islam, we need to have a general appraisal of the classical scheme of taxation and examine whether some parts of the system were meant to be time-bound. This is the task of this section.

The Classical Scheme of Taxation and its Appraisal

The classical scheme of taxation listed in Table 4.1 evolved in the context of the struggle of Muslims initially to ensure survival with freedom of conscience and then to implement a blueprint of justice. The core items of the classical taxation scheme are outlined below.

[illegible]he classical Islamic taxation scheme – core items

	Zakah				*Khums*	*Fay*
	2.5%	5.0%	10.0%	20.0%		
M[illegible] production and treasure trove[a]				√	One fifth (20%) of moveable property confiscated at the war front from the troops of the opposing party.	*Fay* consisted of progressive poll tax, land rent, and a variable share in crops (roughly 30 – 50%) and crafts based on land, crop, and craft surveys
Agricultural produce[b]		√	√			
Livestock	√					
Trade[c]	√					
Industry[c,d]	√					
Cash, gold, silver and jewellery	√					
Rents and wages[e]	√					

Notes

a. This too is sometimes known as *khums* (1/5th). Also some jurists make a distinction between treasures buried by persons and mineral production. It is the former that fetches a *zakah* rate of 20% while the latter only 2.5% (see, for example, Mawdudi, 1994).

b. 5 per cent for lands irrigated with artificial systems; 10% for lands irrigated with natural water. The levy is also known as *Ushr*.

c. Assets and income net of loans, working tools, and permanent fixtures.

d. Given cash/gold, agricultural produce, livestock, and trade capital virtually exhausted the then existing forms of wealth, *zakah* rate on manufacturing is considered analogous to trade. On services involving little traditional capital, one may infer, *zakah* is levied on net profits (see Hasanuz Zaman, 1991, pp. 183-5, for the use, in general, of analogy in *zakah*. For specific juristic details, see Al-Qardawi, 1984).

e. Differences of opinion exist on the issue. Hitti (1970) quoting from Yaqubi states that Mu'awiah used to deduct *zakah* at 2.5%, from the fixed annuities of Muslims.

Zakah

As one of the Five Pillars of Islam, *zakah* is the giving, as an act of piety (worship), a legally (*shari'ah*) stated portion of one's property to the needy in such a way as to preclude for the giver any sort of benefit (Aghnides, 1969, p. 203). The Holy Qur'an (9:60) establishes expenditure heads for *zakah* as follows:

> Alms are for the *fuqara* and the *masakin* (poor and needy), and those employed to administer (*zakah* funds); for those whose hearts have been (recently) reconciled (to Truth); for those in bondage and in debt, and in the cause of Allah; and for the wayfarer: (thus is it) ordained by Allah, and Allah is full of knowledge and wisdom.

The evidence for *zakah* (from the Holy Qur'an as well as *sunnah*) falls under the category of authentic and clear (that is, definite in meaning), with a wide consensus historically among Muslim jurists. Among contemporary writers, Mawdudi (1994, pp. 216–77) and Al-Qardawi (1983, pp. 61–141) establish conclusively that *zakah* is the third pillar after testimony of faith and prayers, and as such is essential to the faith.

Aghnides (1969, p. 204) citing classical Islamic jurisprudence sources, also concludes that the giving of *zakah* by Muslims is *fard* (obligatory) based on evidence found in the Holy Qur'an, the *sunnah*, the *ijma* and in reason. According to the Holy Qur'an, *zakah* throughout history had been one of the worshipping practices of all revealed religions (2:2,3; 21:73; 7:156; 19: 31,55). Islam resurrected it in an advanced form according to some researchers (see Al-Qardawi, 1983, p. 99) as early as the second year after migration (2 AH). In previous religions, the task was entrusted to clergy but they hoarded and amassed wealth on their own accounts and did not distribute it to the poor. In Islam, an organized clergy was disbanded and the task of *zakah* was centralized with the state. The *zakah* rates on a wide variety of items were fixed by Muhammad (pbuh), its expenditure heads were earmarked for charitable causes (9:60), and its collection and management was entrusted to the polity, not to a clergy condemned to have been corrupted (9:34). Note that *zakah* is the only mandatory due on Muslims in the classical scheme and, being a religious obligation, it cannot be imposed on non-Muslim citizens of an Islamic state.

Ghanima

Ghanima[3] are the spoils of war that were specified as the second source of state revenue against the backdrop of the first battle at *Badr* that broke out between Makkans and the Muslim community in 2 AH The Makkans lost, leaving moveable property in the hands of Muslims. The Holy Qur'an (8:1, 41:68) placed one-fifth (*khums*) of *ghanima* at the disposal of Muhammad (pbuh) for his kinsmen, orphans, paupers, and the wayfarers. The remaining four-fifths of the spoils excluded from specific commandments were distributed among the voluntary fighters. *Khums* thus became another source of financing community activities (Hasanuz Zaman, 1991, p. 69, pp. 149–52). Although widely practised by tribes of all faiths then settled in Arabia and by the adjoining empires, on Muhammad's (pbuh) own declaration, *ghanima* was divinely permitted only for the first time with the condition that launching a war for *ghanima* was prohibited (4:94; 8:91). In fact, Islam reformed the then prevailing practice of confiscating all belongings whatsoever of the conquered people to the forfeiture of moveable properties gathered at the war front only (Hitti, 1970, p. 172).

Reformed as well were other practices of war such as the destruction of the human, economic and religious resource base of the target communities. Islam prohibited the killing of women, children, aged, infirm, those who did not fight and those dedicated to worshipping in their own tradition, the cutting down of fruit-bearing trees, the destruction of inhabited places, the slaughtering of sheep or camels except for food, and the burning and scattering of bees (Mawdudi, 1980, p. 35–8). Within the ambit of such moral reforms it can be safely asserted that *ghanima* proved in the then prevailing environment, a very useful fiscal instrument in rewarding voluntary fighters, strengthening the emerging Islamic polity, and striking at the interests of those groups who actively opposed the Prophet.

Fay

In its origin, *fay* consisted of properties or tribute acquired peacefully, that is, without engaging in active warfare, from those parties that reneged at various times from their inter-community obligations under the 'Constitution of Madinah'. The Holy Qur'an (33:50; 59:67) placed such properties entirely at the discretion of Muhammad (pbuh) [the state]. In that capacity *fay* again served to finance the polity-in-making and economically weaken those who tried to rebel. After the death of Muhammad (pbuh), as the Caliphate expanded into the fertile lands of Iraq and Syria, *fay* was standardized under *jizya* (poll tax) and *kharaj* (tax on economic surplus arising out of the cultivated lands), and became the backbone of the taxation system for centuries to come. *Fay* was essentially a benefit tax against guaranteed protection of the life, property, and religious rites of non-Muslims (al-Baladhuri, 1968, I: pp. 210–11). It created horizontal equity between Muslims – who paid *zakah* and defended the state – and the minorities who were free from these obligations. Al-Dawudi (1995) depicts the following specific benefits delivered against land taxes:

> out of which their fighting people were given their allowances, their border-towns were sealed, and subsistence was given to those who looked after them from among their officials, judges, the disbursing officers, all other officials and those who needed them. Then, whatever there remained in excess was distributed among the needy till they became rich. (p. 64)

Other historians add a list of public works such as digging of new canals, construction of water tanks, and dams across rivers both for irrigation and drinking water (Chaudhry, 1996).

The general principles of these taxes were enunciated by Abu Yusuf (731–798) whose thorough study of the taxation system, *Kitab al-Kharaj*; was commissioned by Caliph Harun al-Rashid. According to Abu Yusuf, 'rates of poll tax and land tax are not pre-determined by *Shari'ah*'. They are chargeable subject to ability of 'tax payer' and 'land condition' (pp. 44, 92). A slightly different interpretation comes from Hasanuz Zaman (1991, p.

208): 'The amount of poll tax, if levied on any community without a treaty, could be increased or reduced by the government, but in the case of a treaty, the amount once agreed upon could not be increased'. In line with these principles, the practice varied over time. From Hasanuz Zaman (1991, p. 200), it would seem that the poll tax that Muhammad (pbuh) levied was fixed (for example, in Bahrain, it was one dinar from each able-bodied male). In contrast, Umar I levied progressive poll tax in Iraq: 'The rate of poll tax was fixed at forty-eight dirhams for the well-to-do, twenty-four dirhams for the middle, and twelve dirhams for the poor class, per annum' (p. 217). For this reason, the tax is described in Table 4.1 as a 'progressive poll tax' since it was levied on a per head basis, according to wealth.

In the case of the land tax, the practice again appears to vary from place to place depending on the terms of the treaty. For instance, for Iraq, Hasanuz Zaman (1991, p. 215) reports, 'Umar . . . fixed for each *jarib* of land where water was available a *qafiz* of wheat or barley and a dirham'. This implies a fixed land tax. However, in Syria, the practice appears to have changed. 'Caliph Umar employed two methods of levy in Syria: a fixed tax of one dinar on each man plus a quantity of grain on each *jarib*, and a proportional tax on the harvest (p. 226). One might surmise that varying pre-Islamic tax practices may have influenced such variations in the terms of the local treaties that were forged. Overall, the taxation scheme brought abundant resources to the classical Caliphate, and enabled it to run an expanding state and initiate an Islamic egalitarian society wherein the needy of all faiths received stipends and rations (Abu Yusuf, 1969, p. 87; Zarqa, 1995). In the words of Mahfooz Ahmad (1995), this achievement gave an operational meaning to the state's obligation in Islam to guarantee a minimal sustenance to all of its citizens.

Appraising the classical scheme from an economic perspective, the core taxes are direct and hard to shift. Poll taxes and land rents are classic optimal tax instruments. *Kharaj* on agricultural produce, since that was the major form of enterprise then, is like income tax today. *Zakah* is akin to income-cum-wealth tax. In *zakah* there is earmarking for poverty, foundations of a welfare state, and protection from all the concerns aspired by the fiscal exchange theory owing to permanent fixation of charge rates and specification of eligibility for redistribution. These views are elaborated further in Iqbal (2000).

Ijtihad on Classical Taxation

Ijtihad on public finances started in the early classical period. First, the custom of immediate disbursement of all state receipts was abandoned and *bayt al-mal* (Treasury) was organized on professional lines. Second, pre-Islamic taxes on land and agricultural produce levied by Byzantine and Persian empires were adapted into Islam and construed as *fay* (Osman, 1976). Third, *zakah* was extended to new forms of wealth. Fourth, customs duties, *ushur*, were levied that were not charged during the time of Muhammad (pbuh). In it, there is the principle of reciprocity in international tax competition.

In addition to the above revisions, we find prominent scholars in the Middle Ages such as Ibn Hazm (994–1064 CE) (Gilani, 2000), al-Ghazali (1058–1111 CE) (Ghazanfar and Islahi, 1997), Ibn Taymiyyah (1263–1328 CE) (Islahi, 1988) and Ibn Khaldun (1332–1406 CE) (1967) discussing the *ability-to-pay* and benefit principles, a further widening of the *zakah* base, the validity of taxes in addition to *zakah*, and the disincentive effects of higher taxes on individual enterprise and overall economic growth. In the case of Ibn Khaldun, there was even an early version of the Laffer curve: 'It should be known that at the beginning of a dynasty, taxation yields a large revenue from small assessments. At the end of the dynasty, taxation yields a small revenue from large assessments.' (p. 230). However, the reference point for *ijtihad* remained the classical scheme and its specific bases for taxation and no significant departure from the scheme gained wider approval.

Because our concern has been with the classical Islamic principles of taxation, it is on the classical period that we have focused, and not on the actual practices in later dynasties. In the Ottoman empire, for example, taxes can be grouped in four major categories. First, there were personal or poll taxes levied on persons or households, with rates higher for a married subject with land than for a bachelor or those with no land. Second, there were trade taxes on goods brought to the market, levied per camel load, with rates highest for linen and falling for butter, honey, pots and other goods. Third, there were production taxes on farming and manufacturing activities such as on beehives, animals and vineyards. Finally, there were tributes from vassal states, fees for marriages and criminal fines (Cosgel, 2004). These taxes had some roots in classical Islam but were also greatly influenced by the methods of taxation inherited from the Byzantine states.

Hence, with a great leap in time but without much loss of generality, we now switch to the contemporary studies on public finance in the Islamic tradition. Matters that require immediate attention are, first, what is eternal and what is finite in the classical scheme? And second, can additional taxes be levied?

The Eternal and Finite in the Classical Islamic Scheme

Debate is centred on two major components of the classical scheme, *kharaj* and *zakah* that many consider as essential parts of an Islamic taxation scheme.

Kharaj

On *kharaj*, Kahf (1995) is typical:

> It was total agreement, *Ijma*, of the Companions. . . . Almost all the lands of the Middle East and North Africa with the exception of the Arabian Peninsula are of this category. . . . Consequently, there is no reason for not continuing this rental fee in all countries whose lands are *Kheraji* land, whether this land is used for agriculture, industry, or urban services. (p. 121)

Zarqa (1995) likewise gives *kharaj* a prominent place. Shahab (1998) and Israr Ahmad (1998) too are adamant on its sanctity particularly in the context of a heavy-duty agricultural tax. Nevertheless, Ahmad (1998) construes *kharaj* as a tax in which government has a wide discretion especially in changing its rates.

If the argument of the above researchers is followed, land in every Muslim country may fall under one of the three broad categories: *ushri* land, *kharaji* land, and treaty land. The *ushri* land is that on which inhabitants in early Islam paid *zakah* only, *kharaji* land was conquered in war, and the treaty land is that subject to a mutual agreement with inhabitants for protection in return for a specified tribute. On the basis of this categorization, it is said that the governments have no authority to change the terms and conditions of the first and the third category. But on the second category, they are free to charge whatever '*kharaj*' they consider fair. We disagree.

Kharaj, it must be stressed, originated in a totally different socio-economic and political context that needs re-examination. Arabs, then the only torch-bearers of the new faith, had to be kept free from all other occupations and dedicated to communicating Islam as well as defending its geographical frontiers. This is the reason why Umar, against the recommendations of his contemporaries, banned distribution and purchasing of the invaded lands by Arabs and instead, kept the Arabs in cantonments far away from indigenous settlements. Rulers subsequent to Umar could stick neither with his ascetic style of government (resulting in bigger financing needs) nor with his policies on conquered lands. Three phenomena in particular are worthy of note: first, Arabs were allotted lands of the ex-royal family; second, Arabs purchased lands from the indigenous people; and third, indigenous people began to convert to Islam. Since Muslim owners of land insisted on paying *zakah* (religious due meant for redistribution only) instead of *kharaj* (general taxation at a rate higher than *zakah*), over time the treasury began to suffer a considerable loss of revenue (Qureshi, 1978, p. 37). Nevertheless, payment of *zakah* alone made absentee landlord status affordable for Arabs – the very practice discouraged by the earlier land grant policies of Muhammad (pbuh), Abu Bakr and Umar (Hasanuz Zaman, 1991).

Essentially, the problem was that *zakah* on agricultural land was a maximum 10 per cent of produce (that is, *ushr*) while in conquered lands some 30 per cent of produce was paid in lieu of *kharaj* taxes. There was a 20 per cent difference in tax rates between a Muslim owning the conquered land (paying *ushr* only) and an indigenous owning the same land (paying *kharaj*). Umar prohibited Muslims purchasing the conquered lands. Therefore the question of landlordism never arose.

But later Caliphs, especially Umayyads, allowed Muslims to purchase lands in conquered areas. Muslims insisted on paying *ushr* (10 per cent) only instead of *kharaj* paid by indigenous owners. The lesser tax rate meant that Muslim owners would not need to till the lands themselves. They would pay the tillers/serfs their living, pay (lower) taxes to the state, and still be left with surplus. Such surplus, according to some high profile jurists was *haram* and akin to interest. That is why Umar prohibited it. Later as the practice of 'feudalism' became common, posterity found ways to 'legitimize' the practice.

The other side to the coin is that due to large-scale Muslim purchases of lands in conquered areas, state revenues declined. The end result was another *ijtihad* to the effect that *kharaj* was attached not to owners of land but to land itself. Thus, whoever would own such land (outside the Arabian peninsula) paid *kharaj* and not *ushr*. Consequently, the differentiation on tax rates between Muslims and non-Muslims was abolished in lands outside the Arabian peninsula.

The impact of conversions was no different. As long as converts were small in number, the fiscal solution was simple: the fourth Caliph Ali gave to new converts the option to till the land and pay *kharaj* or migrate to cities and qualify for pension like other Muslims (Chaudhry, 1996). However, when more people wished to embrace Islam, the Arabs began to feel threatened on account of the fiscal implications of conversion (Crone, 1996, p. 16). This inspired resentment and dissatisfaction among the indigenous population who could not reduce their share of fiscal burden even through conversion. Thus state revenues began to decline (Hitti, 1970). Under the circumstances, *kharaj* was re-interpreted not as a tax on the landholder but rather on the land itself because it was pledged in favour of the state (Hasanuz Zaman, 1991, pp. 262–6). This meant Arab conquerors had to pay similar taxes (*kharaj*) as the conquered. As Qureshi (1978) notes, in the then prevailing atmosphere, this was a means to assuage the pride of Arabs in that accepting to pay *kharaj* (that is, taxes on fertile lands) was not a symbol of meekness. Crone (1996) describes this development as the turning point in converting Arabian tribesmen to taxpayers and the original owners of lands to Islam.

This account of the evolution of *kharaj* prompts us to advance three separate arguments against its sanctity. First, the Qur'anic verses (59:6–10) from which Umar exercised *ijtihad* on this issue – of banning Arabs from purchasing it – are very general and not specific. From a methodological perspective, we would be inclined to categorize these verses under *shari'ah* evidence that is authentic yet imprecise (that is, speculative in meaning). In reaching this view, we are encouraged from the evidence cited in early books such as Al-Dawudi (1995) that Umar's *ijtihad* on levying *kharaj* instead of distributing the lands to warriors was not accepted by all contemporaries. Second, we contend that when Arabs became numerous and non-Arabs accepted Islam, the original rationale for differentiation between the two was lost. It is on this account that Ashtor (1976) writes:

> Omar . . . did not take into consideration that the non-Arab subjects would progressively become Moslem and . . . consequently . . . claim the same rights as the Arab Moslems . . . which later caused revolts and civil wars, resulting in much bloodshed. But four generations of Arabs enjoyed the privileges which the regime of Omar bestowed upon them. (p. 22)

But perhaps this is not the case. Umar may have overrated the capacity of his successors to remain ascetic, to not indulge in landlordism, and to maintain simplicity, transparency and accountability (thus small government and lower taxes) in line with the call of Islam. That, however, did not eventuate, especially after the Caliphate was turned into a hereditary monarchy. This brings us to the third reason for emancipation from *kharaj*. The nature and composition of wealth that is generated through mixing labour with nature has drastically changed over time – from predominantly primary production to manufacturing, trading and services. Agricultural taxes can no longer serve as the backbone of a modern taxation system. Although broader land taxation schemes have been promoted at various times in developed countries on economic grounds that the return on land is a pure economic rent and hence taxing it has no disincentive effects (see for example Henry George, 1930), such proposals have found application primarily at a local government level excepting Singapore (the city state status of which does offer some lessons for some Muslim states in the Gulf). Finally, the nature of the markets for agricultural commodities has changed substantially. In classical times and also at the advent of the industrial age, the agriculture surplus was used to fund industry and public goods. Nowadays, more often it is the surplus of the industrial sector that keeps farming going in developed countries. Such policies impact on the developing countries through increases in international supply and depressed prices, not leaving a big margin for developing countries to tax agriculture. The agricultural sector globally has become probably the most distorted in terms of the combined effects of protective support, consumption subsidies, artificial exchange regimes, indirect taxes and speculation through the commodity futures exchanges. While this is not to say that agriculture should not be taxed, it has to be done so in light of all of these factors bearing upon its performance.

For these reasons, we consider *kharaj* only a finite part of the classical scheme notwithstanding the fact that there are important equity, economic and operational issues to be learned from the history of its application in Islam. In particular, absentee landlordism is to be discouraged. Should it be already entrenched, as in the case of countries like Pakistan, then there is merit in drawing upon Stern's (1987) prescription, that as far as is practical, re-distributive and corrective taxation ought to be levied on the source of these problems, that is, large landholdings.

Zakah

On *zakah*, the second item on the classical taxation scheme, there is a broad consensus among Muslims that it is, in character, an obligatory charity in return for which no material reward is expected. Therefore, in a broader spiritual context, it cannot be construed as a tax from a giver's perspective for the very act of giving shows the believer's sense of social responsibility, leaving acquired wealth free of disrepute. This interpretation does not preclude comprehending *zakah*, from a political perspective, in terms of a clearly defined redistributive mechanism akin to the welfare apparatus in a modern Western state and fulfilling many secular goals.

It is in this vein that many contemporary Islamic economists have directed most of their effort towards resurrecting *zakah* as an instrument for need fulfilment and poverty alleviation. To give a few examples, Shirazi (1996) undertakes incidence analysis of *zakah* on poverty alleviation in Pakistan and finds a beneficial impact. Kahf (1997) argues that substituting certain broad categories of social expenditure (education, health, water supply, etc.) against *zakah* proceeds is not appropriate owing to benefits going to many well-off people. Certainly, from a public choice perspective, such a step would open the doors for middle and upper class people to transfer *zakah* benefits back to themselves. Instead, broad market-based economic and budgetary reforms over time – for example, elimination of general subsidies – within the ambit of which a more specific targeting of *zakah* proceeds at the poor and needy could occur. Kahf also suggests that by varying cash versus in-kind collections, adjusting the timing of collection, and in using advance collection, *zakah* can be used as a fiscal tool. In general, it is our contention that the use of such methods except in emergency seem likely to introduce uncertainty. In any case, given *zakah* is earmarked for poverty alleviation, and is disbursed within the year in which it is collected, then collection in kind versus cash will have impact only to the extent that the bundle of goods that the *zakah*-eligible intend to purchase with cash is different from that disbursed in kind. Another suggestion that we reject is that of Anwar (1995) who advocates using *zakah* funds for investment in projects aimed at socio-economic development. The success of his method depends on the extent of the 'float' or funds in excess of dire needs. In that case, the excess may better be channelled through micro-credit targeted at the *zakah*-eligible. As Chapra (2000) says:

> To enable *zakat* to play its role meaningfully, a number of scholars have suggested that it should become a permanent income supplement of only those who are not capable of earning enough through their own efforts. For others it should be used only to provide training and 'seed' capital, either as interest-free credit or grants, to enable them to establish microenterprises and, thus, stand on their own feet. (p. 331)

One major issue surrounding *zakah* is its yield. From Table 4.1 (p. 102), it can be inferred that the scope of *zakah* extends to most heads of GDP. In addition, there is a due on wealth. Thus with most income as well as selected categories of wealth constituting the base of *zakah*, a yield of between 5–10 per cent of GDP ought not to be an over-estimate.[4] Actual collections, however, paint a different picture. Zarqa (1995, p. 217) estimates that the yield of *zakah* in Syria in 1971 was 3 per cent of GDP and in Sudan in 1982 was 3.6 per cent of GDP. Based on a study conducted on Pakistan, the low yield can be attributed to three factors. First, there are operational problems, in particular a disinterested machinery of government. Second, there is lack of public confidence in the government's use of such funds for the prescribed purpose (Shirazi, 1996, pp. 37–40). Many Muslims may prefer to deliver *zakah* on their own rather than through the state. Third, there are *ijtihadi* differences on the appropriate base of *zakah*. As the composition of national income has changed over the centuries, new forms of income and wealth have become more important. Although there have been attempts via *ijtihad* (such as by Al-Qardawi, 1983) on bringing these new forms within the ambit of *zakah*, a consensus is still not in sight. Consequently, there is both a narrow base and a broad base (Salama, 1995) and stark differences of opinion exist among different *fiqhi* schools on which is appropriate (Kahf, 1989, 1997; Ghaffari, 1989, pp. 164–5; Iqbal, 2000).

While these problems have potentially rendered *zakah* a minor instrument in a broader scheme of public finance, from an economic perspective too, it can be argued that there is a safe limit on overall taxation as a percentage of GDP beyond which costs of taxation multiply faster than the revenue growth. In most Muslim countries such a limit may be fairly low. As a result, the potential higher yield from introducing or implementing a wider base of *zakah* may come at the cost of revenue from other sources. *Zakah* issues need to be seen within this larger economic framework.

There is also a related question. *Zakah* is a religious obligation and cannot be levied on non-Muslims. The horizontal equivalent for them is *jizya*. But what if non-Muslim citizens of an Islamic state consider it as discriminatory treatment? As one answer, Al-Baladhuri narrates an example from history:

> Jabalah ibn-al-Aiham al-Ghassani was asked by Umar ibn al Khattab to accept Islam or pay poll tax. He declined to change faith and offered to pay *sadaqa*. Umar refused. Jabalah ibn-al-Aiham al-Ghassani left with 30,000 men to the land of Greeks (Asia Minor). Ubadah ibn-as-Samit gently reproved Umar saying, 'If thou hadst accepted *sadaqa* from him and treated him in a friendly way, he would have become Moslem.' (1968, p. 209)

With this example in mind, Al-Qardawi (1983, pp. 134–41) among contemporary jurists has offered the opinion that if non-Muslim citizens of an Islamic country object to *jizya*, there is scope for charging *zakah/sadaqa* from them in its stead, a point on which we would not demur.

To conclude, we believe that in the light of the widely discussed direct Qur'anic position on *zakah*, there could be no doubt on it being an eternal component of a taxation-spending package in a Muslim country. Nevertheless, differences of opinion exist on extending its base. Also, in countries like Pakistan, where institutions are in place for the central collection and disbursement of *zakah*, public confidence in such institutions is low due to a combination of a narrow tax base and inefficient administration of the tax.

Scope for Additional Taxation

A final question on *ijtihad* in taxation relates to scope for taxation in addition to the classical heads. This issue has been discussed thoroughly in literature and the views are well documented. The overwhelming conclusion is that governments can impose taxes in addition to *zakah* subject to good governance, justice and pressing expenditure requirements for need fulfilment and defence. Among the classical scholars there were some who permitted taxes over and above that which is prescribed by *shari'ah* only in a war-like emergency (Islahi, 2005). Even in such circumstances, Iman al-Nawawi (1233–77 CE) demanded that Sultan Zahir Baybars (1260–77 CE) surrender all ornaments owned by his family to the *bayt al-mal* (al-Suyuti, 1968, vol. 2, p. 105). However, those who did not rule out extra taxes for deficiency of resources in normal circumstances included al-Ghazali, Ibn Taymiyyah, al-Qarafi and al-Shatibi (Islahi, 2005). Al-Shatibi (d. 1388

CE), for example, considered that if circumstances of a public interest nature arose and the public treasury lacked funds, then the government was required to take the money of those who were able to pay, in taxation. We would add that the fact that Umar II restored '*kharaj*' on Muslims in fertile lands where, until then, it had only been paid by non-Muslims is sufficient evidence that taxes, if necessary in addition to *zakah*, are legitimate.

Among contemporary scholars, Mawdudi (1994, p. 262) argues that the Qur'anic concept of '*afw*' (2:219), that is, 'economic surplus' can become the *raison d'être* of taxation under ordinary circumstances. Hasanuz Zaman (1993) elaborates, arguing that general taxation in Islam ought to be based on the concepts of *sadaqa* and *infaq* mentioned in the Holy Qur'an that call for unspecified spending on a broad mix of charitable causes in addition to compulsory *zakah*. He contends that while in the life of the Prophet, moral exhortation was sufficient to raise charitable funds for public goods whenever needed, in contemporary Muslim societies, such endeavours ought to be regulated through general taxation. Al-Qardawi (1984) and Kahf (1995) in particular emphasize this point.

In summary, on the balance of available evidence, *kharaj* is not an eternal component of the classical public finance. *Zakah* alone in our view is the divine core of the classical scheme. However, there are operational issues in collecting and managing *zakah*, and there are differences in juristic opinion on extending the *zakah* base to modern forms of income and wealth. Unless such differences are resolved, yield from *zakah* is likely to remain low.

WEST AND ISLAM: A COMPARISON

The theory of taxation has engaged the efforts of some of the great economists of the past (Ricardo, Mill, Marshall, Wicksell, Edgeworth and Pigou) and present (Buchanan, Meade, Samuelson, Stiglitz). Despite this impressive line-up, it is not obvious that they have greatly influenced actual tax policies, as economists, have done with, say, fiscal policy or cost–benefit criteria for public expenditure. This situation owes itself to two factors: the historical context in which economic governance has evolved and the institutional context of such governance.

Consider, first, the historical context. Both Islam at the time of its origin and the West with the decline of the manor system, faced a similar challenge, that of forging disparate communities with divergent beliefs, interests and patterns of internal regulation into larger polities governed in accordance with certain basic principles. These centripetal forces created a continuing pressure for funds, with taxation the principal – indeed the only permanent – means of financing government activities by transferring resources from the private to the public sector. However, war has triggered the greatest demands on the public purse. For example, the widespread introduction of income tax in Germany coincided chronologically with the Franco-Prussian war of 1870–71. That development, in turn, triggered an extensive literature by academic economists evaluating different concepts of income (Wueller, [1938] 1969). Similarly, Peacock and Wiseman (1961) trace how government expenditures (and tax revenues) as a percentage of GDP increased in Britain with the two world wars. However, those authors also note a 'displacement effect' by which government spending (and revenues) did not return to pre-war levels relative to GDP after the wars but were displaced upwards and continued at the higher levels. Taxpayers' disenchantment with high marginal income tax rates in the post-Thatcher era has promised some reversal of this position, but the more visible manifestation has been the substitution of indirect for direct taxation.

Insofar as the institutional context of taxation policies is concerned, these have been shaped in the West by increasingly democratic institutional structures where policy-making is the prerogative of the executive which is drawn from the political party which can command a majority in the legislature. Periodic elections and the electoral cycle means taking account of community attitudes which are in turn influenced by changes in standards of living, and the opinion-forming activities of research bodies, think tanks, academics, key interest groups and business economists. Within this larger institutional context of policy-making, economists have tried to clarify the scientific basis for levying different taxes and for varying rates of taxation according to capacity-to-pay and sacrifice doctrines. The clearest example comes from ET, which has been most influential in directing debates on tax reform in the post-war era. Its requirement of uniformity and comprehensiveness make it more appealing to popular notions of fairness and less amenable to special interest groups. Also, its valuation requirements are modest compared to the OT framework. Among all the three traditions, ET provides the most detailed practical guidance on implementation. Nevertheless, the underlying assumptions about market efficiency remain perhaps naive. Not every move towards comprehensiveness can be justified if markets are perfectly competitive. Further, with competitive markets, any activity with favourable tax treatment will effectively become a loophole and be exploited to the extent that the rate of return on it will be driven down to normal market rates (Hettich and Winer, 1985).

Much the same can be said of ET writers' somewhat restricted view of the government. By treating it as an exogenous institution, they provided little formal basis for analysing how the political system works and its ramifications for tax recommendations. OT goes a step further and abstracts completely from political realities by assuming a social planner who exogenously provides a social welfare function. In contrast to both ET and OT, a model of government behaviour is the *raison d'être* of the FE approach. Yet it falls short of quantifying the extent to which special interest groups could 'hijack' the majority or the rigidity introduced by tax constitutions that may be used to prevent such behaviour (Hettich and Winer, 1999).

One final point concerns an almost exclusive focus in prevailing Western tax theory on comprehensive income or consumption taxes. This comes at the cost of omitting wealth as a potential basis for taxation, despite the fervent advocacy of such policies by social reformers such as R.H. Tawney (1931). Kiesling (1992) elaborates the impact of this omission:

> Ramifications of it appear everywhere. Wealth data are substandard, and empirical work on wealth issues is lacking. Estate and gift taxation issues have been universally ignored by economists. . . . The distinction between reward for contribution and income from inheritances is everywhere ignored, and the same can almost be said for recognition of the difference between income concentration and wealth concentration, despite the fact that the latter is ten times more concentrated than the former. This is the most serious ethical bias that has been generated by the traditional equal-sacrifice approach as it has been applied in this century. Whether it has been by accident or design is for others to judge, but its effects have been substantial. (p. 327)

In contrast, under Islam, for instance, there can be no doubt about the importance of taxing wealth under the compulsory due of *zakah*. A firm basis exists for redistributive policies, and the obligations are clearly specified in the Holy Qur'an. Meeting them is not just a temporal duty. It is a way of purifying wealth. However, in terms of practical application of these principles, hardly any country with a majority Muslim population (outside the oil-rich kingdoms in the Gulf) can boast welfare state apparatus comparable to that of the West.

There is another contrast between Islam and the West. In Islam, good governance is generally regarded as having peaked in classical times and since then declined. The highly command-oriented vision of governance and control that substituted for the classical consultative vision relied heavily on the support of select tribal groups with their ruling familes and could not uniformly apply the same principles of justice to every one maintaining a *status quo*. This state of affairs deeply influenced the debate on taxation among the jurists of Islam, who did not derive their authority from government writ. Quite the contrary, some were coerced to legitimize government action that they otherwise considered not in conformity with *shari'ah*. In the event, the primary concern of the jurists may well have been saving the common people from the excesses of government. Emphasis on the sanctity of the classical scheme in this environment provided a kind of a safe haven denying a free hand to rulers under the more generic rubric of the ability to pay principle (Chapra, 2000).

Contemporary jurists may have another reason to continue supporting the classical scheme. Here, one may inject a public choice perspective on the issue by bringing in Gellner's (1981) insight that jurists in Islam have always drawn their support from urban centres. The classical scheme depended on agricultural surplus and in particular in the context of *zakah*, was not very explicit on many forms of non-rural income and wealth that assumed significance only after urbanization and the growth of professions, manufacturing, services, etc. Any ideas of broadening the tax base on principles of fairness may have struck at the heart of the jurists' own constituency.

Finally, it can be argued that, notwithstanding the preoccupation of many local level jurists with taxation/*zakah* issues of a secondary nature, a very clear top-down perspective on taxation principles was present in the writings of Al-Ghazali, Ibn Taymiyyah, Ibn Hazm and Ibn Khaldun. But, in itself, clarification of principles can hardly lead to an elaborate tax system in practice. For this to happen, the state must take an initiative. And on this account, it can be safely assumed that in most parts of the world, most of the tax systems and structures were handed down from the governing centre to the governed peripheries and these reflected the interests and agenda of political power groups in the centre. In the West, the arrival of more democratic forms of governance saw tax policies opened up for argument, persuasion, and negotiation through a decentralized series of floating alliances. Whether Muslim countries today can adapt such modes of governance while retaining touch with the religious principles of the classical era, is an issue that does pose a challenge.

A CONTEMPORARY SYNTHESIS

Having discussed Islam, its classical taxation scheme, and post-classical *ijtihad* on it, we turn our attention to investigating a contemporary Islamic perspective on taxation. This raises points similar to those discussed in standard taxation theory that we wish to integrate where appropriate with the Islamic theory of justice and the traditional Islamic schema. Below, we undertake an extended analysis of the Islamic position on various issues. The matters addressed are:

1. What principles of fairness in taxation are acceptable in Islam?
2. Which tax bases are admissible in Islam? Can these bases be integrated into some unified models of taxation?
3. How do such alternative models of taxation fare in light of the conventional literature on tax theory and tax reform?

Principles of Fairness in Taxation

In terms of the theory of justice, three key tenets of the Islamic philosophy are: universal brotherhood for believers, equality before law, and the treatment of the wealth and income distribution from a moral perspective in which is embodied a test for mankind's status as the trustee(s) of God on earth. It is these principles that ought to constitute the basis of a contemporary Islamic taxation framework. On this basis, it can be argued that both the benefit and the ability-to-pay principles are admissible in *shari'ah*. The classic support for the benefit principle comes from Abu Yusuf (731–98 CE) (1969):

> If the main canals and watercourses, from the Tigris and Euphrates, need clearing and cleaning the expenses should be borne by the Treasury and by those directly benefiting from such watercourses. However, the expense of cleaning special canals which supply water to individual fields, orchards, vineyards, vegetable or fruit gardens, must be borne by the owners without any subsidy by the Treasury. On the other hand, the expense of the upkeep of the walls on the river banks, to prevent flooding, of the dams and of the water-locks on the Tigris and Euphrates and similar great rivers, must be borne by the Treasury alone, because it is in the public interest that they should be kept in order as any malfunction will cause damage to agriculture and decrease the income from taxation. (p. 106)

At the same time, on the ability-to-pay principle, Abu Yusuf (1969) writes:

> Umar ordered a general survey of all al-Sawad lands because he thought that an exact survey would benefit the taxpayers, and increase the income of the Treasury without charging the taxpayers more than they could bear. Therefore the right to reduce or increase the taxes, subject to the ability of the land and the taxpayers to pay, as exercised by Umar, is a prerogative of the authorities. (p. 104)

From this standpoint, and keeping sight of the goals of *shari'ah*, it can be argued that the Islamic position on this issue strikes a cord of harmony with the standard theory of public expenditure. Modern economics relates the method of financing a good with three characteristics: rivalry, exclusion, and marginal cost of production. Goods that have the properties of rivalry and exclusion are pure private goods and, with a few exceptions, these can be financed best through market pricing. Then there are mixed goods which share the characteristics of both the private and public goods, and the financing of which depends on the cost of technology to ration such goods. Finally, there are pure public goods which are non-rival and non-excludable (for example, defence and street lights). Their financing through market mechanisms poses the problems of accurate preference revelation, freeriding, and proper level of provisioning. For them, taxation becomes unavoidable leaving open the question of the normative principles of fairness in taxation.

Insofar as the financing of need fulfilment is specified and fulfilled in Islam through *zakah*, one major controversy is out of the way. This leaves financing the general budget. While as we saw above, Abu Yusuf admits the ability-to-pay principle, the question is how to interpret and apply it in practice. Here, perhaps the concept of sacrifice in taxation could be of help. A recent parallel in Islamic literature is Mufti Rasheed Ahmad (2000). He argues that all taxes for which the ultimate incidence as a proportion of personal income (and/or wealth) is higher on the poor than on the rich are prohibited in Islam because it leaves the poor poorer and the rich richer against the explicit command of Allah that wealth must not merely circuit among the rich (59:7). There is, of course, no scope for measuring ability in relation to consumption. Also, one may infer that Ahmad's starting point is that all taxes are prohibited if they affect the before-tax distribution (relative positions of taxpayers) adversely against the poor. We saw a Western parallel to this thought in the maximin principle of John Rawls (1971). A contrast can be made with the framework offered by Hasanuz Zaman (1993), which is that anything goes so long as the poor are taken care of. This latter approach is arguably closer to the prevailing practice in many OECD countries. However, given that there is a clear earmarking for redistribution in Islam, we may ask the question: can the progressivity obtained through such earmarking be offset to a degree by somewhat regressive general taxation based on principles of fairness in Islam, the answer must be a categorical 'No'. Reaching the same conclusion, Hasanuz Zaman (1993) recommends a subsidy in addition to *zakah* from the general budget. This brings us to the question: is progressive taxation (for the general budget) admitted in Islam?

Arguably, on this issue one may draw inferences from *zakah* as well as *kharaj*. With a level (*nisab*) below which it does not apply, *zakah* is itself a progressive tax. Another example comes from the classical application of *kharaj* based on the capacity of the land to bear it, and of poll tax that too was progressive. Jurists, however, have sometimes mentioned 50 per cent as the uppermost 'just' limit on produce (income) that can be taken as *kharaj*. Abu Yusuf (1969), for example, recommended a proportionate share of 40 per cent of crops on naturally irrigated lands and 30 per cent on artificially irrigated lands. These rules of thumb for the then prevailing modes of income do not compare too unfavourably with contemporary views and research findings on income tax progression.

This brings us back to the sacrifice principle interpreted in terms of utility and its extension in the form of optimal taxation. Arguably, every normative prescription that comes through this framework can be challenged on the nature of the social welfare function (SWF). Reflecting such difference of opinion, optimal taxation has been used to provide widely divergent recommendations, from lump-sum taxation and extreme progression in income taxes to heavily taxing the bare necessities of life. Nevertheless, useful insights have been obtained on the relation between SWFs – that incorporate certain views on justice – and the resulting progression in the case of income tax. We, therefore, recommend a case-by-case approach drawing on the optimal taxation literature that may be helpful in elucidating the implications of different assumptions about the nature of an Islamic social welfare function.

Our overall conclusion is that both the ability-to-pay as well as the benefit principles of taxation are admitted in Islam. The latter is applicable for all activities organized on a user charges principle. If redistribution is then taken care of by the religious due, *zakah*, we are left with the issue of raising non-earmarked revenue through general taxation. For this purpose, the ability-to-pay principle ought to be applied. However, there is a caveat. Given a cut-off or minimal income or asset limit required to support necessities on which even general taxation should not apply, progression even in general taxation ought to be accepted as a norm in Islam. Also, on a strict interpretation of Islam, there is a prohibition on all taxes the ultimate incidence of which as a proportion of personal income (or wealth) is higher on the poor than on the rich. This condition might be able to be relaxed on a liberal interpretation, if average household income in a country is in excess of adequate needs and if a welfare state is in operation. In that case, the overall incidence of all kinds of general taxes together must not be regressive. We summarize the above views in Table 4.2.

Tax Bases

We are now left with two questions. First, how to measure ability-to-pay for general taxation? In other words, which of the three tax bases – income, wealth, and consumption – is admissible in Islam for general taxation? Second, how can the *zakah* base be extended? Below we examine these

Table 4.2 The nature of public expenditure and the principles of taxation

The nature of public expenditure	The relevant principle of taxation
Public provision of private and quasi public goods	The benefit principle
Redistribution	*Zakah*
Provision of pure public goods (general budget)	The ability-to-pay rule (proportionate or progressive)

questions by presenting three models: the *zakah* model for comprehensive taxation (that is, both for redistributive and general taxation), the *fay* model for general taxation only, and the integrated solution, again for comprehensive taxation. The *zakah* model attempts to answer both questions raised above – about the basis for general taxation and *ijtihad* on *zakah* – in one solution. The *fay* model addresses only the *ijtihad* on general taxation. The pragmatic approach endeavours to rationalize the entire needs for taxation (redistributive as well as general), acknowledging the difficulty in bringing all schools of thought to a unified stand on *ijtihad* on *zakah*.

The *zakah* model

One way to approximate the ability-to-pay is to undertake *qiyas* (analogical reasoning) on the basis of *zakah*. Table 4.1 gave details of the *zakah* scheme. These items are reminiscent of the distinction that economists make between wealth and capital. Wealth is related to consumption while the capital is geared to production, classified in turn into inanimate capital and human capital. Many jurists when conducting *ijtihad* on *zakah* appear to be indirectly following these distinctions. Thus all agree that among wealth meant for consumption, only liquid wealth (cash, bank deposits, pension assets, etc.), ornaments, and precious metals (that is, stores of non-productive wealth) are to attract *zakah*. Owner-occupied housing, clothes, and consumer durables, etc. are to be exempted. Similarly, insofar as human capital is concerned, there ought to be little objection to levying *zakah* on annual income at the 2½ per cent rate (see Al-Qardawi, 1983, pp. 658–60). This leaves inanimate capital meant for trading and production. Here the dilemma is whether to tax the tree or its fruits. On trading capital, a majority of jurists find that *shari'ah* evidence (in particular, *ahadith*) calls for levying *zakah* (at 2.5 per cent) on all goods specified for trade and income ploughed back. On industry, there is a difference of opinion. Nevertheless, Mawdudi (1994, p. 248) calls for a levy on raw materials, manufactured goods, and cash balances exempting permanent machinery and instruments of a factory. Some suggest a levy on net annual income only. From an economic perspective, in either case, there ought to be some parity in the treatment of various kinds of economic activity so as to instil neutrality as a rule of thumb, that is, in an SHS sense rather than on the basis of an OT framework. On this account, it would seem advisable to set rates of taxation such that the charge on net worth bears some relationship to the charge on income. To give an example, a 2.5 per cent levy on capital would roughly equate to a 10 per cent levy on income from it, if the average nominal rate of return on capital in an economy is around 25 per cent per annum. Once such broader relationships are taken into account, one is inclined to consider the differences of jurists on *zakah* as resolvable. It can be argued, for example, that agriculture apart, the overall framework of *zakah* mentioned above appears to be calling broadly for a levy on adjusted net worth and a levy on wages.

The closest in conventional economic literature to the above suggestion is the recent proposal by Shakow and Shuldiner (2000). They argue that a person's ability to pay is a function of both wealth as well as income but the contemporary system of taxation, by placing an emphasis on income alone, leaves non-productive wealth entirely, and low-yielding wealth largely outside the net of taxation. Nor is all income taxed. Much income on capital manages to escape taxation. These omissions undermine ability-to-pay criteria. US data, for example, show that as income increases wealth increases disproportionately. Instead of seeking a more comprehensive definition of income along the lines of Henry Simons' (1938, pp. 49–58) consumption plus the increase in wealth, the alternative suggested by Shakow and Shuldiner is a tax on earned income (wages and salaries, net business and professional income, pension, unemployment compensation, etc.) and a tax on net worth. Working on US data, Shakow and Shuldiner then run simulations on various combinations of flat tax rates on earned income and net worth (including or excluding various items) that would replace the income tax take in the United States for the year 1994 (= $676 billion of which personal income tax collections amounted to $538 bn and corporate tax collections to $138 bn). For the base case scenario, they assume the following:

- Retirement assets worth an estimated $5.1 trillion are excluded;
- Housing equity up to $1 million is exempted;
- Consumer durables too are excluded;
- Generous tax credits are provided: $1500 for each earning family and $400 for each family member including the family head. Obviously, not all are utilized fully;
- 72 per cent of tax proceeds are raised by wage taxes and 28 per cent by net worth taxes.

If, from their list of simulations, we pick a net worth tax rate equal to *zakah* (2.5 per cent), the tax on income comes to between 14 and 15 per cent. Naturally, there is nothing definitive in these numbers but what we wish to underscore is the merit in adopting this proposal both for *ijtihad* on *zakah* as well as on general taxation in Islam.

The reasons for this recommendation are many.

First, the proposal provides a uniform basis for *ijtihad* both on *zakah* as well as on general taxation. Thus there could be a levy on a common net worth base in lieu of *zakah* and a further top-up in lieu of general taxation. Similarly, there could be a levy on earned income in lieu of *zakah* and a top-up on account of general tax. This would save administrative work and a separate machinery and assessment for both taxation heads. Accounting entries would be enough to credit two separate accounts – *zakah* and general tax – with respective fund raisings.

Second, while integration of all taxes at the individual tax unit level shall be considered more in line with the spirit of Islam, the alternative of indirect taxation cannot be ruled out if there is less administrative cost involved in this option. For instance, *zakah* on deposits with banks can be deducted at source and individuals allowed to integrate it in their personal tax return.

Third, the overall structure is flexible in terms of adjustment to local needs. Properly applied, the net worth tax in itself introduces progressivity. On earned income, preferably there could be a flat rate across the board or, depending on economic profile, different rates (2.5 per cent, 5 per cent, 10 per cent and 20 per cent) for different brackets. Also, while rates on net worth tax could be kept constant, items to be included in it may be adjusted from time to time. For instance, given stark disparities in wealth in the developing countries and a tendency by the rich to store wealth in non-productive (for example, real estate) assets, there is a case for extending *zakah* and general taxation to residential housing and real estate investment beyond a certain level (which might bear a relationship to the median level of value of residence in a country if not the lowest level). Support for this proposition comes from *ahadith* that clearly disapprove of luxurious housing.

Fourth, this approach aligns well with the spirit of *zakah* in terms of integrating both the income and wealth bases as indicators of the ability-to-pay principle. As we saw above, even under the SHS concept applied in practice, non-income yielding wealth escapes taxation and in any case, income on capital is treated lightly. This means that in standard tax analysis, wealth as an indication of economic power is by and large exempted from taxation. Given, as Kiesling (1992, p. 309) points out,[5] the distribution of wealth usually is far more skewed than that of income, the wealth base can be expected to be far wider than that of the income base. In the United States, according to Shakow and Shuldiner, total financial assets alone broadly equal the total GDP of that country. Even if motor vehicles and primary residences are excluded and offset to a degree against liabilities, there is additional wealth equal to GDP invested in real estate and business interests. There is no reason to believe that the profile of wealth-holding in some middle-income Muslim countries would be very different apart from perhaps more low-risk assets dominating their financial portfolios. Thus properly accounted, *zakah* assessable wealth could be worth around double the GDP of a country. The likelihood that wealth concentration is more skewed in developing countries compared to the developed, only widens the potential reach of *zakah*, if it is properly understood by Muslim scholars. Conversely, exclusion of such base as an appropriate indicator of ability-to-pay in the standard taxation systems is inherently at odds with the Islamic position on this issue.

Fifth, standard economic theory by and large downplays using the taxation side of the budget for reducing inequality. In contrast, by levying a modest 2.5 per cent per annum charge on wealth, Islam does favour taxation as a means for reducing inequality. To illustrate the potential of this levy, we have prepared Table 4.3. Without *zakah*, if wealth grows at the rate of 4 per cent per annum, then in 30 years it will be 3.24 times its original value. If, however, *zakah* is levied on the capital and profits ploughed back at the rate of return indicated, then it will grow only 1.52 times of its initial value.

Table 4.3 Redistribution of wealth by zakah *(levied at 2.5 per cent on wealth and return on wealth)*

Rates of return (%)	Value of $1 after 30 years (I)	*Zakah* over 30 years (II = I−IV)	*Zakah* (as percentage of income) (III = [II/(I−1)])	Value of $1 post-*zakah* (IV = I−II)	Wealth redistribution ratio (%) II/I
1	1.35	0.72	206.2	0.63	53.2
2	1.81	0.96	118.8	0.85	53.2
3	2.43	1.29	90.5	1.14	53.2
4	3.24	1.73	76.9	1.52	53.2
5	4.32	2.3	69.2	2.02	53.2
7	7.61	4.05	61.3	3.56	53.2
10	17.45	9.29	56.4	8.16	53.2
25	807.79	429.84	53.3	377.95	53.2

Summing up, based on the *zakah* model, it can be argued that a combination of earned income and net worth provide a fair aggregate basis for taxation in Islam. Note, however, that wealth taxes *per se* have fallen from grace in the West and even their mention risks one being bracketed with the Marxist left. While there are many reasons for this unpopularity – (relatively) wider wealth ownership, the rise of the aspirational class, intrusion into the private space, collection costs and entrenched interests – it can be argued that the academic paucity on this matter is also coloured by the traditional emphasis of economic theory on the role of savings in investment and economic growth. The Holy Qur'an, as we saw above, takes a somewhat different stand on this issue. How this view translates into a unique theory of macroeconomic management is the task that we leave for later, once we have explored the Islamic position on budget deficits.

The *fay* model

Fay in the classical scheme, with all the non-earmarked revenues clubbed under it, provides an alternative way of approaching the problem of general taxation when redistributive needs are mostly taken care of by *zakah*. The following points are worthy of note:

- In *fay*, there are multiple bases: first, income (agricultural or other), second, land rent, third, customs duties, fourth, head count (poll tax), and fifth, income from state lands.
- Since the core financing comes from (agricultural) income, tax rates on this item are high (30–50 per cent), even in comparison with contemporary income tax systems.
- There is proportionality or even progression including the poll tax based on means/ability-to-pay.

In view of these features, it might be thought that the *fay* model of general taxation provides the flexibility to use whatever base that is economically feasible to tax. However, there is one caveat. In the classical Caliphate, a portion of funds raised through *fay* was applied towards providing rations to the poor and needy. This was in addition to *zakah* which was entirely dedicated for charity. Recognition of this fact brings us back to the issue of the principles of fairness in taxation acceptable in Islam.

Our starting point is the argument that if *zakah* is in place, and funds are required to meet non-earmarked needs (general taxation), then whatever combination of taxes is employed, their overall incidence must not be regressive. If it is regressive, then *zakah* would need to be topped up with an additional subsidy that, at minimum, offsets the regressive impact of general taxation. In this recommendation, the *fay* model conforms

Table 4.4 Types of broad-based taxes

Base	Personal form	Indirect form
Wealth	Annual net-worth tax	Property tax Land rent Interest tax Capital gains tax Death and gift taxes Corporate annual wealth tax
Income	Personal income tax	Employer's payroll tax Corporate income tax Interest tax Tithes (on agricultural produce)
Consumption	Expenditure tax (Kaldor model)	General sales taxes (single or multi-rate including wholesale tax (WST), retail sales tax (RST), and value added tax (VAT) Customs duties

Source: Modified from Kahn (1973, p. 134)

broadly with Hasanuz Zaman (1993). Nevertheless, there is a merit in expanding this analysis and explicitly evaluating some forms of taxation that can be levied under it. Consider, for example, Table 4.4 which depicts multiple ways in which each of the three bases – wealth, income, and consumption – can be taxed.

If each tax is evaluated independently, then some forms like indirect consumption taxes do not match well with the Islamic philosophy on three accounts. First, since the incidence may be regressive, they contradict the rule on incidence with which we started. According to Keisling (1992, p. 232), the empirical evidence on incidence tends to confirm the conventional wisdom that sales and excise taxes are regressive. Kazmi (2001) explains the following with reference to Pakistan:

> The predominant share of taxes in Pakistan is that of indirect taxes. Even within the direct taxes, nearly 70 per cent taxes are of withholding nature, which are indirect in their effect. This feature of . . . taxation along with imposition of GST at a larger scale could be considered as the main factors for growing level of poverty in Pakistan. (p. 16)

Second, from the perspective of a giver, there is seemingly an element of *iztirar* as well as *gharar* in indirect taxation. The uncertainty (*gharar*) results because the final (or economic incidence) may be very different from the initial (or legal) incidence.[6] And, if incidence is ambiguous, to what (tax burden to impose on different individuals) are the elected representatives agreeing?[7] There is thus a double governance problem because monies that one is not certain about are being taken without proper consent. Third, some studies (for example, Moore, 2007) find a degree of relationship between bad governance and the overall level of indirect taxes. By contrast, direct taxes are said to raise people's awareness about their right to hold government accountable for the finances that it raises and for what it provides in return to the society. This can only happen when governments and people trust each other and there is transparency in the public finances.

Some may counter, however, that customs duties are indirect and yet are admissable in Islam. Also, dues on agricultural produce and land rent are in fact, *ad rem* in nature. The answer to this objection is that customs duties were levied in reciprocity and formed a minor element in the overall schema. As regards the tax rates on land and agriculture, these were varied in accordance with the crop, method of irrigation, and yield which, although not akin to accommodating 'personal features' in direct taxation, nevertheless were an attempt to bring the overall income estimates closer to allowances for individual circumstances. In addition, books of *fiqh* document that some exemptions were allowed. A parallel in contemporary indirect consumption taxes would be an exemption of necessities and higher tax rates on luxuries.

So far we have discussed the pros and cons of indirect taxes from an Islamic perspective. It must also be admitted that such taxes are sometimes economically more feasible to collect and less easy to avoid. For instance, the experience of many OECD countries shows that when direct (visible) taxes increase beyond a certain level, a sort of citizens' revolt begins to take shape (see next chapter). A switch to indirect forms of consumption taxes as an alternative has been justified subject to five provisos. First, the welfare state is in place. Second, in general, incomes are in excess of subsistence level. Third, consumption taxes constitute a relatively small proportion of the overall tax mix. Fourth, the single largest contributor to overall taxation remains direct progressive tax on incomes. Fifth, the overall tax incidence is close to being proportionate to incomes. In the case of developing countries, one must ask how many of these conditions could possibly apply when regressive taxes are levied. Not surprisingly, the threshold for 'revolt' is much lower in these countries given low per capita income, simmering class-based tensions over stark disparities in wealth that is not necessarily acquired through legitimate means, and a lack of trust in government machinery. Moreover, the potential for economic activities and income to migrate to untaxed sources in the underground economy is high. Nevertheless, indirect taxes ought not to be levied in lieu of better governance and general tax reforms.

We would now like to comment in passing on inheritance taxes. In the West, these taxes are meant to fill a gap in the application of SHS income or increase its fairness in the wake of low taxation of capital income. There is some degree of academic support for such taxes on the basis of an 'equal start' argument. However, actual experience suggests that, given their 'one-off' nature (providing ample time for estate planning), they hardly reach their intended target. The Islamic stand on inheritance would indicate that inheritance taxes as such are unnecessary. The Holy Qur'an (4:11–13) and *sunnah* do not leave the division of inheritance entirely to the discretion of the deceased but rather specify it. These rules proved effective (perhaps too much so) in diluting the concentration of wealth in the Middle Ages, and there is no reason why they should not have much the same effect now. The case for taxing inheritance therefore is weak both operationally as well as from an Islamic perspective. An additional consideration is that *zakah*, if applied effectively, does the same job as inheritance taxes, albeit on a continuous basis.

To summarize then, the *fay* model would admit all kinds of economically feasible taxes for general budget provided good governance, no regression, or at minimum, regression offset by a subsidy from the general budget.

The integrated model

The two models above assume the redistributive scheme in the form of *zakah* is in place. However, as mentioned, due to operational problems and lack of consensus on extending *zakah* to new forms of wealth, redistributive dues collected in the name of *zakah* are dwindling. Collection on religious grounds may also be amenable to legal challenge, as happened in Pakistan. The pluralistic nature of Islamic *ijtihad* and differences of opinion on this matter make us sceptical that there is an easy solution. In any case, from an economic perspective, there is a limit on the size of the total tax take in terms of growth costs to the economy, with the corollary that a separate *zakah* charge has to come from within that limit. It is in this vein that we suggest a different route, that of dispensing with a separate assessment for *zakah* and integrating it with general taxation.

If we keep those activities amenable to benefit charges apart, the entire tax system can be organized on the principle of ability-to-pay accepting the tax bases mentioned in the *zakah* model or in the *fay* model, with a preference for the former. Note that if the *zakah* model is followed, a progressive tax structure will result automatically even if the rates levied are flat (owing to net worth tax). If, however, the *fay* model is followed, it requires the minimum condition of overall non-regression. The suggestion is that for the directly assessed part of the tax on a taxing unit, the taxpayer be allowed to tender (self-assessed) *zakah* (in lieu of the tax liability) to the government. All monies tendered in the name of *zakah* would be credited to a separate account. In case the amounts fall short of a previously stated portion of budgetary allocation for redistribution (say 5–10 per cent of GDP or 10–20 per cent of total tax take given a tax structure that is not regressive), then funds could be transferred from the general budget to *zakah* budget. If they exceed such targets then funds are transferred from the *zakah* budget to the general budget and the government is allowed to benefit from the *ijtihad* (see Hamidullah, 1988) to apply these excess proceeds toward national debt repayments, defence expenditure, and public servant salaries.

Among the beneficial impacts that can be visualized from such an arrangement are the following:

- Complete horizontal equity across all citizens is obtained along one dimension, that is, ability-to-pay interpreted in terms of proportionality (that is, an overall non-regression in taxation) in relation to means (interpreted most likely in terms of income).[8]
- While tax assessment (in accordance with whatever definition of 'means') remains the government responsibility, *zakah* assessment as well as payment becomes a matter of individual conscience. Each can contribute according to his *fiqh*.
- If one considers government worthy of trust, *zakah* could be tendered to government against part of the tax liability which as we suggested above is then credited by the government into a separate *zakah* account. If monies in the *zakah* account exceed a pre-stated limit, the government is authorized to transfer the excess for application to general budget. Note again that insofar as the taxpayer is concerned, the tax liability is fixed according to the tax code. If it is wished to offset part of this liability through paying *zakah* to government, this can be done so relieving the taxpayer from both responsibilities.
- Administrative simplicity can be achieved by abolishing multiple collection procedures, accounts and staff.
- Redistributive dues are earmarked in the budget and subject to accountability at the highest level. They are kept separate and applied only on specified heads.

In principle, the above scheme can be implemented by a simple modification in tax return forms and change in accounting procedures in the tax office.

Tax Reform and the Proposed Models of Taxation

The literature on tax reform lays an emphasis on understanding the motives and philosophy behind alternative proposals for improving tax systems. Cullis and Jones (1992), for example, identify the following three dimensions:

- First, tax reform could be informed by research lying above sectional interests and based implicitly on social optimality. Such studies present the pros and cons of a proposal from the viewpoint of all affected individuals. An example comes from the analysis of an annual wealth tax in Sandford *et al.* (1975).
- Second, there are proposals based on political philosophy, that is, promoting a particular viewpoint on social organization. An example is the different agenda emanating from the conservative wing, moderates and radicals advocating different tax changes so that women are respectively not discouraged from home care to preserve the traditional family, or are made indifferent between home and market production, or are encouraged to work in the market.
- Third, some proposals are avowedly rent-seeking, advancing the preservation or promotion of rents, that is, negative social value (such as barriers to free trade, industrial subsidies, and quotas, etc.).

This framework, along with the standard theories of taxation, enables us to shed some light on the three models of taxation (*zakah*, *fay* and the integrated approach) sketched out above.

From the beginning we made it clear that our analysis aims at elucidating an Islamic perspective on the issues chosen for study. This objective would seem to bring this whole effort within the second of the categories in the previous paragraph. Note, however, that Islam claims that its tenets are general and have a direct link with human welfare. It is in this vein that we consider again the pros and cons of the Islamic tax proposals outlined above. Notably, absent from our discussion is the question of tax incentives or disincentives for women working in the market. This is because Islam at its inception gave women the right to work, have private property, and be known with their own family names. The implication is that the choice between family responsibilities and work depends on the unique conditions of each family unit and ought to be left to them to resolve rather than being encouraged or discouraged through the tax system. Nevertheless, it has to be said that these choices invariably fall upon women, not men, and that other social policies (for example, about childcare facilities) do not encourage female participation in the workforce, which remains low in comparison with the West.

We now move to an evaluation of the *zakah* model which is a tax on earned income and a tax on net worth. In the standard analysis, the impact of an annual net worth tax (ANWT) on work effort depends on why one works. If it is for consumption, then compared to an equi-yield tax on income, an ANWT is less likely to discourage people from working longer hours or applying for more productive and highly-paid jobs because the tax base is not related to their present effort (that is, their current income). However, if the objective is saving, the incentive effect is theoretically indeterminate and empirically far from settled owing to income and substitution effects having opposite effects on behaviour (Sandford, 1971, pp. 179–81). Contrast this with James and Nobe's (1983, p. 238) argument that to the extent that a net worth tax replaces or substitutes for personal income tax, it may actually encourage savings given the latter incurs 'double taxation of savings' (with both the initial income available for saving and the income on the savings itself being taxed). Insofar as the effect of ANWT on investment is concerned, it depends on the tax base. If it is relatively comprehensive then a taxpayer must pay a fixed proportion of his wealth irrespective of how he or she chooses to invest the wealth. This means that although there may be a wealth effect, there will be no substitution effect. Consequently, there will be no distortion in investment decisions. If, however, the base is less than comprehensive, investment in untaxed assets (for example owner-occupied housing, consumer durables, pension rights, insurance policies, foreign bank accounts, financial assets in a bearer form and works of art, etc.) may be encouraged (Smith, 1993). Note that on this account, ANWT performs much like an income tax which faces similar problems. The other side of the argument is that, properly designed, a wealth tax may actually reinforce the profit motive by encouraging owners to transfer wealth from nil or low-yielding assets (money balances, jewellery, business inventories, uncultivated and undeveloped land) to high-earning assets. In this sense, an ANWT may promote a more efficient utilization of capital resources. All in all, from an incentive perspective (but ignoring collection costs), a wealth tax as a substitute for replacing or lowering personal income tax is considered as having lower disincentive effects (Sandford, 1971; James and Nobes, 1983; Cullis and Jones, 1992, p. 343; Smith, 1993).

Table 4.5 summarizes the achievement of different goals – efficiency, horizontal equity, redistribution and administrative control – through a wealth tax. From an efficiency perspective, the tax threshold should be low and rate structure proportionate or mildly progressive, since high progressive rates may deter savings and investments. If the goal is horizontal

Table 4.5 Objectives and structure of a wealth tax

Objectives	Appropriate threshold	Appropriate rates	Ceiling	Additive or substitutive
Efficiency	Low	Low: proportional or mildly progressive	None or 'notional'	Substitutive
Horizontal equity	Low	Low: proportional or mildly progressive	None or 'notional'	Substitutive
Reduction in inequality				
• Limited (relative)	Could be high	Mildly progressive	High	Substitutive
• Radical (absolute)	Could be high	Progressive	None or 'restricted'	Additive
Control	Low	Immaterial	Immaterial	Immaterial

Source: Sandford et al. (1975), Cullis and Jones (1992, p. 343)

equity, again a low proportional charge on wealth is proposed to supplement income tax. Note that to achieve horizontal equity, a wealth tax has advantages over an income tax. This is because the wealth base recognizes assets with low or no money income, and captures those for which the capital base is high but recorded income is low. This feature also makes a wealth tax potentially suitable for a reduction in inequality through progressive rates since the tax could come either from income generated from wealth (relative reduction in inequality) or in extreme cases by liquidating assets (absolute reduction). Finally, if the objective is to use a wealth tax as administrative control, that is, to cross-check data and reduce evasion, progression is not needed and a low charge on wealth could suffice.

In the case of the *zakah* model, the base rate, 2.5 per cent, is certainly not high and therefore matches well with efficiency, horizontal equity, and administrative control objectives. The problem is that it may be seen as diluting wealth over time. It is in this respect that, from a public choice perspective, we anticipate most resistance against the *zakah* model of taxation. Burgess and Stern (1993), for example, remind us that in developing countries, political power and wealth are closely allied and well-concentrated. Attempts to shift the burden of taxation in accordance with equity norms – for example, introduction of land taxes, wealth and property taxes, and progressive income taxes – are severely hampered. Even partial tax reforms are also fiercely contested since those who have spent considerable resources in devising means to evade taxes have a vested interest in opposing measures to close the loopholes. Of course, problems posed by tax shelters are by no means confined to developing countries.

Nevertheless, once the *zakah* base is agreed, this model may be the least vulnerable politically of the three given a potentially flat rate beyond a cut-off limit and clear earmarking for redistribution. Also, if the rich actually pay taxes from their own pocket, they can be expected to constrain irresponsible government fiscal behaviour. The comparison here is with the *fay* model and the integrated solution. The major problem with these models is meeting the condition that the tax burden ought not be regressive. As Rosen (1995, p. 425) observes, measurements of tax burden and tax incidence depend on a large number of assumptions about estimates of elasticity. This provides potential for manoeuvring so that an overall regressive profile of taxes may remain entrenched, yet 'authenticated' as non-regressive. For these reasons, if we were to rank these proposals, we would prefer the *zakah* model over the others because it offers inherent progressivity in a relatively transparent way.

Note that so far our emphasis has been on the broad configuration of a tax system acceptable in Islam. Once we come to sorting out the details, then the ET tradition in conventional taxation has a lot to offer. In particular, one can benefit from its discussion on the level of exemption in relation to need and the number of dependants, treatment of direct expenses, treatment of all kinds of income (personal, corporate, etc.) uniformly or otherwise, admitting fringe benefits and imputed rent, and handling inflation, etc.

CONCLUSIONS

The expanding Islamic state in the classical era had to face many challenges, including taxation and public spending, and it was able to meet them by actualizing the eternal principles of the Holy Qur'an and *sunnah* through institutional means suited to the age. Whether Muslim countries today can recapture this adaptability in terms of the public finances, while retaining touch with the religious principles of the classical era, poses a challenge both for governance as well as for those interested in the betterment of these countries. The preceding analysis has highlighted many issues of direct relevance to evolving a contemporary synthesis of revelation and rationality. In particular, three models of taxation have been advanced that could be considered acceptable in Islam. Ideally, *zakah* should be understood as a broad earned-income-cum-net-worth tax. It could provide the Islamic core of the redistributive portion of the taxation system. A top-up tax on the same base could then fulfil the needs for general taxation. The two taxes collected through the same administrative machinery could save operational costs. Second, there is an alternative possibility of retaining *zakah* on the above base as the redistributive core and organizing general taxation on lines of the *fay* model. This scheme admits all direct and indirect tax bases for general taxation only on the conditions of good governance and the rule that the aggregate incidence of taxes levied for general budget ought not be regressive. If it is regressive, then at minimum, subsidies should offset this effect. Finally, we presented a third model, the integrated solution. This envisages raising the aggregate financing requirements for the general budget as well as for redistribution through whatever tax base is deemed economically feasible. It then allows individuals or households an option to tender *zakah* in lieu of their direct tax assessment. The assessment of *zakah* itself is left to individual conscience. Transfers between *zakah* and general taxation in accordance with a pre-specified rule ensure sufficient allocation of funds for redistribution so that (a) the overall regressive effect of taxes is offset, and (b) by post cash transfers or subsidies, sufficient progression is achieved to alleviate poverty. An important corollary of the above discussion has been that *zakah* is a much misunderstood part of the classical Islamic model of public finance. Comprehended as a due on net worth (excluding housing and consumer durables) and earned income, it offers great potential to mobilize resources for poverty alleviation.

NOTES

1. A clarification is in order here. For Hugo Grotius and Pufendorf, the state was the result of a social contract derived from the moral precept of natural law. Hobbes abandoned natural law and based his contract instead on observations of human nature. Locke attempted to steer between the natural law expression of an Aristotelian conception of the social nature of humankind and the increasingly popular individualistic conception of human beings devised by Hobbes (Musgrave, 1959, p. 63).
2. The argument is elucidated by Lewis and Mizen (2000) as follows:

    Taxpayers might be required to go to the tax office, turn out their pockets, and have their money balances counted. With a tax rate of 50 per cent, the tax collector would confiscate half of the money holdings. This payment would provide the government with the money needed to undertake spending. If the reduction in spending by those taxed is matched by increased spending by the government, zero inflation could be the result.

    An alternative is for the government to undertake the same expenditure and pay for it by printing money. Suppose that the money supply is increased by 50 per cent, producing an increase in prices of 50 per cent. Real money balances are unchanged, but in the meantime the government has acquired command over real resources. It gains real resources when the public hands over goods and services (for example, the provision of teaching services) in exchange for the pieces of paper issued by the government. In this case, the real resources gained are

$$50\% \text{ (that is, } M = P) \times \text{real money balances (that is, } M/P),$$

which is exactly the same as the *explicit* tax on money balances, when the revenue (like any form of taxation) equalled

$$\text{tax rate (that is, } 50\%) \times \text{tax base that is, (that is, } M/P),$$

Accordingly, inflation is regarded as simply another form of taxation, in effect an *implicit* tax on real balances, providing the revenue for government expenditure. (p. 177)

3. Zarqa (1995, p. 203) provides a broad definition of *ghanima* as 'the wealth acquired from the enemy by force during *jihad*'. Hasanuz Zaman (1991) examines the principles and practice regarding war booty in the classical period and compares them to the previous divine religions and the then prevailing Arab custom.
4. This estimate should be valid even after deducting the share in GDP of those not eligible to pay *zakah* since in most economies, the lowest decile contributes less than 3 per cent to national income.
5. For instance, the 1983 estimates for the USA indicate that while the top 5 per cent earned some 15.9 per cent of total income, the top 0.5 per cent held some 23.2 per cent of total wealth and 22 per cent of financial wealth.
6. See next chapter for details. The economic incidence is difficult to measure accurately.
7. Buchanan and Flowers (1980, p. 322) illustrate the other side of the coin with special reference to the corporation income tax. They argue that it is precisely because of the uncertainty concerning its real incidence and economic effects that the tax is convenient for politicians to impose on the general public.
8. Nevertheless, as we saw above in the *zakah* model, Islam calls for something more than this, that is, measuring means in relation to wealth also.

5. Problems of implementing taxation in Islamic countries

INTRODUCTION

So far we have examined the normative principles of governance in Islam and the implications of them for tax bases and rate structures. Now we consider the practical problems of implementing broad-based taxation in Muslim countries. Arguably, this topic cannot be studied in isolation from the socio-political history and milieu of Islamic lands since the patterns of behaviour observed today have deep roots. It is in this spirit that we begin by providing an overview of the fiscal theory and practice in classical Islam. This is followed by an assessment of the growth of government and the structure of taxation in contemporary Muslim societies. Having thus broadly analysed the socio-political and economic backdrop to the fiscal affairs in these nations, we then turn to the difficulties in implementing broad-based taxation schemes such as those developed in the previous chapter. Finally, some recommendations for reform are given.

FISCAL AFFAIRS IN THE CLASSICAL CALIPHATE

Public finance has historically been one of the pioneering independent subject areas (apart from the traditional disciplines built around the Holy Qur'an and *hadith*) that attracted the attention of Muslim scholars. This interest grew out of the unprecedented expansion of the Islamic state in its first century and the need to standardize and harmonize varying taxation arrangements and land policies in these territories. Among the most elaborate titles translated into English are Abu Yusuf's (731–98 CE) (1969) *Kitab al-Kharaj* and Al-Dawudi's (d.1012 CE) (1995) *Kitab al-Amwal*. Among other noteworthy contributions are those of Islahi (1988, 2005) which include a condensation of Ibn Taymiyyah's (1263–1328 CE) views on public finance and Ibn Taymiyyah's work ([1976] 1982) which expands upon public duties in Islam, in particular, regulation of individual and business conduct in market transactions through the institution of *hisba* (essentially an ombudsman's institution). Apart from these titles, there are scores of classical works on exegesis, jurisprudence, ethics, history, sociology, and state-craft that devote a chapter or two to the area of public finance. In this category, Ibn Khaldun (1332–1406 CE) (1967) stands out.[1] Among the more recent investigations, Hasanuz Zaman (1991) provides a record of the fiscal norms as well as practices in the classical period and their relationship with the broader moral foundations of the Islamic economic system. Other noteworthy titles on the classical scheme include Osman (1976), Qureshi (1978), Al-Sayed (1982), Ghaffari (1989) and Ra'ana (1991).

The picture of the classical times depicted in the above studies is that the revenue receipts were disbursed to the needy forthwith[2] under Prophet Muhammad (pbuh) and Abu Bakr, the first Caliph. However, the second Caliph, Umar, organized such disbursements on more professional lines. In the wake of manifold increases in public receipts, he reluctantly agreed to follow the Byzantine precedent of setting up a central treasury (*bayt al-mal*). The Arabic word *bayt al-mal* literally means 'the house of (public) property', that is, the premises where property is stored. However, as Levy ([1957] 1979) explains:

> the term had no reference to any particular building or locality, but was applied to that part of the Caliph's activities concerned with such wealth, either in specie or in kind, as belonged to the community of Islam as a whole and which passed through the hands of the *'amils*, the agents or tax-gatherers of the community. (p. 308)

The *bayt al-mal* financed government activities, disbursed stipends and pensions to the needy and the military personnel in accordance with a register, and performed some of the tasks undertaken by a modern central bank. Borrowing and lending without interest was permissible. However, the oversight of financial intermediation[3] and the issuance of currency lay beyond its jurisdiction. Also, the *bayt al-mal* did not engage in deficit finance (Ghaffari, 1989, pp. 46–7; Ra'ana, 1991, pp. 104–06; Hasanuz Zaman, 1991).

Muslim historians insist that public funds were handled with great rectitude and care in the classical period. This stance, they argue, was consistent with Islamic teachings on taking positions of authority as trust and maintaining small government. Consider, for example, the following traditions:

> Allah's Apostle said, 'everyone of you is a guardian and is responsible for his charge; the ruler is a guardian and is responsible for his subjects; the man is a guardian in his family and responsible for his charges; a woman is a guardian of her husband's house and children and is responsible for them. (Sahih Bukhari (Hadith, 3.733 and 3.592))

> The Prophet mentioned that everyone who had betrayed a trust would have a banner on the Day of Resurrection to the extent of his betrayal in the world, and that no betrayal was greater than that of the ruler of the common people, whose banner would be fixed onto his posterior. (Tirmidhi (Hadith, 5145))
>
> Ali bin Abi Talib said, I heard Allah's Messenger (pbuh) saying, 'Nothing out of public property is lawful for the Caliph except two bowls. In one bowl he and his family will eat and the other one he will place before the people (that is, his guests). (Musnad Ahmad b. Hanbal (Khan, n.d., p. 177)).

Assimilation of such teachings reinforced a kind of disposition in the early Caliphs whereby they looked down upon the pomp and show associated with the worldly empires. Ibn Khaldun ([1332–1406 CE] 1967, pp. 222–3) notes that even the act of delivering the sermon at Friday prayers from a pulpit (by the Governor of Egypt) was questioned because it entailed pride. Such interpretations are supported by H.G. Wells' (1961) account of the second Caliph, Umar, travelling from Madinah to Jerusalem:

> He came the six-hundred-mile journey with only one attendant; he was mounted on a camel, and a bag of barley, another of dates, a water-skin, and a wooden platter were his provision for the journey. He was met outside the city by his chief captains, robed splendidly in silks and with richly caparisoned horses. At this amazing sight the old man was overcome with rage. He slipped down from his saddle, scrabbled up dirt and stones with his hands, and pelted these fine gentlemen. . . . He would not let these popinjays escort him. He went on with his attendant, and the smart Emirs rode afar off – well out of range of his stones. (pp. 612–13)

Wells also cites a letter that Umar wrote to his governor at Kufa:

> 'They tell me,' he wrote, 'you would imitate the palace of Chosroes, and that you would even use the gates that once were his. Will you also have guards and porters at those gates, as Chosroes had? Will you keep the faithful afar off and deny audience to the poor? Would you depart from the custom of our Prophet, and be as magnificent as those Persian emperors, and descend to hell even as they have done?' (p. 613)

Naturally, such ethical standards would place only a modest taxation demand on citizens. A keen sense of justice ensured that such demands were not exceeded by any other means such as gifts and presents to public officials. Appreciating such conduct, as Al-Baladhuri (d. 892 CE) (1968, pp. 210–11) notes, 'in the fight between Heraclius and Muslims at Yarmuk, Christians and Jews of Hims sided with Muslims saying, "We like your rule and justice far better than the state of oppression and tyranny in which we were."'

Again, some Western historians appear to confirm the above records. Ashtor (1976, p. 10), for example, suggests that 'in Egypt and in Syria

. . . the inhabitants . . . did not regard the Arab invaders as enemies, but welcomed them as liberators, or at least remained neutral.' Esposito (1995) elaborates this position further:

> For many non-Muslim populations in Byzantine and Persian territories already subjugated to foreign rulers, Islamic rule meant an exchange of rulers, the new ones often more flexible and tolerant, rather than a loss of independence. Many of these populations now enjoyed greater local autonomy and often paid lower taxes. The Arab lands lost by Byzantium exchanged Graeco-Roman rule for new Arab masters, fellow Semites with whom the populace had closer linguistic and cultural affinities. Religiously Islam proved a more tolerant religion, providing greater religious freedom for Jews and indigenous Christians. (p. 39)

In the light of the above evidence, as well as that presented elsewhere in this book, it can safely be assumed that during the classical Caliphate, rulers considered public property as trust, made minimal demands on treasury on personal account, and spent tax collections on public goods. The classical Islamic state envisaged its role as to implement law and protect the weak rather than wilfully fund and support through public monies a class of lavish government officials, businessmen and merchants. Anyone eager for a better lifestyle was welcome to try his luck in the private sector based on his own efforts rather than under the auspices of the state. Matters were usually decided through mutual consultation (*shura*) following the Holy Qur'an (3:159; 42:38), and citizens could approach public officials freely and question their decisions. The welfare budget (*zakah*) was clearly earmarked and there was a top up from the general budget too.[4] This moral stance, however, began to lose its lustre over time. Mu'awiya (661–680 CE), for example, is considered the last Caliph and the first monarch of the Islamic polity. During his period, the Caliphate assumed an imperial character and drifted into a hereditary monarchy. Two examples would suffice:

> Kingly prerogatives were . . . gradually introduced. Besides the earlier two prerogatives, namely, *khatam* (seal) and *khutbah* (Friday speech), four more were introduced by Mu'awiyah: the *sarir* (throne), the right of the caliph to sit at a higher place (*maqsura*), the right to have an enclosure in the mosque for his exclusive use, and finally, *sikkah* (currency) the right to have his name carved on the country's coins. Arabic was made the court language and the earlier simplicity gradually gave away to luxury and splendor. The only reason advanced for the transformation of a republican or democratic form of government into a hereditary or dynastic monarchy was to avoid communal disintegration through perpetual civil strife. (p. 44)

> . . . Jurists like Shah Wali Ullah regard his method of selection as an appointment through usurpation (*istila*) because according to him, it was obtained through coercion. (Iqbal, 1986, p. 43)

'Mu'awiya asked Ibn Umar as to the constructions he had put up. Ibn Umar observed, "If this is from God's wealth (public treasury) then you have committed a breach of trust; but if it is from your own wealth, you are a spendthrift"' (Hasanuz Zaman, 1991, p. 111).

In comparison to the display of royal authority to which the Persians and the Syrians were traditionally accustomed, it might be thought that Mu'awiya's was a small step. Yet, it was the beginning of a trend that was in conflict with the very spirit of Islam. That is why the then Muslim historians were quick to record and condemn it. The two dynasties that followed Mu'awiya (see Box 2.1) were Umayyads (680–750 CE) and the Abbasids (750–1258 CE). During these dynasties, Islam remained the legitimizing force as well as standard of morality. Nevertheless, an important change had taken place. In the words of Lindholm (1996):

> Although he did claim legitimacy as a member of Muhammad's family, Muawiya's dynasty, the Umayyad, was the first Muslim government to be validated not primarily because of its moral right, but because it commanded the most powerful army.
>
> His advent in 661 inaugurated a secular kingdom that has served the pious ever since as a negative counter to the sanctified rule of his predecessors.
>
> For the pious, under the Umayyad dynasty Mecca gave way to Damascus; faith was displaced by pragmatism and power-seeking; and tribalism and factionalism returned on a vast scale – the period of the charismatic community was over.
>
> The Umayyad dynasty provided the type case for secular rulership to be found from this moment on in Islamic society, wherein authorities rule purely because they have managed to take the throne, without any sacred sanction whatsoever. (p. 87)

Consequently, the ideals set by the early Caliphate were compromised and by a wider margin as we move further in time. Evidence gathered by Hasanuz Zaman (1991, pp. 111–15), for example, suggests the emergence of acquisitiveness among government officials of the Umayyad rule. This development came at the cost of blurring the distinction between the public and the private purse of the rulers, although there are instances to suggest that such violation of the rules of justice was kept within certain limits. Nevertheless, it did not go unnoticed. According to Crone (1996), vociferous protests were made alleging that Umayyads had made God's servants slaves, God's property (public treasury) something to be taken by turns among the rich, and God's religion a cause of corruption. Consider also Ashtor (1976):

> Although the impact of Mohammed's preaching was tremendous and Islam had become a very important factor in the social and political life of a great part of the world, the worldliness of the upper strata of the Muslim society was a phenomenon characteristic of the new caliphal empire. (p. 26)

As the dynasty ended, the ruler conceded:

> We committed injustice to our subjects and they became disappointed with our justice. They wished to get rid of us. Our tax-payers were overburdened so they deserted us, destroyed our estates and emptied our treasuries. (Hasanuz Zaman, 1991, p. 115)

The early Abbasids made attempts to restore justice but further down the line, royal authority became synonymous with luxury (Ibn Khaldun, [1332–1406 CE] 1967, p. 165). Indeed, it became necessary to abolish even the state pensions (Qureshi, 1978, p. 38). By the tenth century CE, the empire had plunged into chaos from a political standpoint. The result was a Caliphate in name, ruled actually by different dynasties across different parts of the empire.

Contenders for power in Islamic lands in the tenth century were the Buyids and their Daylamite allies who conquered the Abbasid empire, centred in Baghdad and ruling most of Persia and the central Middle East, the Qarmati of the Arabian peninsula, and the Fatimads, who eventually were to rule Egypt. In the eleventh century, the Seljuks (Sunni Muslim Ghazz nomads) marched on Baghdad unopposed to take over from the enfeebled Shi'ite Buyids and founded what has been described as 'the greatest empire in Islamadom until the rise of the Ottomans. . . . The Seljuks were the first Muslim dynasty to foreswear completely any pretence of a spiritual sanction for their rule . . . they frankly declared themselves Sultans' (Lindholm, 1996, p. 110). Of the Seljuk (Saljuk, Seljuq) dynasty, Lambton (1968) wrote:

> All the Sultan expected of his subjects was that they should pay their taxes and pray for his welfare, while they expected from him security and justice. The state did not demand, or receive, the loyalty of the common man. Loyalty, so far as it transcended the bounds of the tribe, guild, quarter, or city, was accorded not to the state but to Islam.

Renowned Muslim scholars – Ibn al-Qayyim (1292–1350 CE), Ibn Taymiyyah (1263–1328 CE) (Islahi, 1988) and Ibn Khaldun (1332–1406 CE) (1967) among them – warned rulers about the consequences of excessive taxation and spending for economic activity. Ibn al-Qayyim (Al-Qardawi, 2003, Ch. 3, p. 12 of 13) objected to the greed, oppression and tyranny perpetrated by the rulers and military personnel on farmers. Ibn Khaldun (1967, pp. 230–4) went further and advanced a theory of the interaction between dynastic cycle, taxation, and the rise or fall of economic activity (and civilization). Below is an extended quote from his writing on this issue:

> It should be known that at the beginning of a dynasty, taxation yields a large revenue from small assessments. At the end of the dynasty, taxation yields a small revenue from large assessments.
>
> The reason for this is that when the dynasty follows the ways of Islam, it imposes only such taxes as are stipulated by the religious law, such as charity taxes, the land tax, and the poll tax. These have fixed limits that cannot be exceeded.
>
> The desert attitude requires kindness, reverence, humility, respect for the property of other people, and disinclination to appropriate it, except in rare instances. Therefore, the individual imposts and assessments, which together constitute the tax revenue, are low. When tax assessments and imposts upon the subjects are low, the latter have the energy and desire to do things. Cultural enterprises grow and increase, because the low taxes bring satisfaction. When cultural enterprises grow, the number of individual imposts and assessments mounts. In consequence, the tax revenue, which is the sum total of (the individual assessments), increases.
>
> When the dynasty continues in power and their rulers follow each other in succession, they become sophisticated. The Bedouin attitude and simplicity lose their significance, and the Bedouin qualities of moderation and restraint disappear. Royal authority with its tyranny and sedentary culture that stimulates sophistication, make their appearance. . . . As a result, the individual imposts and assessments upon the subjects, agricultural labourers, farmers, and all the other taxpayers, increase. Every individual impost and assessment is greatly increased, in order to obtain a higher tax revenue. Customs duties are placed upon articles of commerce and (levied) at the city gates. Then, gradual increases in the amount of the assessments succeed each other regularly, in correspondence with the gradual increase in the luxury customs and many needs of the dynasty and the spending required in connection with them. Eventually, the taxes will weigh heavily upon the subjects and overburden. . . .
>
> The assessments increase beyond the limits of equity. The result is that the interest of the subjects in cultural enterprises disappears, since when they compare expenditures and taxes with their income and gain and see the little profit they make, they lose all hope. Therefore, many of them refrain from all cultural activity. The result is that the total tax revenue goes down, as individual assessments go down. Often, when the decrease is noticed, the amounts of individual imposts are increased. This is considered a means of compensating for the decrease. Finally, individual imposts and assessments reach their limit. It would be of no avail to increase them further. The costs of all cultural enterprise are now too high, the taxes are too heavy, and the profits anticipated

> fail to materialize. Finally, civilization is destroyed, because the incentive for cultural activity is gone. It is the dynasty that suffers from the situation, because it profits from cultural activity. (pp. 230–31)

Many elements of Ibn Khaldun's writings anticipate modern economics. First, there is the view that higher taxes prove a heavy toll on incentives to work and invest (that is, on economic activity) and could even undermine a civilization if used to fund luxurious living for the state officials. Second, Ibn Khaldun anticipates public choice theory. The dynastic cycles in his analysis resemble political cycles in democracy. A combination of rent-seeking special-interest groups grows within and with a dynasty (or political regime or party). As time elapses and the dynasty gets more established and relaxed about the continuity of its hold on power, there begins the process by which the special interest groups transfer wealth in their favour from ordinary citizenry. Third, and again in the public choice spirit, Ibn Khaldun warns rulers not to rub shoulders with private businessmen for petty gains. As he puts it:

> Exemption from taxes and customs duties is more likely than anything else to cause one's capital to grow, and it brings quick profits. These people do not understand how much damage is caused the ruler by each decrease in the revenue from taxes. The ruler, therefore, must guard against persons, and not pay any attention to suggestions that are harmful to his revenues and his rule. (p. 234)

Fourth, there is advice for the rulers not to indulge in commercial activity because it would exhaust (in modern jargon, displace or 'crowd out') private capital and undermine private business. Fifth, there is a clear appreciation elsewhere in *Muqaddimah* that once public expenditure assumes a significant role in the economy, its withdrawal can depress private profits and commercial activity.

Ibn Khaldun's insights do not stop at this point but extend further into the coterminous socio-political processes whereby such fiscal rent-seeking ultimately culminates in rebellion. The classical Islamic vision of governance becomes an important political symbol in such a revolt. As the struggle initiated by 'purists' broadens to include less learned sections of the society and other diverse interests, the decline of a ruling dynasty becomes inevitable and so does its replacement by those committed (at least initially) to smaller government. In this way, the value basis of governance, described by us as the 'inner core of governance' in Islam, even though in reality it may have been followed for only a very short period of history, assumes a leading role in shaping and reshaping the political landscape of Muslim societies.

FISCAL MILIEU IN CONTEMPORARY MUSLIM STATES

Having taken stock of the gradual dilution, between the classical era and later dynasties, of the Islamic ethos of small government, we now move to viewing the contemporary situation in Muslim countries. The first point that we wish to stress is that Muslim countries – consisting of some 56 nation states – largely gained independence only forty to fifty years ago. Many being resource-rich and strategically located were later the intense focus of the international rivalry between capitalism and communism. This environment has influenced some countries more than the others, resulting in a compounding of the uneven economic progress that prevailed at independence. At one end of the spectrum is Afghanistan in which some 1.5 million people died in the proxy war between the United States and the Soviet Union fought over some twenty years, with millions more displaced and the country's economic base ruined (Human Rights Watch, 2001, p. 3). At the other end are Turkey, Indonesia and Malaysia that have managed to achieve some stability in spite of earlier unrest. Then there are oil-exporting states which have invested heavily in basic amenities and infrastructure. Yet, they have a long way to go in diversifying from economic dependence on a single resource base. Most also rely on an underclass of immigrant labourers who share few of the rights of the indigenous people. Corresponding to this disparity among Muslim states, some have well-developed taxation and reporting systems while the others are struggling to provide reliable and consistent statistics on public finances. Also, there are major differences in governing structures, from military rule to dynasties to democratically elected leadership. Nevertheless, at least insofar as economic institutions are concerned, almost all are attempting to connect with and embed in the global economic and financial architecture.

Against this unity in diversity, our interest lies only in a broad-based appreciation of the trends in place on the expenditure and tax side of the budget in Muslim countries. The idea is to draw on the literature in conventional economics to investigate the deeper socioeconomic and political undercurrents that may have caused such trends. With this objective in sight, we take Iqbal (1993) and Iqbal and Khan (2004) as a convenient starting point of our investigation. These authors identify five key issues of concern. These are, first, big government that, in general, is the result of central planning in the 1960s and 1970s, second, high debt servicing costs on outstanding foreign and local borrowings that have not yielded projects at all (but have been consumed in current expenditure) or in projects with rates of return below the interest costs, third, substantial defence outlays, fourth, narrow tax bases, and, fifth, tax evasion and corruption. It is these issues together with some general features of Muslim countries outlined earlier that we wish to integrate with the theories of government growth in the West, surveyed, for instance in Lybek (1988).

We see many points in common. First, building from scratch and with the discovery of oil in some countries and gaining freedom in others, there was undoubtedly an increase in citizens' expectations of their respective governments which was tantamount to an increase in the demand for public services. Here, Wagner's (1835–1917) law is pertinent. A transformation from traditional modes of economic organization to industrial ones has tended to shift the responsibility of providing education and health care in particular from the family to the state. In parallel, urbanization has widened the demand for other basic infrastructure such as roads, rail, telephones, public transport, electricity, sewerage and water. Some, such as the Arabian Gulf states, have been more successful in meeting these demands compared to others but overall progress nevertheless has been made in many countries.

Second, insofar as expansion of government is the result of the behaviour of agents on the supply side of the budget, the picture depicted by Iqbal (1993) and Iqbal and Khan (2004) on borrowing becomes the basis for arguing that fiscal illusion – for example, the ease of securing finance through invisible means such as budget deficits, borrowing, inflation – appeared initially attractive for many Muslim countries. For a while, the policy postponed the cost of expanding government, and facilitated the isolation of spending decisions from revenue generation. But ultimately the chickens came home to roost, and adjustments were needed. For example, during the 1980s and 1990s, the central government budget deficits of the Middle East and North African (MENA) countries averaged about 7.6 per cent of GDP compared with 4.4 per cent for developing countries as a whole. By 2001, the (MENA) budget deficits had declined to an average of only 1.1 per cent of GDP (Bennett, 2003). Nevertheless, at around 30 per cent of GDP, spending in 2001 remained higher than the 27 per cent of GDP average in developing countries.

Recall our earlier conclusion that money creation from budget deficits is either taxation (on money balances) or borrowing (at zero interest via seigniorage), and that (in terms of Buchanan) government bond borrowings transfer taxation to the future. In these respects, all government financing amounts in one way or another to taxation in the end. Ibn Khaldun knew that many centuries ago:

> It should be known that the finances of a ruler can be increased, and his financial resources improved, only through the revenue from taxes. (1967, p. 234)

Table 5.1 Selected Muslim countries– central government finance (as percentage of GDP), 1995

	Tax	Non-Tax	Total
Malaysia	20.6	6.6	27.2
Turkey	14.3	7.3	21.6
Lebanon	10.8	1.1	11.9
Jordan	20.4	6.5	26.9
Syria	17.8	8.2	26.0
Indonesia	16.4	6.2	22.6
Egypt	26.3	5.6	31.9
Albania	18.3	9.2	27.5
Cameroon	9.5	2.8	12.3
Pakistan	15.3	7.2	22.5
Gambia	21.8	7.5	29.3

This statement, in its import, includes countries where there is little direct and indirect taxation but the government relies heavily on the monopoly (=taxation) of a mineral resource (for example, oil).

Third, there are the substantial defence outlays mentioned by Iqbal. This is the flip side of Robinson's (1970, p. 93 and 1978, p. 239) argument on the role of the armament industry in influencing the foreign policy of the West. It is the East that has suffered most from the politics of conflict and the sale of armaments, Iraq being a prime example. Timmerman (1991) traces how Western arms trade interests had been complicit in encouraging that country's aggressive military and diplomatic posture (*vis-à-vis* Iran and Kuwait), triggering a regional armaments race and heavy corresponding budgetary outflows.

The fourth issue identified by Iqbal, that of a narrow tax base, needs further examination. Tables 5.1 to 5.3 provide a basis for our discussion. Clearly, the level of taxes in Muslim countries in Table 5.1 is broadly comparable to the sample of developing rather than the developed countries (OECD) given in Table 5.2. In general terms, the level of tax collection in Muslim countries is almost one half that of the developed countries. Also, Muslim countries have a narrow tax base with direct (for example, personal income) taxes constituting only a small proportion of total taxation (Table 5.3), pointing to deep imbalances in economic structure and public governance. As a result, oil producing countries are dependent by and large on taxing one resource, for example, oil, while others rely heavily on indirect taxes on international trade and the manufacturing sector. In the same vein, the level of corporate income taxes is higher and the potential of social security contributions, payroll and

Table 5.2 Comparative composition of tax revenue (as percentage of GDP), 1995–7 average

	Income taxes			Consumption taxes				Social Security	Overall level of Tax Revenue
	Corporate	Personal	Total[c]	General	Excise	Trade	Total[c]		
OECD countries[a]	3.1	10.8	14.2	6.6	3.6	0.3	11.4	9.5	37.9
America	3.0	12.3	15.4	3.7	2.0	0.3	7.0	6.1	32.6
Pacific	4.3	11.4	16.3	4.3	2.6	0.6	8.4	3.5	31.6
Europe	2.9	10.6	13.7	7.3	4.0	0.3	12.4	10.8	39.4
Developing countries[b]	2.6	2.2	5.2	3.6	2.4	3.5	10.5	1.3	18.2
Africa	2.4	3.9	6.9	3.8	2.3	5.1	11.6	0.5	19.8
Asia	3.0	3.0	6.2	3.1	2.2	2.7	9.7	0.3	17.4
Middle East	3.2	1.3	5.0	1.5	3.0	4.3	10.3	1.1	18.1
Western Hemisphere	2.3	1.0	3.7	4.8	2.3	2.6	10.6	2.5	18.0

Notes
a. Excludes the Czech Republic, Hungary, Korea, Mexico and Poland.
b. Sample of 8 African countries; 9 Asian countries; 7 Middle Eastern countries; and 14 Western Hemisphere countries.
c. Discrepancies are attributed to memorandum items.

Source: Adapted from Tanzi and Zee (2000, p. 304).

workforce taxes, and property taxes on the average is not well explored (Table 5.3).

What are the reasons for such differences? The next section looks at the problems of implementing broad-based taxation in Muslim countries. Here, we raise one final question about the fiscal situation in contemporary Muslim societies. So far we have discussed growth of government in these nation states without considering the nature of governance in these countries. Is there a connection between the fiscal position and the quality of governance? This question returns us to Ibn Khaldun and in particular to the scope for a wider application of his model. It can be seen as a forerunner of Toynbee's (1956) study of the genesis, growth, breakdown and disintegration of civilizations. Indeed, Toynbee in volume III of his *Study of History* refers to Ibn Khaldun as 'an Arabic genius' who 'formulated a philosophy of history which is undoubtedly the greatest work of its kind that has ever yet been created by any mind in any time or place' (pp. 321–2).

Ibn Khaldun's political-economic theory of development of dynasties, we recall, proceeds in five stages. First, a new dynasty comes into being by

Table 5.3 Types of revenue as percentage of total revenue

Country	Income profits and capital gains	Individual income	Corporate income	Social Sec. contri bution	Payroll and work force	Property	Goods and services	Gen sales VAT	Int'l trade and transac tions	Other	Non-tax	Entrep. and income	Total
	1	1.1	1.2	2	3	4	5	5.1	6	7	V	8	II
UAE				2.06			19.89				77.31		99.26
Kuwait	0.84		0.84			0.15	0.03		2.41		96.54	93.81	99.97
Oman	16.44		16.17		3.03	0.37	1.63		4.32		73.36	63.9	99.15
Iran	11.91	2.62	9.29	6.84	2.38	1.11	9.15	0.59	9.56	0.85	57.18	44.05	98.98
Bahrain	6.66		6.66	14.01	2.25	0.58	3.74		12.27		60.47	53.74	100
Malaysia	36.32	10.2	25.93	1.23		0.65	26.39	8.8	12.63	4.68	17.92	10.44	99.82
Turkey	31.76	24.78	6.98			0.12	46.05	27.26	2.32	2.1	17.01	1.92	99.36
Lebanon	9.06					8.4	8.38		44.16	4.64	25.35	10.94	99.99
Tunisia	15.66	8.16	4.84	16.84	1.34	0.07	20.78	8.6	25.57	3.28	15.98	13.47	99.52
Jordan	11.4	3.09	8.02		0.71	4.49	31.01		22.72	4.24	25.36	17.95	99.93
Kazakhstan	8.51	1.82	6.69	23.42	3.19	0.08	32.59	26.46	3.71	0.01	2.21	1.03	73.72
Syria	30.15				2.83	0.99	20.72		10.59	2.54	32.19	28.71	100.01
Morocco	19.37	10.32	6.28	6.67		1.95	38.38	19.29	14.44	1	15.99	5.48	97.8
Indonesia	61.3	33.47	25.96	1.77		0.75	24.86	17.66	4.34	0.04	6.92	3.86	99.98
Egypt	20.04	2.13	15.87			0.74	15.89		11.62	10.03	34.19	16.03	92.51
Albania	7.18	1.31	5.87	13.67		0.34	39.69	32.27	15.49	0.19	23.38	19.69	100
Cameroon	16.99	8.29	8.7			1.14	25.14	20.79	27.58	1.48	27.39	16.02	99.72
Azerbaijan	21.87	10.4	11.47	22.1	0.35	1.8	39.91	20.88	8.53		5.44	2.68	100
Pakistan	21.13	3.35	17.57			1.19	26.83	14.47	12.21	14.59	24.06	10.75	100.01
Gambia	14.49	4.22	10.27		0.25		32.41	31.61	42.04	0.2	5.93	2.11	95
Avg (non-oil)	20.33	7.60	9.65	5.36	0.54	1.42	26.81	14.26	16.12	3.06	17.46	10.07	

Table 5.3 (continued)

Country	Income profits and capital gains	Individual income	Corporate income	Social Sec. contri bution	Payroll and work force	Property	Goods and services	Gen sales VAT	Int'l trade and transac tions	Other	Non-tax	Entrep. and income	Total
	1	1.1	1.2	2	3	4	5	5.1	6	7	V	8	II
Switzerland	13.15	9.51	3.64	52.77		2.87	22.79	14.24	1.04		7.32	5.36	99.94
Japan	36.16	23.72	12.45	26.48		4.05	14.43	6.99	1.24	1.6	15.45	8.58	99.41
Norway	21.18	10.39	10.79	20.59		0.93	35.57	20.44	0.52		21.14	18.43	99.93
Denmark	38.78	31.27	4.38	3.88	0.57	1.77	39.78	24.07	0.05	0.52	12.87	8.58	98.22
USA	56.35	45.9	10.45	31.44		1.33	3.13		1.09		6.21	3.24	99.55
Austria	23.81	17.47	4.96	38.01	4.85	0.33	24.85	16.37	0.34	0.59	6.55	3.4	99.33
France	19.34	14.34	4.94	41.16	1.41	1.97	28.23	19.16		0.63	6.07	1.34	98.81
Belgium	36.16	29.08	6.95	33.34		3.02	25.93	15.85			1.57	0.81	100.02
Netherlands	24.81	14.84	9.97	41.11		2.98	22.68	15.25		1.66	6.57	3.93	99.81
Sweden	14.56	6.61	7.95	33.69	6.39	4.92	27.82	16.96	0.07	0.12	10.9	8.72	98.47
Finland	29.71	24.04	5.67	11.04		2.15	44.75	26.89		0.17	12.08	2.66	99.9
Canada	50.98	40.78	9.19	18.13			17.76	11.87	1.85		11.28	5.58	100
Italy	30.02			30.85		1.84	28.67	18.23	0.17	1	6.93	2.74	99.48
Australia	67.14	49.83	16.6		2.26		20.24	9.92	2.56		6.33	3.34	98.53
UK	38.87	27.51	10.81	17.54		6.89	31.3	17.8			5.26	3.26	99.86
Ireland	40.87	31.22	9.64	13.42	1.11	2.5	37.41	20.06			4.69	2.09	100
New Zealand	62.17	45.47	11.18		1.01	0.56	27.44	19.32	2.45		6.07	3.29	99.7

Spain	30.09	23.78	6.14	38.65		0.36	24.2	14.49			6.52	3.39	99.82
Portugal	26.3	16.46	9.65	24.83		0.22	35.65	21.26		2.3	10.01	4.08	99.31
Greece	32.71	17.95	9.33	2.26		4.5	56.72	33.77	0.07	3.59	10.51	5	110.36
Iceland	21.1	18.04	3.06	9.25		4.44	48.99	32.04	1.18	0.36	13.67	6.08	98.99
Luxembourg	33.47	19.41	12.97	24.78		7.27	25.65	13.37		2.86	8.18	5.33	102.21
San Marino	25.75			19.27		0.68	31.78		1.4	0.72	19.86	12.46	99.46
Average	33.63	22.51	7.86	23.15	0.77	2.42	29.38	16.88	0.61	0.70	9.39	5.29	

Source: IMF *Government Finance Statistics Yearbook 1999*

strengthening group feeling and social cohesion, defending property and providing military protection. Second, stability is established and the new ruler gains complete control. Third, there is a period of economic prosperity and enjoyment of the 'fruits of royal authority'. Taxes are collected and public revenue is administered under the total authority of the ruler. Fourth, contentment sets in, there are few initiatives and some stagnation begins. Fifth, there is extravagance, wastage and decadence. Taxes increase, but revenues decline as the economy falters. Underpinning this cyclical view of history is the concept of '*asabiyyah*' (group feeling, social cohesion), which provides stability to the political order. At the dynasty's genesis, group feeling and solidarity is strong. But *asabiyyah* grows weaker after reaching its zenith. Eventually, excessive taxation, luxurious living and corruption lead to the downfall and replacement by a new dynasty, supported by cooperation and strong social cohesion. The 'political-economic cycle' begins again (Spengler, 1964).

While Ibn Khaldun's cyclical interpretation of history is cast in terms of dynasties, it can be recast and extended into and supplemented by a public choice theory of the political process that models fiscal behaviour among democratically chosen governments. Moore (2007) reviews contemporary literature on this issue. In brief, the thesis is that governance outcomes are influenced by the struggle between the ruling elite who wish to exercise unrestrained power and the citizenry who want to limit such power. In the absence of ready sources of revenue such as mineral wealth, the reliance on general taxation as the only continuing source of revenue may provide strong incentives for the ruling elite to bargain and negotiate with taxpayers. This dependency creates an opening for more accountability, responsiveness to public demands, and state capacity-building to identify and implement such demands. In other words, under certain circumstances, the state's need to rely on broad-based taxation can become an impetus for improving governance outcomes. Such, at least, has been the history of some European nations. In contrast, according to some interpretations, the irony of resource-rich states (which suffer the 'resource curse') as well as those dependent on foreign loans and aid is that they do not need to tax and engage the general public. Hence, governance suffers.

Yet, many countries are undemocratic but pro-enterprise. As Usher (1992, pp. 131–2) argues, the reason is that if the sole objective of a ruler is to maximize the state revenue then there is every reason to expect protection of property rights and encouragement of entrepreneurs regardless of the form of government. Hence the *de facto* protection of property rights, especially for foreign investors, in countries such as China (Chiu and Lewis, 2006). However, if there is a danger for a regime of being overthrown, then it will be prepared to sacrifice a good deal of national income and growth to hunt down conspiracies against it (the military rulers in Pakistan and monarchical governments in the Middle East can be cited as good examples of this phenomenon). Equally, there is reason to contend that the latter insight can be applied to weak democracies under the threat of not being able to finish their full term or being re-elected. Also, looking into the mirror of world history, it applies to military and imperial powers on the cusp of their decline.

To summarize, while strains of contemporary economic thought can provide explanations of the trends in taxation and government growth in Muslim countries, they strike a surprising degree of harmony with the wisdom embodied in the classical and the post-classical Muslim thought on this issue and in fact build further upon them. The overall contribution of such analysis is that it both identifies imbalances in the fiscal governance of Muslim nations and gives a basis for a deeper reflection on the problems of redressing these imbalances.

PROBLEMS OF IMPLEMENTING TAXATION IN MUSLIM COUNTRIES

These connections between governance and taxation provide a convenient backdrop to examining the questions that we raised earlier in relation to problems of implementing a broad based taxation regime – such as the one we advanced in the previous chapter – in contemporary Muslim societies. Below, we list some issues that are, in the ultimate analysis, a reflection on the quality of governance in Muslim nation states.

Economic Structure and Organization

There is a marked difference between the developed and the developing countries in terms of economic organization. As Tanzi and Zee (2000) elaborate, many low-income economies are organized around large numbers of small agrarian and production units that work at subsistence level, are prone to seasonality, lack formal documentation of transactions, and make only a limited use of the banking system. Wages make only a modest contribution to national income, the informal economy is sizeable, literacy rates are low, and the tax administration staff is less skilled and poorly paid. These features introduce dependence on one economic sector (for example, agriculture, manufacturing or oil), promote indirect taxation, arbitrariness in tax assessment, increased collection costs, and face-to-face interaction between assessor and tax payer facilitating bargaining and corruption.

Skewed Distribution of Income and Wealth

The preceding explanation for the small share of direct taxes in terms of economic structure and low per capita income means that the potential for taxation at the upper end of the wealth and income scale is overlooked. Drawing again upon Tanzi and Zee (2000):

> it is well known that developing countries tend to have income distributions that are much less even than industrial countries. In the former, Gini coefficients that exceed 0.5 are not rare. This highly uneven income distribution has two implications: first, that to generate high tax revenue, the top deciles would have to be taxed significantly more proportionally than the low deciles; second, that economic and often political power is concentrated in the top deciles so that richer taxpayers are able to prevent tax reforms that would affect them negatively. This partly explains why personal income taxes and property taxes have been very little exploited in these countries and why tax incidence studies of developing countries have found tax systems rarely achieve effective progressivity. (p. 300)

Many, if not most, of the problems can be traced to self-seeking political behaviour and, in particular, the substantial amounts of monies that are misappropriated by rulers, bureaucrats and military generals and either hoarded in unproductive forms of wealth (for example, real estate in Pakistan) or placed in foreign bank accounts. The behaviour of prominent businessmen, many with monopoly rights that allow them to operate like oligarchs, is often little different. Having such large amounts of funds withdrawn from circulation within the domestic economies results in chronic 'capital starvation' and high interest rates. Consider, Jackson *et al.* (1994):

> Those fortunate few with astronomical incomes – the tribal chieftains, the kings, the large land-owners, the oil-rich sheiks and the political leaders – do have ample capacity to save. Unfortunately, these high-income receivers frequently dispense their wealth on the hoarding of precious metals or the purchasing of existing properties in the form of land or urban real estate. The monetary saving that does occur often flows abroad for safe-keeping or to take advantage of the more convenient saving outlets provided by the securities markets of the advanced nations. The important point is that those few who have the ability to save are often unwilling to do so or, if they are willing, do not make their savings available for investment in productive facilities. (p. 453)

This behaviour results in a reduction of the amount of capital available to work with labour, depressing wages. It then becomes difficult to broaden the economic and tax base by speeding up development and bringing those most vulnerable out of the vicious circle of poverty.

Poor Governance

Of course, the situation is more complex than one of venal officials and oligarchs simply abusing their position of power, important though that is. Money – even that obtained by legitimate enterprise – may be subject to seizure and appropriation if one falls out of favour with, or actively opposes, the current political regime. Wealth and the position of the whole family, and not just that of the individual concerned, may be at risk. Then, compounding the insecurity of property rights, there are the risks of the domestic investment environment. Inflation risk and exchange rate uncertainty may encourage funds to leak offshore in search of a safer haven. Banking and financial systems may also militate against domestic placement. For example, an assessment in the IMF's *Finance and Development* (Creane *et al.*, 2003) found that in nearly one half of the Middle East and North African (MENA) countries, the banking sector is not well developed, and is highly concentrated and dominated by public sector banks subject to extensive government intervention and marked by wide interest rate spreads. In most of the MENA countries, the development of the stock market, corporate bond markets, insurance companies, pension funds and mutual funds (unit trusts) is embryonic. In the IMF's definition (Abed, 2003), MENA comprises the Arab states in the Middle East and North Africa – Algeria, Bahrain, Djibouti, Egypt, Iraq, Jordan, Kuwait, Lebanon, Libya, Mauritania, Morocco, Oman, Qatar, Saudi Arabia, Somalia, Sudan, the Syrian Arab Republic, Tunisia, the United Arab Emirates and Yemen – plus the Islamic State of Afghanistan, the Islamic Republic of Iran, Pakistan, and the West Bank and Gaza.

Table 5.4 classifies the MENA countries according to their level of financial development in 2000–1 using principal components analysis.[5] In effect, problems of economic governance, financial governance and monetary governance reinforce the underlying issues posed by poor political governance and the vast concentrations of wealth and power.

Lobbying and Corruption

Obviously, a major stumbling block in the way of reforming taxation on ability-to-pay basis is the concentration of power and wealth in developing countries. This point needs to be corroborated further by way of an example. We cite the case of Pakistan. Khan and Khan (1998) estimate that provincial governments can increase the tax contribution of the agricultural sector to their revenue base from the present around 6 per cent to somewhere between 17–29 per cent. Some other experts consider the potential far greater (Osman Ghani, *Dawn*, 20 March 2000). The problem,

Table 5.4 A ranking of Middle Eastern and North African countries according to their level of financial development, 2000–1

Level of financial development		
High	Medium	Low
Bahrain	Algeria	Iran, I.R. of
Jordan	Djibouti	Libya
Kuwait	Egypt	Sudan
Lebanon	Mauritania	Syrian Arab Republic
Oman	Morocco	Yemen
Qatar	Pakistan	
Saudi Arabia	Tunisia	
United Arab Emirates		

Note: Of the 24 MENA countries listed on p. 153, Afghanistan, Iraq, Somalia, and the West Bank and Gaza were omitted due to lack of data.

Source: Creane et al. (2003).

however, is that the agricultural lobby wields considerable political influence that it has used pervasively to block land reforms and evade agricultural taxes. As *The Economist* (28 August 1993) notes:

> since independence in 1947, finance ministers have been trying to tax agricultural incomes and the big landlords . . . who have dominated every government have fiercely and successfully resisted. (p. 36)

It can be argued that the position when taxing industry is not much different. The influence of lobbies has manifested many a time in the form of ad hoc and continuously shifting tax and tariff policies through the notorious use of SROs (statutory regulatory orders). In reforming this state of affairs, Kazmi (2001), the joint chief economist (operations) of the Pakistan planning commission, finds not only a lack of interest at the highest level but rather an active resistance and collusion. Supported by statistics, he takes aim directly:

> Over the last fifty years, the overall cultural orientation in Pakistan has been toward self-centeredness, greed, lust for money and power, corruption, exploitation and complete disregard for public welfare. The power hungry ruling classes have been self-seeking . . . with the result that the very viability of the country is at stake. When the Central Board of Revenue published the Directory of Income Tax Payers in 1994, it . . . showed that all those who wielded economic and political power either did not pay any tax at all or paid just peanuts as compared to their assessed tax liabilities. . . . In the case of Pakistan, it seems that all

Table 5.5 Causes of tax evasion/pilferage

Administrative (I)	Tax Laws (II)	Socio-Cultural (III)	Economic Env. (IV)	Miscellaneous (V)
Lack of documentation	Exemptions	Personal greed for wealth	High rate of Inflation	Easy virtue of tax officials
Complexity of tax system	Direct tax exemptions Indirect tax exemptions	Black money/ ostentatious consumption/ living patterns	Poor public Service	Political will and commitment of the ruling elite
Poor legal framework	Exemptions of legislators on their own incomes	Corruption/ degeneration of moral values	Low level of Literacy	
Secrecy of personal/ corporate finances	Discontinuation of publication of tax directory		Inconsistency in government policies/ regulations	Role of tax consultants/ tax lawyers and systematic tax evasion, etc.
Lack of right mix of reward and punishment	Tax amnesties: their repeated use Premium on tax pilferage	Lack of faith in the socio-political system		No use of cross-country experience in tax reforms/ administration
Squeezing more and more revenues from small number of taxpayers				
Lack of audit/ computer facilities				

Source: Kazmi (2001, p. 26)

> the ideas, customs, skills, arts or collective intellectual achievements are related to evading our social responsibilities. . . . The guiding principle of our rulers has been 'the greatest unhappiness of the greatest number'. (pp. 16–17)

Not surprisingly, tax collection until recently has been in disarray, the cumulative foreign and domestic debt has reached almost the level of GDP, and interest payments constitute some one third of the current expenditure of the government. Table 5.5 lists the major causes of tax loss identified by Kazmi. Kazmi's analysis is supported by anecdotal evidence too.[6] An ex-President of Pakistan, Farouq Leghari once estimated that some US$50 billion worth of public monies had been diverted by politicians, bureaucrats and military generals, and deposited overseas. This broadly equals the country's debt, the interest payments on which have been crippling budgetary allocations for development and poverty alleviation (*Dawn*, 12 March 2001). When, occasionally, attempts are made to recover such amounts from abroad, the obstructions faced are enormous.

Imbalances in International Trade

One important dimension of taxation in some Muslim countries are the high tariffs on international trade. While economic literature has criticized this trend, in some cases they may reflect the other side of the subsidies game. Consider an example.

Developed country X announces a multi-billion dollar programme for subsidizing its private car manufacturing industry (and perhaps providing export credit finance as well) to increase its competitiveness. At this point, one may ask: why look a gift horse in the mouth? If X wants to tax its own citizens and offer a subsidy to car buyers in other countries, why complain? However, cars are manufactured in some developing countries too. Take, for example, the case of country Y. With its GDP less than 20 per cent and per capita income some 2.25 per cent of the country X, there is no way Y can even conceive of engaging in this subsidy game. Nevertheless, the domestic car industry in Y will likely put pressure on government to maintain tariffs or slow down their planned reduction. Country Y may then be open to the claims of muddying the waters of international trade, but the subsidies given by X may be forgotten.

In our view, country Y will be rightly aggrieved, but it may be unwise to pursue that course of action. It will be denying its consumers and producers the benefits of cheaper cars, cheaper trucks, cheaper tractors and cheaper transportation and production costs generally. It will aid its car manufacturers (although that is problematical in the long run) only at the price of rendering other sectors less competitive, hindering their export and import substitution potential. While the appeals for help are difficult to resist, tariff protection often hurts those levying it more than the competitors by encouraging a hand-out mentality and discouraging the search for greater productivity.

Presumably, for such reasons, Tanzi and Zee (2000) recommend that the developing countries ought to raise revenues in ways that do not deviate substantially from international norms. The recommendation made is that developing countries compensate reduction in tariffs on excisable imports by a commensurate rise in excise rates both on imported and domestic goods and if there is still a shortfall, raise the VAT or GST (which, we saw, is regressive). Naturally, this formula removes protection of domestically produced goods in developing countries and opens them to foreign goods, the cost of which may have been artificially lowered by governmental support. It would be better if such matters were made part of a more careful, globally agreed and monitored, mutually beneficial regime of trade. In the absence of such desideratum there is at least a case to be made for resisting the pressures for tit-for-tat retaliation, and instead in this particular case, accepting the money handed out by foreign taxpayers as embodied in the cheaper imports.

Fiscal Morass: Is There a Third Stakeholder?

So far in this and the previous chapter, it has been suggested that the economic case for altering the fiscal structure in Muslim countries is compelling. The question, however, is how to break the ice? Where does one begin? A radical Marxist solution would call for breaking the nexus between property and political power. Historically, this has happened through building pressures on politically apathetic regimes. If governments are smart they see the writing on the wall and begin to constrain themselves by agreeing to follow clearer rules and constitutions. Representation is increased and there is the appearance of policy responsiveness to needs, transparency and accountability. In short, in the conception of Moore (2007), increased dependence on broad-based taxation compels governments to be responsive to the calls of the taxpayers thereby opening up the way for reforms in the quality of governance. Almost invariably, however, considered in the light of European history, this phase of the reform process has been conflict-ridden. Perhaps, many Muslim countries today may allow a milder version of that historical process to be repeated. What may be different in the case of Muslim countries is that there is a third stakeholder (broadly 'the West') apart from the people and their rulers. Bernard Lewis (1993) provides a comparison of the past and the present:

> Modernization in the nineteenth century, and still more in the twentieth, far from reducing this autocracy, substantially increased it. On the one hand, modern technology, communications, and weaponry greatly reinforced the rulers' powers of surveillance, indoctrination, and repression. On the other hand, social and economic modernization enfeebled or abrogated the religious constraints and intermediate powers that had in various ways limited earlier autocracies. No Arab Caliph or Turkish Sultan of the past could ever have achieved the arbitrary and pervasive power wielded by even the pettiest of present-day dictators. (p. 96)

> There are two temptations to which Western governments have all too often succumbed, with damaging results. They might be called the temptation of the right and the temptation of the left. The temptation of the right is to accept, and even to embrace, the most odious of dictatorships as long as they are acquiescent in our own requirements, and as long as their policies seem to accord with the protection of our own national interests. The spectacle of the great democracies of the West in comfortable association with tyrants and dictators can only discourage and demoralize the democratic opposition in these countries. (p. 98)

The situation depicted by Bernard Lewis did not happen overnight. Some, perhaps many, rulers in Muslim countries, at their origin, may have been close to their people. Later, the non-representative style of governance and disregard for the letter and spirit of their relevant constitutions has gradually allowed these rulers to fall prey to the trappings of office and the kind of fiscal behaviour that Muslim scholars throughout history had always warned against. As a result, domestic economic problems have risen (albeit concealed by the oil market) and there has been a drift away from people and seeking of legitimacy beyond borders accompanied by dependency on energy, for some, and debt and foreign aid for others. Foreign stakeholders cannot be expected to advance legitimacy without realizing their 'own national interests'. As a result, the rulers find themselves between a rock and a hard place. Pressures to reform from within are on the rise while, in our reading, demands to serve foreign interests keep on increasing. The solution would have been to revive genuinely representative national assemblies. This would, in one go, constrain ever increasing domestic and foreign pressures for change and, over time, tilt the balance in favour of realizing the interests of local communities. The reality, however, is different. The solace is sought in repression. Kuran (1998) has depicted the consequence of this state of affairs: ordinary people in many Muslim countries have to falsify preferences under brute force. By implication, reform is repressed but the temperature within the crucible keeps rising.

We would go further. There is another side to the analysis which is completely missed by Kuran. The comfortable association between what Bernard Lewis calls the great democracies of the West and rulers and dictators (of the East), it may be argued, puts subtle pressures on Western governments to somehow justify their actions before voters and human rights associations. In our reading, a solution to this dilemma is sought in giving the struggle for reforming Muslim polities a twist that somehow makes repression palatable to the voter-audience in the West. In other words, voter preferences are falsified. How that happens is a research problem that requires detailed investigation in its own right. What we would like to emphasize is that in analysing the prospects for reform in Muslim countries, researchers must keep the implications of this double falsification of preferences in sight. On one side of the divide, it occurs under duress; on the other, it takes place under the semblance of free choice. This situation is not a good omen for indigenous, independent (that is, impartial) movements for reform in Muslim countries, nor for that matter is it good for harmony in international affairs.

Summary

In summary, there is indisputably an urgent need for reforming taxation in many Muslim countries. However, when considering the issues involved it soon becomes apparent that the fiscal structure is a reflection on the broader political and property relationships in these countries. In this event, it is our contention that unless these relationships are reformed and the nexus between property and political power is cut, there is little hope for meaningful reform. While this conclusion might indicate a rather bleak outlook for reform, this pessimistic note is not the direction we essentially intend to take in this book. Rather, we keep alive the possibility that these societies can make an orderly transition to better governance.

POLICY RECOMMENDATIONS

In the final analysis, hopes for a brighter future in Muslim countries are integrally linked with the scope for reform. Although the external environment is important, the first step is for Muslim countries to put their own houses in order and implement taxation and expenditure policies that reflect the norms of equity and the aspirations of their own people. This means work on a number of fronts: rethinking governance, re-establishing supremacy of law, reforming taxation in line with domestic income and wealth profile and economic priorities, facilitating an appropriate investment profile and climate, and reconsidering expenditure priorities. To this end we propose an agenda for action that accords with the original vision of Islam, starting with the connection between taxation and governance.

Reinvent the Politics of Gains and Losses

Earlier we considered contemporary views on taxation and governance (for example, Moore, 2007). The starting premise that the ruling elite in resource-rich countries and nations dependent on foreign aid and loans have no need to engage the general public on taxation issues. As a result, governance suffers, resentment in the general populace keeps on rising, and the gulf between the rulers and the ruled widens. At the limit, rulers seek legitimization not from within their borders but from outside, seeking external props for the status quo. Such an association can come at a heavy cost to internal unity and peace within such communities. In this context we recall the perceptive advice of Bhutto (1976):

> . . . our vocation as Muslims is not to harbour hostility against other human communities, East or West, North or South, but to conduct ourselves that we can help build bridges of communication and sympathy between one set of nations and another. We draw our inspiration from the Holy Qur'an . . .

Muslims need to respond to such advice on multiple fronts. First, they ought to look inward and build pressure for reforming the state-citizen relationship on a more equitable and participatory footing through democratic reform. Second, on the international front, they should revive non-alignment as a cornerstone of foreign policy and settle local and regional disputes in the spirit of international brotherhood so as to alleviate the basis for diverting substantial expenditure away from human development into international armaments and conflict. This, however, must not come by compromising the right of Muslim countries to organize their collective affairs on Islamic lines, while accepting different views on social organization across countries, and freedom of belief and religious practice for minorities all over the world. Third, and, again in line with the spirit of Islam, Muslims ought to play an active role in promoting free trade and be ready to self-examine and dispose of protection and cartels (hopefully) in return for tangible and significant world-wide progress on free trade. And, fourth, Muslims should work on a medium term policy goal of creating an equitable international taxation regime. In particular, they need to support building international consensus on and mechanisms for bringing capital *pari passu* with labour in terms of tax treatment. As Zee (1998) argues:

> Policymakers in an increasing number of countries have become alarmed by the responsiveness of the domestic capital income tax base to international differences in tax policy . . . thus limiting their degree of freedom in setting domestic capital income tax rates and in mobilising revenue. . . . [Any politically viable solution] probably have to be adopted within a broad multilateral framework to address the difficulties associated with non-participatory countries, and possibly supplemented by bilateral agreements to address the revenue distribution issue. (p. 587)

Rediscover the Power of Moral Renovation

Any attempt to alter the incidence of taxation in accordance with equity norms is likely to encounter opposition. Standard views on taxation offer some advice on how to blunt this resistance. The basic trick is to anticipate the likely behaviour of potential gainers and losers and seek to balance their conflicting demands. For example, measures such as widening the tax coverage and broadening the tax base can be supplemented with a lowering of tax rates such that the overall tax 'grab' is largely unchanged at inception (Feldstein, 1976; Burgess and Stern, 1993; Tanzi and Zee, 2000). While such practical recommendations have merit, they explore only one side of the human psyche, that of calculating material risk-and-reward. Islam, we have stressed, offers an alternative methodology, and a complementary dimension by appealing to people's moral conscience through the use of education, media and pressure groups to bring about over time a change in culture and attitudes. On this account, the Islamic call to people and nations to count their gains and losses over a longer-than-life horizon and within an origin-destiny-accountability framework remains largely unexploited. Perhaps one reason for this situation is the active involvement of religious groups in politics at the cost of neglecting to paying attention to reforming people from within.

By way of contrast, on this particular issue, the history of Muslim civilization records that when the post-classical Muslim polity veered to be more or less secular in nature, religious reformers exhibited great tenacity by focusing on reforming the morality of the public in general and, in this way, exercising an indirect influence on government. Ibn Taymiyyah, for example, asked people not to evade taxes (but instead struggle against them) because evasion would only increase the share paid by fellow citizens.

What is needed today is a revival of this tradition to raise domestic and international awareness against inequity, corruption and money laundering. Specifically, normative principles of distributing the tax burden should be elevated to the centre of the tax reform debate in Muslim countries so as to make those with the greatest ability-to-pay conscious of demands on them to fulfil their social obligations. With extreme disparities in income and wealth distribution in developing countries belying the overall low per capita income, the scant proceeds from direct taxation reinforce the impression that the privileged are above the law and can evade their tax bills. This imbalance ought to be highlighted by the reformists in order to generate momentum in favour of constitutional, legal, and administrative changes.

Peaceful ways of exerting pressure may include broadening cooperation with like-minded political and civil liberties movements in the West. With such co-operation, the chances of reckless political behaviour occurring in developing countries may be reduced. Is it too much to expect the *umma* in general to exercise self-control, exhibit civic virtue, and share social obligations? The importance of ethical reform can be seen from Table 5.5

where the root cause of all socio-cultural and legal issues, and most administrative and miscellaneous matters, can ultimately be traced to the (bad) example set by the privileged ruling elites. Such attitudes erode whatever institutional structures are set in place although as we shall argue later in this book, there is great scope to improve on that front too.

Gain the Trust and Confidence of Taxpayers

A successful tax system relies on the government credibility in delivering public goods against the revenues raised. From an ethical perspective, a tax system can be conceived as part of a social contract or a constitutional arrangement that specifies how the cost of public services ought to be shared among the citizenry. Viewed in this larger context, the full potential of taxation as a means to mobilizing resources for economic development can be explored only if (a) taxation arrangements do not depart drastically from accepted norms of social justice, (b) there is a broad perception that the ruling elites are not above the law but paying their due share to the Treasury, and (c) the public at large supports and identifies with the government's economic policies.

If there is a lacuna in the application of the above principles, it is that the political costs of taxation begin to impose an even lower limit on the overall level of taxation than that feasible on economic grounds (Holcombe and Mills, 1995). It is no accident of history then that perceptions on unjust taxation played an important role in the American and French revolutions in the eighteenth century and in Australia's Eureka rebellion in the middle of the nineteenth century. Earlier, and the observation gains significance in view of the writings of Muslim scholars on taxation at around the same time, it is interesting to note that the distinction between absolute monarchy (France) and limited monarchy (Britain) was defined by Sir John Fortescue (*c.* 1394–1476) according to whether taxes could or could not be levied without the consent of Parliament.[7] Against this backdrop, the reality on taxation in many Muslim countries needs to be recognized. All too often, the privileged consider themselves above the law and the need for greater revenues has arisen on account of repayment of growing interest and principal on debt that was not secured in the first place with the consent of the potential taxpayers or their representatives. Taxpayers have good reasons to feel frustrated with governance arrangements and for not identifying with the immediate goals of taxation. As a corollary, all too often, for their part, this situation provides a moral justification (of sorts) for many of them to migrate to the underground economy to evade taxation. Nevertheless, this stand-off underlines the case for reform and the need for political will and the skill required to sell it to general public. In the end, however, nothing short of good governance can regain public confidence.

Close the Constitutional Gates to Rent-seeking

Use (or perhaps more correctly, misuse) of legislative power offers a lucrative venue for rent-seeking through legislative direct and indirect exemption from taxation. Ideally, the revenue system of a country as enacted by the legislature should be regarded as an essential part of the social infrastructure of a country and a public good of utmost importance. Frequent ad hoc changes in tax policy generate uncertainty, encourage corruption, breach public trust, prevent individuals from making far-sighted plans, and undermine taxation as an instrument for altering economic incentives. On corruption, every time policy is open to changes, substantial economic benefits are put up for grabs for organized lobbying groups. On incentives, certainty is needed as responses build only gradually over a lengthy adjustment period as the allocation of investment responds slowly to changes in net-of-tax returns. In the case of intertemporal efficiency, the achievement of significant benefits may take decades as higher savings ratios gradually increase the stock of capital. Keeping these issues in sight, it can be argued that, as far as is possible, the basic structure of the revenue system and its individual components should remain essentially unchanged over a sequence of budgetary periods. Few alterations ought to be made in tax rules between major structural tax reforms. Also, the task of evaluating alternative policy options should be entrusted to authoritative expert commissions who adopt a principled rather than rent-seeking approach to taxation (Head, 1997; Head and Krever, 1997). Public choice literature seeks to address this problem through enacting voting rules or embedding a fiscal framework within a country's constitution. An example comes from a prominent Islamic scholar, Khurshid Ahmad (1994b, p. 38), who recommends legal enactment to put a ceiling on deficit-financing.

Reform Public Expenditure as Well as Taxation

Historically, public sector savings played an important role in many developed countries for financing economic development. However, as Bird (1987) argues, the bulk of evidence shows that the developing countries nowadays are acting quite to the contrary. Instead of increasing public savings, they have been more than matching increases in tax revenues with current non-developmental expenditure. The drive for tax reform and emphasis on increasing tax revenues is therefore in many a case, misplaced. The priority ought rather to be on reforming the expenditure side of the budget. Tanzi and Zee (2000) likewise recommend that developing countries focus more on the ways that the revenue is utilized than on the (low) level of taxation per se.

In fact, considerable changes have taken place in these aspects among MENA countries. By 2001, budget deficits on average were closer to balance and much lower than that of other developing countries. Nevertheless, despite declining as a percentage of GDP, central government spending and net lending to the private sector remained above the average for developing countries. In part, this would seem to reflect a combination of a slower rate of privatization and thus continued subsidies to state-owned enterprises (SOEs) from the public purse. Also, the size of the government bureaucracy is a problem. Central government wage bills among MENA countries averaged around 11 per cent of GDP in the second half of the 1990s, roughly double that of developing countries generally (Bennett, 2003). There is clearly scope for further change, if only because the MENA countries in general have lagged behind international standards in promoting transparency in the public finances and the reporting of fiscal data. On these grounds, expenditure ought to be prioritized and reconfigured, one reason being to identify the potential application of the benefit principle, which is more difficult to apply if non-flexible items (transfers, defence and interest payments) constitute the bulk of spending.

However, at times, even non-flexible items may allow considerable scope for reform. For instance, Tahir (1995) points out that in Pakistan, combat-related defence budgets (expenditures on armaments, border defence and the like) need to be separated from the rest of the defence budget (expenditure on maintenance of cantonments in main cities, garrison schools and colleges for wards of defence forces, military hospitals, etc.). The same is true of the considerable administrative expenditure attached to executive offices, so much so that scores of assistants accompany Presidents and Prime Ministers on performing strictly personal religious rites – the discretionary *Umrah* to Makkah – on public exchequer. Such expenditure leaves little for spending on mass education and infrastructure and it bestows benefits not offered to society in general (overlooking the non-political, non-military personnel's role in building the country). From a *shari'ah* point of view, the sums involved should be charged to the beneficiaries rather than levied on the public at large through the national exchequer.

In a similar vein, the redistributive budget could usefully be segregated from the rest of the government budget. On this issue, Muslim countries need to exploit the full potential of *zakah* as per proposals given in Chapter 4. Anecdotal evidence suggests that even in poor countries like Pakistan, substantial amounts of *zakah* escape the government net but are nevertheless delivered through the private sector. Collection of such monies might instead be centralized, their net widened to impart progressivity to the tax structure, and their account separated from general budget and channelled to those most deserving in accordance with national policies and priorities. This step would require a parallel action on subsidies. In particular, there is need for undertaking a dispassionate review of subsidies on consumer goods in favour of targeted *zakah* disbursements to deserving families. Also, production subsidies ought to be thoroughly evaluated professionally and advanced only sparingly (Tahir, 1995).

Institutionalize Savings

So as to encourage savings, a fully funded regulated compulsory superannuation scheme in the public as well as the private sectors (beyond a certain cut-off wage level) should be instituted. The funds so raised can be channelled into real business activities through professional management.

Promote Investment

Case-by-case exemptions from taxation against committed funds in real business investment should be considered. Such incentives to capital cannot be avoided given the realities on the ground. Harberger (1998) elaborates some of the issues that we mentioned earlier in terms of onshore-offshore investment choices:

> In many developing countries, even their own nationals require a significant risk premium in their own market, *vis-à-vis* London and New York . . . . If such investors are willing to accept a 5 percent real return in New York, they may very well insist on the expectation of a 10 percent net-of-tax return on their industrial and similar investment at home. This means that if there is no tax, investment projects will face a likely cut-off rate of expected return of around 10 percent. If now a 33 percent corporation tax is imposed, this cut-off rate of return will be 15 percent, and many investments will now be rejected, though they would have been accepted at a 10 percent cut-off rate. The capital that would have gone into these investments will likely flow abroad (or fail to flow from abroad). Less capital will thus be working with the labor force in the developing country in question, and the equilibrium real wage accordingly will be lower. This is the mechanism by which labor comes to bear part, or all, or more than all, of the burden of the tax. (p. 217)

While there is little scope for disagreeing with the above analysis, the question faced by designers of taxation in Muslim countries is whether in fact it is taxes on capital income that are preventing investment in their countries. It could be argued, for example, that the capital made by 'rent-seekers' is exported from local jurisdictions with little intention of being 're-invested' back again. In fact, as someone observed many years ago, rent-seekers usually have coupon-clipper rather than competitive entrepreneurial mentalities. Low-risk tranches of investment offered in stable and profitable public sector commercial organizations or new infrastructure projects can help attract such investors back to the home market.

However, as King Canute famously demonstrated, the 'state' has limited powers in the face of the tides. Should a similar recognition be made of the 'financial waves' by promoting bearer securities and safe-custody arrangements to address secrecy requirements for financial investments by domestic investors? Even New York and other major national markets have been forced to this position by the power of the international markets.

These recommendations have an underlying focus on constraining the ability of the state to employ fiscal illusion and of special interest groups to divert budgetary allocations in their favour. Emphasis is also placed on arranging public finances so as to promote transparency and create awareness among the general tax-paying public of the costs of the policies that they support as well as the kinds of expenditure allocations that have likely evolved historically without their consent. Such principles – transparency, discipline, political accountability, and efficient administration – are in complete harmony with the precedents set by the Prophet Muhammad (pbuh) and the early Caliphate. In them, and in their revival, lies the recipe for the success of Muslim countries.

NOTES

1. Ernest Gellner (1981, p. 16–48) provides a comprehensive discussion of Ibn Khaldun's sociological and economic theories, and their influence on and relationship with modern Western thought.
2. Narrated Anas: Some goods came to Allah's Apostle from Bahrain. The Prophet ordered the people to spread them in the mosque. It was the biggest amount of goods Allah's Apostle had ever received. He left for prayer and did not even look at it. After finishing the prayer, he sat by those goods and gave from those to everybody he saw. . . . Allah's Apostle did not get up till the last coin was distributed. (*Sahih Bukhari* (Hadith, 1.413)).
3. This function was performed under *hisba*. Historical records depict regulators laying down guidelines for *riba*-free transactions; depicting forms of permissible barter, cash, and credit agreements in *shari'ah*; and overseeing honouring of credit transactions (Khan, 1982).
4. In spite of such ethos, resistance to taxation began early in Islamic history. The tribal revolt against *Zakah* had to be quelled by force soon after the death of Muhammad (pbuh). And, fiscal issues did play a role in the *Kharajite* struggle against the third Caliph, Usman.
5. Creane *et al* construct a 'comprehensive' index of financial development that combines six different indices (covering the banking sector, non-bank financial sector, regulation

and supervision, monetary policy, financial openness, and institutional environment), each of which in turn is a composite of four to nine different indicators, both quantitative and qualitative, collected over the 2000–1 time period. Countries were then grouped into three categories (high, medium and low) as reported in Table 5.4.

6. In the seven years since Kazmi's paper, taxation has become a prime area of government's reform programme with some encouraging results.
7. Chief Justice of the Court of the King's Bench under the English King, Henry IV, from 1442 to 1461, he later made a plea for limited monarchy in his study *Difference between an Absolute and Limited Monarchy* (*c.* 1471). First published (that is, issued publicly) in 1714, the volume was later issued under the title *The Governance of England* (1885).

6. Islamic position on budget deficits

INTRODUCTION

Taxation constitutes the major source of financing government activities in many countries. Nevertheless, it is quite common in any one year or over a period of time that a government's outlays exceed its revenues, resulting in a budget deficit. Are such deficits bad for an economy? Do they reflect deeper problems of public governance? Or, to the contrary, do they stimulate economic growth by providing a tool for economic management? These questions have occupied scholars for centuries. Historically, three schools of thought have emerged on the economic consequences of budget deficits, viz. Neoclassical, Keynesian and Ricardian. These paradigms are then supplemented by the public choice theory that studies the dynamics of deficit and debt creation with reference to the decision-making/governance structures of modern polities. The goal of this chapter is to undertake a critical examination of these competing secular positions on budget deficits and then evolve a normative Islamic perspective on the issue in order to achieve three end results. First, the standard economic theory on this issue is synthesized with the normative Islamic perspective. Second, the underpinnings of the prohibition of fixed interest debt in Islam are assessed with reference to the conventional theory of public debt. Third, the Islamic position on budget deficits is integrated with the taxation models of the previous chapter to arrive at a model of macroeconomic management that is embedded in the Islamic ethos. The chapter concludes on policy recommendations and conclusions.

WESTERN PERSPECTIVES

Governments follow a budgetary process to make fundamental decisions about raising and allocating money for their activities. Some operate in terms of 'five-year plans', but the normal situation is that, once a year, the government presents a budget that measures its annual cash flow in the form of receipts in tax and non-tax revenue and expenditure. While many outlays (for example, non-welfare) are by and large fixed, revenues

Table 6.1 The public debt in selected developed countries (percentage of GDP)

	1991	1996	2001	2005
Japan	47.1	68.3	122.3	152.3
France	29.0	44.6	49.1	53.2
Germany	20.1	23.4	35.3	41.0
Italy	97.6	119.7	107.9	106.3
Netherlands	59.3	58.5	43.1	48.0
UK	32.3	48.8	40.1	43.3
USA	45.7	48.0	33.0	38.5

Source: Jaimovich and Panizza (2006)

are much more uncertain and depend on a number of factors including profits and the performance of the economy. As a result, policy-makers determine a planned excess of revenues over expenditure or vice versa and economic conditions settle the actual outcome as the fiscal year progresses. When in deficit, governments can use multiple modes to finance their activities: levy additional taxes, print money, sell public assets or borrow. Borrowing results in public debt. Having once been created, debt requires servicing through interest payments and refinancing unless retired. As shown in Table 6.1, public debt relative to GDP has grown in many developed countries, and will do so over time if budget deficits persist.

The public debt may be owed to nationals (internal debt) or foreigners (external debt). In the case of internal debt, no claim against the productive resources of a nation, or the income and output that these resources generate, arises from outside the political jurisdiction of a country, whereas external debt does give foreigners a claim on the wealth and productive resources of a nation. These distinctions have assumed importance in debates on the economic impact of budget deficits, although Buchanan (1958, 1992) argues that there is no effective difference between internal and external debt as both transfer taxes to future generations. In the Western tradition, such debates go as far back as to the mercantilist and classical economic thought. The core ideas presented then have continued to set the agenda for research. Although the contemporary formulations of this problem are theoretically far more succinct, this has not helped to narrow down differences among extreme positions on this issue. Before proceeding further, we examine the basic theoretical structure and contributions that various schools of thought have made toward understanding the problem of budget deficits.

Neoclassical and Monetarist Thought

Neoclassical theory draws its inspiration from the writings of classical economists who considered public debt analogous to the debt of a private household. They argued that public debt reduced capital formation in the private sector, facilitated government profligacy, financed international wars, and burdened future generations for interest payments. In the event, debt was considered permissible only in emergencies barring which a year-on-year balancing of public budgets was considered essential (O'Brien, 1975).

The Neoclassical model provides a formal basis for these views. It analyses a self-adjusting economy populated with farsighted individuals – each belonging to a specific generation and having a finite life which overlaps with the successive generation – optimizing inter-temporal consumption over their life cycles through borrowing and lending in perfect capital markets. In such a setting, bond-financed budget deficits shift taxes to future generations, reduce savings, raise interest rates[1] and lower the stock of capital, thereby decreasing welfare in the long run. This result was first derived by Diamond (1965) based on lump sum taxes but reinforced by Auerbach and Kotlikoff (1987) who use a 55-period life-cycle simulation model to show that even temporary budget deficits in the presence of distortionary income taxes also reduce welfare in the long run. Other research based on loanable funds theory raises issues about 'crowding out', namely that government spending displaces private spending by competing for scarce resources and raising interest rates. Under a flexible exchange rate regime, high interest rates may in turn attract foreign capital inflows driving the exchange rate higher and changing the balance of trade in goods and services. Hence persistent budget deficits result in either reduced private investment and, depending on the exchange rate regime, an increased current account deficit (Fischer and Easterly, 1990; Ball and Mankiw, 1995).

Should the budget deficits be monetized instead of bond-financed, the money supply is increased at a rate greater than its demand (at current prices), resulting in excess cash balances. The public's attempt to reduce these balances restores a new supply-and-demand equilibrium whereby current (and likely expected) prices rise in proportion to the change in the quantity of money. If expected prices increase, the results do not end there. Bondholders build the new expected inflation rate into nominal interest rates resulting in a further once-for-all increase in prices additional to that from the policy action. Ironically, nominal interest rates finish up higher (at least in a closed economy context) than they would have from a bond-financed rise in public spending. Monetizing the deficit, therefore, inflicts an 'inflation tax' on the holders of money balances, which is arbitrary and inequitable. The value of the revenue from this tax equals the proportional rate of change of the high-powered nominal money stock times the real stock of money balances. It is paid by the holders of money balances to the issuers of money when recipients of the money balances surrender command over real resources in return for the money (Lewis and Mizen, 2000, pp. 177–8).[2] Note that as people reduce their holdings of the thing taxed (real money balances) the tax revenue declines. There is a temptation for money issuers to attempt to restore revenue by inflating faster. The end result of this process is accelerating inflation (ibid., pp. 172–7).

Where might the above findings lead in terms of the role of fiscal or monetary policy in stimulating growth and reducing unemployment? The monetarist school spearheaded by Friedman (1962, 1963, 1968, 1977) addresses this question with reference to a theory of the causes of unemployment and whether the factors responsible can be tackled through fiscal or monetary policies. The focus essentially is on the concept of 'natural rate of unemployment' that an economy tends to have in a state of equilibrium. It is argued that this rate depends on the 'real economic forces' at play, that is, structural characteristics of the economy such as market imperfections, institutional arrangements (unemployment-insurance schemes), and trade unions and the preferences of its members. Activist fiscal and monetary policies can do little to influence these arrangements. Instead, such policies result in rising prices and, if sustained, inflation. Also, as the role of government expands over time as a result of interventionist policies, taxes cannot be continuously deferred to future generations and eventually rise in turn causing heavy disincentives for private enterprise and economic growth. An appropriate policy to alleviate microeconomic rigidities causing unemployment would be to abolish production, trading, wage and price monopolies, and regulation that interfered with *suo moto* clearance of markets.

To sum up, in the Neoclassical and monetarist models, permanent budget deficits are 'bad' for an economy as they raise interest rates and inflation, crowd out private investment, and shift taxes to future generations. Also, there is little scope for activist fiscal and monetary policy to work to the extent that unemployment stems from microeconomic rigidities that lie outside the purview of these policies. In other words, there is no long-run trade-off between inflation and unemployment in terms of the Phillips curve. In the long run this relationship is considered as vertical in the Phillip's curve space because agents adapt to the ongoing inflation rate: 'since you can't fool all the people all the time, the true long-run Phillips curve is vertical' (Friedman, 1975, p. 28).

The Keynesian Revolution and Functional Finance

Developed in the wake of a depression that resulted in widespread unemployment across all advanced industrial economies in the 1930s, the Keynesian model differs from the Neoclassical model in two respects. First, a significant proportion of the population is construed as myopic or liquidity-constrained having a high propensity to consume out of current disposable income. Second, the starting position is one in which economic resources are considered involuntarily under-employed. Keynes in the *General Theory* (1936) saw the full employment equilibrium of classical and Neoclassical theories as far from the rule. The level of aggregate demand was subject to swings in the 'animal spirits' that drove investment, while consumers may choose to save rather than consume. In Neoclassical models, falling prices may expand real money balances and lower interest rates, but the economy may be caught in a liquidity trap in which money balances are hoarded rather than spent or invested. If prices fall enough everyone holding a dollar could be (potentially at least) a millionaire, but the process is slow to operate and, in the interim, expectations could collapse. Perhaps in 'normal' conditions, markets may adjust more rapidly, but in the circumstances of the 1930s the opposite seemed a reasonable description of reality.

Under these conditions, the merit in sticking to the classical rule of balancing the budget lost favour. Instead, it was advocated that the budget ought to be used to stimulate a level of aggregate demand consistent with full employment output using a combination of increased spending and lower taxes (although taxes were sufficiently low in the 1930s to rule this out). Such budgetary deficits would influence aggregate demand in two ways. First, government demand for goods and services would raise incomes and through the 'multiplier' effect increase household spending through the circular flow of income. Second, any decrease in taxes would directly increase disposable income stimulating consumption.

It took a while to sway the scholarly opinion in favour of activist fiscal and monetary polices (helped significantly by Alvin Hansen, 1949), but once it happened, it marked an end to the classical commitment to the principle of balanced budgets. In fact, many following in the footsteps of Keynes extended the scope of government intervention to a broader range of economic conditions than had been envisaged by Keynes. In particular, Lerner (1943) synthesized Keynesian insights with mercantilist views on government borrowing creating a doctrine of functional finance. The doctrine advocated that:

- A government should adjust its taxing and spending measures such that the aggregate demand is maintained at a level consistent

with the full employment output of the economy (without causing inflation).
- A government should borrow money or repay debt to change the proportion in which the public holds money and bonds so as to maintain interest rates at a suitable level.
- A government should print money or destroy it to conform with policies pursued via functional finance.

Lerner's (1948) views on the burden of public debt were essentially a derivative of this philosophy. Effectively, the classical analogy between the private and the public debt was abandoned and mercantilist doctrine that the debt held by the citizens of the issuing state created no burden in aggregate was resurrected. 'We owe it to ourselves', said Lerner. The same rationale was used to dismiss concerns about the burden of debt on future generations. According to Lerner (1948):

> A variant of the false analogy is the declaration that national debt puts an unfair burden on our children, who are thereby made to pay for our extravagances. Very few economists need to be reminded that if our children or grandchildren repay some of the national debt these payments will be made to our children or grandchildren and to nobody else. Taking them together they will no more be impoverished by making the repayments than they will be enriched by receiving them. (p. 300)

Of course, in an accounting sense this is true. But is it correct to 'take them together'? Those receiving the payments no doubt feel better off. But do those making the payments feel so sanguine? Here we are led back to the issue of interpersonal comparisons of utility so compellingly questioned by Lionel Robbins (see p. 97).

On the link between public debt and increase in inequality, Lerner made the value judgement that holders of debt (to whom interest is paid) are different from the payers of additional taxes (to service the debt). As a result, in his view, public debt retirement entailed adverse distributional consequences. The fact that the recipients may be widows or orphans or holders of pension funds and insurance policies seemed not to signify. Convinced that they were rich rentiers, undeserving of interest on their saving, Lerner went on to suggest that taxes could be made progressive to diminish the resulting inequality.

Finally, Lerner presented the 'new orthodoxy' (still reflected in our view, in much questionable thinking on the balance of payments) that external debt is different precisely because we don't owe it to ourselves:

> A nation owing money to other nations (or to the citizens of other nations) is impoverished or burdened in the same kind of way as a man who owes money

> to other men. . . . An external loan enables an individual or a nation to get things from others without having to give anything in return, for the time being. The borrower is enabled to consume more than he is producing. And when he repays the external debt he has to consume less than he is producing. (Lerner, 1948, p. 256).

Of course, the external borrower does not 'get things from others without having to give anything in return, for the time being'. He or she gives a promise to repay, just like a government gives to a domestic lender or like a corporation gives to a bank financing its investment expansion. The reader is referred to Iley and Lewis (2007) for an analysis of the similarities and differences.

At a theoretical level there is much to question in the Keynesian orthodoxy. There is little theoretical explanation of the microeconomics of markets and the nature of the rational-irrationalities that might lead to rigidities in the labour market. The A.W. Phillips' curve (1958) gave empirical force to an historically inverse relationship between the rate of unemployment and the rate of inflation against which it could be countenanced that activist monetary and/or fiscal policy could be employed to reach full employment at some bearable inflationary cost. However, Friedman and Phelps simultaneously argued in 1968 that the empirical relationship was an historical accident of an environment in which people were originally slow, but later reacted much faster and perhaps almost instantaneously, to bring inflation expectations into line with the actual inflationary effects of monetary policy. The argument seemed to doom activist policy. An aggregate supply curve that appeared horizontal in the short as well as the long term led even the most steadfast Keynesians to agree that at full employment (or its rational expectations equivalent), real deficits crowd out private investment and raise inflation.

However, events seem to have a way of intervening in quite unexpected ways. The *entente cordiale* between the monetarists and the dwindling ranks of the Keynesians was ruptured by the policy-makers and the ever growing population of market economists who pressure them to act. Policy-makers (and the chorus of critics who want instant answers) appear to be less enamoured of the self-regulating propensities of free markets and of the mean reversing full employment tendencies of the macro-economy than the academic theoretical macroeconomists. Precisely why this cleavage has occurred is unclear but the proximate reasons are Japan, Alan Greenspan and Ben Bernanke. Japan's lost decade of growth in the 1990s, with its economy stuck in what seemed, to most observers, a Keynesian liquidity trap, with zero nominal interest rates unable to act as a stimulus, obviously struck a chord with American policy-makers and ushered in the era of asymmetric monetary policy initiated by Alan Greenspan of 'ride the boom and cushion the bust' (Iley and Lewis, 2007, p. 59).

A useful point to start the story is the dotcom boom of the late-1990s. Global factors, by dampening inflation and boosting the terms of trade, certainly played a part and helped spur the investment and stock market boom. Where Iley and Lewis depart from this account is in recognizing that the Federal Reserve, both temperamentally and institutionally (with its mandate as it interprets it for maximum sustainable growth), was predisposed to 'ride the boom'. Indeed, judging by the expansion of liquidity after the Long-Term Capital Management (LTCM) crisis, it would seem that it gave the boom more than a helping hand.

Having ridden the boom, Fed officials perhaps then felt that they had little choice other than to cushion the bust' given the uncertainties of September 11 and their desire to put in place a 'deflation-insurance policy' against the perceived risk of a Japanese-style stagnation. Whether or not their perception of 'looking down the abyss' is tinged with some degree of self-justification is probably unimportant now. The results are there to be seen. The Federal Funds rate was lowered in a series of steps from 6.5 per cent in 2001 to 1 per cent in 2003. What can be described as the '0–1–2' pattern of policy interest rates then ushered in (0 in Japan, 1 per cent in the United States and 2 per cent in Europe) produced results that were striking. The real Federal funds rate in the United States was set below zero for the first time since the 1970s and then held there for 12 successive quarters. Monetary policy was easily the most expansionary since the policy-makers' misguided attempts to inflate the economy out of the first oil price shock in the mid-1970s – a parallel few modern policy-makers would be eager to acknowledge. Accompanying this policy stance was an associated surge in global dollar liquidity. The standard measure of global US dollar liquidity, which adds growth in the US monetary base to increases in US dollar reserves held in custody at the Federal Reserve Bank of New York, peaked at an annual growth rate of almost 21 per cent in August 2004, its most rapid rate of increase since the 1970s. In a world awash with liquidity, funds have to go somewhere, and on this reading the expansionary policy drove down US (and world) long-term interest rates (Iley and Lewis, 2007).

Another serious charge is that the Greenspan era saw a reorientation of monetary policy away from 'putting a floor under labour markets' towards 'putting a floor under financial markets' (Palley, 2005). On this view, the so-called Greenspan 'put option' has generated moral hazard, triggered over-exuberance and the mis-pricing of risk in successive asset markets and so underwritten the explosion of household debt and housing boom of 2004–6. In turn, rising asset prices and the enhanced access to credit of US households pumped up the US economy by accelerating consumption spending. The legacy, in the shape of the biggest economic imbalances in

American history (negative household savings, external deficit), underpin the 'sub-prime' crisis of 2008.

Nor can the Greenspan era be seen as an aberration. As of the end of 2008, the Federal Funds rate was again significantly negative in real terms as a consequence of the Bernanke Fed lowering the Federal Funds target rate from 5.25 per cent per annum in September 2007 by (over) 5 percentage points to an unprecedentedly low rate of between 0 and 0.25 per cent (set as a range rather than a level) and, despite an inflation rate for 2008 of 4.1 per cent, injected massive amounts of liquidity into the financial system in an attempt to stave off a US slump and shore up the balance sheets of financial institutions which have lost hundreds of billions of dollars on securitized assets. Moreover, the (outgoing) Bush administration sought to provide assistance to over-extended borrowers in much the same way that it rushed through tax cuts in 2001. How long this activist stop-go policy and cycle of easy–tight money will be perpetuated remains to be seen, but it is a very different world to that visualized in the neoclassical framework that underlies most economic analysis (as explored further in the next section). Consequently, for the moment, at least, economic theory and economic policy seem to be moving in very different universes.

Ricardian Equivalence and the Incidence of Public Debt

We now return to the question of the burden of the public debt, an issue on which Keynesian and classical views differ. The tenets of functional finance on the nature and burden of public debt have been closely examined by Buchanan (1958). Contesting the claim that public debt is different from private debt, Buchanan argues that, to reach this conclusion, the proponents focus only on one side of the balance sheet – in case of private debt, on the liability side and in case of the public debt, on the asset side. If both the asset and liability sides are considered together, the issue all boils down to whether debt-funded investment generates, at minimum, sufficient returns to service and amortize the debt. It is in this respect that Buchanan sees no difference between internal and external debt, or, public and private debt.

Buchanan draws on Adam Smith's insight that investors in government paper do not incur any sacrifice since they purchase it voluntarily. Transposing this insight into a utility-choice framework means that members of say, Generation I who purchase government bonds on their own volition, move to a higher indifference curve since their purchases increase their utility compared to investing in any other available alternative. This is quite the opposite to what happens to the utility of the members of Generation II who inherit the burden to service this liability by paying taxes. While the purchasing of government bonds is voluntary, paying part of income in taxes to service government debt previously contracted is compulsory. Since Generation II participates neither in the decision to issue debt nor in decisions as to what projects to which the proceeds are applied, its members incur a sacrifice in servicing such debt. They are literally 'bonded' into these tax payments without consent. Naturally, their utility decreases.

But, what if future generations are the children and the grandchildren of the present generation, and the latter behave altruistically towards them, that is, the utility of the current generation depends not only on its own consumption but also on the consumption of future generations extending the consumption–savings decision-making horizon for the members of Generation I practically to the infinite lives of their families (continuing in future) rather than to the finite life of their own? This is precisely the formulation explored by Barro (1974) to reach the conclusion that if a debt-funded tax cut raises income over an individual's lifetime but keeps the family's permanent income unchanged, then the individual will save rather than consume the incremental amount and leave it as a bequest for descendants. Thus government bonds enter an individual's portfolio, not as 'net wealth' but together with the corresponding (fully anticipated) tax liability in future. From this perspective, when a government runs deficits by cutting taxes and keeping spending constant, individuals will not increase their spending because their permanent family income will not have changed. Similarly, when a government increases its spending funded by deficit financing, individuals correspondingly reduce their spending leaving no effect on aggregate spending. There is no difference therefore between issuing public debt and raising taxes. Nor is there is a burden of public debt on future generations.

Barro's formulation is known as Barro–Ricardo or the Ricardian equivalence theorem due to Ricardo's analysis of the theoretical equivalence of public debt and future taxes.[3] Buchanan (1958, pp. 161–2) pre-empted and dismissed the Barro viewpoint. Elmendorf and Mankiw (1998), Brennan and Buchanan (1987), and Buiter (1990) also deal at length with the tenuous nature of the assumptions about intergenerational family permanent income underlying Barro's framework. Empirical evidence on Ricardian equivalence is inconclusive. It has not been possible categorically to reject the hypothesis because it simultaneously denies the impact of some forms of fiscal policy (temporary cuts in taxes financed by debt) while admitting others (such as anticipated permanent cuts in government purchases). Overall, evidence from the United States (and the expectations of policy-makers) are that tax cuts do increase aggregate demand (given accommodative monetary policy) although perceptions about the permanence of such cuts play some role in determining the extent to which increased income flows into consumption (Fischer and Easterly, 1990).

In contrast to the mixed response for the Ricardian equivalence theorem, the Buchanan view of the shifting of the debt burden to future generations receives support from intergenerational redistribution in basic overlapping-generations models such as that formulated by Diamond (1965). When a government (from a balanced budget position) lowers taxes without corresponding cuts in expenditure, its inter-temporal budget constraint requires that taxes be increased in future. Such an increase, however, may fall on those who are younger or not yet living enabling those living or older to consume more at the cost of the young.

Mankiw (2000) provides a middle path between the two extremes above. He argues that both the Diamond–Samuelson model of overlapping generations and the Barro–Ramsey model of infinitely-lived families contradicts one or more of the following empirical findings: (a) actual consumer spending follows more closely the current incomes of households; (b) many households do not have sufficient financial means to enable them to undertake inter-temporal consumption smoothing; and (c) the vast majority of aggregate US capital formation stems from intergenerational transfers. Obviously the bequest motive is active although only for that small part of the population that owns most wealth (the top 5 per cent hold some 60 per cent of economic and 72 per cent of financial wealth). Mankiw argues for developing a third alternative – the 'savers–spenders' model of fiscal policy – that recognizes the great heterogeneity in consumer behaviour. Essentially, the economy is visualized to be populated both by savers, whose behaviour generally conforms with the Barro–Ramsey model of infinite horizons (smoothing not only across one's own life but also across descendants) and spenders, who live from pay-cheque-to-pay-cheque consuming their entire income in every period.[4] Such a model yields the following theoretical results:

- Temporary tax changes have large effects on the demand for goods and services.
- Government debt increases steady-state inequality in income and consumption; and
- Substantial long-run crowding-out can occur if taxes are distortionary. If, however, taxes are lump sum or levied entirely on inelastically supplied labour, then government debt need not crowd out capital in the long run.

This theory retains the scope of fiscal policy to operate in the short run but ties its long-run effects to the nature of taxation regime. However, insofar as the burden of public debt is concerned, there is no escape from the result that the distribution of income and consumption is influenced to the detriment of spenders and in favour of savers.

The above literature leads to other important issues relevant for developing a normative perspective on budget deficits. First, there is the question of the conditions under which deficits funded by public loans become feasible. In the economic literature, this problem is usually tackled by asking to what uses the funds are put and emphasizing the distinction between loans for consumption and loans for investment in capital goods. From this perspective there is an associated call for capital budgeting and a more comprehensive public sector balance sheet (Wolfson, 1979, pp. 102–3; Buiter, 2001). Interestingly, although Buchanan (who we have been using as our basic point of reference) initially admitted the scope of public debt for the financing of capital goods, he later rejected this proposition in large degree because most government expenditure does not comprise capital investment, but also in part because in a democratic setting populated with self-seeking agents, political lobbyists and vested interest groups, the efficient spending of such monies for capital formation becomes a questionable proposition. This raises the question of how the dynamics of the politico-institutional framework influence the economics of deficit and debt creation. A final issue concerns the appropriate level of budget deficit and public debt. Given the significance of the last two points, we examine them separately, below.

Appropriate Level of Deficit and Public Debt[5]

If public borrowing implies postponing taxes, we are left with the question of how the problem will be dealt with in future. Only a portion of future national income can be taxed to service public debt while maintaining primary public expenditure consisting of (producing, purchasing, providing of) public goods and services, and transfers to households and businesses (for example, through income support and subsidies). To the extent that the total (primary and interest) expenditure in a single year exceeds tax revenues and seigniorage, it must be met by issuing new debt. This gives us our first identity of the one period public borrowing requirement:

$$\text{New borrowing} = \text{Primary expenditure} + \text{Interest expense} - \text{Tax} - \text{Seigniorage} \quad (6.1)$$

For simplicity, let us combine seigniorage (profits from money issue and any inflation tax) together with taxation. Also, let D be the outstanding stock of debt (that is all of short maturity) and i^* the nominal interest rate on it. Then the above equation can be rewritten as:

$$\text{New borrowing} = \text{Primary expenditure} + i * D - \text{Tax} \qquad (6.2)$$

Note, however, that an increase in debt in one period has implications for the government's budgetary policy in the subsequent periods. In particular, to service the debt, either government spending must decline in the future or taxes must increase. But public expenditure cannot be reduced to zero and taxes cannot rise forever. By implication, there is a prudent limit on the level of debt in relation to the productive capacity of the economy. What is that limit?

Obviously, as Buiter (2001) notes, the prudent level of the public debt-to-GNP ratio depends on many structural features of the economy, its international environment, and its history or the inherited initial conditions (time dependency). Among the structural features are the private saving propensity, the degree of financial development of the economy, the growth rate of productivity, a government's ability to expand the tax base, raise tax rates and compress public spending, and finally demographic developments. Clearly no one-size-fits-all figure exists. In fact, if history provides any guidance, in Britain, the debt-to-GNP ratio reached as high as 282 per cent in 1821 (after the Napoleonic wars) and 272 per cent after World War II. These, however, were extraordinary times. Under normal circumstances, the Maastricht Treaty for the EU offered a model of a ceiling on deficits of 3 per cent of GDP and on net public debt of 60 per cent of GDP for member countries, although the latter was not honoured as we saw in Table 6.1. Importantly, the debt here is not just the debt exclusive to the national government, but the combined debt of all levels of government in the nation including national, state and local authorities. Whether state and local authorities borrowing in their own name without national guarantees should be subject to global limits is handled differently in various federations (Australia, Canada, Germany, the United States and the EU). Neverthless, given the complexity of the problem, it is possible to argue that any calculated number is not sacrosanct but rather arbitrary from an economic standpoint.

Once it is accepted that in terms of economic analysis, there is no single prudent debt-to-GNP level equally applicable for all nations, the focus shifts to the so-called 'sustainability' conditions under which a given debt-to-GNP ratio can be stabilized. This calculation is more tractable but not necessarily more meaningful.[6] In a growing economy, stabilizing debt-to-GNP would mean that the level of the deficit to be financed by issuing new debt in each period should equal the existing stock of debt (*D*) multiplied by the rate of growth of nominal GNP (say, '*z*'). This gives the identity:

$$\text{New borrowing} = z * D \tag{6.3}$$

Combining (6.2) and (6.3), we get the long-run budget constraint as follows:

$$z * D = \text{Primary Expenditure} - \text{Tax} + i * D \tag{6.4}$$

$$\text{or, } (i - z) * D = \text{Tax} - \text{Primary Expenditure} \tag{6.5}$$

$$\text{or, } (r - g) * D = \text{Tax} - \text{Primary Expenditure} \tag{6.6}$$

where r and g represent real interest and economic growth rates respectively,[7] and the primary deficit (surplus) equals the excess (shortfall) of primary expenditure over tax revenue.

These equations provide some guidance on whether the current level of taxes and expenditure can be sustained in future with a specified upper level constraint on the debt-to-GNP ratio (although precisely how that figure is arrived upon remains at least problematical). With this premise, the following points are noteworthy:

- The change in the outstanding public debt is the sum of two components: borrowing to finance primary deficit and borrowing to finance nominal interest on the outstanding debt.
- If the economic growth rate exceeds the real interest rate that is, $z > i$ or $g > r$, then either taxes can be lowered relative to primary expenditure or existing debt can be refinanced with more debt (without the need for raising taxes)[8] or up to a certain level, primary deficits can be sustained, all without impairing the debt-to-GNP ratio.
- If, however, the real interest rate is greater than the growth rate of real GNP growth that is, $i > z$ or $r > g$, then taxes have to rise relative to primary expenditure. Alternatively, the debt ratio will increase even if the issuance of new debt is required only to service the outstanding debt stock. Hence, primary surpluses will be required (that is, taxes will have to rise relative to primary expenditure) to service the debt and stabilize the ratio. Otherwise, interest rate risk premia may increase and at some point it may become impossible for the government to sell more debt.

Such analysis shifts our focus to the conditions under which the level of real interest rates could remain below the rate of economic growth. On this issue, Fischer and Easterly (1990) contend:

> There are some who believe that the real interest rate should normally be below the growth rate, and that this eventual return to normality will provide an escape from the debt crisis. But an economist's instincts, rightly, are that such a free lunch is not possible. Real interest rates can be temporarily below the growth rate and could be below the growth rate for a long time in a rapidly growing economy – this is part of the virtuous circle of growth. But market forces tend to prevent the real interest rate from remaining below the real growth rate permanently. As more debt piles up, the pressure on bond markets drives up the interest rate and growth declines. If a rapidly growing economy attempts to exploit the apparently favorable debt dynamics by borrowing excessively, the growth rate will eventually fall below the real interest rate. At the level of the world economy, the normal situation should be thought of as one in which the real interest rate exceeds the growth rate. (p. 136)

Macklem (1994/95) adds:

> Taking a longer view, it is clear that periods in which growth has exceeded the real interest rate are the exception. . . . There is . . . an economic argument for the real interest rate to exceed the growth rate of real output in the long run. If the real interest rate were below the growth rate of the economy, then firms and households could borrow, pay the interest on their debt with the additions to output stemming from growth, and still have a surplus left over. In such circumstances, everyone would want to borrow, in which case the demand for loans would exceed the supply, putting upward pressure on the real interest rate. The rise in real interest rate would encourage individuals to save while discouraging borrowing, thereby balancing the demand and supply of loans. Market forces will tend to push the real interest rate above the growth rate of real GDP if households prefer current consumption to future consumption on average, since lenders will have to be compensated for deferring their consumption to the future. These considerations suggest that a prudent assumption on which to base fiscal policy is that the real interest rate will exceed the real growth rate over the long term. (p. 4)[9]

The message seems clear. There are risks that interest-based financing of government activities may ultimately turn out badly, as there is real danger that interest costs in the long run may exceed the economic growth rate resulting from additional investment.

This brings us to a related issue. It is generally the case that governments can borrow at less than diversified private institutions (from a general equilibrium perspective, at a rate less than the marginal productivity of capital (r)). Does this represent a genuine social saving? Wagner (1987) considers that the answer depends on whether the government enterprises in which the borrowed funds are invested can surpass the economic constraints – the inherent uncertainty in investment – that apply to other private firms in an economy. Given that the public sector does not work under the same incentive structure as does the private sector, it is not misleading to suggest that government is a rather more costly and riskier enterprise. In this case, the idea that the lower government borrowing rate represents opportunities for social gain is ruled out. Instead, the rationale for a spread between the private and public borrowing rates is found in the limited liability of the former and the unlimited liability of the latter which covers up higher cost and riskiness through present and future taxation.

On such grounds, a number of writers consider that the 'lower government borrowing cost' argument is seriously flawed (Kay, 1993; Gilibert and Steinherr, 1994; Grout, 1997; Klein, 1997; Grimsey and Lewis, 2004). Both Grout and Klein adopt a position that in some ways is analogous to the famous Modigliani–Miller theorem about the cost of capital. Modigliani and Miller (1958, 1963) argued that the 'true' value of a firm is governed by the risk characteristics of the underlying stream of returns, and (in the no tax regime case) is independent of how finance is raised. Somewhat similarly, Grout and also Klein argue that what is important is the 'true' risk of the project, which is independent of whether the public sector or the private sector provides the funding. What differs is that the private finance explicitly builds the risk into the cost of funds. By contrast, the public sector masks the risk because the government can fund the project at a risk-free rate independent of the actual risk position.

Why, then, can the government generally borrow at such favourable terms? The answer would seem to be that for private debt there is a risk of default, whereas for government debt there is little or none (at least in the case of governments of most developed countries) because the government can raise the taxes to meet the obligation. The government is risk-free in the eyes of the investor lending funds because the risk is transferred to the taxpayers, who bear the cost through the risk of higher future tax payments and different consumption outcomes. In Klein's words, taxpayers have assumed a contingent liability for which they are not remunerated. They become, in effect, shadow equity providers. This residual risk imposed on taxpayers is a cost, which ought to enter into any true economic analysis. If this were done, the real cost of government borrowing would be the same as the private sector if the underlying risk of the projects were the same. After all, taken to its limit, the lower government borrowing cost argument would seem to imply that all activities should be undertaken by government as the cost of capital is so low. Were this to happen, would the debt then still be regarded as riskless? Clearly not. For sovereign risk to be downplayed, there is the implicit assumption that the government sector stays within reasonable bounds and good public governance rules.

Pulling the threads together, the equations in this section provide useful insights on the long-run (steady-state) dynamics of public debt and its relationship with economic growth, taxes, and expenditure on the one hand and government's cost of borrowing on the other hand. Overall, we reach the conclusion that it appears doubtful that governments, through fixed-interest borrowing and investment, can boost economic growth on a sustained basis. Somewhere, the limit is reached as real interest rates rise beyond the real growth rates and taxes have to rise relative to public expenditure to finance public debt.

Deficits, Debt and Public Choice

Turning now to more normative aspects, the substantial literature on budget deficits covers a wide gamut. In the words of Bernheim (1989), from among the three prevalent schools of thought on budget deficits, one can justify any conceivable normative position, that is, whether the deficits are good, bad, or irrelevant. It all depends on one's choice of a paradigm. Yet if deficits can have either positive or negative economic consequences (and are perceived by the markets as such), then the management of economic policy cannot be assumed away. Budgets are the outcome of a political process but that hardly surfaces in the Keynesian analysis. At best, underlying this analysis is the presumption that politicians are dedicated to serve the public interest and they and the administration have no motives of their own in manipulating the state institutional structures and decision-making for personal gains. Allan Meltzer (1988) called this the 'goodwill' or 'benevolent dictator' theory of government which was dominant in the early post-war years.

In reality, politicians represent an electoral constituency, aligning closely with its economic interests, and working through democratic decision-making process to secure these interests so that their chances of re-election are improved. When this understanding of political behaviour – akin to the behaviour of rational self-interested economic agents – is brought to bear on the public expenditure decision-making process, then three asymmetries emerge. First, democracies tend to favour decisions that deliver benefits to small groups (special interest groups) with costs spread over a large number of taxpayers, each bearing a small portion. The converse of this rule is that since the cost of cutting government spending falls on a small number of beneficiaries while society as a whole benefits, it is the former who have the incentive to form pressure groups and deter cost-cutting. Second, democracies tend to favour decisions entailing visible (headline-creating) benefits and invisible costs. The former coalesce the beneficiaries while the latter neutralizes the opponents. Third, there is a tendency to favour decisions producing immediate gains, the cost of which is paid in the distant future. Budget deficits and public debt provide opportunity for the realization of these tendencies. Deficits spread costs over a large number of taxpayers, hide the costs from those who bear it, and create an impression of producing immediate benefits at the expense of consequences (rising taxes, lower private capital formation, increased trade deficits) in the future. It is not surprising therefore that as Bennett and DiLorenzo (1984) argue, 'Debt is a politician's delight' (p. 219). It provides an opportunity to redistribute income from future (possibly unborn) generations to the current electorate.

Similar insights emerge while analysing the debt problems of developing countries in the larger context of international political economy. These countries succumbed to the Keynesian model of debt financed government expenditure in the 1950s and 1960s under the impression that internal debt and monetary finance provided the required resources for economic development through forced savings. At the same time, the external debt alleviated constraints on domestic resources and provided expanded opportunities for investment and faster development. These high hopes, however, rarely materialized. A number of reasons can be offered. It is useful to focus first on the era of central planning that marked the 1960s and 1970s, and then on some current issues.

In the years of experimentation with central planning, many issues arose. First, foreign loans became a tool for promoting the foreign policy objectives of donor countries in the cold war context. Second, a significant amount of loans was 'tied aid', that is, tied to purchasing goods only from the donor countries and forbidding shopping for less expensive or most appropriate equipment. Third, consistent with central planning, the aid favoured big capital intensive projects, for example ports, dams, and roads at the cost of rural development. Fourth, the demise of the Bretton Woods fixed exchange rate system in 1973 resulted in the heavy depreciation of many developing countries' exchange rates impairing capacity to service loans denominated in a foreign currency. Fifth, the response of the industrialized world to the second oil price cycle of 1979/80 had two main consequences: world trade actually declined in 1982 after expanding steadily for nearly three decades, hurting exports from developing countries; and anti-inflationary monetary policy raised LIBOR and the borrowing costs of developing country debtors (Lewis and Davis, 1987, Chapter 10). Sixth, corruption and economic mismanagement of borrowed funds by developing nations detracted from them obtaining the full benefit from loans. Seventh, as many developing countries began to compete in exporting more or less similar products, commodity prices fell. Eighth, capital flight worsened the plight of developing nations. Substantial amounts of funds 'flew' back to the banking system in the industrialized countries harming the capacity of debtor nations to repay interest and principal amounts. Prominent owners of offshore funds were the rank and file of the political elite of developing countries, and few questions were asked as to the legitimacy of such wealth by members of the financial or the political system of the developed world. Ninth, the many financial crises that have since resulted from this poor ability of developing countries to service their debts have almost invariably ended up in these nations abdicating their economic and fiscal freedom to international institutions such as World Bank and IMF. In particular, through a coordinated effort on political, educational and training fronts, these institutions have successfully installed technocrats in the economic ministries of many developing countries who share much of the ideology and outlook of these organizations – not necessarily a bad thing in terms of earlier corruption and economic mismanagement. As a result, while both the North and South shared in the follies and failures of the developing country debt experiment, the burden of debt has fallen exclusively on developing countries (Lairson and Skidmore, 1993). This situation was quite different to the nineteenth century when the cost fell on British depositors who had funds in failed Australian banks or upon those who invested equity and bought bonds issued by North and South American railway companies when those ventures collapsed.[10]

A public choice analysis of the preceding points could focus on many aspects. First, debt did indeed prove to be 'a politician's delight'. For future generations (including the present current generations), however, it is proving a burden, especially since the earlier loans were not necessarily spent on productivity enhancing investment. Second, returns often failed to match either expectations or the interest financing costs. Third, tied aid frequently did not meet the 'economic feasibility' test from the recipient's perspective. Fourth, with loans linked to cold war politics, developmental aims and accountability suffered.

Not surprisingly, creditors build their case for the continuing enforcement and legitimacy of their claims exclusively on the first explanation above, that is, bad governance (especially given the amounts wasted on military expenditure), while borrowers emphasize the second, third, and fourth points when seeking remission of such claims and a fresh start. Lindert (1991), for instance, sees default on sovereign debt as primarily a property rights problem. If developed countries could have, within their reach, sufficient developing country assets to seize, incentive for default could be mitigated. On the other hand, Versi (1998) appeals for mercy in the following words:

> Every baby born in the developing world owes $485. What chance do future generations have of ever clearing such mountains of debt? What chance do they have of being able to live off the entire fruits of their own sweat without having to give most of it away to the perpetually extended palm of the moneylender? . . . All the pleading from the developing world has fallen on deaf ears.

> Arguments that the debts were contracted by earlier, despotic regimes are ignored; evidence that bad advice by the Bretton Woods organisations has led to the debts is produced to no avail; proof that loans were given without due responsibility similarly fails to impact. . . . There is no mercy in the heart of the men who deal with money. (p. 7)

To some analysts, (for example, Toussaint (1999) and Rowbotham (2000)), the above outcomes are not surprising. History is replete with instances where, in the broader international struggle for power and wealth, external public debt has been used as a convenient tool to seize fiscal and political control and create dependency in lands where an otherwise overt political control is not possible. Historically speaking, Benjamin Friedman (1989, p. 13) may be right in saying that 'World power and influence have historically accrued to creditor countries'. Nonetheless, his observation sits uneasily with the obvious present-day fact that the world's greatest economic power, the United States, is the world's largest debtor, absorbing 80 per cent of world saving that crosses borders (Iley and Lewis, 2007).[11]

So much for the past and the ramifications of the central planning/Keynesian heritage. What of the present? Rather than try to span the range of developing and newly industralizing countries, along with transition countries of Eastern and South Eastern Europe, Central Asia, China and Vietnam, we focus again on a sample somewhat more representative of this volume, namely the 24 Middle East and North Africa (MENA) countries. An assessment of their performance in *Finance and Development* called 'Unfulfilled promise' (Abed, 2003) and 'Failed legacies' (Bennett, 2003), while recognizing the wide gap between richest (Qatar with GDP per capita of $27,900) and poorest (Djibouti, $350 per capita GDP), nevertheless identified some common cultural and social challenges that have stunted their economic progress. These are:

- *Poor integration with the world economy* FDI is on average two-thirds less than might be expected for developing countries of equivalent economic size. Tariff and non-tariff barriers remain high.
- *Delayed political reforms* Failure to develop democratic institutions is seen to be a major obstacle to economic reform. According to the *Arab Human Development Report*, published by the United Nations, the region lags badly in gender equality and political and civil freedoms.
- *Bureaucracies* The region is marked by 'bloated' bureaucracies, narrow tax bases and expensive subsidies. State-owned enterprises have a dominant economic role, acing as employers of last resort, inflating public payrolls and wage bills.

- *Underdeveloped financial markets* Financial markets are adjudged to be shallow and fragmented, with outdated regulatory systems and too many state-owned banks. Banks are poorly linked to international markets, and exchange rates are controlled and inflexible.
- *Population growth* Due to Islamic views on contraception, the population growth of the MENA region is one of the fastest in the world. Jobs have not kept pace, producing what is described as a 'bleak job picture' fuelling social tensions.
- *Education* There is thought to be an imbalance in the provision of education between urban and rural areas, and inadequate preparation of students to meet the requirements of modern market systems. Overall, there is considered to be an overemphasis on tertiary education and an oversupply of university graduates, with the large proportion of graduates with degrees in human and social sciences symptomatic of a skill mismatch.

Nevertheless, some 'ghosts' of the central planning era have escaped. As noted in Chapter 5, budget deficits in the MENA countries have declined significantly. Accompanying this revised fiscal situation has been lower inflation, smaller balance of payments deficits and faster economic growth. Rising world commodity prices (notably for oil) have reinforced these trends, and for the GCC countries have turned fiscal deficits into surpluses.

At the same time, however, not all old problems have gone away. As noted earlier, the MENA region has been slow to introduce openness into public governance and report fiscal data in a transparent way. This is at variance with the historical Islamic stance on such matters, as explored in Chapter 8. Another perennial issue is corruption, encouraged in no small part by the opulent living standards of the ruling families and political elites, whose behaviour contrasts sharply with the example set by the Prophet and the early Caliphate. Chapter 9 explores the corruption and governance link.

For the present, however, we stay with budget deficits and government borrowing, turning first to the Islamic position on budget deficits.

ISLAMIC POSITION ON BUDGET DEFICITS

Drawing on the methodology developed in Chapter 2 and the standard economic theory of budget deficits given above, it seems to us that the Islamic perspective on budget deficits should constitute at least three building blocks. The first is a clear and deep understanding of the basic principles and precedents of Islam that have a bearing on the deficit question. Second, Islamic principles need to be synthesized with the research on the economic consequences of deficits if the nature and scope of budget deficits in Islam is to be appreciated. Third, attention needs to be given to the political economy ramifications of budget deficits. With these components in place, one can hopefully integrate and develop them into a composite Islamic view on budget deficits. This is the agenda that we tackle below, one by one.

Principles and Precedents

Readers will now be familiar with the fact that, in Islam, the Holy Qur'an and *sunnah* constitute the two primary sources from which to seek normative guidance on all matters. In keeping with that methodological framework, we extract below some basic principles and precedents in Islam that have a bearing on the issue of budget deficits.

Islamic democracy

In Islam, *shari'ah* defines limits to popular sovereignty or governmental authority of any kind (including its fiscal authority) (Bahlul, 2000). The special role of government leadership is to implement a blueprint of justice as elucidated in Chapters 2 and 3.

Islamic norms of governance

Justice requires that government does not burden the general public for the provision of goods the benefits of which accrue only to a select group of people (Tahir *et al.* 1999). Naturally, *zakah* transfers to the needy are an exception to the rule. Justice also demands that public offices be construed as a trust. Accordingly embezzlement or the corruption of public funds is severely reprimanded. Wastage of resources (in particular, pomp and show by government officials funded by citizens' monies) is similarly censured (see Chapters 3 and 9).

Islamic modes of transaction

For trade and commerce, interest, that is any stipulated excess (increase) on the principal amount in money lending is prohibited (2:274–79; 3:130; 4:161; 30:39). The ideal replacement for interest-based loans is interest-free loans (*qard hasan*) for a charitable cause (2:245; 57:11; 64:17; 73:20), and profit-and-loss sharing arrangements for commercial purposes (*sunnah*). Buying and selling and commodity trading are considered different in essence from money lending (2:275; 4:29). Although the determination of price in this activity is left to the mutual agreement of the buyer and seller, there is a difference of opinion on whether deferred payment sales agreed at a price higher than spot, are permitted. Contemporary Islamic banking legitimizes such activity but there is at least some evidence that scholars of Mawdudi's (2002, p. 251) stature considered such differential pricing to be doubtful, at minimum.

Fiscal precedents set by the Prophet (pbuh)

In terms of precedents, Muhammad (pbuh) borrowed in both cash and kind in his capacity as the leader of Muslim community for emergency needs and public purposes. At times, such borrowing was undertaken to repay maturing loans. The main purpose of borrowing was to fulfil the basic needs (livelihood) of those who sought help from Muhammad (pbuh) as well as to strengthen defence against aggression. There was no coercion involved in such borrowings. The borrowing was undertaken on an interest-free basis and there was no instance of repudiation of borrowing. Debts incurred were always repaid. Also, Muhammad (pbuh) left no outstanding borrowings at the time of his death. There is also no indication that any of the borrowings that he undertook as the head of the Muslim community adversely influenced the political struggle of the community to live life in accordance with its conscience.

Fiscal precedents of early Caliphs

In view of the substantial improvement in public finances subsequent to Muhammad (pbuh), there is no evidence of borrowing during the reign of the four rightly-guided Caliphs (Siddiqi, 1996, pp. 77–96). Perhaps for this reason the early Islamic writers on public finance such as Abu Yusuf and Abu Ubayd al-Qasim bin Sallam (774–838 CE) are silent on this issue (Islahi, 2005). The earliest writers to talk about borrowing by the state were Abu Yala al-Farra (990–1066 CE) and al-Mawardi (974–1058 CE) who saw it as a last resort in very rare circumstances. Their reasons seem to revolve around apprehension that the authorities may either fail to repay the loans or resort to extra taxation to do so (the burden of debt argument). Nevertheless, public borrowing was seen as permissible should regular income or payments to the *bayt al-mal* be temporarily delayed (Islahi, 2005). In this way the Prophet's 'urgent needs' motive was upheld. Because the *bayt al-mal* did not operate as a central bank, there was no concept of deficit financing by money creation, as can occur in the present era.

Contemporary practice

Despite these seemingly clear rules, contemporary *shari'ah* scholars have proven adept at using *ijtihad* to come up with certain asset-based debt to finance public expenditure based on trading, leasing and partnership instruments. While it is not easy to provide outright support or condemnation of many of these instruments by direct reference to the Holy Qur'an or *sunnah*, there can be no doubt that their innovation and use has revolutionized Islamic finance generally and the financing of public expenditures, in particular.

Has Islamic finance at last found a solution to the problem of *riba* in the financing of public sector deficits by the issue of government bonds (a practice that was almost universally condemned only ten years ago)? This is an issue that we take up in the next chapter.

In the meantime, it can be safely inferred, although with some important qualifications noted from the historical heritage, that budget deficits are permitted in Islam subject to a prohibition upon fixed-interest debt. The question at issue that we have deferred to later is the legitimacy in terms of *shari'ah* of the means used in recent innovations to circumvent the prohibition while allowing Islamic bonds to be issued on a regular basis.

That leaves the question of the nature and scope of budget deficits.

Nature and Scope of Budget Deficits under Islam

The ban on fixed interest debt leaves four alternatives in terms of financing budget deficits: zero rate debt, profit and loss sharing arrangements, asset-based debt instruments evolved through *ijtihad*, and monetary finance. How would the introduction of such instruments change the economic impact of budget deficits? We begin with the simplest case of zero rate debt and rework in Table 6.2 the example on equivalence between debt and taxes quoted in Ricardo (1888).[12]

Even though conceived as a thought experiment, this example illustrates how the burden of debt defined in terms of equivalent taxes to service the debt reduces drastically as the interest charge moves closer to zero. Even so, the question of intergenerational inequity caused by debt is not

Table 6.2 Ricardo's comparison of debt and taxes

David Ricardo in Funding System	Equivalent amounts given discount rate equals zero
'In a point of economy, there is no real difference in either of the modes; for 20 millions in one payment, 1 million per annum forever, or 1,200,000, for 45 years, are precisely of the same values . . .'	In a point of economy, there is no real difference in either of the modes; for 20 millions in one payment, a negligible amount per annum forever, or 444,444, for 45 years, are precisely of the same values.

completely resolved. In this respect, an Islamic stance can be discovered from many complementary principles and precedents. For instance, in Chapters 2 and 5, we elaborated the *shari'ah* concepts of trusteeship and guardianship. In Chapter 3, we described Ghazali and Shatibi's list of the objectives of *shari'ah* that lie in protecting religion, life, freedom of conscience, family and property. To these concepts, we can add the standard of duty and care specified in *shari'ah* in terms of an orphan's property. The appeal to an orphan, while emotive, has some resonance since at the political decision-making level, the constituency of future generations does not receive the attention that it deserves. By *qiyas* (analogy), it can be said that the property of future generations in relation to the current operations of government can be considered akin to an orphan's property in relation to the guardian or trustee of that property. On this point, the relevant injunction from the Holy Qur'an is clear:

> Come not nigh to the orphan's property except to improve it until he attains the age of full strength; and fulfil (every) engagement for (every) engagement will be enquired into (on the Day of Reckoning). (Al-Isrāa, 17:34)

> To orphans restore their property (when they reach their age) nor substitute (your) worthless things for (their) good ones; and devour not their substance (by mixing it up) with your own. For this is indeed a great sin. (Al-Nisāa, 4:2)

> Make trial of orphans until they reach the age of marriage; if then ye find sound judgment in them release their property to them; but consume it not wastefully nor in haste against their growing up. If the guardian is well-off let him claim no remuneration but if he is poor let him have for himself what is just and reasonable. When ye release their property to them take witnesses in their presence: but all-sufficient is Allah in taking account. (Al-Nisāa, 4:6)

> Those who unjustly eat up the property of orphans eat up a fire into their own bodies: they will soon be enduring a blazing fire!' (Al-Nisāa, 4:11)

As ordained, the prime task of a trustee is to improve an orphan's property not detract from it. Only in case of dire need is the trustee allowed to take even remuneration from the trust. What are the equivalent circumstances of dire need in case of a government?

If we recall the precedents of borrowing in the time of the Prophet Muhammad (pbuh) mentioned above, Ghazali and Shatibi's list of the objectives of *shari'ah* proves apposite. Muhammad (pbuh) borrowed to assist the poor or to defend against aggression; in brief, to protect religion, life, and freedom of conscience. In such action, too, the principle of interest-free finance was never compromised! Herein lies the *shari'ah* scope for using public borrowing.

Notably, the verses quoted above call not merely for retention but for an improvement in the orphan's property. To the extent that this obligation means improving living standards through investment in utilities and infrastructure, as Lewis and Algaoud (2001, p. 100) contend, this end could be achieved by activating PLS method through a variety of operational modes. However, insofar as improvement through the route of deficit finance is concerned, the answer lies in reflecting on the history of Third World debt mentioned above, if not that of the role (or abuse) of sovereign debt in general in the history of mankind. It comes as no surprise therefore in the precedents of the classical Caliphate, in whose time a broad tax system had become established, that we find no instance of borrowing. This is irrespective of the fact that Umar bin Khattab wished to build long-distance roads in compliance with Muhammad's (pbuh) developmental vision narrated in *Bukhari*, namely that the day is not far when a woman shall travel from Hirah (in Iraq) to Makkah – a distance of more than 1500 km – fearing none but Allah. It can safely be presumed that Umar was depending on taxes. We are encouraged in reaching this conclusion from the fact that many dams, canals and roads were completed during the early Caliphate without need of debt financing.

Another implication of borrowing through interest-free debt is revealed by recalling our earlier analysis of the conditions for the sustainability of public debt, namely

$$(r - g) * D = \text{Tax} - \text{primary expenditure} \qquad (6.6a)$$

In the long run, the real interest rate might be expected to exceed the real economic growth rate. Debt once contracted will go on compounding at a rate higher than the growth rate, increasing the debt-to-GNP ratio unless a primary surplus is produced, that is, taxes are increased relative to expenditure to pay periodic interest or redeem the debt. In the case of interest free debt, $r = 0$. This implies, assuming a growing economy, that the debt ratio will contract if there is no primary deficit. In other words, there is some margin to create additional primary deficit without jeopardizing the debt-to-GNP ratio. Borrowing to pay existing borrowing therefore does not become a Ponzi scheme.

This observation leads us to the second classical Islamic instrument which is the profit and loss sharing arrangement. Leaving the complexities of how to use this instrument for deficit finance aside, at the level of a given project, if r is considered as profit-and-loss sharing (PLS) ratio, and g is considered as the overall return on the project, then r is always going to be a fraction of g making the left-hand side of equation (6.6), a negative value. If the entire budget deficit is funded in this manner, the general result obtained in the case of interest-free borrowing holds, that is, assuming a growing economy, the debt ratio will contract if there is no primary deficit. Alternatively, taxes can fall relative to expenditure to maintain a stable debt-to-GNP ratio or there will be some margin to create additional PLS funded primary deficit without jeopardizing the debt to GNP ratio.

We now analyse a surrogate asset-based *ijtihadi* financing instrument based on say, a buy-and-sell transaction. If, as is typical nowadays, such an instrument prices off a Treasury yield curve, then the implicit fixed rate (say r) that it incorporates (as the difference between buying and selling price) is no different from the corresponding fixed interest rate. Certainly, once settled, r will not change (if late payment penalties are excluded from consideration) but there is no protection that in the long run it will be a fraction of g. In particular, r may be more than g, less than g, or even vary over the economic cycle, resembling in this essential respect with the prevailing fixed interest government instruments. This correspondence is even closer in the case of *sukuk*, considered in the next chapter.

Finally, let us explore a possible Islamic stance on monetary finance. A strict Islamic interpretation on money would be not to allow its debasement, that is, target a zero monetary inflation regime permitting a rate of change in money supply only to match with the demand for money. This derivation comes implicitly via analogy (*qiyas*) from the general prohibition in the Holy Qur'an (7:85; 11:85; 83:1–4) of corrupting the standards of weights and measures. A more permissive stance, drawing on the views on taxation, would allow monetary base finance as long as the needy are compensated. However, given the arbitrariness of an inflation tax as well as the absence of transparency in this mode of operation (that is, what Greenspan (1966) refers to as hidden confiscation of wealth), we consider the former interpretation as more consistent with Islamic notions. This position does not necessarily rule out the use of monetary finance under circumstances of depression when the immediate inflationary cost is low. Within the parameters of the prevailing fractional reserve system, one can find a similar proposal floated in literature – sometimes called the sovereign proposal – which aims to shift the 'monetary grant' from private banks to the public purse for a rule-based financing of specific desirable public infrastructure projects. Since private banks have no intrinsic right to benefit from this grant in the first place,[13] we see no contravention of rules of justice in this activity, as long as the strict (non-inflationary) framework for regulating it is maintained. This conclusion links up with the opinion of Tahir *et al.* (1999) who permit monetary finance on the following conditions: (a) exhaustion of all other means of revenue on legitimate expenditure; (b) unsatisfied and pressing needs of a public good nature (that is, to assist the poor, defence, debt servicing); and (c) stability of money and keeping inflation within acceptable limits.

Summing up, there is inherent in the classical Islamic preference for zero rate loans and PLS contracts, an element of economic sustainability – potential to withstand cyclical ebbs and flows of economy – that neither the interest-based loans nor the buy-and-sell based *ijtihadi* alternatives offer. Let us now explore the potential of these instruments in the context of the public choice theory surveyed earlier.

Protection against Political Irresponsibility

Once we abandon the 'benevolent dictator' view of government, the political decision-making process has some well-known deficiencies: it favours special interest groups at the cost of the general public; it supports decisions with visible benefits but less visible costs; and is biased towards immediate gains, the cost of which is shifted to the distant future. Fixed-interest debt borrowings might be seen to play a special role in reinforcing these tendencies since they permit large amounts of spending to occur immediately (during the politician's current term of office) with the problems associated with repayment spread over a long period in the future (more likely when someone else is in office to deal with the costs). There is the temptation to redistribute wealth from future generations to the current generation. A question arises: how do the Islamic alternatives for deficit finance reinforce or curb such tendencies?

Insofar as zero rate advances to government are concerned, Siddiqi's (1996) comments are pertinent:

> Since the lender receives no worldly return, public borrowing presumes the lender being motivated by moral and religious considerations. Projects directly related to jihad, those directed at feeding, clothing and housing the poor and providing medical care to those who cannot buy the same, as well as educational and moral-spiritual orientation programmes are most likely to motivate people to give *qard hasan* (free of interest loan). The social authority should, therefore, make public borrowing specific and select purposes most likely to motivate lenders, in order to succeed in mobilizing interest-free loans to the government. (p. 94)

Of course, there has to be an underlying trust that the government will apply the proceeds most efficiently for such causes. That in-built requirement *per se* appears to be a sufficient deterrent not only against the public choice concerns but also against the possibility of raising (large amounts of) monies that bear a meaningful relationship to GNP. It is also conceivable that people will be more willing to advance interest-free loans to charities than to government. In this case, Siddiqi's elucidation of the role of the voluntary sector in Islam becomes more pertinent. In spite of these limitations, it is possible that zero rate loans have a wider validity than is presently conceived. Their application in the case of intra-government transactions is clearly possible. But more importantly, it can be argued that varying amounts of (tax funded) government sponsored zero rate loans can be used as part of an incentive package to attract large private investment into social infrastructure such that the pecuniary return on such investment does not fall below a certain floor rate of return (for some period). The amount of the loans can be adjusted so that the anticipated rate of return to the private sector has a meaningful relationship to the estimated risk and social rate of return on the project. To protect against public choice issues, an upper limit on such subsidies ought to be specified at the time of project approval.

When it comes to PLS contracts, in any case, there is an implicit assumption that the private sector's invitation to participate with the government in infrastructure is on a profit-and-loss sharing basis. This condition again incorporates a very high level of protection against the public choice concerns. A PLS participant is due a stipulated share in profits contingent only upon a project's success. No private contractor will enter such an arrangement unless, in his subjective assessment, the project will yield a reasonable return on investment. If, however, the project fails, a PLS partner has no lien on future taxes, no leverage to seize fiscal flexibility of a nation and no avenue to forfeit political independence. It is a partnership taken in good faith by both parties and results in either win–win or lose–lose. There is no intermediate outcome to give one party leverage over the other. This is as much applicable to internal investments as to external investments. In case of the latter, the benefits of foreign direct investment over debt are substantial. As Lairson and Skidmore (1993) contend:

> As for direct foreign investment, the physical assets transferred to a host country . . . are unlikely to be dismantled and removed. Direct foreign investment often produces a transfer of skills and technology as well. While stream of profits from the investment may leave the country, this will occur only so long as the investment is productive and generating output, wages, and tax payments locally. If the investment goes sour, the outward flow of profits ceases and costs of coping with a bad business decision are shared between the multinational and the host nation. (p. 285)

Of course, it can be argued that the PLS method also has some limitations. First, it creates moral hazard problems. Given that venture capital and equity modes of finance are not uncommon in real practice, however, an overemphasis on such problems is misplaced. They can be overcome through incentive structures and institutional means. Second, PLS typically is suited for production and delivery of goods that are closer to the private end of the private–public goods dichotomy. It is also applicable where the user-pays principle is intrinsically feasible or made feasible through regulation. For cases where the social return is expected to be high but pecuniary returns low, pure PLS may become inapplicable although, as we said before, a combination of regulation and/or zero rate financing and/or subsidies can possibly be worked out.

This brings us to the question of financing a range of quasi-public goods where social returns may be very high but pecuniary returns or returns that can be captured through taxation or user-pay principles are below the hurdle rate. Pure PLS and its intrinsic protection against waste does not work in this case because feasibility is driven not by pecuniary returns but by social returns. Here, *ijtihadi* instruments offer a way out. Contrary to interest-based debt that can be used to finance consumption, the *ijtihadi* instruments are linked strictly to asset financing and in this respect are a definite improvement over fixed-interest debt. Nevertheless, given that the choice of project in which to invest resides with the government, that is, the outcome of a political decision, there is no guarantee that inefficient public investment will not be undertaken. Seen from another angle, financiers are not motivated to finance such projects because, in their subjective assessment, the expected pecuniary return on a given project as a whole is above their hurdle rate but rather because the government is prepared to compensate them above the hurdle rate whatever the pecuniary and social returns.[14] All public choice concerns listed in the first part of this chapter therefore remain. Some would say that these issues are doubly reinforced by buy-now-pay-later kind of propositions embodied in *ijtihadi* instruments. The search to minimize such concerns brings us back to the solutions offered by the public choice literature, that is, enactment of constitutional rules for fiscal responsibility. This conclusion is reached also through another route. If we assume that all capital public expenditure is undertaken in projects that are feasible on an expected pecuniary return basis, it is a substantial challenge even then to run such projects funded entirely through debt even though many project-financed vehicles are highly geared. Certainly, a profit-oriented private corporation funded entirely by debt would be considered a highly risky proposition, and this has been amply demonstrated in the fallout in 2008 from the sub-prime crisis. The need to set an upper constitutional limit on state assumed debt – contracted through whichever transactional arrangement – in relation to the productive capacity of the economy therefore becomes self-evident.

To sum up, in the principle of the prohibition of fixed interest debt, there is an inbuilt protection against political irresponsibility. By mitigating the use of fixed interest debt, Islam closes doors to two kinds of exploitation. The first occurs when the natural risk of investment failure is shifted entirely to the borrower. The second comes about if a coalition of the wealthy and the politically powerful not only can avoid being taxed in the present in accordance with their ability-to-pay but can also, through profligacy and fiscal illusion, burden future generations of those who pay taxes. The fact that fixed-interest debt has assumed greater significance in recent years poses important issues in terms of Islamic principles.

A Composite Position on Budget Deficits

Now that we have discussed the different aspects of the Islamic position on budget deficits and its implications, we pull the threads together and attempt to arrive at a composite Islamic perspective on the issue. The ban on fixed interest lies at the core of the Islamic stance. It offers protection against many ills described above – extravagance, large governments, fiscal illusion, disregard of public opinion and seizure of political and fiscal flexibility. The solution to the finance of deficits instead is found, on the one hand, in encouraging zero rate loans that test the inner moral strength and whether an individual really is prepared to help fellow beings in need. On the other hand, there is the permission of PLS arrangements which pave the way to harness self-interest in the task of general economic development. PLS allows only those projects which private investors consider, in their subjective assessment, as profitable.[15] Implicit in these two forms of financing are the activities at two extremes that a government would like to undertake but cannot, due to insufficient taxes. Governments need funds either for social support in which case they ought to tax, receive donations or borrow at zero rate or if they cannot do better than the market and through PLS, they ought to impose that constraint upon themselves. Since there is no precedent of government engaging in any other form of borrowing in the classical Islamic era, there is no trap in which to fall. If the precedents are strictly followed then anything that lies between zero rate loans and PLS is to be funded through taxes, managed by government by in-kind community participation in tasks of common interest, or undertaken by the voluntary sector.

It can be argued that while such a purist perspective is admirable, certain realities have to be recognized:

- Gone are the days when people used to lend monies at zero rates;
- The entire financial system is based on fixed interest lending;
- Governments have put themselves into a situation where a significant portion of their tax take-up goes to servicing past loans; and

- There are projects of the kind and size for which government involvement becomes unavoidable.

In the face of such pressures, contemporary Muslim jurists have focused their efforts on coming up with innovative interest-free debt financing modes and others that have the appearance of being interest-free in name only. While the former seem more 'Islamic' (in binding finance directly rather than more cosmetically with capital assets), there is still no protection in them against inefficient investment or public choice issues. That shortcoming can be addressed directly by constitutional or rule-based solutions that limit debt from exceeding a country's ability-to-pay.

Note, however, that the focus on designing debt instruments that 'conform' to *shari'ah* offers only one solution. A more permanent solution lies in creating conditions so as to mobilize private investment in industry and infrastructure. Large private investments in infrastructure, at times on a PLS basis, have been made in developed countries. There is no reason why this cannot be done in developing countries. Indeed, there is a well developed literature on project finance geared especially for Islamic countries in a *shari'ah*-compliant way (McMillen, 2007). The biggest impediment to such investment is uncertainty on property rights that flows from the inability of Muslim countries to put their political systems on a sound footing. Going hand in hand with this governance issue is the inability to tax genuinely on an ability-to-pay or even user-pays basis leading to widespread cynicism, abuse and evasion. If that state of affairs can somehow be reformed, along with greater security of macroeconomic performance, then attracting the return of large amounts of funds invested by domestic residents abroad could offer one avenue to increase investment. Also, governments can initiate large infrastructure projects through private participation by laying out the legal and regulatory framework to ensure that property rights are clearly specified and respected. To this end we made some policy recommendations in Chapter 5.

A COMPARISON

How does the above Islamic perspective on deficit finance compare with that of conventional economics? It is our belief that the Islamic system aims at striking a balance between the classical and the Keynesian visions of economic management through a moral-cum-pecuniary incentive approach.

In the classical economic framework, markets are self-adjusting and the system rebounds quickly to full employment. There is little scope for government intervention in the economy except to make markets more flexible. In the Keynesian system, the persistence of involuntary unemployment and cyclical fluctuations in the economy result from alternating swings in optimism and pessimism due to a combination of consumer sentiment, risk and liquidity preferences and instability in investment expenditure ('animal spirits'). Planned investment–savings gaps open up due to changing preferences for liquidity in the face of fluctuations in the prospective marginal efficiency of capital.

In both the classical and Keynesian system, interest and debt play a major role. In the Keynesian system, if private households and businesses borrow enough (and spend) to absorb savings so as to purchase the total output produced by an economy, then full employment is maintained. If, however, private borrowing and investment falls short of savings, government steps in to take up the slack either by lowering interest rates (money creation) or by public spending (borrowing) so that public debt plays a positive role in acting as a conduit to applying savings to the purchasing of output when private agents are not willing to do so (Buiter, 1990). In the classical system, the adjustments take place through price movements which lower interest rates through expanding real money balances or by stimulating private spending and borrowing through wealth effects. Public debt still is a conduit but through changes in real rather than nominal variables.

Islam comes close to classical economics in terms of its call for small government and minimal intervention in private property rights subject to certain reforms on exchange. At the same time, however, repeated castigation of hoarding behaviour in the Holy Qur'an indicates that there is no presumption that *laissez-faire* in itself is adequate. The Keynesian concern for under-consumption and preference for liquidity in the face of uncertain economic conditions or low prospective returns on capital is not inconsistent with, and provides a rationale for, Islamic views on this issue. Nevertheless, the solution is sought in different ways. Take, for example, the institution of *zakah.* Should the rich have a lower marginal propensity to consume (higher propensity to save) compared to the needy, a flow of resources from the rich to the poor can be expected to feedback on aggregate demand (through a multiplier effect). Since the redistribution occurs voluntarily, the question of a negative impact of *zakah* on incentives does not arise. Such a feedback could potentially raise incomes faster than otherwise, offsetting the reduction in wealth envisaged in Table 4.3. Here we have one explanation of the claim made frequently in the Holy Qur'an that *zakah* does not reduce wealth but rather increases it. There is a side benefit too. To the extent that resources flow to the poorer sections of the society, the structure of production in a country would start gearing towards fulfilling such needs.

Such suggestions need to be tested empirically to gain deeper insights into *zakah*. However, the potential to do so depends on how closely the underlying model approximates the consumption and savings behaviour of households. On this issue, as we saw above, Mankiw (2000) may prove instructive. To recall, he argues that the assumption of inter-temporal consumption smoothing (through financial markets) that underlies both the Diamond–Samuelson model of overlapping generations and the Barro–Ramsey model of infinitely-lived families conflicts in three ways with the findings from empirical studies. First, actual consumer spending follows more closely the current incomes of households. Second, many households do not have sufficient financial means required to enable them to inter-temporally smooth consumption. For instance, in the United States, the mean net worth of the lowest two quintiles of the wealth distribution is a mere \$900. Excluding home equity, this falls to a negative \$10,600. Third, the great accumulation of wealth by a small part of the population (the top 5 per cent hold some 60 per cent of economic and 72 per cent of financial wealth) suggests motives beyond life-cycle smoothing, in particular a bequest motive.[16] In the presence of such significant deviations of the actual from the theoretical, Mankiw suggests an alternative: the savers–spenders model of fiscal policy. In this model, the economy is considered to be populated simultaneously by savers whose behaviour conforms with the Barro–Ramsey model of infinite horizons (smoothing not only across one's own life but also across descendants) and of spenders who live from pay-cheque-to-pay-cheque consuming their entire income in every period.

The savers–spenders model, with its split between the consumption–savings behaviour of the lower and upper strata of society (that is, *zakah*-givers and takers), enables us to see the role of *zakah* as being the Islamic parallel to Keynesian income redistribution policy. In addition, *zakah*, one may surmise, provides a different set of incentives to link savings to investment by penalizing hoarding or under-consumption through imposing a tax on wealth. Variants on this line of thinking can be sought from models exploring growth dynamics and income distribution. For example, Kaldor (1956) demonstrated that by assuming a zero marginal propensity to save on the part of wage earners, capitalists earned what they spent and workers (wage earners) spent what they earned. A distinguishing feature of this approach is that it explains how the nexus between savings and investment (which breaks down in the Keynesian model) is brought about through changes in the distribution of income as relative factor rewards become independent of productivities. At another level, *zakah*'s inherent focus on human development can better be appreciated in the light of endogenous theories of economic growth that underline the role of human capital in economic growth. *Zakah* fits into this type of approach too because in its original conception, it is a centralized, state-managed institution amenable to dovetailing in accordance with the modern understanding of reasons of poverty and means of its elimination through educating people and removing credit constraints to actualize their potential. Understood in this manner, *zakah* can bring planned and organized development of human capital within reach, given proper implementation and institutional structure. Modern theories thus tend to reinforce the Islamic emphasis on this matter.

Apart from *zakah*, Islam also elicits other moral and economic measures. The prohibition of conventional fixed-interest debt, the associated promotion of profit-and-loss-sharing participatory business arrangements and the advocacy of interest-free loans (*qard hasan)* to the poor stand out among these measures. In terms of the savings–investment gap, the ban on traditional fixed-interest lending and borrowing limits the Keynesian solution of large issues of non-asset based public debt. No longer can Islamic governments solve the problem of 'hoarding' by, in effect, reinforcing the mentality that produces it, and simply lowering 'the rate of interest' and raising the value of financial wealth held by savers. No longer can government transfer the 'real risk' of investment to itself, that is, burden taxpayers (with the unknown) through a higher 'risk-free' reward to induced savings. Rather, there is a levy on wealth (*zakah*).[17] Assuming that the tax authorities can reach most savings, what ought savers do to protect their savings from diminishing (through *zakah*)? Must they invest? In the absence, at least in principle, of a fixed-interest outlet, investment in any project having net positive expected rate of return thus becomes feasible. Alternatively, if the marginal return from capital is very low in one location, it will be transferred to another region in search of higher expected returns, thus spreading economic growth. The main economic concern with this solution is that the savings ratio will drop owing to *zakah*, which may not be a worry in the short run. Consequently, embedded in the tenets of Islam is a unique, automatic stabilizing model of fiscal management that overcomes some issues of classical and Keynesian economics.

POLICY RECOMMENDATIONS

Issues surrounding the budget deficit and public debt have been matters of intellectual concern and debate for centuries. On balance, theoretical argument and empirical evidence point to the validity of the Neoclassical, monetarist and the public choice positions. Researchers have illustrated that budget deficits have mainly adverse influences on inflation, interest rates, private investment, and the current account deficit. Also, as deficits cumulate, interest payments on the accumulated stock of debt raises the burden of taxation and is likely to have inequitable distributional consequences. In fact, the very capacity to create deficits can be seductive and have unfavourable implications for governance. Nevertheless, there are exceptions to the rule. Under well-defined circumstances, deficits can be employed to support economic activity and employment. Yet, the risk remains that, within the modern political decision-making framework, such definitions will be stretched liberally leading to an expanding public sector and a later rise in taxation initiating a vicious circle. In effect, in the words of Buchanan (1992) 'the idealized Keynesian policy set – deficits in depression, surpluses in booms – proved to be unworkable in democratic politics. The regime of apparently permanent debt-financed deficit spending was born' (p. 231).

For more than a century and a half beginning roughly with the publication of *Wealth of Nations* by Adam Smith in 1776, both in Great Britain and the fledging United States, budget deficits and public debt were viewed with disapprobation and resorted to only in emergencies such as wars (although a notable exception was the debt issued by the United States for the Louisiana Purchase). Invariably, the resulting debt was retired through budget surpluses in normal times. In Victorian Britain, budget protocol aimed at balancing the annual accounts of the central government at the lowest possible figure (Taylor, 1972, pp. 60–2), and the subject lost interest for economists. That situation contrasts with the debates that surrounded the debt accumulation occasioned by the Napoleonic Wars. The United States first borrowed money in 1777 to buy supplies to fight the Revolutionary War. However, this early debt was retired quickly. With the war of 1812, the debt rose substantially and by 1816, it was 13 per cent of national income. Nevertheless, a 'puritan budget ethic' prevailed overall in the nineteenth century and for many years the United States remained debt free, although the Civil War saw the accumulation of debt of almost $2.8 billion by 1866. During World War I, US public debt rose conspicuously from 3 per cent of national income in 1917 to 41 per cent in 1921. But the greatest increase in the national debt came during World War II. This connection between deficit, debt and war reasserted itself during the Vietnam war, but the US federal budget deficit actually declined with the second Iraq war to a level below its 45-year average of 2 per cent of GDP (Iley and Lewis, 2007).

What can Muslim countries learn from these insights on the budget deficits and public debt? We believe that four lessons emerge. First, if a distinctively Islamic approach is to emerge, there is need to rediscover the real spirit of Islam and the fiscal model underpinning its ethos. Second, governments should, ideally, define the circumstances under which they should be able to borrow or create deficits. Third, the state should submit itself to a fiscal constitution that promotes austerity in budgetary economics. Fourth, macro- and microeconomic reforms facilitating the role of the private and voluntary sectors should be the top priority of governments, laying foundations for a sustained generation of wealth and prosperity embedded in self-respect, personal responsibility, and preservation of individual incentives. We discuss these recommendations in turn.

Discovering the Real Spirit of the Islamic Economic Model

One can detect, as explained in the next chapter, in Islamic business, financial and governmental circles, a heavy emphasis on designing so-called *ijtihadi* debt surrogates to substitute for interest-based debt. This approach does not necessarily tap the real spirit of Islam. If Islamic finance is to be distinguished from conventional methods, the research ought to be focused on institutional means to implement the goals of Islam that lie in fulfilling moral obligations to the poor, implementation of *zakah* and prohibition of fixed-interest debt. Together these elements constitute the unique fiscal component of the Islamic economic system.

Another area to be explored is in-kind finance. There are many examples from the life of the Prophet (pbuh) and the early Muslim community which point to a willingness to pool labour for works of community interest. Among these were rendering help and assistance (social work) to the old, widows, and orphans. Marshalling efforts for defence, the biggest challenge facing the early community, also fell within this ambit. *Ahadith* depict that the Prophet Muhammad (pbuh) himself participated, alongside many, in digging trenches so as to prevent Makkan's march on Madinah. In these precedents lies a great potential for the building of infrastructure in many poor countries which are unable to raise sufficient taxes to mobilize monetary means for such tasks. Prophet Muhammad (pbuh) demonstrated to his community that monetary scarcity is no hindrance to joint participation in works of community welfare.

Some modern economists agree with this emphasis. Basic infrastructure – utilities, housing, public health, roads, railways and communications – takes up some 60 per cent of investment in industrialized countries and can be seen as a prerequisite for the remaining 40 per cent of investment in manufacturing, agriculture and commerce. Jackson *et al.* (1994) argue that given the difficulty in mobilizing monetary resources to undertake this task, there is potential to accumulate infrastructure through non-financial investment. To quote:

> Given the pre-requisite leadership and willingness to co-operate, capital can be accumulated by transferring surplus agricultural labour to the improvement

> of agricultural facilities or the construction of basic social capital. If each agricultural village would allocate its surplus labour to the construction of irrigation canals, wells, schools, sanitary facilities and roads, significant amounts of capital might be accumulated at no sacrifice of consumer goods production. Non-financial investment simply bypasses the problems embodied within the financial aspects of the capital accumulation process. Such investment does not require consumers to save portions of their money income, nor does it presume the presence of an entrepreneurial class anxious to invest. In brief, provided the leadership and co-operative spirit are present, non-financial investment is a promising avenue for the accumulation of basic capital goods. (p. 454)

Many schemes suiting local requirements can be built around this basic idea. Local councils in developing countries can pool some technical equipment and basic finance, state governments can provide planning expertise, and local people can provide the labour to begin building streets and schools, lay sewerage systems, and arrange for cleaner water. These are works that have benefits with which people can immediately identify. For tasks of a higher order, incentive schemes like preferential treatment for entry into public employment or admission into a public-sector university or remission of fee at a university, etc. can break the ice.

When Should Governments Borrow or Resort to Deficit Finance?

The classical and new classical approaches are at one in emphasizing that access to public debt may lead to irresponsible executive and legislative spending decisions. Buchanan (1958, 1992) sees the public borrowing decision in essence as being no different than that facing an individual, that is, borrow when you want to transfer repayment to the future and there is a viable economic case for doing so. This conclusion keeps sight of the shortcomings of the (democratic) political decision-making process, that is, overvaluation of the present benefits and undervaluation of (or applying a high discount rate to) the future benefits and costs. Since these proclivities find in the public debt instrument a useful artefact to shift the real cost of short-term or consumption expenditure to future generations, funding of such expenditure through debt is clearly ruled out. Thus Buchanan (1958) states:

> In the 'classical' model which assumes substantially full employment of economic resources, public debt issue should never be allowed to appear as an alternative method of financing public expenditures, the benefits of which are presumed to accrue, in whole or even in part, to individuals making the choices. The tax is the only appropriate financing medium for such expenditures. (p. 158)

Conversely, tax financing of genuine very long-term investment opportunities the benefits of which occur in future periods is not disfavoured.

In such cases, the use of public debt is said to offer merit. However, protection against opportunistic political behaviour requires that the Wicksellian tradition be revived. In this event, it is recommended that some method of debt servicing and amortization or earmarking is specified and approved together with the decision on public expenditure that is to be funded by debt. To give an example, a call for increasing salaries for school teachers (that is, increase in current expenditure) ought to be met through tax increases while that for a new school building (capital expenditure) through public debt with a pre-specified tax increase schedule to service such debt approved simultaneously with the expenditure decision. A real life example comes from the United States where roads have been funded by dedicated taxes on motorists (but now need tolls for new roads since road demand has outstripped taxation) (Grimsey and Lewis, 2004, 2005).

Wagner (1987) examines at length the microeconomic justification and stabilization motive for debt finance. On the former, he argues that the government's ability to borrow at a better rate than other borrowers is not a sign of its less riskiness but rather of its ability to cover up through taxation what is in reality a greater cost and riskiness of carrying a project in the public sector. On the latter, he reminds us that even if we assume (unrealistically) that policy-makers have a full grasp of the nature of economic fluctuations and can put together an appropriate fiscal policy response in time with them, a programme of money creation and destruction is alternative to that of fixed-interest finance. This is largely what has happened, with monetary policy acting as the 'swing instrument', although the worldwide stimulus packages of 2009 are evidence that fiscal policy has not been dispensed with entirely. Buchanan (1958) too finds the use of public debt in depression as inefficient. He argues that since government's purchase of resources under these circumstances does not come at a cost to the private sector, the real cost of such an operation ought to be zero. The only way for a government to entail zero cost when acquiring command on real resources is by expanding the monetary base. That is precisely what is recommended in depressions.

All in all, the call is first, to limit government borrowing for long-term capital expenditure only, second, to subject such expenditure to either the Wicksellian supra-majority constraint or to joint expenditure-(future) taxation schedule approval, and third, place constitutional limits on borrowing (see below). Some question government borrowing even for investment purposes given well-known incentive problems in the public sector. They call for outright balanced budgets. Only under conditions of severe recession is there support for deficit finance but not in the form of borrowing but through monetary finance.

Promoting Fiscal Discipline through Constitutional Rules

We mentioned above the gradual weakening of what Buchanan (1992, p. 230) called the 'old-time fiscal religion' which acted as a constraint against debt in classical analysis. In addition, the fall of the gold standard, and the widespread adoption of fiat money removed an important check against government profligacy. Greenspan (1966, 1981) argued that the gold standard served as protector of property rights and a shield against 'hidden' confiscation of wealth through inflationary finance and wasteful public spending. However, there are substantial resource costs in commodity money that make a return to gold unlikely (Lewis and Mizen, 2000).

Buchanan (1992) was convinced that the classical principles of public debt must return to general acceptability if the fiscal irresponsibility of governments is to be circumscribed, but saw little sign that 'fiscal religion' had been rediscovered. In fact, there has been greater recognition of the political economy position on the misuse of budget deficits and public credit, and a professional momentum in favour of reviving rule-based fiscal policy. Buchanan *et al.* (1978) and Niskanen (1992) led the way. Kopits and Symansky (1998) review the literature and conduct simulations. They define a fiscal policy rule as a permanent constraint on fiscal policy, typically defined in terms of an indicator of overall fiscal performance. Box 6.1 summarizes some fiscal rules that could be embedded in a constitution to provide automatic restraint against the 'Leviathan' tendencies of governments. Naturally, there are calls for exemption from these rules in the case of emergency to avoid temptation for external aggression.

Facilitating Markets and Limiting the Role of Government

The final recommendation is the importance of rules, enforcement mechanisms, and organizations in general that facilitate and promote economic development by transmitting information, enforcing property rights and contracts, and managing competition (World Development Report, 2002). Such architecture provides the core of governance structures in a country. Iqbal and Lewis (2002) examine research in this area and highlight an agenda for domestic reforms consisting of four items: limit concentration of powers, constrain discretionary powers, strengthen institutions, and enhance and enforce monitoring and accountability. The first requires a workable and balanced separation of powers among the executive, the legislature, and the judicial arms of the government, on one hand, and among central, state, and local authorities, on the other hand. Each level of government in turn requires appropriate checks and balances. Leaving

BOX 6.1 MAJOR TYPES OF FISCAL POLICY RULES

Balanced-budget or deficit rules

- Balance between overall revenue and expenditure (that is, prohibition on government borrowing); or limit on government deficit as a proportion of GDP.
- Balance between structural (or cyclically adjusted) revenue and expenditure; or limit on structural (or cyclically adjusted) deficit as a proportion of GDP.
- Balance between current revenue and current expenditure (that is, borrowing permitted only to finance capital expenditure).

Borrowing rules

- Prohibition on government borrowing from domestic sources.
- Prohibition on government borrowing from central bank; or limit on such borrowing as a proportion of past government revenue or expenditure.

Debt or reserve rules

- Limit on stock of gross (or net) government liabilities as a proportion of GDP.
- Target stock of reserves of extra budgetary contingency funds (such as social security funds) as a proportion of annual benefit payments.

Source: Kopits and Symansky (1998, p. 2)

much discretionary power in the hands of both politicians and civil servants provides opportunities for evasion and waste of public funds. A properly functioning system incorporating a separation of powers protects against such abuse of discretionary powers. The judicial system is a case in a point. Not only does it resolve disputes between private parties but also between private and public parties. In doing so, it provides a check on public excess. The components of an administrative reform programme aim at bringing civil service as close as is possible to the Weberian model, that is, politically neutral, professionally competent, goal-oriented, dedicated, and functionally sound. Limiting concentration of powers and strengthening institutions contributes significantly to accountability and

BOX 6.2 CHOOSING THE TOOLS FOR ACCOUNTABILITY

Ends To facilitate/ enhance	Means/Tools
Legitimacy of decision-makers	Constitutions; electoral systems for government and decision making bodies; bureaucratic systems of representation; Royal Prerogative; legislation; letters of appointment; formal delegation of authority; standing orders
Moral conduct	Societal values; concepts of social justice and public interest; professional values; training/ induction programme
Responsiveness	Public participation and consultation; debates; advisory bodies; public meetings; freedom of speech
Openness	Parliamentary question times; public information services; freedom of information laws; public hearings; Green and White Papers; annual reports
Optimal resource utilization	Budgets; financial procedures; rules of virement; parliamentary public accounts committees; auditing; public inquiries and participation; formal planning systems
Improving efficiency and effectiveness	Information systems; value for money audits; setting objectives and standards; programme guidelines; appraisal; feedback from public

Source: M. R. Hayllar (1991) modified by Turner and Hulme (1997)

transparency. Nevertheless, complementary help from deterrence is also required. Detection and enforcement priorities ought to feature in the reform agenda (Becker, 1968). Box 6.2 summarizes the tools available to facilitate accountability.

The World Development Report 2002 brings into sharper focus the need for:

- Actualizing an open, transparent and friendly environment for commerce, trade and foreign investment;
- Effective government oversight of corporate governance practices so as to promote transparency and increase public confidence in the private sector;

- Improving the prudential framework for financial institutions so as to ensure a timely, accurate and reliable flow of information from financial intermediaries and prevent economic and financial crises;
- Evolving institutions that alleviate information asymmetries, which retard access of the poor to credit markets;
- Promoting trade liberalization and removal of entry and exit barriers for firms so as to expand opportunity for participation in the market, facilitate free market competition and reduce transaction costs of doing business.

In the final analysis, the key to boosting economic growth for nations and in reducing poverty for individuals lies in following the classical advice in expanding the role of free market competition so that more and more people are voluntarily engaged in productive effort that is rewarded by the market. Governments can do a lot in facilitating such an environment by ensuring property rights, lowering transaction costs and promoting competition. To this end we have provided some suggestions and alluded to research in this area.

CONCLUSION

We began by considering the differences between the classical and the Keynesian views. In the classical analysis, government is perceived as an inefficient player when it comes to taking on some of the functions assumed by the market. It therefore ought to limit its activity to the prior conditions necessary for an orderly operation of free markets – responsibility for law and order, delivering justice, and ensuring defence. To fulfil these roles, there is allowance for levying taxes. Beyond that, there is little role for government *per se* in economic development and no allowance for deficit finance. By contrast, the Keynesian model (or at least how it evolved) allocates a substantial role to government in economic stabilization and development.

The budget deficit became the primary policy instrument of Keynesian economic policy, necessary in circumstances such as depression, with public debt the main means of financing demand-inducing deficits. The 'new orthodoxy' focused on the immediate transfer of resources at the time when the spending occurred and, since this has already taken place, denied that the public debt embodied any subsequent burden on taxpayers when the debt is repaid. This conclusion was contrary to classical analysis which focused on the voluntary nature of the initial resource transfer when funds are exchanged for promises of future interest, and the involuntary nature of the later re-exchange when taxes are imposed. The paradigm shift led to two problems. First, if the macroeconomic situation is what is prompting the creation of budget deficits, then the demand-inducing deficits could be financed by money creation. There would then be no need to shift to future taxpayers the tax burden that the debt interest financing implies, for money creation (without an inflation tax) carries with it no such burden on future generations. Instead, the government takes advantage of seigniorage gains to the central bank (as issuer of fiat money), as a source of revenue. Interestingly, the extensive use of monetary policy in the twenty-first century suggests that this lesson has not been lost on present day policy-makers.[18] Second, the new orthodoxy carried with it no fiscal 'religion'. Strictly speaking, the logic of the Keynesian position would be to run deficits in recession and surpluses in booms. Not only was this stricture overlooked, but many governments in the 1970s and 1980s explicitly used public debt to finance outlays for public consumption.

Not surprisingly, the problem of public debt (in particular sovereign debt) has at times plagued the entire global financial system and indirectly influenced economic growth for the worse. In reality, the very act of allowing the state to engage in debasing money and borrowing aligns poorly with the incentives for efficient spending of monies so raised. The Islamic stand on this issue is that governments cannot borrow on fixed interest. They must impose either moral or market constraints upon themselves for any investment not funded through taxes. Savers may join hands with government on a PLS basis, if they wish to do so. This provides government with an opportunity to have greater investment in its preferred categories than it can afford through taxation.

The bearings of the Islamic stance on economic strategy are very clear. First, fiscal austerity ought to be accepted as a driving force in state financial management. Second, there should be a prime stress on instituting a sound tax system based on principles of equity. Neither inflation nor borrowing can substitute for it. At minimum, all current expenditure ought to be financed through taxes. Third, steps ought to be taken, on the one hand, to institute preconditions for inviting private investment (rule of law and clear property rights) and on the other hand, promoting means for increasing private savings, in particular of small business operators, wage earners, and farmers. Fourth, creation of deficits for capital expenditure ought to be restricted by rules of fiscal responsibility. Fifth, to the extent deficits are created, PLS modes (regardless of internal or external participation) ought to be preferred over debt finance and internal debt preferred over external. Sixth, at the level of each deficit finance proposal, expenditure estimates ought to be accompanied with schedules for servicing the liability. Seventh, for many infrastructure projects, governments can make

PLS workable through zero rate loans and regulatory mechanisms. The former could render the pecuniary return attractive and the latter could make the user-pay principle feasible. Eighth, in developing countries with spare labour, monetary scarcity ought not to be an excuse for inaction on infrastructure.

NOTES

1. Orr *et al.* (1995) estimate that an increase in budget deficit by 1 per cent of GDP could raise real interest rates by around 1/6 per cent when funded through internal debt and by approximately 1/3 per cent when funded through external debt that worsens the current account deficit.
2. See note 2 in Chapter 4.
3. Ricardo illustrated the interdependence of debt and taxes by elaborating that a lump sum borrowing by the state was equivalent to the present value of a future stream of (additional) annual taxes required to service the debt (to perpetuity). He thought that if the public appreciated such equivalence, then it would fully capitalize future tax payments. Otherwise, therein lied the source of deluding the members of a nation into greater spending and lesser savings (Buiter, 1990, pp. 230–1).
4. One is tempted to add that the 'sub-prime' phenomenon of 2004–8 gave them the opportunity to own and then be dispossessed of real estate.
5. Unless mentioned otherwise, most of this section is based on Macklem (1994/5) and Fischer and Easterly (1990).
6. For a critique of such measures in the context of the US deficit, see Iley and Lewis (2007, Chapter 6).
7. Note that equation (6.6) replaces $(i - z)$ in equation (6.5) with $(r - g)$ since $i = r +$ inflation and $z = g +$ inflation.
8. Borrowing to pay interest on outstanding debt is sometimes referred to as a Ponzi scheme, after Charles Ponzi of Boston, USA who made a fortune in the 1920s by inventing a pyramid scheme but ultimately ended up in jail and became penniless.
9. Page numbers refer to the HTML version of the article available through EBSCO Host Research Database.
10. In the former case, 54 of the 64 Australian banks closed or suspended payment (Lewis and Wallace, 1997, Chapter 1). In the other episode, to consider how different it was then, we quote Blatt.

    > The expansion of the US railway system in the mid-nineteenth century was a highly risky proposition, and plenty of people got stung; but not the promoters of the major railway companies. It was common practice to form two companies: (1) a railway company proper, which issued and sold shares, mostly in London, and (2) a railway construction company, in which the shares were closely held by the promoters. The railway company, having raised capital in London, commissioned the railway construction company to construct a railroad. By no accident at all, the construction turned out to be extremely expensive, so the railway company paid out huge sums to the railway construction company. In due course, the railway company went bankrupt, the shares were worthless, the English investors had lost their money; the American promoters had their railroad and the money'. (Blatt, 1983, p. 268)

11. This chronic situation is the basis for Bonner and Wiggin's (2006) argument that the United States is the 'Empire of Debt'. Unable to exact tribute from the peripheral states, it has instead borrowed from them to finance its wars and global hegemony. While

borrowing to finance an imperium is not unknown in the past (England and Holland in the earlier times), the scale of US borrowing from overseas is unprecedented. See Iley and Lewis (2007, pp. 109–14) for a discussion of these views.

12. Ricardo is, of course, comparing the equivalence of a lump sum (present value), perpetuity and a 45-year annuity. The present value of a one million annual perpetual stream at 5 per cent (0.05) is 20 million. With a zero interest rate, a perpetuity is undefined. For the Islamic parallel, using a very small rate, for example, close to zero (0.01 per cent p.a.), gives a perpetuity of 2000 versus 1,000,000 in the Ricardian case. In the case of the annuity, the Islamic parallel with a zero interest rate would be a straight division of 20 million by 45 or 444,444.
13. At a theoretical level this issue formed the basis of the debate around the Pesek and Saving (1967) view. Harry Johnson (1969) argued that any 'monetary grant' (that is, seigniorage) accruing to private banks would be competed away through competition.
14. Note that in this respect, there is an asymmetry between the private and the public use of *ijtihadi* financing instruments. In the private use, borrowers assess the cost of such instruments *vis-à-vis* their subjective estimate of pecuniary returns. In the case of public use, return estimates come out of the political process and are prone to its adverse tendencies.
15. The need for the state to get involved in such projects could be due to many types of market failure that are typical of developing economies.
16. Thus studies indicate that the vast majority of aggregate US capital formation stems from intergenerational transfers. Note that the greater importance of the bequest motive is inconsistent only with the Diamond–Samuelson model.
17. On the moral side, hoarding is prohibited and wealth is to be considered a gift from God and must be kept in circulation (see Chapters 3 and 5).
18. Thus the huge expansionary fiscal stimulus packages launched in early 2009 in the United States and the United Kingdom in the face of what the IMF call 'the great recession' have been accompanied by unprecedentedly low official interest rates (0–0.25 per cent p.a. in the US, 0.50 per cent in the UK) and by open market operations (the buying of government bonds) to inject money into the economy, a policy understatedly called 'quantitative easing.'

7. Financing methods for government bodies

INTRODUCTION

This chapter is a direct extension of the previous one on government budget deficits. Tax and non-tax revenues frequently fall short of the needs for public expenditure. In view of the constraints upon Islamic financing methods, especially the prohibition of fixed-interest debt, there is the question of how such shortfalls ought to be financed especially if they result from spending of a developmental nature. Contemporary *shari'ah* scholars have devised solutions to this problem by adapting the classical Islamic modes of trading (buying and selling) for financing purposes, resulting in 'asset-based' finance. To some critics, such adaptation is tantamount to a reinterpretation of Islamic teachings on *riba*, bringing contemporary Islamic finance very close in essence to conventional interest-based financing.

In this chapter, we examine these Islamic alternatives against the twin backdrop of the history of interest-free finance and the Western critique based on the theories of optimal financial contracting. The idea is, first, to study a range of *shari'ah* compliant techniques to mobilize resources for public expenditure and the market forces driving the evolution of such instruments. Then, second, it is to examine the implicit Western critique of Islamic finance from the theoretical standpoint that fixed-interest debt contracts facilitate the micro-dynamics of corporate governance and alleviate agency problems. Third, after reviewing the role of fixed-interest debt we propose some alternative approaches to financing commercial and public sector activities. We begin with a brief history of Islamic finance.

HISTORY OF ISLAMIC FINANCE

Usury or interest has attracted the close scrutiny of religious scholars and philosophers for centuries. The oldest scriptures of Hinduism, based on the Veda, condemned interest lending as a major sin (Rangaswami, 1927; Gopal, 1935). Plato and Aristotle opposed interest on the grounds that it contravened natural law and retarded the development of higher moral values. Judaism and Christianity banned interest (usury). Hebrew law prohibited it, at least among Jews ('brethren'). Christianity was even more unequivocal on the topic of usury. In fact, based on canon law and arguments of Church scholars such as St Thomas Aquinas, the medieval Christian could offer at least ten reasons against the practice: (1) it was contrary to the teaching of Jesus; (2) usury was prohibited by the law of Moses; (3) the Church strongly opposed loan-related activities such as taking collateral; (4) money-lending was an unnatural act, not part of Aristotle's natural economy; (5) collecting interest along with principal was contrary to Roman law; (6) usury violated natural justice since profits rightfully belong to those who make money productive; (7) it leads to inequality for the needy; (8) earning interest violated medieval views on productive work and labour; (9) the time value of money implicit in interest exploited time itself, which belongs to God; and (10) interest is fixed and certain which means that a usurer takes his 'pound of flesh' regardless of the outcome – that is, without sharing the risks – of a commercial venture (Lewis, 2007). Such views came under increasing pressure with the growth of commerce, and the reformation and the rise of Protestantism. Eventually the Church relented and usury was re-defined as excessive interest. In this way, the charging of interest became legal although some restrictions against charging exorbitant interest rates remained in place until fairly recently (Lewis and Algaoud, 2001, pp. 203–10).

Islam, on its own claims of being the final revelation (33:40), and the touchstone and torch-bearer of all the essential truth communicated in the past, preserves the ban on interest (3:03, 130; 42:13). In doing so, it does not discriminate between a Muslim and a non-Muslim (3:75–6). Also, it distinguishes itself from the ancient Greek and Christian positions by declaring trade with mutual consent as being not only legitimate but to be encouraged (2:275). Nevertheless, transactions containing *gharar*, that is elements of uncertainty as regards the possession, quality, quantity, price or delivery date of the goods being transacted are prohibited (*sunnah*) and so is outright speculation, effectively gambling (5:90). Such a search for justice in exchange constitutes part of the broader Islamic ethos of justice elaborated earlier.

In conformity with the above principles, early Islam approved two of the then prevailing modes of business partnerships: *mudarabah* and *musharakah*. Both were organized on a profit and loss sharing basis. Evidence suggests that such partnerships were practised in the early and Middle Ages both in the Islamic and the Christian domains (Udovitch, 1970; Gerber, 1981; Lewis and Algaoud, 2001). Evidence also suggests that there was a well-established tradition in Islamic societies to extend interest-free credit to the needy. Village mosques used to play a key role in this charitable activity (Cunningham, 1990). This integration of piety with entrepreneurship did not escape the eyes of Jean Chardin, a French traveller in the Ottoman, Mughal, and Iranian territories in the late seventeenth century. He observed, 'In the East Traders are Sacred Persons' (Dale, 1996, p. 64). For sure, traders were not alone in receiving their motivation from Islam. Nor did all traders adhere to the new rulebook. El-Gamal (2005) likens many present-day Islamic banking practices to 'medieval ruses'. Certainly, medieval Christians employed many tricks to circumvent the Church's ban on interest. But it would seem that they were not alone. Schacht (1964) finds evidence of 'legal fictions' in use in Madinah as early as the time of Malik b. Anas (d. 796), founder of the Maliki school of law.

At another level, from Islam's inception, intellectual pursuits on a wide range of subjects, economics included among them, were inspired by the Islamic call for synthesizing religion with rationality (Ebrahim and Safadi, 1995). Chapra (cited in Kuran, 1996) claims that 'Islamic Economics remained primarily an integral part of the unified social and moral philosophy of Islam until after World War II'. Esposito (1987) seems to pre-empt that conclusion:

> from Muhammad's seventh-century Arabia to the dawn of European colonialism in the sixteenth century, Islam was an ascendant and expansive religio-political movement in which religion was part and parcel of both private and public life. (p. 15)

Nevertheless, if not quite apparent before, it was obvious by the end of the sixteenth century that Muslim civilization was in decline and we have already investigated some reasons for this state of affairs in Chapter 5, the origins of which can be dated to at least the tenth century CE when the empire began to disintegrate and Ibn Khaldun's 'dynastic cycle' entered into the downswing phase. Thus gradually weakened, Islamic civilization was then to fall prey to the European incursions which culminated in military occupation and complete subjugation. By the late nineteenth and twentieth centuries, the spiritual, cultural, and institutional framework of Islam was thoroughly penetrated in terms of the structure of education, law, economy and military. From the viewpoint of the present discussion, the prohibition of fixed interest too was challenged. In particular, for example, Imam Muhammad Abdu (1849–1905), who was appointed Editor-in-Chief of the Egyptian government official gazette in 1880, was 'encouraged' by the then British rulers of Egypt to issue a controversial *fatwa* (an Islamic ruling) in favour of interest-bearing post office certificates (Cunningham, 1990). Mallat (Warde, 2000) sees such rulings in the following perspective:

> Egyptian muftis writing in the 20th century acknowledge that they are treading a delicate path and are dealing with powerful economic actors and institutions that have strong supporters in new, as well as in established, commercial sectors. Because a fatwa that unilaterally condemned interest-bearing transactions would be totally ineffective, most muftis have taken care to formulate their opinion in language that is either cautious or ambiguous. (p. 57)

Whatever the rationale, by World War II, the superimposition of Western institutions on an Islamic substructure had been producing at least three kinds of people. There were those who eagerly learnt and adopted Western values and there were those who rejected them completely and remained loyal to the erstwhile Islamic vision, albeit with low visibility. Somewhere in the middle were those making the best of both worlds. They believed that to a degree there was scope for a synthesis through *ijtihad*, and perhaps foresaw that a culture which rejected or mistrusted new techniques and ideas from Christendom (the West) would ultimately be self-destructive. In spite of these differences, all groups resented foreign occupation. In this environment, 'Islam became a rallying point for anti-colonialism' and in this form was thrust back into Muslim public life (Esposito, 1987, p. 16). By the middle decades of the twentieth century, many lands with Muslim majority population had to be granted independence.

This atmosphere proved a boon for private scholars to set the agenda for *ijtihad* with a new vigour. Development of an elaborate theory of interest-free finance was an integral part of this agenda. Sayyid Qutb from Egypt, M. Baqir al-Sadr from Iraq, and Mawdudi from the Indian subcontinent and later from Pakistan, made significant contributions. In 1963, an early experiment in interest-free banking was conducted in Mit Ghamr in Egypt combining the idea of German savings banks with the Islamic value framework. Wohlers-Scharf (1983) notes the background to this experiment:

> A precondition . . . for any change of behaviour from hoarding and 'real-asset saving' to 'financial saving' was the creation of a financial institution which would not violate the religious principles of large segments of the population. Only then could the majority of the population be integrated into the process of capital formation. (pp. 79–80)

The project made impressive progress but it was abandoned for fear of stimulating Islamic fundamentalism. Egypt again became the seat of experimentation in 1971 with the establishment of the Nasser Social Bank in the public sector. Notably, in an era of Arab socialism and nationalism, both experiments made no direct reference to religion (Warde, 2000, p. 74).

The real boost to Islamic banking came in the 1970s and 1980s. Newfound wealth in the form of petrodollars provided at least the means if not the motive. Suffice it to say that there was impatience by the late 1960s, and recognition by even the most secular Westernized leadership, of what was perceived as the unchanging colonial character of the industrialized nations. Add to this mix the Arab–Israeli conflict and support was ripe for a pan-Islamic financial structure to foster indigenous institutions that could mobilize resources for economic development, for which oil revenues then provided a capital base.

The first institution that emerged as a result was the Organization of the Islamic Conference (OIC), established in 1970. In 1972, at the Third Islamic Conference held in Jeddah, a plan to reform the monetary and financial systems in light of Islam was presented before the Foreign Ministers of Islamic countries. The study had been undertaken by experts from 18 Muslim countries under the leadership of the Egyptian Ministry of Economics. In consequence, the 1974 OIC summit held in Pakistan voted to create an intergovernmental Islamic Development Bank (IDB). IDB was established in Jeddah in 1975. A raft of commercial and investment banks followed (Wohlers-Scharf, 1983).[1]

In general, this pursuit of pan-Islamism in the 1970s was received positively in the West, in particular by the US administration. The key players, Saudi Arabia, Iran, and Egypt were then all strong supporters of the West. They identified their ideological orientations more closely with the 'free world' as against secular communism and were keen on having their economies embedded within the US-centred international economic order. This was evident from Saudi Arabia and Iran recycling their oil wealth back into the West through military and civilian contracts and making significant investments in US Treasury bonds and Western banks. As far as IDB was concerned, its statutes explicitly asked for coordination and collaboration with the International Monetary Fund (IMF) and other international organizations. The operations of the private Islamic banks as well were pro status quo, reliant on government and ruling family capital for their formation and compliant with the local political, economic, and regulatory framework. All in all, the very structure and operations of these organizations (much conducted in US dollars) took place within the rules of the international game, albeit from an Islamic normative stand as far as was practical.

In financial terms, the vision to conduct banking on Islamic principles has met with success. Including all forms of Islamic financing, estimates of the global assets in 2009 that comply with Islamic law range from US$700–1000 billion (*New Straits Times*, 11 April 2009, B13). Yet the system is facing many challenges too. First, there are pressures to standardize products (often to Western norms) so as to facilitate regulatory supervision. Second, with the entrance of leading conventional banks into the business – through subsidiaries and 'Islamic windows' – the 'pure play' Islamic banks must lift standards of service, product innovation and delivery. Third, given the international focus on terrorism, the level of transparency must be increased. Fourth, not all experts agree that Islamic banking is really Islamic. To the credit of the industry, it is aware of these challenges, while remaining under pressure to adapt to conventional modes of financing.

A point of significance that flows from the above outline is that from the perspective of political economy, the business of Islamic banking is to some degree walking on a tightrope. While its goal is to provide financial intermediation in conformity with the value system of Islam, it has to execute that task within the bounds of the broader economic, financial, legal, and prudential supervisory system that is not necessarily based on Islamic tenets. This situation may have implications for the solutions that are sought to avoid fixed interest. However, the issues also go to the heart of Islamic banking, for many of the questionable practices can be observed in countries such as Iran and Sudan that have 'Islamicized' their economies (see Lewis and Algaoud, 2001, Chapter 5).

INSTRUMENTS OF ISLAMIC FINANCE

The essence of Islamic finance is that loans should be advanced free of interest for charitable purposes and on a profit and loss sharing (PLS) basis for commercial purposes. PLS arrangements, however, cannot exclusively cater for the peculiarities of a modern economy which is inherently cast in an interest-based mould. Accordingly, the first challenge facing Islamic finance was to design a more diversified set of interest-free instruments. This challenge has been met by adapting permissible trading contracts, originally designed for buying-and-selling of real goods, for financing purposes. Many writers on Islamic finance provide details of the presently widely accepted modes of transacting. One key reference in this regard is the report of the Council of Islamic Ideology (CII), Pakistan (Ahmed *et al.* Khan, 1983) on the elimination of interest which provides extensive discussion of the various contracts suitable for commercial, agricultural, and investment banking. Tahir *et al.* (1999) provide an excellent update. Lewis and Algaoud (2001) and Hassan and Lewis (2007a) can be cited as more recent contributions on this issue.

The prevailing instruments of interest-free finance relevant for public sector financing can be divided broadly into four categories: the classical

PLS modes of *mudarabah* and *musharaka*; the different buying-and-selling arrangements adapted for financing through *ijtihad* in the last three decades; leasing (rental) operations; and Islamic bonds (*sukuks*). Below we describe these instruments in a somewhat greater detail.

Profit and Loss-sharing Arrangements

Profit-and-loss sharing methods, used appropriately, lie at the heart of the Islamic philosophy on money and finance. They are the techniques most consistent with the value system and the moral economy of Islam and, in another sense, the most 'modern' as well, given they have some similarities with the merchant banking and venture capital segments of contemporary finance. In theory, such ethos can revolutionize socioeconomic structure by opening access to funding based on merit rather than on collateral and connection. Ironically, the problems discussed later in this chapter mean that such finance constitutes a relatively small proportion of the assets of Islamic financial institutions. Nevertheless, two instruments serve as models: m*udarabah* and *musharakah*.

Mudarabah

A *Mudarabah* arrangement is a partnership between an investor (*rabb-ul-mal*) who brings money and an entrepreneur (*mudarib*) who contributes his business expertise. The entrepreneur acts in the capacity of investor's agent to manage the business exclusively in accordance with a contract. In case of profit, the *mudarib* returns the principal amount along with a predetermined share of the profit to the investor. The *mudarib* himself takes the remainder as a reward for his labour and entrepreneurial contribution. Monetary losses are borne entirely by the investor. Liability for losses, however, is limited to his investment unless he has given the *mudarib* an express permission for incurring debts (Usmani, 2000).

Musharakah

A *Musharakah* is a contract among two or more parties, all contributing some of their capital in a joint commercial venture. Profit ratios have to be specified in advance but in case of a loss, it must be shared in proportion to the capital contributed. There are differences of opinion in *fiqh* as to whether profit ratios can differ from ratios of capital contribution. Among the classical jurists, Imam Malik and Shafi'i do not permit it, Imam Ahmad makes it subject to free consent, while Imam Abu Hanifah caps the share of a perpetual sleeping partner to no more than the proportion of his investment (Usmani, 2000).

Credit Instruments

On a strict interpretation there is no scope for interest- or discount-based financing instruments in Islam. Given teething difficulties of operating PLS contracts in developing economies, however, jurists adapted some contracts for finance that in the classical interpretation were meant for engagement in the real business of buying and selling. For instance, *bai' bi-thamin ajil* (BBA)/*bai'muajjal* is a deferred payment sale of goods permitted in *shari'ah*. According to some *shari'ah* scholars, the mutually agreed price could be different than the spot price.[2] Likewise, *shari'ah* does not object to a *murabahah* arrangement wherein a seller discloses his cost of goods to a buyer and a mark-up is mutually agreed in lieu of profit for the seller. These concepts, combined and adapted for Islamic banking, allow a prospective trader or a potential real asset purchaser to approach a bank specifying his need for a real good. The bank purchases the asset and on-sells it to him adding its mark-up for deferred payment and the risk that it takes in owning the goods between the original purchase and its on-selling to the customer. There are a number of variations on this basic idea. For example, in a *bai'salam*, clearly defined goods are sold at a specified price for future delivery.

While the mark-up may seem to be just another term for interest as charged by conventional banks, the legality of the traditional type of *murabahah* or trading-based financing is not questioned by any of the schools of Islamic law. What makes the traditional *murabahah* transaction Islamically legitimate in *fiqh* is that the bank first acquires the asset for resale at profit, so that a commodity is sold for money and the operation is not a mere exchange of money for money (Wilson, 1983, pp. 84–5). In the process the bank assumes certain risks between purchase and resale; for example, a sudden fall in price could see the client refusing to accept the goods. That is, the bank takes responsibility for the good before it is safely delivered to the client. The services rendered by the Islamic bank are therefore regarded as quite different from those of a conventional bank which simply lends money to the client to buy the good. That is, the mark-up is not in the nature of an additional amount paid on the principal amount of a loan but is in the nature of a profit charged in a trade transaction, with attendant risks attached.

It is the associated risk-taking that legitimizes the reward. As the Prophet (pbuh) said 'profit accompanies liability for loss' (Vogel and Hayes, 1998, pp. 83–5, 112–14). This *hadith* means that one can earn profits (*al-kharaj*) from possession of property only if one also assumes the risk of loss (*al-daman*). In practice, however, the following actions have been found possible within the premises of Islamic law. First, the Islamic bank may appoint the client himself to purchase on behalf of the bank the commodities that the client wants the bank to finance so that there is no risk of purchasing something that the client may not want. Second, arrangements can be made that, as soon as the goods are purchased on behalf of the bank, they are immediately sold to the client on an agreed cost-plus mark-up basis so that the period of ownership of physical goods by the financial institutions and risks associated with the ownership are reduced to a minimum. These two elements allow the risks in the transaction to become almost negligible for the Islamic financial institutions and the return on the financing provided by the financial institution becomes almost fixed and predetermined (Khan, 2007).

Against this backdrop, the original conditional approval in 1983 of *murabahah* by the Council of Islamic Ideology, Pakistan is worth noting:

> although this mode of financing is understood to be permissible under *Shari'ah*, it would not be advisable to use it widely or indiscriminately in view of the danger attached to it of opening a back-door for dealing on the basis of interest. Safeguards would, therefore, need to be devised so as to restrict its use only to inescapable cases. (Ahmed *et al.*, 1983, pp. 118–19).

Quite to the contrary, such instruments constitute a sizeable (normally the largest) proportion of the portfolio of Islamic banks nowadays. This widespread use has in itself given the instrument a kind of legitimacy that it was never accorded in the first place.

Leasing Operations (*Ijarah*)

Leasing (*ijarah*) is also commonly practised by Islamic banks. *Ijarah* literally means 'to give something on rent', and technically it relates to transferring the usufruct of a particular property to another person on the basis of a rent claimed from him. The difference between sale (*bay*) and *ijarah* is transfer of ownership *vis-à-vis* transfer of the usufruct (*manfa'a*). That is, the leased property remains in the ownership of the lessor and only its usufruct is transferred to the lessee for specified rental payments which incorporate an element of profit.

This profit element in the lease is permissible, despite its obvious similarity to an interest charge. According to Islamic jurists, the *shari'ah* allows a fixed charge relating to tangible assets (as opposed to financial assets) because by converting financial capital into tangible assets the financier has assumed risks for which compensation is permissible. Classical Islamic jurisprudence permits the sale of usufruct from an asset on the grounds that the exchange involves risk, and this risk legitimizes any profits obtained. The conditions attached to *ijarah* clarify the risk involved to the lessor: first, the duty of repair is incumbent upon the lessor, second, the lessee is free to cancel the lease if the usufruct proves less beneficial than expected, and third, the price of the asset at the termination of the lease period cannot be fixed in advance (Warde, 2000, p. 135).

As in the case of the *murabahah*, the financier is able to ameliorate most risks. The requirement that the lessor is responsible for maintenance can be circumvented by the lessor appointing the lessee as its agent to undertake the maintenance, and by taking out an appropriate insurance policy. Uncertainty with respect to the scrap or residual value of a leased asset can be taken care of if the contract can be made for a period during which the financial institution will recover the principal amount as well as an appropriately benchmarked rate of return. The asset at the end of the lease period can then be transferred to the lessee. This makes the contract generate a fixed return for the financial insituion on its investment. Strictly speaking, the rental charges cannot be set on a floating rate basis (pegged to LIBOR for example) because the rules on *gharar* (uncertainty) deem that the contract has to fix and define the terms of the lease. However, this requirement can be bypassed by a non-binding 'gentleman's agreement' to renew the lease from time to time throughout its life at a new rate.

Leasing has become an integral part of Islamic finance, for two reasons. First, Islamic banks have made extensive use of the *ijarah* conract to finance an array of activities ranging from devising solutions to the financing of cars and residential homes to 'big ticket' items such as construction equipment, aeroplanes and ships. Once the banks adapted to the restrictions on Islamic leases in ways described above, the instrument emerged as a very flexible mode of finance, eminently adaptable to different uses, and which solves the problem of collateral by generating its own specific to the asset. *Ijarah* contracts are now being standardized and the documentation merged with that for conventional leases (Tag El-Din and Abdullah, 2007). Also, when combined with the permissible modes of buying and selling, the contract provides the basis for synthetic *sukuk* transactions with cashflows akin to conventional fixed interest securities. Such instruments (along with leasing itself) have received wide application in public sector finance.

Islamic Bonds (*Sukuk*) and Financial Engineering

Muslim jurists subject the buying and selling of debt obligations to certain conditions in order to comply with the prohibition of *riba* (interest), *gharar* (uncertainty) and *maysir* (gambling). Rosly and Sanusi (1999) specify these conditions in detail. In summary, the debt must be a genuine one, that is, it must not be a subterfuge to borrow money such as an asset-linked buy-back arrangement. The debtor must acknowledge the trade and creditors must be known, accessible, and sound. Trading must be on a spot basis and not against debt. Importantly, the price cannot be other than the face value. In line with these principles, early doctrine on interest-free finance disallowed corporate or government bonds and the discounting of bills. Pressures for innovation have resulted in finding a way out of these limitations, admitting 'financial engineering'. In particular, *ijarah* (leasing) bonds (*sukuk al-ijarah*) have been devised that are backed up by the ownership of an underlying asset and serviced by the usufruct received from it. Other *sukuk* have been issued, for example, *sukuk al-mudarabah, sukuk al-musharakah, sukuk al-murabahah*, and also *sukuk istisnaa*.

Sukuk means participation certificate, and is commonly referred to as an 'Islamic bond'. In order to construct them techniques similar to conventional asset-backed securities are employed, with *sukuk* actually more akin to pass-through certificates because of the ownership characteristics. A *sakk* simply represents a proportional or undivided ownership interest in an asset or pool of assets (McMillen, 2007). Islamic bonds are more useful if they can be traded on the secondary market, thus gaining liquidity. Certain conditions must be met with respect to the trading capacity of the bonds on the Islamic financial market. Specifically, unlike conventional bonds, they cannot represent a debt claim (in Islam, the buying and selling of debt obligations is forbidden except at face value). Instead they must constitute property of an approved asset. Such a bond is obtained through the securitization of the asset, the property of which is divided into equally valued units and incorporated in the *sukuk* certificates. The value of the *sukuk* thus remains anchored to the value of the underlying asset. While they come in zero coupon and coupon versions, the productivity and return is linked to the profit returns of the underlying asset and not to an interest rate (although an interest rate such as LIBOR can be used as a 'benchmark').

AAOIFI (the Accounting and Auditing Organization for Islamic Financial Institutions) has issued a 'Standard for investment *Sukuk*' (AAOIFI, 2003), which defines investment *sukuk* as certificates of equal value representing receipt of the value of the certificates, which value is applied to a planned and designated use, common title to shares and rights in tangible assets, usufructs and services, equity of a given project, or equity of a special investment activity (Adam and Thomas, 2004). So far AAOIFI has issued standards for 14 types of *sukuk*. These can be broadly grouped into *sukuk* that bear predetermined returns and *sukuk* that allow for sharing of profit and, in some instances, loss. *Sukuk al-musharakah* and *sukuk al-mudarabah* are examples of profit-and-loss-sharing *sukuk*. To date, most issued *sukuk* have borne predetermined returns, and a large number of such *sukuk* have been *sukuk al-ijarah*, frequently at a predetermined rate of return.

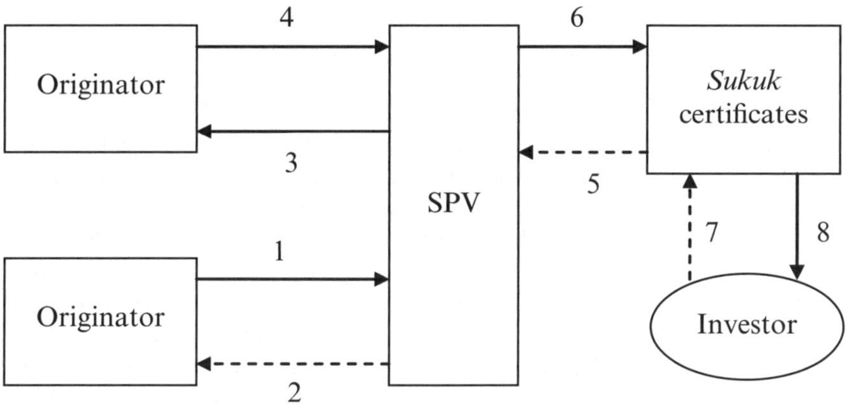

Key
1. Originator sells assets to be leased to the SPV.
2. Originator receives payment for assets sold.
3. The SPV leases assets back to the originator.
4. The SPV receives rent payments from the originator under a term-specified contract.
5. The SPV collects funds from the issuances of *sukuk* certificates to finance the purchase of assets from the originator.
6. The SPV utilizes the rent payments from the originator to disburse distributions on the *sukuk* certificates.
7. Investors (both conventional and Islamic) secure the *sukuk* certificates.
8. The investors are reimbursed periodically by the distributions from the SPV which are funded by the originator's rental payments on the leased assets.

Source: based on Tariq and Dar (2007)

Figure 7.1 Generic arrangement of sukuk *structure*

A *sukuk* uses methods that are now well-developed in conventional markets for structured finance. Structured finance comprises three steps: '(1) pooling of assets (either cash-based or synthetically created); (2) delinking of the credit risk of the collateral asset pool from the credit risk of the originator, usually through the transfer of the underlying assets to a finite-lived, standalone special purpose vehicle (SPV); and 3) tranching of liabilities that are backed by the asset pool' (Fender and Mitchell, 2005, p. 69). The first two characteristics are present in most securitizations and feature in Islamic structured instruments, but not the third, since they are organized to 'pass through' the returns on the underlying assets. As such, there are three parties to a *sukuk* arrangement: the originator of the *sukuk*, the SPV which is the issuer of the *sukuk* certificates, and the investors that buy these certificates. The basic arrangement is shown in Figure 7.1.

Consider, for example, the case of the *sukuk al-ijarah*. The originator holds assets (land, buildings, aircraft, ships, and so on.) that are to constitute the basis of the returns to the *sukuk* investor. These assets are sold by the originator to a SPV and then are leased back at a specified rental. The SPV securitizes the assets by issuing *sukuk* certificates that can be purchased by investors. Each *sukuk* certificate represents a share in the ownership of the assets, entitling the investor to periodic distributions from the SPV funded by the originator's rental payments on the leased assets. The returns can be either fixed rate or floating rate (often referenced to LIBOR) depending on the originator.

Ironically, devout Muslims refuse to buy conventional bonds because they violate the prohibition against earning interest. However, the fixed rate or LIBOR-linked *sukuk* do comply with Islamic laws by virtue of the ownership of the underlying assets. For example, the certificates for the first *shari'ah*-compliant securitized market financing of US assets are structured so that Islamic investors effectively get a fixed rate of return (11.25 per cent annually) while considering themselves owners of the underlying assets. An official *shari'ah* adviser issued a *fatwa*, or declaration, certifying that the instrument 'will yield returns, Allah willing, that are lawful and wholesome' (*Business Week*, 17 July 2006, p. 9). A press report on a later issue referred to 'so-called Islamic bonds – or *sukuk* – that are structured to avoid overt *riba* payments' (*The Australian*, 19–20 August 2006, p. 47). The word 'overt' is interesting.

The basic structure of a *sukuk* is very flexible and can be varied in a number of ways. The underlying assets that are pooled and securitized can be *ijarah*, *murabahah*, *istisnaa* or *musharakah* receivables, or combinations of them, and the rates of return can be fixed, floating or zero coupon. Investment risks (credit risk, interest rate risk, foreign exchange risk, market price risk, liquidity risk) are much the same as those of conventional bonds, and depend on the way the securitization is structured, although one unique risk is that of *shari'ah* compliance, a factor which also governs the tradeability of the *sukuk*.

It is the potential for tradeability that primarily makes for the popularity of *sukuk al-ijarah. Ijarah*, though less commonly employed than *murabahah* as an asset in Islamic banks' balance sheets, offers much greater flexibility for the Islamic bond market. Each security called *sukuk-al-ijarah* represents a pro rata ownership of physical assets as against a pro rata share in financial claims or debt in the case of *sukuk-al-murabahah*. While debt can only be transferred at par, ownership in physical assets can always be transferred at a mutually negotiated price (Obaidullah, 2007). Thus *sukuk-al-ijarah* allow for creation of an active secondary market since they represent a share in the ownership of a physical asset.

In addition, this mode of financing provides the most suitable basis to develop fixed-income securities for mobilizing funds for government. A large part of the government budget is devoted to acquiring fixed assets, machinery, industrial plants, and basic infrastructure such as buildings, roads, bridges and so on. All expenditure designated to acquire such assets could be financed through resources mobilized on the basis of leasing-based securities.

It is on such grounds that many in government and finance welcome *sukuk* as a valuable addition to the range of Islamic instruments, allowing the creation of an Islamic bond market with secondary trading, something which did not exist before. El-Qorchi (2005), viewing them from a multilateral bank perspective, recognizes the competitiveness of many of the new products in attracting both Muslim and non-Muslim investors, while the asset-based Islamic bonds are seen as a particularly innovative, rapidly growing market sector tapped by sovereign and corporate borrowers alike. In the Islamic financial industry itself, such innovations are hailed for allowing vast sums of money to be raised from Islamic investors. A press report in 2006 says 'a construction frenzy in the oil-rich Gulf region has triggered a boom in the market for *sukuks*, or Islamic bonds, as devout Muslims increasingly demand financing instruments that comply with their religion' (*The Australian*, 12 July 2006, p. 23).

A less flattering assessment comes from academics such as Hamoudi (2006). Hamoudi speaks of 'the failures of Islamic finance' which have led to the creation of 'a bizarre and highly artificial construct that does nothing to address the social concerns that are the central reason for the creation of Islamic banking and finance' (p. 8). It is fair to say that not so long ago, it was unthinkable to even talk about an Islamic financial instrument, especially a bond, that would guarantee a fixed return. Since 2001, when the Bahrain Monetary Authority issued Islamic leasing certificates with a five-year maturity to the value of $100 million, it has become a reality to financially engineer financial instruments offering *shari'ah*-compatible fixed returns. By 2006, the total value of *sukuk* on issue globally was estimated to be over $25 billion, and the market has grown since then (Tariq and Dar, 2007).

One interpretation of this development is that there has been a change in the special system of religious governance that an Islamic financial institution must put in place to reassure investors that God's laws are being followed in financial transactions. Volker Nienhaus (2007), in particular, argues that the behaviour of the *shari'ah* supervisory boards, that monitor adherence to Islamic principles, has altered markedly over the years. In the past, they were somewhat conservative. Now he wonders whether in recent years the boards have become rather too permissive, and accommodating to the bankers. One only has to recall the 'capture' theory of regulation (Stigler, 1971) to think of reasons why the *shari'ah* board members might be inclined to give bank managers the benefit of the doubt when approving new product innovations, so blurring the ideological purity of the Islamic system.

However, this behaviour may not be a new problem. In his commentary on the activities of the Religious Supervisory Boards (RSBs), written well before the advent of the *sukuk*, Abdullah Saeed (1996) reached the following conclusion:

> At times it appears that there is a tendency on the part of RSBs to solve practical problems by resorting to *hiyal* (legal fiction). Even though the RSBs sometimes appear to be averse to *hiyal* in their problem solving function, some *fatwas* pronounced by the RSBs are akin to *hiyal*. Utilisation of *hiyal* seemingly comes from the RSBs' preoccupation with moulding the solutions which are suggested by the management of the banks, or by the RSBs themselves, into legal forms which are acceptable to various forms of contracts developed in *fiqh*. A solution to a particular problem can be made acceptable if it is in a certain form, while the same solution cannot be acceptable in another form. The RSBs, at times, after declaring a particular transaction unlawful, go on to declare the same transaction lawful if it is presented in a different form even though no modification was made to any of its constituent elements. (p. 116)

While one can discern unease in some circles as to the pace of innovation and the direction of change in Islamic capital markets in the current decade, specific concerns about the legitimacy of *sukuk* in terms of the spirit if not the letter of the law may be misdirected. It is not *sukuk* as such which are controversial, but rather the trading-based financing methods which underlie both them and the great bulk of Islamic banking practice, at least as interpreted by *fiqh*. This leads us to the next issue.

HOW ISLAMIC IS ISLAMIC FINANCE?

Like any market system, Islamic finance relies on a spirit of entrepreneurship if it is to grow; there must be innovation and new products designed that meet customer needs. Certainly, recent developments in Islamic financing pass this particular test. Many innovative new products such as *sukuk* built around mark-up financing methods have allowed banks and their clients to engage in investment, hedging and trading activities that would have been almost incomprehensible not so long ago. But do these instruments go too far? Unlike other financial arrangements, the Islamic system must meet another test, the religious test, and remain within the scope of Islamic law.

Consider, for example, the innovations that have taken place in the area of government financing. Fahim Khan (2007) sets out the case for

Table 7.1 Some Islamic money market instruments

	Objective	Non-islamic security equivalent	Popularity
Sukuk structures	Create a secondary market and liquidity for debt collaterized by real and financial assets	Asset-backed securities	High
Mudarabah inter-bank investment (MII)	Inter-bank borrowing and lending	Negotiable certificates of deposits (CDs)	Medium
Wadia inter-bank acceptance	Liquidity management facility between the central bank and an Islamic bank	Islamic bank reserves at the central bank	Medium
Bank Negara negotiable notes	Manage liquidity of the Islamic banking system	Treasury bills	High
Islamic accepted bills	Finance foreign trade transactions	Bankers' acceptances	Medium
Islamic negotiable instruments of deposit (INID)	Provides a return on maturity time deposits	Time deposit with fixed maturity	High
Rahn agreement	Liquidity management	Repurchase agreement	Low

Source: Hakim (2007)

sukuk and other newly developed instruments enabling participants in Islamic financial markets to borrow and invest and manage liquidity along conventional lines. (These instruments are surveyed by Hakim (2007) and summarized in Table 7.1.)[3] Khan is convinced that fixed-interest rate government debt along conventional lines has to be replicated with fixed return, negligible risk, Islamic securities, based upon mark-up arrangements, if a successful secondary market is to develop that can rival those in conventional financial systems. A fixed return is attractive to borrower and lender alike, and in the absence of liquidity the demand for the securities from ultimate investors and financial institutions will be greatly reduced.

He is probably correct in this judgement. But the question then becomes one of whether, in the process of achieving this objective, desirable as it may be, the 'baby is thrown out with the bathwater'.

Let us consider the reasons given for Islamic fixed-return contracts being regarded as acceptable, as explained by Khan:

> The pricing mechanism of Islamic financial instruments, including those of government securities would, basically, be similar to that for conventional financial instruments. The time value of money in economic and financial transactions is recognized in Islam. The only difference is that the time value of money cannot be realized as a part of the loan contract. It can be realized only as an integral part of a real transaction. Thus, in a trade transaction, if the payment of price is deferred, then the time value of money will be included in the price of the commodity. Similarly, in a leasing contract, time value is an integral part of the rent that parties agree upon. (p. 295)

This is correct, as far as it goes. But the issue then becomes whether this is really a trade transaction, or is it a loan in disguise masquerading as a commodity deal to conform to legal rules? A recent commentary on such practices comes from El-Gamal (2007). In his eyes, the Islamic finance industry has degenerated into one that is dominated by form over substance, the chief aim of which is to circumvent, rather than comply in any meaningful way, with the Qur'anic injunctions against *riba* (interest) and *gharar* (excessive uncertainty). This aim is realized when conventional lending practices are replicated in Islamically-acceptable ways in the balance sheets of Islamic financial institutions – a process that he calls '*shari'ah*-arbitrage'.

Some might want to blame the entry of conventional banks to the industry for this state of affairs. An expanding array of conventional banks competes head on with purely Islamic banks by providing Islamic financial services in a variety of ways. Some are best described as 'hybrids', offering Islamic 'windows' or 'counters' hand-in-hand with conventional banking operations. Others have opened special branches that sell only Islamic banking products. In locations that restrict the operations of 'hybrids', conventional banks have established separate Islamic financial institutions with distinctive legal identity and management. Others have created separate brands for their Islamic activities, such as Amanah (HSBC) and Dar al Istithmar (Deutsche Bank). In these different ways, new banks or subsidiaries or offshoots of conventional banks rapidly are appearing and widening their market presence (Hassan and Lewis, 2007b).

Faced with this competition, Islamic institutions perceive the need to match the innovation and marketing structures underpinning conventional financial services. This desire has led to the search for Islamic financial instruments that essentially replicate the characteristics of conventional financial products, while remaining within the purview of acceptability in terms of *shari'ah* oversight. Examples given earlier are the adaptation of conventional hire purchase and leasing contracts to *ijarah* (Islamic leasing) structures, and the development of *sukuk* by modifying and utilizing techniques developed in conventionally structured finance arrangements. These adaptations both simplify the workings of the contractual forms and standardize the payoff profiles, generating returns to bankers and investors that are, being derived from the levying of a 'cost-plus' rate of profit formula, as fixed, certain and safe under Islamically-compliant financing modes as any interest-based conventional loan.

While it is true that the pace of financial adaptation has accelerated over the last decade, the reality is that conventional banks have long been involved in the industry at the wholesale level, offering commodity-based and other Islamically acceptable investment vehicles, and acting as intermediaries between the commodity brokers and the purely Islamic banks. Moreover, the issues date back to the early days of Islamic banking in the 1970s and 1980s when only 'pure play' Islamic banks occupied the field. Their adoption of trading-based instruments, in which the financial risk taken by the banks has been minimized (if not altogether removed) in ways described in the previous section, has invoked considerable hostility from Muslim scholars. A number of the critiques are reproduced below.

First, Dr Ghulam Qadir (1994, p. 105) on practices in Pakistan:

> Two of the modes of financing prescribed by the State Bank, namely financing through the purchase of client's property with a buy-back agreement and sale of goods to clients on a mark-up, involved the least risk and were closest to the old interest-based operations. Hence the banks confined their operations mostly to these modes, particularly the former, after changing the simple buy-back agreement (prescribed by the State Bank) to buy-back agreement with a mark-up, as otherwise there was no incentive for them to extend any finances. The banks also reduced their mark-up-based financing, whether through the purchase of client's property or through the sale of goods to clients, to mere paper work, instead of actual buying of goods (property), taking their possession and then selling (back) to the client As a result, there was no difference between the mark-up as practised by the banks and the conventional interest rate, and hence it was judged repugnant to Islam in the recent decision of the Federal Sharia Court.
>
> As banks are essentially financial institutions and not trading houses, requiring them to undertake trading in the form of buy-back arrangements and sale on mark-up amounts to imposing on them a function for which they are not well equipped. Therefore, banks in Pakistan made such modifications in the prescribed modes which defeated the very purpose of interest-free financing. Furthermore, as these two minimum-risk modes of financing were kept open to banks, they never tried to devise innovative and imaginative modes of financing within the framework of *musharakah* and *mudarabah*.

Next, Professor Khurshid Ahmad (1994a, pp. 46–7) writes:

> *Murabaha* (cost-plus financing) and *bai'muajjal* (sale with deferred payment) are permitted in the *Shari'ah* under certain conditions. Technically, it is not a form of financial mediation but a kind of business participation. The *Shari'ah* assumes that the financier actually buys the goods and then sells them to the client. Unfortunately, the current practice of buy-back on 'mark-up' is not in keeping with the conditions on which *murabaha* or *bai'muajjal* are permitted. What is being done is a fictitious deal which ensures a predetermined profit to the bank without actually dealing in goods or sharing any real risk. This is against the letter and spirit of *Shari'ah* injunctions.
>
> While 1 would not venture a *fatwa*, as I do not qualify for that function, yet as a student of economics and *Shari'ah* I regard this practice of buy-back on mark-up very similar to *riba* and would suggest its discontinuation. I understand that the Council of Islamic Ideology has also expressed a similar opinion.

Dr Hasanuz Zaman (1994) is more critical still:

> It emerges that practically it is impossible for large banks or the banking system to practise the modes like mark-up, *bai'salam*, buy-back, *murabaha*, etc. in a way that fulfils the *Shari'ah* conditions. But in order to make themselves eligible to a return on their operations, the banks are compelled to play tricks with the letters of the law. They actually do not buy, do not possess, do not actually sell and deliver the goods; but the transaction is assumed to have taken place. By signing a number of documents of purchase, sale and transfer they might fulfil a legal requirement but it is by violating the spirit of prohibition. (p. 208)

Again:

> It seems that in large numbers of cases the ghost of interest is haunting them to calculate a fixed rate per cent per annum even in *musharakah*, *mudarabah*, leasing, hire-purchase, rent sharing, *murabaha*, (*bai'muajjal*, mark-up), PTC, TFC, etc. The spirit behind all these contracts seems to make a sure earning comparable with the prevalent rate of interest and, as far as possible, avoid losses which otherwise could occur. (ibid., p. 203)

He sums up in the following words:

> many techniques that the interest-free banks are practising are not either in full conformity with the spirit of *Shari'ah* or practicable in the case of large banks or the entire banking system. Moreover, they have failed to do away with undesirable aspects of interest. Thus, they have retained what an Islamic bank should eliminate. (ibid., p. 212)

In considering these criticisms, the first thing that should be resisted is the notion that the financing techniques violate the *shari'ah*. While the Holy Qur'an prohibits usury, it actively encourages trade. The criticized financing methods are the principal ways by which Islamic banks finance trade. A letter of credit under the *murabahah* principle enables buyers to take delivery of goods for trading purposes with the bank acting as intermediary. Financing of trade is a major activity of some Islamic banks. It follows that the more international the bank, and the greater is its involvement with the financing of trading and commercial activities, the larger is likely to be its usage of mark-up instruments. Similarly, the more international the region, for example the Gulf countries, the greater are likely to be the trade financing activities of the Islamic banks in the area.

Nevertheless, the use of trading-based financing does extend way beyond this traditional function. Whether by trial or error, it would seem that Islamic bankers have discovered that PLS financing is not practicable for all economic activities, and that it does not always guarantee the banks a reliable return available for distribution to depositors. This consideration, after all, is especially important in Islamic financing since depositors with investment accounts, not shareholders, bear the cost of any losses incurred by banks under PLS modes. Even Umer Chapra, one of the leading supporters of the 'pure' model of Islamic banking, concedes this point (Chapra, 2007). While Dr Chapra advocates that Islamic banks ought to do more financing by equity participation, and much less by the alternatives, he accepts that not all financing requirements are amenable to PLS methods. Indeed, he admits that debt is 'indispensable'; in practice it constitutes the greater part of Islamic finance, involving *murabahah*, *ijarah*, *bai'salam* and *istisnaa* and other sales-based financing modes. These are less risky than PLS financing because the rate of return is fixed in advance and built into the deferred payment price on a cost-plus (or 'mark-up') basis. By the same token, with the banker receiving (or expecting to receive) a predetermined rate of return, the sales-based modes have every appearance of interest-based instruments.

This leads us to the next question. If Islamic banking merely modifies conventional financing in such a way as to satisfy the *shari'ah* scholars, what is there that remains distinctive about the Islamic system? In short, what is the essential point of departure between the two systems? Should the adaptive devices come to dominate the system and come to be regarded as tantamount to legal fictions (*hiyal*), there is the danger that Islamic banking looks like an issue of branding, like Mecca Cola instead of Coca Cola. Then there is the issue of the social charter that inspired many who help found the system. Although the term '*halal* banking' has sometimes been used as a description for Islamic banking operations, the broader term 'Islamic banking' has been preferred to signify that the system also stands for the furtherance of religious and social goals involving various charitable foundations, economic development and the alleviation of poverty. This broad social ethos is a potential differentiating factor in the market that runs alongside strict legal compliance with Islamic jurisprudence.

These are matters, it has to be admitted, that rebound through the centuries for the '*shari'ah*-arbitrage' referred to by El-Gamal (2007) is not a new problem. Many of the issues go back to the early days of Islam when, according to Schacht (1964), attempts to circumvent the prohibitions on *riba* by legal devices (*hiyal*) began. A popular technique consisted of the double sale (*bay'atan fi bay'a*). For example, the (prospective) debtor sells to the (prospective) creditor an item for cash, and immediately buys it back from him for a greater amount payable at a future date. This amounts to a loan with the particular item concerned as security, and the difference between the two prices represents the interest. Schacht, as we noted earlier, dates this custom in Madinah as early as in the time of Malik (d. 796) and claims that there were 'hundreds' of such devices used by traders *cum* money-lenders, all with a scrupulous regard for the letter of the law. Parallels to the present-day situation are complete when Schacht goes on to observe the role of the religious scholars in ensuring the legality of the transactions.

> The first and simplest *hiyal* were presumably thought out by the interested parties who felt the need for them, the merchants in particular, but it was quite beyond them to invent and apply the more complicated ones; they had to have recourse to specialists in religious law, and these last did not hesitate to supply the need. Once the system of religious law had been elaborated, the religious zeal of the first specialists was gradually replaced and superseded by the not less sincere, not less convinced, but more technical, more scholastic, interest of professionals who took pride in inventing and perfecting small masterpieces of legal construction, The inventors of *hiyal* had to calculate the chances of legal validity to a nicety if the *kadi* (Islamic judge), who was bound by the sacred Law, was not to upset the real effects of the business transaction, which their customers, the merchants, had in mind, effects which depended upon the validity of every single element in an often complicated series of formal transactions. (p. 80)

What is the solution (if one is sought) to the practice of *shari'ah*-arbitrage? To Western eyes an obvious answer would be to admit the substance and abandon the form, by Islam following Christianity, effectively bowing to what may seem the inevitable, and relinquishing the religious prohibitions upon *riba* financing – except, that is, for excessive (usurious) interest charges. Islamic finance would then resemble the ethical investment movement in the West, by excluding *haram* activities (finance of alcohol, pork production, gambling, and so on.) but allowing loans to be made at reasonable commercial rates. In effect, *riba* would be associated with the usury 'doubled and multiplied' and other such exorbitant interest rate practices condemned in the Holy Qur'an (3:130) Despite such a resolution being consistent with the line argued over 40 years ago by Fazlur Rahman (1964) and other revisionists on the issue of *riba*, this prospect is, however, one that is universally unpalatable both to critics of the current trends in the industry (who wish to preserve the specialness of Islamic financing) and practitioners (who benefit from *shari'ah*-arbitrage) alike.

It is more likely, indeed virtually certain, that the present situation will continue and that innovations will propel Islamic finance along its present path, which would appear to be one of asymptotically approaching conventional financing, albeit with different terminology. Is this purely a face-saving, essentially cosmetic, solution to retain the semblance of conformity with the strictures of the Holy Qur'an, or is there some real purpose served? Chapra argues the latter. He considers that differences do remain between conventional lending and sales-based financing (via, say, *murabahah* or *ijarah*), and that these are important in two respects. First, because the seller of goods (the financier) must own and possess the goods being sold, speculative short-selling is ruled out, helping to curb the type of excessive speculation that takes place in conventional financial markets.[4] Second, the sales-based financing methods do not involve direct lending and borrowing but comprise purchase or lease transactions based on real goods and services. Financing in the Islamic system thus tends to expand *pari passu* with the growth of the real economy, constraining excessive credit creation and limiting one of the causes of instability in the international markets. In similar vein, El-Gamal (2007) sees some mitigating elements in synthetic loan structures based on credit sales and leasing, since they represent a form of secured lending that limits excessive borrowing by virtue of the fact that debt-based financing rises in line with the growth of the assets financed.

This, then, leads us to the final question. Why is interest lending apparently so seductive? Why were Christians attracted to fixed interest lending, and why are Muslims (or at least Islamic bankers) today so keen to replicate fixed interest financing? Is it simply the difficulty of putting aside old habits? Or, are there incentive compatibility issues that make it difficult to implement the preferred Islamic financing modes?

THE PROBLEMS OF ISLAMIC FINANCE

The theoretical basis of interest free finance and the compliance of Islamic banks with the letter and spirit of *shari'ah* have been subject to scrutiny by researchers on conventional economics and finance. Kuran (1993,

1995, 1996, 1997) and Aggarwal and Yousef (2000) are cases in point. The critique has two dimensions. One is that most instruments employed for Islamic finance – for example, *murabahah*, *ijarah*, *istisnaa*, and *salam* – while different in some respects from conventional fixed-interest finance are nevertheless a far cry from the Islamic ideal of the genuine profit and loss sharing arrangements, for example, *mudarabah* and *musharakah* contracts. The other is that a major reason for quasi-fixed financing patterns lies in the prevailing low standards of honesty and trustworthiness. In such an environment, human interactions increasingly become akin to game theoretic economic models populated with self-seeking individuals who are bent upon maximizing their own payoffs. Typically, a gap in information (asymmetric information) between those who run a business (entrepreneurs or managers) and those who finance it (investors), places the latter at the risk of being disadvantaged by the former through the choice of an adverse project (adverse selection or hidden information) or by shirking work, spending on personal benefits, and hiding the true level of project profitability (moral hazard or hidden actions). Islamic banks working alongside conventional banks face an additional dimension of adverse selection since entrepreneurs with below average earnings expectations seek financing through PLS modes in order to minimize losses in case of failure. Conversely, businessmen with above-average profit expectations prefer fixed interest (conventional) financing in order to maximize their gains in case of success. In these circumstances, financial contracting becomes a matter of designing mechanisms that more closely align the incentives of entrepreneurs with financiers at least possible transaction costs. It is in this context then that a debt contract may be seen to offer an advantage over simple PLS contracts in many conditions.

The Theoretical Basis of Debt Contracts

The theoretical backdrop to the above analysis is interesting. It began with Kenneth J. Arrow's brilliant (1964) demonstration that in the presence of risky securities payable in money, the existence and optimality of classical competitive equilibrium can be achieved by indexing the return on securities to the state of nature, that is, actual outcomes. This result is tantamount to the optimality of equity contracts. Yet, debt contracts – the interest on which is not ordinarily contingent on investment returns – are pervasive in the real world. How can this anomaly be explained? This question led to the rise of information economics which focuses on the implications of one particular market imperfection, namely, the presence of asymmetric information among the parties to a transaction, the existence of which exposes the parties to the risks of moral hazard and adverse selection. Several stylized models then depict how parties will use different features of debt and equity contracts to alleviate such risk. Four contractual settings are common.

In costly state verification (CSV) models (see, for example, Townsend (1979)), it is assumed that it is costly for investors to verify the *ex post* income of borrowers. Use of debt economizes on verification costs by eliminating the need to verify in states of nature when returns are higher than a critical level, making it possible for the borrower to pay a constant stream of income to the investors. Conversely, when such payments fall short of the constant amount, the financier has the right to audit. By identifying the states in which an audit is carried out with bankruptcy and the costs of audit with bankruptcy costs, debt can be shown as the optimal contract. Given that bankruptcy is tantamount to the borrower's loss of right in the project, it is in his interest not to misrepresent his income. The fixed interest contract is thus incentive compatible.

In agency cost models (such as Jensen and Meckling (1976) and Jensen (1986)), debt can be shown to alleviate the friction that exists between a firm's owners and managers. Managers have an incentive to seek personal benefits through perquisites – luxury offices, first class air travel, 'empire' building and so on – at the cost of extracting shareholder value. Issuance of debt can reduce this tendency as it commits managers to pay out cash, reducing the free cash flows available for personal consumption.

Adverse selection models focus on private information (for example, quality of the project) possessed by managers or entrepreneurs. With this information, low-quality firms have an incentive to issue equity contracts. Firms that for some reason intend to under-report (distort) their profits may likewise favour equity contracts over debt. When such behaviour is widely anticipated, the market for contingent contracts shrinks (the problem of 'lemons') and all firms have to issue debt contracts. Alternatively, better quality entrepreneurs use debt financing as a signal of their superior quality (Banks and Sobel, 1987; Allen and Gale, 1992). In some other contracting environments, issuance of debt is made optimal because equity sells at a discount (Myers and Majluf, 1984). On another hand, equity contracts dominate debt in the case of adverse selection in relation to the riskiness of a project (Lewis and Algaoud, 2001, Chapter 4).

Control and ownership models assume that the pattern of allocation of certain rights among different stakeholders is an important variable in explaining and designing financial contracts. For example, Aghion and Bolton (1992) model incomplete contracting (all future contingencies cannot be specified) between an entrepreneur and an outside investor in which entrepreneurial effort and reward cannot be specified. The outside investor is interested only in cash flows, while the entrepreneur is interested both in cash flows and private benefits (including reputational enhancement, patronage, diversion, and so on). These private benefits create a conflict of interest between the two parties which is resolved through the allocation of two variables: cash flow and decision rights. Efficiency is achieved by allocating decision rights to the entrepreneur when earnings and future prospects are good, leaving him to evaluate if additional payoffs are worth the extra effort involved. However, when earnings and prospects are bad, control transfers to the investor. This occurs through the prespecified right to institute bankruptcy that comes with the debt contract. Thus the investor's decision to liquidate is not influenced by the entrepreneur's private benefits and maximization of value occurs in bad states. Debt contracts emerge as optimal.

Challenges to Debt Optimality

The preceding analysis points to the 'inevitability' of fixed interest contracts and underpins the critique of PLS contracting in Islamic banking. However, this is not the final word on the matter. The microeconomic rationale for debt optimality can be queried in certain respects and fixed-interest debt contracts may at times have a negative impact on macroeconomic stability. Below, we consider each of these aspects.

Critique of the microeconomic rationale for debt optimality

Almost all contracting models can produce contrary results if the initial assumptions about the contractual arrangements are varied. For example, Mookherjee and Png (1989) demonstrate in the context of CSV models that if random audits are permitted, equity contracts actually dominate debt contracts. Nevertheless, despite this result, Dowd (1992) remains unimpressed:

> If debt is indeed sub-optimal, one is forced to conclude that agents in the real world are making wide use of an inefficient contract form, and have done for a very long time, and many economists would find this conclusion disturbing as well. (p. 672)

> It is clear, then, that there are reasonably plausible circumstances in which debt contracts appear to be optimal, and this point needs to be emphasised in view of the recent work of Mookherjee and Png (1989) and others which suggests that they are usually inferior. Many economists would also find it reassuring that debt contracts are defensible given that they figure so prominently in real-world financial arrangements, and it is useful anyway to be able to explain why debt is so widely used. (p. 689)

On agency problems, the second of the contracting models, Hart (2001) argues that the conflicts of interest pointed out by Jensen and Meckling can be more conveniently resolved by putting the insider agents (that is, managers) on optimal incentive schemes. Thus the financial structure can be spared from the burden of resolving agent-centred design problems. It can be argued that this is in fact what the Islamic *mudarabah* contract does; it attempts to resolve agency problems by giving the entrepreneur a share in profits aligning their incentives more closely with the shareholders. The challenge for Islamic finance lies in adapting this concept to a wider range of conflicts of interest that exist in today's business structures.

Adverse selection models are said to suffer the same theoretical shortcoming as the agency models, that is, insiders (in particular managers), behave in a particular manner because they are responding to an implicit incentive contract that ties their interests more closely with the existing shareholders. For instance, Dybvig and Zender (1991) question much usage made of adverse selection to explain financial contracting. They illustrate that for a wide variety of insider–outsider conflicts, the use of capital structure and dividend policy can be rendered irrelevant by designing compensation schemes that do not tie the interests of insiders (managers) with the existing shareholders alone.

Macroeconomic rationale for sub-optimality of debt

While the theory of optimal contracting examines reasons for the observed prevalence of debt contracts or a combination of debt and equity in corporate financial structure, a related strain of research seeks to explain how in the presence of asymmetric information, differences in debt and equity, and inside and outside funds, translate small adverse shocks to the economy into large investment finance and output fluctuations. The starting point is that the conflict of interest between parties to a debt contract may lead to situations of excessive risk-taking since for a given expected net present value, any increase in risk that reduces the expected return to creditors equally increases the expected return to borrowers (Milgrom and Roberts, 1992, p. 495). Equity contracts, insofar as the choice of a project is concerned, mitigate such conflict of interest since either party's payoff is maximized by selecting the same project.

Stiglitz and Weiss (1981) demonstrated how the adverse incentive in debt contracts may result in failure of price (interest rates) and non-price (collateral) mechanisms to allocate bank credit, resulting in credit rationing. Other research examined the role that fixed-interest contracts play in business cycles via variations in the proportion of income allocated to debt and equity holders, hurdle rates and net worth, which are linked in the following way. First, a rise in interest rates raises the hurdle rates for investment in new projects. Second, interest expense rises on existing floating rate and short-term debt reducing corporate cashflows. Third, net worth reduces owing to falls in asset values. Fourth, agency problems worsen. Fifth, the premium required on raising external finance is increased. All these factors constrain capacity to borrow further and spend (that is, break the link between savings and its circulation, triggering recession). Households and small firms that face high agency costs – and are dependent on bank debt – are particularly affected since a flight to quality occurs. This leaves these sectors allocated a relatively lower share of the credit when they need it most at critical points of the business cycle (Stiglitz and Weiss, 1992; Bernanke *et al.* 1996). It can be argued that to the extent that equity finance becomes a part of the financing mechanisms to households and commercial sector ventures, it provides capacity to withstand external shocks and (obviously) lessens the adverse impact of leverage.

Compound Interest and Sustainability

The call of Islamic finance to abolish interest is primarily on religious grounds. Nevertheless, Islamic scholars have sought to provide a theoretical basis for the prohibition in terms of morality and economics. The reason for this endeavour is straightforward: while the basic source of the ban is the divine authority of the Holy Qur'an, it gave no conceptual rationale for why interest is unjustified.[5] Early writers such as Ghazali emphasized the social welfare aspects and the violation of justice in money-lending at interest. Twentieth-century scholars, such as Ahmad (1952), Abu Su'ud (1980), Siddiqi (1980, 1982), Chapra (1985) and Khan (1985) moved away from equity considerations, and have taken the conventional theories of interest to task for equating interest with either 'impatience' or 'waiting', on the savings side, or with the 'productivity of capital', on the investment side. Instead, they argue, interest is paid on money, not on capital, and has to be paid irrespective of capital productivity.

The difficulties that can arise from this last obligation is readily apparent to anyone who has toyed with the arithmetic of compound interest. Lietaer (2001) gives an example of the 'impossibility' of compound interest. One pfennig (that is, one cent) invested by Joseph at the birth of Christ at 4 per cent would have grown to the value of one ball of gold equal to the weight of the Earth by 1749 CE and to 8190 balls of gold of the weight of the Earth by 1990 CE. The underlying thesis advanced here is that once we start talking about long-run sustainable economic growth (that is, without incurring negative externalities in particular, environmental degradation and pollution) and start comparing it with prevailing interest rates, debts costing even 4 per cent p.a. (real) compound appear difficult to service.

Such arguments, we should note, have a very respectable heritage in conventional economic theory. As to whether interest is paid as the return on money or as the return on capital we can note the opinion of Sir Dennis Robertson (1951). He asked whether interest is governed by the classical forces of productivity and thrift or by liquidity preference theory with its focus on the money market and the quantity of money. He answers in a typically Robertsonian wry manner: 'we must have a classical theory to tell us why there is a rate of interest at all, and a liquidity theory to tell us why it is what it is' (p. 200). Next, as to the distinction between interest and profits, we turn to Adam Smith in the *Wealth of Nations.* He stated that the share of income derived 'by the person who employs it is called profit. That derived from it by the person who does not employ it himself, but lends to another is called the interest, or the use of money' (p. 52). He continues by pointing out that the reason a lender can secure interest is because a profit can be made. Conard (1959) draws the obvious implication that then follows: 'the former could demand a return for his funds essentially equal to the profits that the capitalist was able to acquire from their use, with the result that the rate of interest would be roughly equal to the rate of profit, and determined by it' (p. 12). Thus, in equilibrium, any statement about interest becomes one about profit, and in this respect Islamic finance is not immune from the 'impossibility' of compounding (whether it be of interest in conventional analysis or re-invested profit in the Islamic system).

However, again this is not the end of the matter. There is left what Schumpeter (1934) called the 'dilemma' of interest. He argued that wherever competition exists, it will drive to zero (or normal profits) the profit on any particular product or productive method. Since interest is derived from profits – being paid by the entrepreneur in order to acquire them – how can it be a permanent flow when profits themselves are always temporary? In this case, the question remained unresolved. Schumpeter himself was unable to determine whether the equilibrium rate of interest is positive, that is, whether interest could exist in equilibrium.

Summary

Before moving on, let us summarize key points of the preceding discussion. First, there would appear to be certain conditions that govern when a debt contract is optimal, but the argument can be overstated. Some research on security design makes assumptions that virtually guarantee the optimality of a specific contract (Allen and Winton, 1995). Others focus on conflicts of the type that can more conveniently be resolved by changing managerial compensation schemes rather than adopting a certain mix of financial instruments in corporate capital structure. However, if the 'optimality of debt' (in certain circumstances) view is rejected, we are left with no answer to the question of why debt contracts have proven to be so attractive for so long. Second, any optimality of the debt contract in the microeconomic context comes at a cost to the macroeconomic system where debt and leverage can magnify small economic shocks into larger investment and output fluctuations (and the highly levered collateralized debt obligations (CDOs) at the centre of the sub-prime crisis of 2008 remind us all too vividly that this particular issue has not gone away). Third, while debt is not necessarily the best way to resolve the kind of problems highlighted – that is, moral hazard, adverse selection, and agency conflicts – the existence of these problems cannot be denied. Research on financial contracting remains valuable and sheds light on a variety of arrangements that can be employed to alleviate these problems. Fourth, financial contracts should be viewed not only in terms of the way they split cash flows among the parties but also in terms of control rights that they assign to them at various stages of the project life. Both components must be kept in sight for incentive compatibility and efficiency of resource allocation in security design. Fifth, organizational design (for example, insider/outsider conflict) and information distribution can have an important bearing on financial structure.

What is the Matter with Islamic Finance?

Leading Islamic scholars have taken the system of Islamic finance to task on the grounds that the contractual solutions offered by Islamic bankers are, in essence, no different from conventional solutions. What is the reason for such similarity? In our view one major reason is that (within the constraints of the prevailing system) the PLS concept is not readily adaptable to consumer and trade finance, as well as for public sector finance. The adaptation of classical deferred price merchandising contracts for financing has changed the landscape in two ways:

- The risk of merchandizing is retained by the traders but the risk of credit is shifted to the bankers. This is precisely what happens in conventional interest based finance.
- Banks' profit rate comes from the charging of a difference between the deferred price and the spot price. Controversial even by classical standards, this practice leaves the system open to the charge that there is seemingly only a hair's breadth of difference between conventional and Islamic finance. One difference is that in Islamic finance, deferred price once contracted does not change, while in conventional finance delays incur additional interest.

One alternative could be that Islamic banks purchase shares (on a profit and loss sharing basis) in merchant/trading concerns which deal directly in consumer durable goods. In this way the institution would take on merchandizing risks associated with sales activity and unambiguously earn income that is *riba*-free. However, such activity may induce a host of legal, regulatory and prudential supervision issues that the industry may prefer to avoid, and the same is true of financing commercial trading business. Instead, the financing of infrastructure or industry holds more potential for the application of PLS contracts within the existing system, although these are not areas in which Islamic finance has a significant presence. In any case, if PLS contracts were to be moved to the centre of Islamic banking, problems of adverse selection and moral hazard re-emerge.

In order to address adverse selection and moral hazard in a *shari'ah* compatible manner, a number of alternatives need to be explored. First, one must recognize that moral hazard is not a problem specific to equity contracts but is embedded in all institutional and transactional arrangements. Perhaps this fact points to a missing dimension of the modern socio-economic and political architecture, with an overemphasis on 'self-interest' and the 'commercial' needs of the society. We leave this thought for others to ponder. However, the importance of having to curtail moral hazard within-jurisdiction is supported by the evolution of modern equity markets, for instance in the United States. A wider market in equity participation was made possible by the development of the accounting profession and the establishment of watchdogs like the Securities and Exchange Commission. At a second level, it may be possible to bring financial transactions closer to the community. In particular, for micro finance, *masjids* and community organizations could play an important role in providing integrity checks on individuals. Third, there is a need to develop innovative bank and inter-bank strategies to alleviate moral hazard. As examples, clients may be required to have regular audits from bank-approved auditors, key accounting staff for leading borrowers may be recruited jointly by the bank and its client, and banks may standardize client risk ratings and share information on bigger clients and their past dues. Fourth, there may be a need to implant an entrepreneurial culture among those who have money in many Muslim countries, which can be addressed through a combination of appropriate research, training and incubator facilities.

ALTERNATIVE MODELS OF PUBLIC SECTOR FINANCE

If PLS contracts are to be brought to the forefront of Islamic banking, solutions should be sought at the transactional and organizational level if the status quo in the larger socio-economic and political system is to be overcome. In this section, we illustrate how insights from the theory of financial contracting can be integrated with Islamic requirements to avoid interest in order to design a PLS contractual structure for financing a commercial public sector organization or for that matter, any commercial venture.

Suppose that we need to set up a new public sector commercial organization. Is it possible to segregate its capital structure into parcels of different risk-return profile without contravening *shari'ah*? In other words, can the same underlying 'going concern' or 'business' offer different profit sharing ratios to investors with different risk profiles?

It is our belief that the answer to the above question is in the affirmative if we differentiate risk by a combination of control rights and redemption schedules. For instance, parcels of securities (shares/bonds) can be issued that give their holders right to share profits in a specified ratio for a specified period (1, 2, 3, . . . years). The rationale for this differentiation is given below.

Profit prospects over one time horizon may be different from those over a different time horizon. If this is the case, then attaching different PLS ratios to different maturity parcels seems fair. Control rights can similarly provide another basis for segregating equity (as we saw above under *musharakah*, only the sleeping partner cannot have more than the ratio of capital contribution). Second, the market value of common stock at a given time is affected by a host of temporary and permanent factors including monetary policy and 'irrational exuberance'. There is little 'fairness' (or justification) in taking such value – that in any case is 'forward looking' – as a reference for redeeming stated maturity shares or bonds the holders of which are parting with participation in a company's future. To them, it is the breakup value that matters. Stated alternatively, enterprise value is built or lost usually owing to aggregate decisions taken over a much longer period than that for which a limited-maturity stock remains in issuance. Thus to the extent market value reflects intangible goodwill and investments yet to be made or 'growth assets' over and above that of breakup value or 'assets in place', it is due to common stockholders on account of their expertise in providing leadership via prudential supervision and choice of management team as well as on account of their risk taking to perpetuity. The key condition for the legitimacy of this proposal, however, has to be compliance with the *shari'ah* edict that in case of winding up or bankruptcy of a firm, the loss ought to be shared in proportion to the principal amounts contributed.

ILLUSTRATIONS OF CAPITAL STRUCTURE DESIGN

On the basis of the above assumptions, the design of capital structure for a commercial organization is outlined in Boxes 7.1 and 7.2. Two scenarios are presented. In the first (Box 7.1), it is assumed that the taxation authorities treat stated maturity shares akin to common stock. In the alternative scenario (Box 7.2), it is assumed that the dividend on stated maturity shares is treated as tax deductible by the taxation authorities.

BOX 7.1 ALTERNATIVE 1: DIVIDEND ON STATED MATURITY SHARES IS NOT EXPENSED

Assumptions

Total equity/capital	\$300 million
After tax average ROE	15%
After tax profit	\$45 million
Tax rate	30%

Table 7.2 Illustrative PLS capital structure when dividends on shares are not expensed

Share type	Face (\$ mn)	Maturity	Profit sharing ratio (%)	Target rate of return (%)	Loss ratio (per face/ total) (%)
Class A	100	2 Years	17	7.65	33.3
Class B	100	5 Years	25	11.25	33.3
Class C	100	Ordinary	58	26.10	33.3
Total	300		100		100

Key terms and conditions

- Voting rights initially belong to shareholders of Class C only. This assigns them the customary responsibility of prudential supervision through the appointment of board of directors, key managers and auditors.
- Class A and Class B have no voting rights under ordinary circumstances.
- Target rates of return are indicative rates for comparison (say with LIBOR), signalling and control purposes only.

These rates should not be confused with sharing ratios that alone matter for cash flow transfers to relevant parties. Also, instead of one target rate of return, there is scope for specifying rate corridors. For example, the target return-corridor for class A shares could be 7–8 per cent.

- One or more of the following will be considered as default events:
  - The firm fails to deliver indicative target rate of return to A and B holders over any pre-specified period (say 6 months);
  - The firm fails outright to redeem A or B at stated maturity dates;
  - The firm uses a company valuation for calculating redemption at stated maturity date of A or B tranches that gives the holders of these share classes less than amounts they subscribed in the beginning (face or par value);
  - The firm declares bankruptcy or bankruptcy protection.
- In case the above mentioned prespecified default event(s) materialize, shareholders of class A and B are entitled to one or more of the following rights:
  - To convert their shares into common stock with full voting rights (one share–one vote) as for class C shareholders. This dilutes the control of class C shareholders.
  - To trigger an upper limit on voting rights of class C shareholders. To give an example, C could not have more than 20 per cent of the aggregate voting rights. The remaining 80 per cent being split between class B and C giving them overwhelming control of the corporate affairs. Of course, it means the latter will have more than one vote one share. This is not unusual. Many precedents exist (Emmons and Schmid, 1998).
  - To strip class C shareholders altogether from voting rights and pass on the full control to class A and B shareholders giving them prestated multiple votes per share. The position of C *vis-à-vis* A and B is thus completely reversed. This may be termed as soft bankruptcy.
  - To trigger formal bankruptcy procedures. This is akin to CSV models as in Townsend (1979).

- Since the initial basis for risk differentiation now falters, there is scope for redefining maturity structure and profit sharing ratios for A and B parcels in case the firm remains a going concern. In a simple case, default may lead to control rights as stated above but trigger *pari passu* rights of all classes of shareholders on cash flows generated from the company. A and B become common stock. More complicated alternatives can be designed subject to unanimous trustee consent (see below).
- Holders of all classes of shares bear losses in proportion to the capital invested in case of liquidation/bankruptcy.

- There is scope for setting a trustee board on which all classes of shareholders elect their representatives. The trustee board decides on allocating rates of return to each class within specified corridors subject to yields satisfying the specified sharing ratio. Trustees have the right to transfer profits to reserves in case they exceed the lower limit of the target corridor. This is done with the view of smoothing out dividend fluctuations. From a *shari'ah* perspective it may be possible to give trustees the right to vary sharing ratios (with mutual consent) on fairness grounds under extraordinary circumstances.

BOX 7.2 ALTERNATIVE 2: DIVIDEND ON STATED MATURITY SHARES IS TAX DEDUCTIBLE

In case dividends on Class A and Class B become tax deductible akin to conventional bonds (requires changes in tax laws), then:

Total profit after tax from previous scenario	45.0
Total profit before tax (45/(1–tax rate))	64.3
Dividend expense on A and B (64.3 * (17 % +25 %))	27.0
Profit before tax on tranche C (64.3–27)	37.3
Company tax ($37.3 * tax rate)	11.2
Profit after tax	26.1

Table 7.3 Illustrative PLS capital structure when dividends on shares are tax deductible

Share Type	Face ($ mn)	Profit sharing ratio (%)	Expected profit ($ mn)	Expected return (%)
Class A	100	17	10.9	10.9
Class B	100	25	16.1	16.1
Class C	100	58	26.1	26.1
Total	300	100		

Note that the government can specify rules that to the extent benefit to shareholders A and B accrues from taxation rules, the company is authorized (but not bound) to transfer such benefit into a reserve fund for smoothing out dividend payouts on fixed maturity shares. Alternatively such benefits may be tied to approved R&D schemes, social welfare contributions, environmental protection, and so on. Note also that in the example given above, such benefit amounts to 30 per cent of $27 million = $8.1 million, that is, 2.7 per cent of total capital and 12.6 per cent of before tax profit!

Advantages of the proposed scheme

- The scheme provides a comprehensive solution to corporate capital structure. Both the equity and quasi-fixed instruments are tradable in secondary markets. The return on quasi-fixed instruments is expressed as a ratio of the total return in accordance with *shari'ah* requirements.
- Given the PLS method, only those projects will attract attention that in the subjective assessment of private investors are economically feasible.
- Control rights are arranged so as to mitigate moral hazard.
- Shareholders C are always in a position to expand or leverage the company further by taking a cut in their profit-sharing ratio and offering it to a new group of investors. Such 'leverage' needs to be distinguished from conventional leverage. In our proposed case, all parties have predetermined share in profits and bear real losses in proportion to capital. This is expected to alleviate the macroeconomic problems of the kind mentioned in Stiglitz and Weiss (1981, 1992) and Bernanke *et al.* (1996), and summarized above.
- There is scope for widespread application. The method offers a holistic approach to corporate finance, project

finance, and infrastructure finance. Corporations can issue short-term CDs or medium-dated paper by employing this method.

- The solution offered works at the contracting party level and puts minimal extra demands on the legal or regulatory system. Given constraints implied in the history of Islamic banking, this ought to be considered a definite plus.

Possible objections

- It could be argued that redemption at par for tranches A and B is not compatible with *shari'ah* and redemption should occur at the then prevailing market value. At the heart of this debate lies the question as to which class of shareholders should bear the brunt of fluctuations in market value – positive or negative – as long as the firm remains a viable going concern. This objection can be dealt with by referring to the fundamentals of corporate valuation bringing in the question of breakup or book value versus market value. According to our proposed design, the former becomes the concern of A and B holders while the latter that of the C holders. This is because market values are forward looking and at any given time reflect a host of temporary and permanent factors such as the state of local and international economy, monetary policy, goodwill, and so on. For example, take the case of goodwill. Under non-default circumstances, it is unjust to attribute any portion of it to stated-maturity shareholders of class A and B since it owes a positive value only to the valuable contribution over a long period of residual shareholders (class C). It therefore rightly belongs to those who in theory have a perpetual stake in the company and are responsible for prudential supervision of its affairs and appointment of its key managers.
- The objection stated above also loses weight if we reflect on the widely accepted and practised model of Islamic banking. The overall concept cannot necessarily be fitted into any of the standard Islamic contractual forms, although the two-tier *mudarabah* is usually cited in support. Bank shareholders' funds work side by side with depositors' funds in earning profits. Yet depositors are customarily redeemed at par while common stock trades at market value. Depositors have no voting rights while common

stockholders have these rights. If this model is transposed to corporate capital structure with some amendments, there should be no objection.

- It can be argued that given the design, the tendency will be for C holders to compensate A and B close to fair market values in particular under a worse-case scenario. Suppose A and B have rights to trigger bankruptcy only if the valuation for redemption at stated maturity gives them below par value. Suppose that there have been losses for the first two consecutive years. Shareholders in Class A will have lost some capital by the redemption date. However, Class C shareholders may still highly value the long-term potential of the company as a going concern. They may not be willing to lose control through dilution or bankruptcy. Accordingly, they may still be interested in redeeming class A at face value through purchasing or refinancing. Alternatively, if the company prospects have significantly deteriorated by the end of two years, then a bargain at less than face value is possible through mutual consent or an outright liquidation will happen in which each bears the loss in proportion to the original capital invested.

Summary

The framework in this section has demonstrated how insights from optimal contracting literature can be used to divide equity into parcels of different risk-return profile in a potentially *shari'ah* compatible manner. Many variations of the basic theme are possible. Also, there could be a widespread application of this method both in the public as well as the private sector. However, there is one caveat. To utilize this method, one has to focus on the abstract principles of Islamic finance underlying PLS. Only then can the full benefits of this technique be realized and the flexibility required in today's financial world for a holistic approach to corporate finance and commercial public sector finance be delivered.

CONCLUSIONS

The focus of this chapter has been on examining contemporary *ijtihadi* methods for financing government bodies. In the process, we have discovered that Islamic finance has drifted a long way from its goal of shunning interest. Cashflows and returns very similar to conventional fixed interest bonds and loans have been 'legitimized' on a large scale employing techniques that seem tantamount to legal subterfuges, that is, *hiyal*. While this development has provided plenty of scope for innovation, valued from a Muslim practitioner, public sector and investor perspective by expanding the range of instruments available for public finance to a variety of asset-based debt finance, *shari'ah* scholars are merely 'treading a well beaten path' developed over many years in conventional finance, and for reasons explained to a considerable degree in the recent literature on financial intermediation and optimal contracting. Can Islamic finance rise beyond its passion to replicate the conventional system and instead come up with an alternative vision of economics and finance, the prized goal that it set for itself many years ago? We doubt it. Perhaps the direction of this movement was sealed on the day when trade-based formulations – *murabahah*, *salam* and cost plus sales – gained *fiqh* approval for financing purposes. The rest is history. As R.H. Tawney (1926, p. 99) said many years ago: 'The children of the mind are like the children of the body. Once born, they grow by a law of their own being, and, if their parents could foresee their future development, it would sometimes break their hearts.' On a positive note, the end result of such 'innovation' has been a rapid growth of this nascent industry and its seemless integration into the global village of finance, which can now be tapped more readily for developmental projects. The next big challenge faced by the industry is to improve its standards of accountability and governance, a topic to which we turn in the next chapter.

NOTES

1. Lewis and Algaoud (2001), Table 6.1, lists the institutions established from 1963–99, which reached a peak of 20 new banks formed in 1983.
2. 'A group of jurists are of the opinion that, should the seller increase his price if the buyer asks for deferred payments, as is common in instalment buying, the price differential due to the time delay resembles interest, which is likewise a price for time; accordingly, they declare such sales to be *haram*. However, the majority of scholars permit it because the basic principle is the permissibility of things, and no clear text exists prohibiting such a transaction. Furthermore, there is, on the whole, no resemblance to interest in such a transaction, since the seller is free to increase the price as he deems proper, as long as it is not to the extent of blatant exploitation or clear injustice, in which case it is *haram*. Al-Shawkani says, "On the basic of legal reasons, the followers of Shafi'i and Hanafi schools, Zaid bin 'Ali, al-Muayyid Billah, and the majority of scholars consider it lawful." (Nayl al-awtar, vol. 5, p. 153. Al-Shawkani said, "We have compiled a treatise on this subject and have called it 'Shifa al'ilal fi hukum ziyadat al-thamam li mujarrad al-ajal' (The reason for increasing the price due to lapse of time), and have researched it thoroughly.")' (Al-Qardawi, 2003, Chapter 3: Business Transactions, p. 6).
3. From the viewpoint of central bank monetary management one of the most interesting

is the *rahn* agreement. This works as follows. 'Under this structure, the lender provides a loan to the borrower, based on the concept of *qard hasan*. The borrower pledges its securities as collateral against the loan. Should the borrower fail to repay the loan on the maturity date, the lender has the right to sell the pledged securities and use the proceeds to settle the loan. If there is surplus money, the lender will return the balance to the borrower. The *rahn* agreement is predicated on the concept of a repurchase agreement (or Repo), a very popular instrument in traditional money markets, though its use by Islamic banks is more limited. The Central Bank uses these instruments as a tool for liquidity management for money market operations. Any returns realized from these securities are considered a gift (*hiba*) and determined according to the average inter-bank money market rates' (Hakim, 2007, p. 168).

4. However, even this feature may have been overtaken by events. Shariah Capital is an Islamic hedge fund that trades out of London but is headquartered in New Canaan, Connecticut, USA. Hedge funds typically generate returns in a falling market by short-selling, buying the shares back at profit when they have subsequently fallen in value. This practice poses a problem for Muslims because the short-selling step entails borrowing a security that one does not own, which is prohibited because it violates the *hadith* 'sell not what is not with you' (Kamali, 2007). Apparently, the Shariah Capital solution uses a down-payment – to establish ownership of the stock – before the 'short sale' (Morais, 2007).
5. The prohibition of 'riba' is mentioned in four different passages in the Holy Qur'an, all forthright and clear on the subject. The first of the verses (30:39) emphasizes that interest deprives wealth of God's blessings. The second (4:161) condemns it, placing interest in juxtaposition with wrongful appropriation of property belonging to others. The third (3:130) enjoins Muslims to stay clear of interest for the sake of their own welfare. The fourth passage (2:275–8) establishes a clear distinction between interest and trade, urging Muslims, first, to take only the principal sum and second, to forgo even this sum if the borrower is unable to repay. The ban on interest is also cited in unequivocal terms in the *hadith* or *sunnah* (Algaoud and Lewis, 2007).

8. Accountability and governance

THE IMPORTANCE OF ACCOUNTABILITY

This chapter explores the relationship between accountability and governance in the Islamic economic and political system. We argue that accountability is central to governance under Islam, and the chapter develops the basic principles of Islamic governance whether applied to public governance or to corporate governance.

Our starting point is the observation that every society has features that shape and define it. In the case of the Islamic social and economic system, Siddiqi (2006) argues for freedom, equality and justice, and what these values imply, as being the characteristics of the Islamic approach to life, for Islam has (at least to modern-day Western thinking), a very distinctive stance on these matters. To Siddiqi's characteristics of freedom, equality and justice we would add a fourth, accountability to God, as reinforcing, indeed underpinning, those attributes.

Individual Freedom

Consider first, freedom. The concept of freedom in Islam needs to be understood and put in the context of Islam's central idea, that of *tawhid*. *Tawhid* is the commitment to the life-giver and the sustainer of life as the essential source of value. A corollary of such commitment is freedom, in the sense that freedom from domination by others is a necessary first step to commitment to Islam or the inner peace that comes from submission to God. By virtue of being the servant (*abd*) only of the one God, mankind is liberated from other commitments and obligations and bondages. In their dependence on God, all humans are equally free and independent of one another. Such individual freedom of choice is the natural precondition of individual accountability to God in the life after death. Consider the following verses:

> Not one of the beings in the heavens and the earth but must come to The Most Gracious as a servant.

> He does take an account of them (all), and hath numbered them (all) exactly.

And everyone of them will come to Him singly on the Day of Judgment. (Maryam 19: 93–5)

Equality

With this freedom comes equality. Individual freedom of decision-making is not absolute and has to be moderated and constrained by rules which are designed to ensure that others enjoy similar freedoms. That, in essence, is what the *shari'ah* achieves. But such restrictions are non-discriminatory, for they treat everyone equally. Thus equality is a necessary consequence of *tawhid*, placing all humanity at a par in their relationship with God, so that no human being can claim essential superiority over other human beings. Spiritual equality provides the basis for social equality. Such equality follows from people being subjects of the one and only God to whom all shall return and be answerable. That essential truth puts them at par in their relationship with God. Umar makes the point succinctly:

> God has no relationship with anyone. The only way to relate to Him is to obey Him. All human beings, the elite as well as the lowly, are equal in God's system (*deen*). God is the lord of all of them and they are all His servants. (Ibn Kathir, vol. 8, p. 35)

Nevertheless, equality is not absolute, at least in terms of achievements and possessions. Rather, the emphasis in the Islamic economic system pertains to equality of opportunity without expectations as to any particular set of outcomes. What A. Ali (2005, p. 52) describes as the 'Islamic work ethic', implies that work is a virtue in light of a person's needs, and is a necessity for establishing equilibrium in one's individual and social life (Nasr, 1984). Islam requires every individual to work and to produce. Prophet Muhammad (pbuh) teaches: 'Never be lazy and helpless' (Rahman, 1994, p. 9). There is no good in an individual who does not want to produce and earn money. To Muslims, the unproductive hand is an unclean impure hand. The route to economic achievement is hard work and assumption of risk. It is not through inheritance.[1] This principle, and the centrality of work and deed in Islamic thinking, is addressed in the Holy Qur'an:

> Is it they who would portion out the Mercy of thy Lord? It is We Who portion out between them their livelihood in the life of this world: and We raise some of them above others in ranks so that some may command work from others. But the Mercy of thy Lord is better than the (wealth) which they amass. (Az-Zukhruf, 43:32)

In this context, useful work is that which benefits others and society. Subsequently, those who work hard are acknowledged and are rewarded.

At the same time, however, increasing inequality in the distribution of income and wealth is strongly disfavoured, and there are inbuilt mechanisms for counteracting such tendencies. Islam preaches moderation and a balanced pattern of consumption. Luxury and over-consumption is condemned, as is poverty. Every being has a minimum requirement to be able to live in dignity. As we have seen, the system is balanced out through the act of *zakah* (almsgiving as an essential part of the system and faith). If this source is not enough, the Islamic government would apply a temporary tax on the rich and affluent to balance the budget as a religious duty (*fard-e-kifaya*).

In these ways the pursuit of economic activities must be based on moral and legitimate foundations. Individuals are expected to feel socially responsible for others in the community. One cannot enjoy life while others cannot. In general, the aim of the Islamic economic system is to allow people to earn their living in a fair and profitable way without exploitation of others, so that the whole society may benefit. The welfare of the community over individual rights is also emphasized, allowing the protection of the essential dignity that God conferred on all humanity.

Justice

Chapter 3 examined Islamic views on justice at some length and we will not dwell extensively on them again except to note that justice – the objective of *shari'ah* – is what the religion of Islam seeks for human relations. The Arabic word *adl* and *qist* both mean 'to act justly' and both have been used in the Quranic verses. Says the Holy Qur'an:

> Allah commands justice, the doing of good, and giving to kith and kin, and He forbids all indecent deeds, and evil and rebellion: He instructs you that ye may receive admonition. (An-Nahl 16:90)

> O ye who believe! Stand out firmly for justice, as witnesses to Allah, even as against yourselves, or your parents, or your kin, and whether it be (against) rich or poor: for Allah can best protect both. (An-Nisa 4:135)

> Of those We have created are people who direct (Others) with truth, and dispense justice therewith. (A'raf 7:181)

These verses are clear on justice as fairness, justice as non-discrimination, and justice as equity in order to ensure balance and harmony, something at which Islam aims.[2]

> We sent aforetime our messengers with Clear Signs and sent down with them The Book and the Balance (of Right and Wrong), that men may stand forth in justice. (Al-Hadid 57:25)

The last two verses also make clear that the central role of the Islamic political system is the establishment of socio-economic justice. The term 'politics' (*Siyasah*) has been used in the Prophet's *hadith* where he said: 'The children of Israel used to be politically guided by their prophets (*tasusuhum al-anbiyaa*), and there is no prophet after me.' On this basis, 'politics' can best be defined as the 'means to offer leadership and guidance to people towards the attainment of good both in this life and the Hereafter' (Tag el-Din, 2006, p. 1). Correspondingly, justice has been tied up with three necessary requisites: representation of the ruled ones, consultation with them, and accountability towards them.

Accountability

This brings us to accountability. Accountability to God and the community for all activities is paramount to adherents to Islam. To Muslims, *shari'ah* is the essential guiding force as it encompasses all aspects of human life and accountability is ultimately to Allah, as all deeds will be accounted as stated in the Holy Qur'an:

> To Allah belongeth all that is in the heavens and on earth. Whether ye show what is in your minds or conceal it. Allah calleth you to account for it. (Al-Baqarah 2:284)

Of course, accountability is not confined to Muslims and occurs in all walks of life and all societies. Those in charge of economic resources must give account of their stewardship, irrespective of whether the transactions and resources in question are those of a government organization or a private sector entity. This stewardship function has been a regular feature of organized human activity from the earliest times (Brown, 1905; Brown, 1962; Stone, 1969). Originally specified at the level of the individual property owner and his agent or representative, accountability also has broader economic and social purposes and objectives and no more so than under Islam in which economics, politics, religious and social affairs all fall under the jurisdiction of the divine law of Islam. Calder (2002, p. 1981) defines Islamic law as 'a hermeneutic discipline which explores and interprets revelation through tradition'. The Holy Qur'an (the revelation) and *sunnah* (the Prophet's example as recorded in *ahadith* or the traditions), define clearly what is true, fair and just, what are society's preferences and priorities, what are individuals' and business enterprises' roles and responsibilities, and also, in some aspects, spell out specific accounting standards and accounting practices.

In the Holy Qur'an, for example, the word *hesab* is repeated more than eight times in different verses (Askary and Clarke, 1997). *Hesab* or 'account' is the root of accounting, and the references in the Holy Qur'an are to 'account' in its generic sense, relating to one's obligation to 'account' to God on all matters pertaining to human endeavour for which every Muslim is 'accountable'. All resources made available to individuals are made so in the form of a trust. Individuals are trustees for what they have been given by God in the form of goods, property and less tangible 'assets'. The extent to which individuals must use what is being entrusted to them is specified in *shari'ah*, and the success of individuals in the hereafter depends upon their performance in this world. In this sense, every Muslim has an 'account' with Allah, in which is 'recorded' all good and all bad actions, an account which will continue until death, for Allah shows all people their accounts on their judgement day (S4:62). This adds an extra dimension to the valuation of things and deeds compared to those already embodied in conventional reporting obligations.

Hence the basic similarity between *hesab* in Islam and 'accounting' lies in the responsibility of every Muslim to carry out duties as described in the Holy Qur'an. Similarly, in a business enterprise, both management and the providers of capital are accountable for their actions both within and outside their firm. Accountability in this context means accountability to the community of believers (*umma*) or society at large. Muslims cannot, in good faith, compartmentalize their behaviour into religious and secular dimensions, and their actions are always bound by *shari'ah* obligations and responsibilities.

ISLAMIC GOVERNANCE

After his *hijra*, the Prophet Muhammad (pbuh) worked to construct as strong and enduring an Islamic state as he possibly could. He laid down all the necessary principles of good governance and gave an example to his followers in such a way that after his death they established a Caliphate based on precepts like those outlined above, namely justice, individual freedom, equity, *shura* (mutual consultation), and accountability to the one true God.

It follows that the original sources of Islamic political thought (which in turn inform political and public governance) are to be found in the Holy Qur'an, the traditions (*sunnah*) and the practices of the four 'rightly-guided' Caliphs who contributed to the development of the Islamic state in the footsteps of the Prophet. The laws of Islam as embodied in the Holy Qur'an and the *sunnah* are above man but, in the absence of an official church or clergy in Islam, their understanding, interpretation and implementation is entrusted to the community of believers. Muslims have been instructed to decide their affairs through consultation (*shura*) among themselves. That in turn requires freedom of thought and expression, rights to assemble and converse, and encouragement to engage in healthy criticism and fruitful counsels among followers, be they rulers or subjects. For these reasons, Siddiqi (2006) argues that democratic decision-making should be added 'as a pillar of the free society of Islam' (p. 4).

It further follows that all who comprise the community are required by God to participate in the formation of an educated, economically successful and ethical society. Witness the Holy Qur'an:

> Revile not ye those whom they call upon besides Allah, lest they out of spite revile Allah in their ignorance. Thus have We made alluring to each people its own doings. (Al-An'am 6:108)

> Of the bounties of thy Lord we bestow freely on all – these as well as those: The bounties of thy Lord are not closed (to anyone). (Al-Isra 17:20)

To this end, pursuit of knowledge is made compulsory for every Muslim.

> Proclaim! And thy Lord is Most Bountiful, – He Who taught (the use of) the Pen, – taught man that which he knew not. (Al'Alaq 96:35)

The Prophet (pbuh) declared:

> Pursuit of knowledge is a duty of every Muslim' (Ibn Majah: *Sunan*, Bab 17, al-Muqaddimah, *Fadl al-Ulama wa'l Haththàla Talab al-Ilm*, Hadith no. 220).

Accordingly, humans must use reason to bring about a just Islamic social order, and the advancement of that aim will depend on the extent to which individual Muslims participate in the determination of social affairs. As noted, achievement of socio-economic justice necessitates three conditions: representation, consultation and accountability. It is on such grounds that the Holy Qur'an mandated the pre-Islamic concept of *shura*, that is governance by mutual consultation and consensus, as a central aspect of an Islamic system of government as epitomized by the actual practice of the Prophet and the four rightly-guided Caliphs. *Shura* involved the use of elections or consultations to select representatives to discuss, debate and formulate public policy on the *umma*'s behalf. Using this example, each specific community or fraternity should decide, via *shura*, what structure of governance is appropriate for it. In effect, what must be decided is the process of establishing mutual consultation on political decisions, and the role of *ahl al-hal wa al-àqd*, the persons eligible to participate in the process of *shura* (Tag el-Din, 2006).

The upshot, according to Askari and Taghavi (2005), is a system of governance in which the primary political authority must collaborate with a pluralistic governing body of representatives (*shura*), and by such means enable the *umma* to prevent a single individual or entity from seizing control over the community and establishing a dictatorship. They cite Imam Muhammad Shirazi, a renowned Islamic scholar, who strongly supports this position as illustrated by the following quotation (2001, pp. 92–3):

> The decision making process must be that of mutual consultation (*Shura*) so that every individual has an opinion which must be considered. . . . Everything should be in equilibrium [with] free and fair elections within the movement itself and a balance of power. Naturally splits will form in the movement. However, between these splits there must be equality, balance and competence so that a single group is not able to take control of the movement and derail the movement towards dictatorship.

If the core values upon which the *umma* base its economic and social policies stem from *shari'ah*, an ethical social and economic order will be established in which a pluralistic government can check and balance the power of the ruling order. Because God is the ultimate authority, political officials presiding over the welfare of the Muslim state are unable to claim absolute power and must respect *shari'ah* when formulating state policy.

The Holy Qur'an makes the obligation of brotherhood among Muslims a major religious duty which has to be pursued with wisdom in accordance with stipulated rights of brotherhood. Thus the concept of *umma* lies at the heart of the Holy Qur'an and that of the Prophet's tradition where believers are looked upon as true brothers. In this respect, the importance of representation and accountability becomes even more significant in *shura* than it is in Western democracy. The *umma* must study Islamic ethics and fully understand Islam's moral, social and fiscal standards before deciding whether to adhere to rules based on Islamic principles. As a corollary, the institution of *shura* can be seen as the genuine Islamic counterpart of political democracy, even though the working mechanism of *shura* and the extent of public acountability of *shura*-appointed offices need to be actualized in modern political environments.

In broad terms, however, the essential principles of the system of Islamic governance are clear. Quranic verses are revelatory only after they have been interpreted, understood and explained by human reason, known as *ijtihad*. The ruling authority chosen by the *umma* is therefore required to ensure financial resources for a class of scholars that has devoted its professional and personal life to the study, analysis and verification of history and Islamic doctrines, ethics and law.

> Bring me a Book (Revealed) before this, or any remnant of knowledge (ye may have), if ye are telling the truth! (Al-Ahqaf 46:4)

Employing *ijtihad*, Islamic strategists and scholars can discern how to amend specific doctrines in order to meet a community's particular socio-economic and political needs while remaining true to basic Islamic ethical standards. By this means, the *umma* can ultimately put a check on the power of the political authority when it comes to comprehending Islamic principles on justice, equity and social responsibility, and can therefore ascertain if the policies or conduct of the ruling authority violate justice and are therefore un-Islamic. Indeed, the Prophet Mohammad is reported to have said 'Their highest kind of *jihad* (personal struggle for self-improvement) is to speak the truth in the face of a government that deviates from the right path' (Ul Haq, 1995, p. 57).

ISLAMIC DECISION-MAKING

In Chapter 1 we argued that, viewed from its widest perspective, governance – the act of governing – refers to the relationship between the governors and the governed, such as that between the government and the people, and has at its basis the decision-making powers ceded by individuals to those in authority so that the common interests of society can be served. However, the same issues arise whether we are dealing with multilateral bodies, the governing of a nation state or region, or the governance of an organization such as a business enterprise. In all instances, governance is essentially about the nature of decision-making.

In turn, decision-making involves finding answers, in our preferred frame of reference, to three questions: by whom, for whom, and with what resources. 'For whom' decisions are made depends on the underlying context, constitution or charter. 'By whom' decisions are made is dependent on the decision-making structure developed. 'With what resources' determines 'to whom' accountability is due for the usage made of them.

An examination of the principal legal sources of the Holy Qur'an and *sunnah* reveals clear guidelines about decision-making processes in an Islamic context. In particular, Islamic law and its distinctive Islamic institutions imply very different implications for decision-making than conventional approaches. Specifically, the concepts of *shura*, *hisba* and the *shari'ah* supervisory process and religious audit establish the basic building blocks of a system of Islamic governance and rules and procedures for making decisions. This framework becomes apparent when we consider the three dimensions of decision-making that we introduced in Chapter 1: decision-making by whom, for whom, and 'with what' and 'to whom'.

By whom

The Holy Qur'an is very clear on the issue of 'by whom'. Consider the following verses:

> And consult them on affairs (of moment). Then, when thou has taken a decision, put thy trust in Allah. (Al-Imran 3:159)

> Those who respond to their Lord, and establish regular prayer; who (conduct) their affairs by mutual consultation; Who spend out of what We bestow on them for sustenance. (Ash-Shura 42:38)

In fact, according to The Presidency of Islamic Researches in the commentary on Sura Ash-Shura, 'consultation' is the key word of the Sura, and suggests the ideal way in which a good man should conduct his affairs. The commentary goes on to note that this principle was applied to its fullest extent by the Prophet Muhammad (pbuh) in his public and private life, and was fully acted upon by the early rulers of Islamic society. The *Shura* or Consultative Council had its origins in pre-Islamic times where it comprised a council of tribal elders. Originally, it constituted an informal forum of deliberation where decisions were arrived at when discussing new problems. During these deliberations, the problems in question were thrown open for general discussion. Members of the council were invited to express their considered personal opinions, and these opinions were thrashed out until a consensus of opinions was reached. Islam introduced improvements in accordance with the moral principles enunciated by the Holy Qur'an (Stork, 1999).

Thus the basic message of Sura Ash-Shura, to 'live true in mutual consultation and forbearance, and rely on Allah', contains the essence of governance from an Islamic perspective. Those who wish to serve Allah must ensure that their conduct in life is open and determined by mutual consultation between those entitled to voice, for example, in affairs of business, as between partners or parties interested, and in state affairs as between rulers and ruled. Since the Holy Qur'an clearly specifies that any decision involving more than one party requires access and consultation on the basis of principles of *shura*, Islam encourages the participants to work together freely and frankly when arriving at decisions (Shaikh, 1988). Institution of a shuratic decision-making process explains how decision-making in government, business and other activities can meet Islamic moral values. Decision-making is an important trust from God, and Islam demands from those holding this trust to engender truthfulness, justice, consultation and a spirit of consensus-seeking among participants during group decision-making. On the basis of *shura*, leaders must encourage others to participate in decision-making.

Islahi (2005) observes that, in order to promote this end, a chain of writings on statecraft embodying rules for governance appeared in the Islamic tradition. Abu Yusuf's (731–98 CE) *Kitab al-Kharaj* most certainly qualifies in this category. Some other works that he identifies are *Da'aim al-Islam* by Abu Hanifah al-Nu'man al-Isma'ili (d. 974), *al-Ahkam al-Sultaniyyah* by both Abu Yala al-Farra and al-Mawardi (974–1058), *Siyasat Namah* by Nizam al-Mulk al-Tusi (1018–92), *al-Tibr al-Masbuk fi Nasihat al-Muluk* by al-Ghazali (1058–1111), *Siraj al-Muluk* by al-Turtushi (1059–1126), *Qabus Namah* by Kay Kaus b. Iskander (written 1082), *al-Siyasah al-Shar 'iyyah* by Ib Taymiyyah (1263–1328), and *Tahrir al-Ahkam fi Tadbir Ahl al-Islam* by Ibn Jama'ah (1241–1333).

In addition to rules for good governance, these works have been a rich source of Islamic political economy. Political discourses by Muslim scholars have always emphasized that the authority of the ruler is not absolute. Rather, it is a trust from God. Addressing Caliph Harun al-Rashid, Abu Yusuf (1392, p. 5) said: 'Take care of what Allah has assigned to you and fulfil the obligation of authority entrusted to you'. An associated theme in the writings is on the maintenance of 'justice'. 'The just government will stay even if it is non-believer, and unjust government will never prolong even if it is a Muslim government' (Ibn Taymiyyah, 1976, p. 94). Another special feature of the literature is that it gives much attention to economic issues, especially supervision of markets, development of the economy and public finance. This leads to the institution of *hisba*, which refers to the 'control function of the government through persons acting especially in the field of morals, religion and economy, and generally in the areas of collective or public life, to achieve justice and righteousness according to the principles of Islam and commonly known good customs of time and place' (al-Mubarak, 1973, pp. 73–4 quoted in Islahi, 2005). This role is apparent when we consider the issue of 'for whom'.

For whom

All human activity belongs to Allah. A code of approved social behaviour was developed by the Prophet Muhammad (pbuh), and his companions were later appointed, when the Islamic community expanded in the early days of the Islamic state, to institutionalize, perpetuate and preserve the codes and ensure compliance with the principles of *shari'ah*. Under the early Abbasids (750 CE onwards), the institution of *hisba* was established to ensure compliance with the requirements of *shari'ah*. An office of local administration, the office of the 'inspector of the market', continued into Islam from Byzantine times (Schacht, 1964). Its holder was given the title *muhtasib* (and his office called *hisba*), and the functions were Islamicized by entrusting its holder with discharging the collective obligation in the Holy Qur'an to 'encourage good and discourage evil', making the *muhtasib* responsible for enforcing Islamic behaviour in terms of community affairs and behaviour in the market, such as accuracy and honesty in business dealings. It is in terms of protecting the public interest that Murtuza and Abdallah (2007) compare the role of the *muhtasib* with that of modern-day certified public accountants (CPAs).

Hisba was a very important institution of Islamic statehood. It was through this department that the state exercised a comprehensive socio-economic control on trade and economic practices. The Prophet (pbuh) was conscious of this reality when, after his *hijra*, he began to build the foundations of a new Islamic order. In order to accomplish this goal, he signed a treaty that some contemporary researchers have called the 'Constitution of Madinah'.[3] Through this pact, the Prophet managed, in a relatively short space of time, to establish a market where Muslims could dominate and where their own rules would be implemented. Over time, some Quranic verses regarding economic matters were revealed, some laws were made, some rules were created, while some of the pre-Islamic conventions and values were abolished, modified, or left intact. The existence of an autonomous market where the Muslims could dominate and the *shari'ah* prevail, was vital in putting Islamic rules into effect.

The next concern was the administration of the market to ensure that the economic rules of the *shari'ah* were actually carried out. An institution, later named *hisba*, was devised for monitoring the economic system. The word *hisba* is a noun derived from *ihtisab*, and both are derivatives of the root *hsb* meaning reward, good deed, or judgement and measure. *Ihtisab* also means taking into consideration, hoping for a reward in the Hereafter by adding a pious deed to one's account with God, and shaming and preventing a bad deed (Ibn Manzür, I, pp. 310–17). From this source use of the noun *ihtisab* came to be associated with the activities of a person who invites others to do good and advises them not to do evil. Somewhat more technically, *hisba* came to mean a socio-economic institution established by the state to promote good and forbid evil (al-Mawardi, [1405 AH] 1985, pp. 299–300; Khan, 1982, p. 135). From this root, the official in charge of *hisba* was called *muhtasib*.

In effect, in establishing an Islamic state, the task of the Prophet was to reshape earlier institutions, lay down standards of behaviour, and provide arrangements for the continuation of those standards. Besides devising a code of approved behaviour, the Prophet took care to institutionalize the preservation of this code by commanding everyone to engage in *al-amr bi'l-ma'ruf wa al-nahy 'an al-munkar*, that is, doing good and forbidding evil (Akram Khan, 1982, p. 135). In a number of traditions, he is reported as having emphasized this duty for every Muslim (Muslim, *al-Iman*, 83,85). Economic functions of the *muhtasib* included: ensuring the supply and provision of necessities (Ziadeh, 1963, p. 40), supervision of industry (Ibn Taymiyyah 1976, p. 21), resolution of industrial disputes (ibid., p. 34), supervision of trading practices, standardization of weight and measures (ibid., pp. 21–2), prevention of injurious economic activities like adulteration (ibid.), check on interception of supply through forestalling, hoarding or coalition of oligopolists (ibid., p. 23) and fixing of prices, wages and rentals if necessary (ibid., p. 24, Ziadeh, 1963, pp. 54–96). Overall, though, the *hisba* functions included religious duties and affairs regarding municipal administration such as keeping the roads and streets clean and preventing the construction of buildings in public areas (al-Mawardi, pp. 303 ff.; Ibn al-Ukhuwwah, 1976, pp. 73 ff.; Akram Khan, p. 138).

Hisba, like the institution of *shura*, is a long-standing tradition of Islamic society that can be seen to represent a core element of Islamic corporate governance. The role of the institution became significant during the expansion of the Islamic state as the number of business and commercial activities expanded, exemplifying the nature and extent of the adoption of an ideal system of sacred law in early Islam. No single office currently really can be compared with the *hisba*. Its multifarious activities are now done by different ministries and their special departments. The nearest group of offices are the regulatory agencies which oversee financial markets, trade and commerce and ensure weights, measures and standards. Consequently, to what extent the office could be revived in its traditional form is problematical. Nevertheless, and in our view importantly, the institution of *hisba* survives in terms of the right of every Muslim, irrespective of the presence or absence of an officially appointed *muhtasib*, to come forth as a 'private prosecutor' or enforcer of Islamic standards of governance (Schacht, 1964, p. 52).

With what and to whom

The third plank of the Islamic governance system is the process of religious supervision to guarantee that all operations, contracts and procedures conform with the Islamic moral code. To a Muslim, all resources are God-given, and ownership of wealth belongs to God. Individuals are only trustees and it is to God that accountability is ultimately due. The purpose of a religious audit is to assure both insiders and outsiders that God's laws are being followed. This function is exemplified most clearly in the case of Islamic corporate governance, considered below.

CORPORATE GOVERANCE[4]

The three dimensions of decision-making that has served as our frame of reference – 'by whom', 'for whom' and 'to whom' – apply irrespective of whether we are governing a nation, a social organization, or a business enterprise. Nevertheless, just as governance of the nation state is informed by a theoretical model of the ideal state and the proper way to run a country (political democracy in the West and its Islamic counterpart in the form of *shura*), so too corporate governance is rooted in the conceptual basis of the firm. Here we distinguish three alternative frameworks, covering the firm as a legal entity, the firm as an economic entity, and the firm as an accounting concept. Each of these concepts produces a perspective on one of the three decision-making aspects.

The Legal View

Decision-making 'by whom' is implicit in the legal notion of the firm. For the lawyer, a firm is either an association of persons, a partnership, a limited partnership or a corporation, as well as several variants attached to each type. However, the corporation is distinguished by virtue of the fact that it is assigned a distinct legal personality by the law, whereas a partnership is not. The corporate shareholders own the corporation as a legal entity, but the corporation as the legal body in turn owns the corporate assets. Every corporation has the same contractual rights as an individual under law and is treated as capable of owning real property, entering into contracts, suing and being sued, all in its own name, separate and distinct from its shareholders. There is consequently a fundamental difference in legal structure between a firm that is incorporated and one that is not (Iwai, 2002).

Nonetheless, while the corporation has a separate personality under law, it is in reality a mere abstract body, incapable of performing any act except through flesh-and-blood humans. As a result, corporate law requires a corporation to have a board of directors as the ultimate holder of power to act in the name of the corporation. The board, in turn, hands over power to a class of specialist managers who act on the board's behalf under the control of the CEO, who is often also the chairman of the board of directors and supported by the executive directors. CEO and managerial control was not always the case. In the United States before 1914, bankers and institutional investors held sway in the boardroom and executives had little real decision-making powers (Hawkins, 1997; Simon, 1998). It was not until the 1950s and 1960s that the 'imperial' CEO emerged. Prior to that time, most companies selected one person as chairman of the board and another, typically younger, executive as president.

Thus the legal position of the incorporated firm is straightforward, and provides for three sets of participants:

1. Shareholders, who supply risk capital under conditions of limited liability;
2. Directors, who are responsible for the stewardship of the company's resources; and
3. Employees, especially managers, who conduct the company's operations and manage corporate assets on a day-to-day basis under powers delegated to them by the directors.

Moreover, there is a strict two-sequence line of the delegation of authority, running from shareholders to directors to management, which is designed to prevent shareholders from interfering directly in the management of the company.

The Economic View

Decision-making 'for whom' flows from the economic view of the firm, which envisages a firm as a business enterprise in pursuit of profits that then accrue to shareholders as claimants of the residual income from corporate assets. The economic rationale is that the organization replaces a large number of market transactions that would otherwise be undertaken by individuals (and usually are in a simple economy). As societies and technology grow more complex, the problem of coordination by the price system becomes increasingly difficult and costly, pushing the firm to the forefront as an organizing device. By gathering functions within its corpus, the firm reduces the transactions costs of negotiating the individual transactions. Instead of numerous separate contractual relations between owners, employees, suppliers, customers, creditors and governments in order to generate profits, the corporation is able to act as an independent holder of property rights, and (by virtue of its legal status) form contractual relations with others. The complex network of contractual relations is greatly simplified, leading to a large reduction of transaction costs for all participants, shielding outside parties from the disruptions posed by internal disputes, illness, death or the entry of new partners or owners.

While efficiency enhancing, the separation that is thereby introduced between ownership and control requires a governance framework to ensure that the decisions of the directors and management are compatible with the interests of those supplying the corporation with economic and financial resources. Since the managers are the ones who, in the name of the corporation, make decisions about the employment of corporate assets and what contracts to undertake, there is the danger that they may mistake the decision-making powers entrusted to them for their own power, which can be exercised at their discretion and for their own benefit rather than in the best interests of the corporation as a whole.

The Accounting View

This leads us, finally, to the question of 'with what' resources and thus the issue of 'to whom' accountability is due for the use of resources. In the accounting view of the firm, the enterprise is viewed as a collection of resources for business activities, and information on those assets and the uses made of them is kept, maintained and reported for the benefit of participants and other parties. As such, the concept clearly predates the development of the joint stock company, and grew out of the commercial necessity to treat a group or association of persons as a single entity for record keeping and continuity of business transactions. This 'mercantile notion of the firm'[5] enabled merchants and their accountants to assign partnerships and other forms of collective business activity a personality in their books, and allowed financial contributions to become the capital of the firm and maintain this status in the books over time. It facilitated the flow of information to a range of contracting parties and meant that a number of persons (in the legal sense) could be regarded in practice as one individual in the rules of trade.[6]

Of course, the informational and accountability function assumed even greater importance when the agglomeration of resources widened beyond a relatively closed circle of partners or traders, and public corporations began to raise vast sums of capital from financial institutions and thousands of small investors. They rely on the accuracy of the information supplied to them, under conditions where the liability of shareholders to repay them is limited to their contributed capital. At the same time, the liability of the corporate managers is also limited and restricted to those of 'duty of loyalty' and 'duty of care' – the former requires managers to control corporate assets in the best interests of the corporation, and the latter obliges them to administer corporate assets with reasonable care and skill. While those in charge of economic resources must still give account of their stewardship, the accounting by management would nowadays be described in somewhat different terms, as assisting in the efficient allocation of resources by providing information, either for *ex post* monitoring of performance or for *ex ante* decision-making by those responsible for making investment decisions (Whittington, 1992).

COMPARING MODELS OF GOVERNANCE

Models of corporate governance can be distinguished in their approach to the three dimensions of decision-making that we have identified as the essence of corporate governance: decision-making 'by whom', 'for whom' and 'with what' resources, the latter governing 'to whom' accountability is due. Our primary concern is one of contrasting the principles of Islamic corporate governance with the Western approach. While there is undoubtedly a dominant Western approach to corporate governance, at least in Anglo-Saxon countries, there is more than one model. Thus we consider, first, the 'managed corporation' paradigm and then what may be termed the 'socially responsive' corporation. Table 8.1 compares these two models with the Islamic system.

The Managed Corporation

By whom

What may be called the 'managed corporation' model (Pound, [1995] 2000) of corporate governance has dominated the American corporate arena for decades, and is a legacy of the rise of large public companies and dispersed share ownership. In the model, managers lead and directors and shareholders follow. Boards, to a large degree, and shareholders, most certainly, are kept distant from the corporate decision-making process, and are excluded from strategy formulation and policy setting. Senior managers provide the leadership and make the decisions. The board's role is to hire top-level managers, monitor their performance, and dismiss them if they perform poorly. Shareholders' only function is to replace the board members if the corporation does not perform well. There is little attempt to take into account the opinions of outside shareholders. In effect, the role of the governance mechanism is to put the right managers in place, give them room to implement their chosen strategy, and monitor their progress.

Table 8.1 Alternative approaches to corporate governance

Decision-making basis	Managed corporation model	Socially responsive corporation	Islamic corporate governance
Legal concept of firm: decision-making by whom?	CEO and senior management	Executive and supervisory processes	*Shuratic* decision-making process: consultation and consensus-seeking
Economic concept of firm: decision-making for whom?	Maximize profits Maximize shareholder value	Stakeholders	Institutions of *hisba*. Role of *muhtasib*
Accounting concept of firm: decision-making with what resources and to whom is accountability due?	Financial governance by shareholders and suppliers of finance	Corporate responsibility Triple bottom line: economic, social and environmental accountability	*Shari'a* supervision process Religious audit

For whom

Milton Friedman's (1970, p. 32) well-known aphorism 'the social responsibility of business is to increase its profits' provides a classic statement of the economic position, although it has been replaced by one that firms should maximize shareholder value. The OECD Principles of Corporate Governance emphasize that corporations should be run, first and foremost, in the interest of shareholders (OECD, 1999). It is not surprising that the concept of shareholder value is enshrined as the principle of corporate governance and the yardstick by which management performance should be measured among companies based in the United States, Britain and the Anglo-Saxon countries, and has become more prominent in discussions of corporate governance in Europe and Japan. This trend has been driven in large part by the growth of investor activism and the rise of the institutional investors (pension funds, mutual funds, hedge funds and private equity firms) and a class of fund managers who are themselves subject to performance scorecards and must satisfy individual clients pushing for higher returns. The institutions are happy to see portfolio firms put under equivalent performance tests. For their part, the target companies are given a clear market directive to improve the returns earned on existing capital, to invest in projects that promise to earn returns above the cost of capital, and to sell assets that are worth more to others (Lewis, 2003).

With what and to whom

Accounting can be seen as the process of identifying, measuring and communicating information to permit informed judgements and decisions by users of that information, but in the managed corporation model, disclosure is often limited and focused on the needs of the individuals and bodies that control resources (Baydoun and Willett, 2000). In fact, corporate governance issues are typically concentrated on those with a direct financial stake in the corporate entity, and especially those supplying capital and finance to the firm. In the standard paradigm 'corporate governance' is synonomous with 'financial governance'. For example, 'corporate governance deals with the ways in which suppliers of finance to corporations assure themselves of getting a return on their investment' (Shleifer and Vishny, 1997, p. 737). Others narrow the topic down to shareholders alone; 'good corporate governance is the stewardship of an enterprise's assets for the benefit of its owners' (Pardy, 1992, p. 15).

The Socially Responsive Corporation

The governance framework above has not gone unchallenged, and in the alternative Western paradigm of the socially responsive corporation, shareholders and others are encouraged to exert influence over policy, and board members and managers are not discouraged from taking their opinions into account. Such an approach has long been entrenched in some European systems of corporate governance. In Anglo-Saxon countries, shareholders are largely confined to the use of 'exit' (in terms of Hirschman's (1970) dichotomy between 'exit' and 'voice'), but not all market systems inhibit shareholders (and others) from directly influencing management. In Germany, for example, the use of 'voice' is encouraged through the accountability arrangements of the *Aufsichtsrat* (supervisory tier). In the Germanic countries (Germany, Austria, Switzerland, Netherlands), there is a separation of executive and supervisory responsibilities. The executive board encompasses the top-level management team, whereas the supervisory board is composed of outside experts, such as bankers, executives from other corporations (for example, interlocking directorships) along with employee-related representatives. There is reliance on the supervisory board for oversight and disciplining of the management as well as for a cooperative conflict resolution between shareholders, managers and employees.

In general, the cornerstone of German corporate culture is 'the concept of the interest of the company as a whole' (Schneider-Lenne, 1992, p. 15). The company is seen as a combination of various groups, the goals of which have to be co-ordinated and do not stop at maximization of the return on investment. Survival, and the long-term interests of employees, customers, suppliers, and the general public have to be taken into consideration. 'This commitment is rooted in the German constitution which says that ownership entails obligations' (Schneider-Lenne, 1992, p. 16).

Even in the 'managed corporation' model that has held sway in the United States, institutions (and the many thousands of individual investors they represent) are no longer passive constituents and have emerged as serious participants in the governance process. Both directors and managers have seen the value of actively seeking the input of institutional shareholders. This interaction can take the form of exchanges of information and analysis, company visits and special private briefings. (Canella, 1995; Brancato, 1997). These linkages are taken further and given a different emphasis in the 'stakeholder' model (Blair, 1995; Monks and Minow, 1995; Gelauff and den Broeder, 1997). In this framework, corporate governance can be seen as the whole system of rights, processes and controls established internally and externally over the management of a business entity with the objective of protecting the interests of all stakeholders (Lannoo, 1995). Such a system recognizes more diverse groups of 'stakeholders' or 'constituents' than simply management and shareholders, including workers, banks, non-financial companies with close ties to the corporation, local communities and the central government. The systems may be characterized by relatively concentrated shareholding, with cross-holding among companies not uncommon. Close family links often add an extra dimension.

Consequently, in this alternative paradigm, oversight of decision-making is vested in a wider grouping, and the firm is seen to have obligations which extend beyond the interests of shareholders alone. The 'triple bottom line' agenda, with its economic, social and environmental dimensions, broadens the picture by emphasizing that the corporation draws on social and environmental resources and has broad citizenship responsibilities to ensure that these are maintained and replenished. 'Sustainability' and 'corporate responsibility' are the watchwords. 'Extended producer responsibility' and 'product stewardship' are concepts that focus on the manufacturer's responsibility for the entire life cycle of products, covering packaging and the life of the product through to end use. Accountability to the community for the use of natural, human and civic resources involves the preparation of valuations of social capital, human capital, the natural environment and cultural heritage in the form of full cost accounting or environmental accounting. In terms of 'international corporate responsibility' there is organizational awareness of health, safety and industrial standards and the development of social accountability standards (AA 1000, SA 8000), 'responsible indices' (FTSE-4-Good), 'corporate sustainability' rankings (Corporate Monitor), 'corporate governance' quotients (Institutional Shareholder Services), and other voluntary codes (Caux Principles, the Global Sullivan Principles, Keidanren Charter, Global Reporting Initiative guidelines).

The Islamic Perspective

The preceding comments make clear that Western approaches to corporate governance are not quite as one-dimensional as many accounts from the Islamic side often suggest (Abdul Rahman, 1998; Baydoun and Willett, 2000). To illustrate, Peter Drucker, for one, regarded 'shareholder value' to be unduly preoccupied with short-term results and called for a balance between these and the long-range prosperity and survival of the enterprise (Heller, 2000). Another leading management guru, Charles Handy, speaks of the 'citizen company' operating in an environment in which businesses are communities not properties (Handy, 1999). The various principles of good governance and codes of best practice developed internationally over the last decade[7] can be seen as embodying the notion that best practice is not just about attaining maximum profitability or economic efficiency or fair dealing, but is about endeavouring to make sure that companies are directed and controlled according to moral standards acceptable to the general community (Gooden, 2001).

Nevertheless, despite these distinct ethical undertones underlying the concept of best practice in governance, there remain three difficulties from an Islamic viewpoint (Haniffa and Hudaib, 2002). First, the ethical foundations of Western business morality stem predominantly from socially derived 'secular humanist' values rather than being based on religious moral authority. As such, the central source of authority and the basis of accountability differ from that of Islam, for which *shari'ah* is the guiding force. Second, the basic beliefs and values of Western corporate culture remain rooted in self-interest and, even if modified to a smaller or larger degree, there is no overarching requirement to take account of wider interests of society. Third, the major theoretical model of corporate governance is based on agency theory rather than stewardship theory (Davis *et al.*, 1997). Thus the major actors are conceived not as stewards who can be motivated to act in the best interests of the principals in a spirit of partnership for the good of the firm, but as self-interested opportunistic agents who have to be watched over and controlled. This characterization is not one that ought to be appropriate for Muslims.

A defining feature is that Islam commands authority over the totality of a Muslim's being, not accepting any distinction between the sacred and the secular. As noted earlier, the New Testament injunction to render unto

Caesar the things which are Caesar's, and unto God the things that are God's, has led to a divergence in the West between sacred and secular that is anathema to Muslims. In Islam, the realms of God and Caesar are not separate jurisdictions. Islamic law, the *shari'ah*, claims sovereignty over all aspects of life, ethical, social, political and economic. Every act of believers must conform with Islamic law and observe ethical standards derived from Islamic principles. These ethical principles define what is true, fair and just, the nature of corporate responsibilities, the priorities to society, along with some specific governance standards. Second, in addition to providing a set of business ethics, certain Islamic economic and financial principles have a direct impact upon corporate practices and policies. Included here are the institution of *zakah* (the alms tax), the ban on *riba* (usury) and the prohibition on speculation, calling for the development of an economic system based on profit-and-loss sharing.

By whom

Turning to the three dimensions of decision-making that have served as our points of reference, *shüra*, *hisba* and the *shari'ah* supervisory process and religious audit establish the basic building blocks of a system of Islamic corporate governance. The type of involvement implicit in shuratic decision-making procedures provides a vehicle for ensuring that corporate activities and strategies are fully discussed and that a consensus-seeking consultative process is applied. Directors and senior managers would be expected to listen to the opinions of other executives before making a decision and *shura* members would include, as far as possible, representatives of shareholders, employees, suppliers, customers and other interested parties.

Islamic corporate governance necessarily has a wide commission, with obligations extending beyond shareholders, financiers and management to suppliers, customers, competitors and employees, embracing the spiritual as well as the temporal needs of the Islamic community. An employee, for example, would be expected to contribute his or her knowledge to the formulation and implementation of the organizational vision, and consultative procedures should be applied to all affected, that is, shareholders, suppliers, customers, workers and the community (Baydoun *et al.*, 1999).

Mawdudi argues that there are three reasons behind the shuratic decision-making process (Mawdudi, 1974, cited in Shaikh, 1988). First, on ethical grounds and in line with the basic Islamic precept of justice, those most affected by a decision, and/or those whose duty it is to implement the decision, should participate in its making. Second, consultation and consensus-seeking prevents one or a small group of individuals from overriding others' rights and imposing their will on others for selfish motives or because of a belief that their views carry more weight. Such behaviour is unacceptable in Islam. Third, as noted earlier, the making of decisions is a trust from God, and Islam requires those in receipt of this trust to ensure that truthfulness, justice, consultation and a spirit of consensus-seeking rules among those participating in the group decision-making process.

For whom

'For whom' is straightforward in Islam because the starting points are from Allah. The ultimate ends of business and economics, indeed that of any form of human activity, are to Allah, and the means employed should not deviate in any way from the sacred law of Islam. The institution of *hisba* offers a framework of social ethics, relevant to monitor the corporation, with the objective of encouraging the correct ethical behaviour in the wider social context. Historically, the scope of *hisba* extended beyond economic matters to encompass moral and spiritual concerns, as well as the supervision of social and civil works. *Muhtasibs* oversaw municipal services (street lighting, building design, garbage and water supply), organized places of worship (mosques, appointment of imams) and implemented justice and fair play in society by preventing price manipulation, incorrect weights and measures, and so on (Murtuza and Abdallah, 2007). *Hisba* can thus be seen as the exercise of wide-ranging administrative control over members of society – a kind of grand 'auditor-general' or 'grand ombudsman' – in order to ensure that they observe what is 'good' (*al ma 'ruf*) and avoid what is bad (*al munkar*) across a large number of areas and activities (Ghazanfar and Islahi, 1997, pp. 19, 20). At the same time, however, *hisba* is more than this since the institution empowers individual Muslims to act as 'private prosecutors' in the cause of better governance by giving them a platform for social action.

With what and to whom

The third pillar of the system is the discipline provided by Islamic religious auditing, which is a device to solicit juristic advice, monitor compliance with Islamic precepts and collect *zakah*. This extra layer of auditing and accountability for resource use ensures that the enterprise operates as an Islamic concern in its business dealings. The processes involved in religious supervision are illustrated most clearly in the case of Islamic financial institutions (Algaoud and Lewis, 1999), but the governance principles operate across the full range of business activities. The functions of the religious auditors, as spelt out in the organization's articles of association, are threefold. First, the religious supervisors give advice to the board and the management about the religious acceptability of the firm's contractual arrangements and new product development. Second, an independent report is provided to inform shareholders as to the compliance of management with Islamic principles and to the extent that the business is run Islamically. Third, there is an audit involved with the special almsgiving levy, *zakah*, to establish that the *zakah* fund is being correctly assessed and properly administered and distributed. In these various ways, the religious supervisory process will testify that the articles of association, stipulating that the organization run its business in accordance with Islamic law, are in fact met.

Yet no system of governance, however well conceived, will influence organizational behaviour unless it is embedded in an appropriate ethical or moral climate and unless the principals involved in decision-making set the pattern in the priorities and attitudes. Ethics in Islam, like everything else Islamic, is deeply rooted in the Holy Qur'an and *hadith* (Nasr, 2002). Just as Islam regulates and influences all other spheres of life, so too it governs the conduct of business and economics. The distinctive characteristics of Islamic economics are that it is Godly, ethical, humane and moderate and balanced (Khaliffa, 2003). Business should reflect all of these four characteristics, and be conducted by Muslims in accordance with the requirements of their religion to be fair, honest and just towards others.

Business activity, in consequence, must be broadly inspired and guided by the concepts of *tawhid* (oneness and unity of God), *ihsan* (goodness) and *tawakkal* (trust in God) while regulated, within those boundaries, by a legal framework committed to values such as justice and the ban on *riba* (interest) and the prohibition of *ihtikar* (hoarding) and other malpractices. In fact, a large number of Islamic concepts and values define the extent and nature of business activity (Rahman, 1994). There are many positive values such as *iqtisad* (moderation), *adl* (justice), *amanah* (trust, honesty), *infaq* (spending to meet social obligations), *sabr* (patience) and *istislah* (public interest). Similarly there are a number of values which are negative, and thus to be avoided: *zulm* (tyranny), *bukhl* (miserliness), *hirs* (greed), *iktinaz* (hoarding of wealth) and *israf* (extravagance). Economic activity within the positive parameters is *halal* (allowed and praiseworthy) and within the negative parameters *haram* (prohibited and blameworthy) which has to be moderated. Production and distribution which are regulated by the *halal–haram* code must adhere to the notion of *adl* (justice). Collectively, these values and concepts, along with the main injunctions of the Holy Qur'an, provide a framework for a just business and commercial system.

IMPLEMENTING THE VISION

When Muslim countries emerged from World War II, the social, political and economic organization and the business and commercial practices in operation were overwhelmingly those inherited from the Western colonial powers. Islamic economics developed as a social discipline in response to this environment, with the aim of establishing or restoring Islamic authority in areas where Muslims increasingly were falling under the sway of Western ideas (Mawdudi, [1947] 1975; Nasr, 1994; Kuran, 1995).

In the political arena, virtually all of the post-Ottoman literature shares the view that the Islamic political system ought to be rediscovered from original sources – the Holy Qur'an and the Prophet's *sunnah* – and partly from the practices of the rightly-guided (*Rashidun*) Caliphate. The pursuit of socio-economic justice within the framework of *shura* stands out as the focal theme of these views. This is in recognition that the institution of *shura* is to be advocated as the genuine Islamic counterpart of political democracy. Nevertheless, the working mechanisms of *shura* and the extent of public accountability of *shura*-appointed offices remain open questions in current writings on the Islamic political system (Tag el-Din, 2006).

Tag el-Din also argues that, in the economic sphere, the challenges facing Islam bring the issue of *shura* to a much sharper focus than the way it has been posed in the traditional sources. The real issue is how *shura* is to be institutionalized, and he identifies the importance of representation and accountability as of significance for implementing and activating *shura.*

Allied to this issue, especially in the context of the revival of the received heritage of the early Muslim civilization, is the status of the concept of *umma* and the accountability of Islamic institutions to the *umma.* One manifestation of this relationship that is central to corporate governance is the interface between the firm and the general community as reflected in the financial reporting obligations needed for full accountability to the *umma*. In an Islamic society, the development of accounting theory should be based on the provisions of Islamic law along with other necessary principles and postulates which are not in conflict with Islamic law. It perhaps goes without saying that Islamic law has very clear views on the basic principles as to how financial reporting and accounting practice should be undertaken in terms of objectives based on the spirit of Islam and its teachings (Lewis, 2001).

Disclosure

If the purpose of accounting information is to serve the public interest, it follows that in an Islamic context the *umma* has the right to know about the effects of the operations of the organization on its well-being and to be advised within the requirements of *shari'ah* as to how this has been achieved. Accountability is thus interpreted as being, first and foremost, accountability to God through making information freely available.

Truthful and relevant disclosure of information is important, in different aspects of Islamic life. There are responsibilities such as paying *zakah*, the calculation of which requires disclosure of the worth of assets and liabilities in terms of the religious obligation to succour the poor, for it indicates a Muslim's capacity to do so. Full disclosure is necessary for predicting future obligations and assessing investment risk.

Six verses in the Holy Qur'an refer to 'relevance'. One meaning of the 'relevance' referred to is disclosure of all facts (S2:71) 'Now hast thou brought the truth' also, based on (S4:135) 'O ye who believe! Stand out firmly for justice' Essentially, these are directives to call it 'how it is' in all things. Financial information is relevant from an Islamic viewpoint only when it includes the attribute of 'truth', and fair and accurate disclosure of the matters at hand. On this basis, doubt must arise whether compliance with the conventional accounting practice of being 'conservative' regarding asset valuation and income measurement can conform with *shari'ah*, any more than would deliberate optimism and overstatement.

Materiality

Adequate disclosure requires that a financial statement should contain all material information necessary to make it useful to its users, whether it is included in the financial statements, the notes accompanying them, or in additional presentations. Since the Holy Qur'an discloses the truth and best way for living in the world (S5:16), so disclosure of all necessary information for the accomplishment of faithful obligations and the making of economic and business decisions consistent with that ethos is the most important tenet of an Islamic accounting system.

Sura 2:282–3 in particular puts commercial morality on the highest plane as regards the bargains to be made, the evidence to be provided, and the doubts to be avoided. Understandable information is an accountability necessity applicable to financial information in an Islamic accounting framework, in which the information is not to deceive the user, nor decrease understanding in such a way as to lead to a wrong decision. By decreeing that financial information should be disclosed part by part, materiality of financial affairs should be obvious in the context of the disclosure. In general, the materiality of accounting information in an Islamic framework is considered relevant if it is related to *shari'ah* requirements.

Record Keeping

According to the Holy Qur'an, followers are required to keep records of their indebtedness:

> Believers, when you contract a debt for a fixed period, put it in writing. Let a scribe write it down fairly . . . and let the debtor dictate, not diminishing the sum he owes. (Al-Baqarah 2:282)

Islam thus provides general approval and guidelines for the recording and reporting of transactions. Underpinning Islamic belief is the requirement that doubt and uncertainty be removed from interpersonal engagements. In business affairs, trading and the like, it is clearly evident that all parties' rights and obligations are to be fully documented for verification and exploration. Verses place an emphasis on recording material credit loans and transactions, and advise that these transactions should be signed by debtors (to acknowledge their indebtedness and the amount thereof), the ultimate in verification processes.

Reliability

Askary and Clarke (1997) identify 19 verses in the Holy Qur'an placing emphasis on the reliability of matter (2:283; 3:122,159; 4:58,81; 7:89; 8:2,27,49,61; 12:11,64,66; 23:8; 27:39; 33:72; 65:3; 70:32; 81:21). As with every other aspect of Islamic secular life, reliability extends into the area of accounting. If published financial information is unreliable, many followers will be unable to accomplish their religious responsibilities, and they will be unable to assess their capacity to assist the disadvantaged, or their capacity to pay *zakah*. If the managers of business entities are to be honest to the business entities' owners, *Sura* 4:58 indicates that they must produce true and complete, reliable, financial disclosure for them. This verse places an emphasis on making over trusts to their owners ('Allah doth command you to render back your Trusts to those to whom they are due'). In other verses, there is an emphasis on the need to fulfil obligations.

Transparency

Reliable information must also be presented correctly and fully, including details of all the transactions undertaken. *Sura* 11:84–85, for example, says 'give full measure'. True disclosure of financial facts, and the provision of them without any deceit or fraud in order to satisfy users' requirements, is thereby essential for accomplishing such obligations and to facilitate the making of decisions on investment and business matters.

Balance Sheets

Islamic financial statements must show the financial impact of financial transactions and other consequences of Islamic economic activities. Accurate changes in the financial position must be determinable from the balance sheet, along with how those changes arose from the income statement. Under Islam, the elements of financial position would include all items which are subject to financial evaluation, assets, liabilities and the residual benefits, based on the Holy Qur'an. Many verses in the Holy Qur'an deal with various aspects of property and assets. An Islamic asset includes all valuable property resulting from previous events belonging to the owner. Such an asset should not be usurped and if obtained in a lawful (*halal*) way has economic benefits for its owners. Lawful acquisition is a critical aspect of 'asset' in this context; rights to interest income are never recognized. Liability is defined in Islam either as a faithful obligation, or any debt to other persons or business entities. Again, in respect to both, the paying of interest is prohibited under the prohibition of *riba* (Algaoud and Lewis, 2007). Finally, equity in residual benefits is obtained directly from the financial evaluation and contrasting assets and liabilities. Legality is again an issue: *sura* 2:275 decrees that Muslim equity should not be mixed with unlawful (*haram*) properties.

THEORY AND REALITY

How are we to reconcile these religiously-derived principles with the practical reality of political and commercial life in Muslim countries? The institution of *shura* (mutual consultation in political and other decisions) can be commended as a genuine Islamic counterpart of pluralism and political democracy, yet it would appear that '*Shura* was indeed the weakest link in the experience of the early Caliphate after the end of the Right Guided Caliphate and, hence, the key element in the current revivalist movements of political Islam' (Tag el-Din, 2006, p. 2). Much the same can be said of pluralism. 'Islam, if practised as written in the Qur'an, is an inclusive and not an exclusive religion. Pluralism is at the root of Islam. Yet today and throughout recent history, Muslim fundamentalists, both those that rule and those who aspire to rule, have adopted a posture that is anti-pluralist, and thus in our view anti-Islamic' (Askari and Taghavi, 2005, p. 194).

In business life, also, the rules are clear. If Islamic principles were applied, business organization would be marked by the concept of *shura* and the application of shuratic decision-making processes involving consultation and consensus-seeking, along with the institution of *hisba* providing a framework of social ethics and empowering individual Muslims to act as 'private prosecutors' in the cause of better governance and social action. These principles would be enforced by a fiercely independent process of religious supervision by auditors who are not beholden to management for their appointment and reappointment and who are not reliant on management when assessing the Islamicity of business and financial contracts.

This is the ideal. The reality falls short of these standards and is probably closer to what A. Ali (2005, p. 172) calls a 'sheikocracy': hierarchical authority, rules and regulations contingent on the personality and power of the individuals who make them, subordination of efficiency to personal relations and personal connections, indecisiveness in decision-making, informality among lower level managers and a generally patriarchal approach. Nepotism is often evident in selecting the upper-level managers. Tradition plays a significant role in the life of individuals and groups. Extended families, friendships and personal relationships reinforce group orientation and duties. Class origin and kinship is significant.

> The Arab executive lives in a society where family and friendship remain important and prevalent factors even in the functioning of formal institutions and groups. Consequently . . . the Arab executive relies upon family and friendship ties for getting things done within his organization and society. (Muna, 1980, p. 12)

Such divergences between theory and practice has resulted in two responses (at least) among Muslims. One is a fatalistic acceptance of the status quo. Ali considers that Muslims, and Arabs in particular, hold two sets of identity. One is immediate, social and spatially particular. The other is historical, cultural and global (Ahmad, 1984). Violation of particular principles, cherished in the early days of Islam, is common because the basic aspects of the reality of Arab politics and organizations are the personalized nature of authority, tribalism, and fluidity and alternating fission and fusion of group coalitions and alliances (Ali, 2005, p. 124).

He argues that the two identities are reconciled by the Islamic equivalent of 'doublethink'.

> Doublethink, a term used by George Orwell [in the classic work *1984*] for holding two contradictory beliefs simultaneously, in Arabia and other Muslim countries, depicts a condition where the ideal (Islamic principles) is held officially, but violated in practice. At the organizational level, this situation produces what Child (1976) calls mental cheating. Managerial behaviour, which remains strictly within the framework of the authoritarian and hierarchical structure of the organization, seeks to prepare subordinates to accept decisions already made by managers and to improve the individual manager's images in a society where Islamic and tribalistic values still have some important influence.

> The intention of managers, in this case, is not to create a situation of real consultation, but rather to create a feeling of consultation. (Ali, 2005, p. 122)

The other response to the gap between theory and practice is what Deepak Lal (1998) refers to as the call to purify Islam from all the corruptions that have crept in over the centuries into Muslim lives, and thereby recreate the 'golden era' of Islam. The period of the four rightly-guided Caliphs (Abu Bakr, Umar ibn-al-Khattab, Uthman and 'Ali) is generally regarded as an ideal time, when Islam was practised perfectly and, with the dramatic conquests and the expansion of the Islamic state, it appeared that 'God smiled on Muslims' (Lal, p. 50).

The difficulty with this latter response is the potential for perpetual disappointment. As Lindholm (1996) observes:

> In the memory of Muslims ever since, this period appears as a divine ordered social formation flowering under the benign regime of the community's duly elected representative – the Caliph.
>
> Muslim thought is saturated with longing for a return of this idealized era when ordinary men and women are imagined (in the soft glow of collective memory) to have acted together selflessly under the leadership of just and divinely guided Caliphs to realize the will of Allah in the world of human beings – a realization validated concretely through the vast power and wealth acquired by the victorious army of the faithful. (p. 80)

Even allowing for 'apocryphal exaggeration' (Atiyah, 1955, p. 36) and some less than ideal circumstances ('three of the four caliphs were assassinated', Watt, 1996, p. 40), suggesting that 'the early Caliphate was not devoid of wordly struggles over power and glory' (Lindholm, 1996, p. 87), the fact remains that the hold of this period of history over Muslim thinking remains strong, and there are good reasons for this admiration. In the words of one (generally unsympathetic) Western observer: 'Its [Islam's] rise is one of the wonders of world history – a chain reaction of conquest and conversion, an amassment not just of territory but of millions of hearts and minds. The vigour of its ideal of justice allowed for levels of tolerance significantly higher than those of the West' (Amis, 2008, p. 81).

From a Muslim perspective, there was much more. It was a golden period that saw *wahy*, that is, revelation (guidance of God) come to man, Muhammad (pbuh), after a break of some 600 years, and he interpreted, disseminated and implemented that message in the life of individuals and a community in a way that provided a benchmark and blueprint for all generations. The *Rashidun* Caliphs tried their utmost to follow the path that their leader had demonstrated. In terms of governance, the period was marked by good conduct and a responsible attitude to the public purse. It was also a period of small government, and the four rightly-guided Caliphs were circumspect in the powers that they exercised.

> For six months, until the community decided to contribute to his sustenance, Abu Bakr was a part-time leader in Medina, continuing his usual work as merchant, and milking his neighbors' sheep for additional income. Later Caliphs were not much more powerful. Abu Bakr's successor, Umar, was obliged to count the camels sent as tribute by himself, with only voluntary help. (Lindholm, 1996, p. 85)

In short, they were free of the trappings and the seductions of empire to which later Muslim dynasties were to succumb.

To what extent the 'golden era' can be reconstructed seems at best an open question, but there is no doubt that the achievements of this period result in a very different worldview from that held by most Christians. As Lindholm goes on to remark:

> Remembering their glorious world-conquering past, Muslims have not pictured the 'City of God' in the Christian manner as beyond ordinary ken, achieved in the radiant future by faith and renunciation. For them, God's mandate was actually realized in historical reality, under the authority of the Prophet himself and the four pious rulers after him. (p. 79)

> Recalling their millennial past, the Muslim devout, unlike their Christian cousins, have never inwardly consented to the disjuncture between the religious experience of the community of believers (equal before God, led by the Prophet and his deputies) and the reality of power-seeking secular rulers prone to political intrigue and the use of physical coercion. (pp. 80–1)

These differences may be reflected in responses to public policy thinking, not only in terms of public governance and social affairs but also on matters relevant to business and commercial affairs. In many Islamic accounts of corporate governance the Islamic position based on the principles of classical Islam is contrasted with the most extreme 'self-interested agents' models of corporate governance, operating in what Samuelson calls the 'ruthless economy' with a 'cowered labour force' (Samuelson, 1997, p. 6). In these models, competition and market disciplines force the players into line so that the cult of 'shareholder value' prevails. Such accounts ignore the 'stewardship theory' of corporate governance, the counter-views of management gurus such as Peter Drucker and Charles Handy, the work of corporate reformers such as Margaret Blair and Nell Minow, and the normative codes and principles of best practice and good governance drawn up in a number of settings. Then there are the diverse approaches to corporate governance at a global level, which offer different perspectives again. One study identifies six basic models of corporate governance internationally, of which one is the Islamic model of corporate governance.[8] Rather than drawing the strongest possible contrast between Islamic principles and what is, in effect, one particular paradigm of Western corporate governance, a potential exists to examine the parallels between the Islamic approach and the 'stakeholder' and 'socially responsive' corporate paradigms. For example, the view of Kay and Silbertson (1995, pp. 90–1) that the large public corporation is a 'social institution' and should be governed by 'the concept of trusteeship' to 'sustain the corporation's assets', including 'the skills of its employees, the expectations of customers and suppliers, and the company's reputation in the community', would seem to sit comfortably with Islamic thinking on these matters.

Finally, corporate governance cannot be divorced from broader governance issues. One commentator (although not a Muslim) has drawn attention to the 'sharp practices' of companies such as Enron, the 'misdeeds' of auditing firms such as Arthur Andersen, and what would seem to be an 'immoral core' at the heart of capitalism, contrasted with the moral certainty of Islam with respect to business ethics (Wilson, 2003). However, any claims to a moral high ground on matters of principle must be tempered by the practical reality of the poor record of many Muslim countries in terms of corruption and economic and public governance. These are the issues explored in the next chapter.

NOTES

1. That is why Islamic law (by a detailed description in the Holy Qur'an) defines exactly how the estate is distributed after death. An individual's power of testamentary disposition is basically limited to one-third of the net estate (that is, the assets remaining after the payment of funeral expenses and debts) and two-thirds of the estate passes to the legal heirs of the deceased under the compulsory rules of inheritance, providing for every member of the family by allotting fixed shares not only to wives and children, but also to father and mothers.
2. Consider also the verses:

   > And the Firmament has He raised high, and He has set up the Balance (of Justice), in order that ye may not transgress (due balance). So establish weight with justice and fall not short in the balance.
   >
   > (Ar-Rahman S55:7–9)

3. This discussion has been greatly informed by the entry 'The Market of Madinah' prepared for the *Encyclopedia of Islamic Economics.*
4. This section and the next draws on Lewis (2005).
5. In Lindley, *Law of Partnership,* see Schamell (1962).

6. In effect, under Islamic law, the accountant assigned a *dhimmah* (personality) to the firm, leading to the creation of a legal capacity or *ahliyyah*. See Nyazee (1999).
7. The UK Cadbury Code is a prominent example. For Sir Adrian Cadbury's later thinking see Cadbury (2002).
8. Lewis (1999) examines the Anglo-Saxon model, the Germanic model, the Japanese model, the Latinic model, the Confucian model and the Islamic model.

9. Governance and corruption

INTRODUCTION

One of the themes that has recurred in this book is the need for corruption-free governance. Unfortunately, however, corruption is a fact of life. It is a deeply rooted age-old phenomenon that exists in innumerable forms, knows no cultural boundaries, operates in the private as well as the public sector, applies to rich countries and poor, and defies a comprehensive definition. Given this universality, it is perhaps surprising that in the published literature, the problem has been approached almost exclusively from a secular viewpoint. It is the purpose of this chapter to present an Islamic perspective on corruption insofar as its definition, causes, and remedies are concerned and compare and contrast this standpoint with the understanding reached within the Western social scientific paradigm.[1] We begin with the latter by defining corruption and examining changing views about its significance, causes and remedies.

WHAT IS CORRUPTION?

In common usage, the word 'corruption' is associated with a range of acts such as bribery, extortion, buying influence, nepotism, favouritism, fraud and embezzlement. Nevertheless, it is at root evidence of a moral failure. The word 'corruption' comes from the Latin verb *rumpere*, to break (Tanzi, 2000). By implication, then, something is broken – presumably a prevailing ethical, moral, social or administrative code of conduct. In this respect, corruption can be thought of as the betrayal and abuse of trust for private benefit (Wolf and Gurgen, 2000). A number of corollaries follow. First, there can be no clear distinction between perpetrator and victim. If ethics are good for you, then corruption must be corrosive to the perpetrator, along with society as a whole. Second, there is necessarily a cultural dimension. Some actions for example, officials demanding bribes are considered corrupt in virtually all societies, whereas attitudes to gift-giving and cronyism, for example, vary from country to country (Camerer, 1988). Third, the definition makes clear that corruption takes place not only by public officials but also by those in a position of trust in private enterprises or non-profit organizations. Indeed, most government corruption involves a private sector entity.

Arnold J. Heidenheimer (1970, p. 4) classifies the analysis of corruption into three basic models: public-office-centred, public-interest-centred and market-centred models. The key focus of public-office-centred concepts of corruption is on the behaviour of public officials which deviates from accepted norms in order to serve private ends. Thus J.S. Nye (1967) defines corruption as:

> behaviour which deviates from the formal duties of a public role because of private-regarding (personal, close family, private clique) pecuniary or status gains; or violates rules against the exercise of certain types of private-regarding influence. This includes such behaviour as bribery (use of a reward to pervert the judgement of a person in a position of trust); nepotism (bestowal of patronage by reason of ascriptive relationship rather than merit); and misappropriation (illegal appropriation of public resources for private-regarding uses). (pp. 566–7)

Tanzi (2000) prefers to define corruption in the negative:

> the intentional noncompliance with arm's length relationship aimed at deriving some advantage from this behaviour for oneself or for related individuals. (p. 94)

We return to this definition later. The essence of public-interest-centred definitions is on the damage done to the public interest by corruption. As Rogow and Laswell (1963) point out, corruption is violation of the common interest for special advantage. Friedrich (1966) argues that corruption exists whenever a responsible functionary or office-holder, is by monetary or other rewards not legally provided for, induced to take actions which favour whoever provides the rewards and thereby damages the public interest.[2,3]

The market-centred definitions are an attempt to bypass the ethical violation in corrupt behaviour and instead use social choice or public choice methods to analyse corruption. For example, Leff (1964) argues that corruption is an extra-legal institution that individuals or groups use to gain influence over the actions of the bureaucracy. Its existence *per se* indicates only that these groups participate in the decision-making process to a greater extent. The result, according to Tilman (1968), is that corruption involves a shift from the bureaucratically determined, centrally allocated, mandatory pricing model to a model that is akin to a free market in which clients risk sanctions to pay bureaucrats higher than mandatory prices to assure desired benefits.

This type of approach led to attempts to classify the character or seriousness of the act. Alatas (1990) distinguishes between 'transactive' corruption, that is mutually arranged, agreed and advantageous, and 'extortive' corruption that involves some kind of compulsion. 'Investive' corruption is not linked directly to an immediate transaction but is instead an investment for obtaining favours in the future. 'Nepotistic' corruption involves unjustified favoured treatment for friends and relatives, while 'autogenic' corruption refers to benefits obtained from pre-knowledge of policy outcomes and 'supportive' corruption protects and strengthens existing corruption. Another distinction has also been made between administrative or bureaucratic corruption and political corruption, the latter occurring when politicians betray the electorate by selling their votes to pressure groups while undertaking regulatory or budgetary legislation. Tanzi (1998) associates the words 'petty' with bureaucratic corruption and 'grand' with political corruption, although he accepts a certain ambiguity exists between corruption and rent-seeking, at least in some eyes. As Heidenheimer (1970, p. 6) asks, 'Which norms are the ones that will be utilised to distinguish corrupt from non-corrupt acts?'

Philip (1997) takes up Heidenheimer's question and canvasses three main candidates for attributing meaning to the normative content of 'corruption'; these are 'public opinion, legal norms, and standards derived from modern Western democratic systems' (p. 441). All have problems. Public opinion may be coloured by partisan considerations and be both culturally-dependent and time-specific, allowing no consistency across countries and through time. Legal standards share these faults, along with the perennial one of the difference between the letter and spirit of the law where an action may not be prohibited but is nonetheless offensive to public expectations. This factor is accentuated by country-to-country differences in constitutional and judicial precedents.

We now move on to evaluate the standards incorporated in Western democratic systems as a potential basis for attributing a widely accepted normative content to the terms 'public office' and 'public interest'. Most Western researchers tend to view the democratic system as the culmination of an evolution whereby a variety of pre-modern monarchical, patrimonial, and feudal political arrangements that confused the boundaries between the private and the public interest succumbed in favour of a system that draws a sharper boundary between the two. Whereas in earlier centuries, public offices had been objects of sale, trade and exchange, during the nineteenth century, such practices gave way to bureaucratic structures across Europe wherein employees were obliged to commit to a set of norms and rules that inhibited potential conflicts of interest. Public or political office came to be viewed as a relationship distinguishable from all other kinds of arrangements and exchange such as absolute monarchy, patrimonial domination, and market exchange.

Philip (1997) interprets this development as a conflict resolution apparatus to avoid potential 'disorder' originating from factional strife or from the powers of Leviathan itself:

> political corruption involves substituting rule in the interests of an individual or group for those publicly endorsed practices which effect an ordered resolution to conflicting individual or group interests. (p. 458)

Substituting these rules for individual or group gains erodes the legitimacy and the capacity of the public domain to resolve conflict. One may add, in such a case, the state itself becomes a source of conflict rather than a mechanism for conflict resolution. Nevertheless, this conception of the state as a conflict resolution mechanism offers the most fruitful ground for attributing normative content to the concept of corruption.

IS CORRUPTION A SERIOUS MATTER?

Many analysts have echoed Leys (1965) who asked 'what is the problem about corruption (p. 215)?' It has long been argued, for example, that corruption can have a beneficial effect, especially in oiling a malfunctioning or developing economic system (Leff, 1964). Leys himself envisaged that, in bad conditions, bribery may be socially and not just privately beneficial. Huntington (1968) considered that 'in terms of economic growth the only thing worse than a society with a rigid, overcentralised, dishonest bureaucracy is one with a rigid, overcentralised, honest bureaucracy' (p. 69).

Nowadays there is a greater recognition that these short-term advantages of accepting the existence of corruption are acquired at a longer-term cost, since corruption distorts the economic system and erodes faith in democracy and the rule of law. Rather than being the 'grease' that lubricates the 'squeaky wheels' of a rigid bureaucracy, corruption in fact fuels the growth of excessive and arbitrary regulations which can then be exploited for corrupt purposes (Ades and Tella, 1997).

For the purpose of analysis we call the first conception the 'benign' view of corruption (corruption as oil) and the second corruption as 'malignant' (corruption as sand in the machine). Over time, an emerging body of theoretical and empirical research on the phenomenon has shifted the balance in favour of the latter view. Table 9.1 provides a summary of these studies and also compares the two views on the impact of corruption upon a number of aspects of political and economic development.

Table 9.1 Views on the impact of corruption

Benign view	Malignant view
A: Political impact	
Corruption is conducive to political development	Political corruption shakes the very foundations on which a state is established: state is an apparatus to resolve conflict. Bribery results in arbitrary action that inspires conflict rather than resolves it (Philip, 1997).
	Corruption violates public trust, corrodes social capital, and undermines state legitimacy by eroding confidence in playing by the rules (World Bank, 1997). Thus, the state's capacity to perform basic functions such as protection of property rights and enforcement of contracts that are crucial for economic growth is impaired. Corruption weakens prudential supervision of banks and financial markets and debilitates implementation of useful regulation such as building industry codes and food inspections (Tanzi, 1998).
	It can be argued that given increased access to information, corruption's ability to 're-engineer' political and economic scene has become doubtful, even if it ever worked in the past. In particular, in a developing country where military and bureaucracy are strong players in power politics, 'political corruption' cannot be contained. By default, it extends to these organs of the state. Since police and judiciary are the enforcement apparatus, they too have to collude to facilitate corruption. Also, because 'banks are where the money is', nationalized banks and development finance institutions become targets of corruption as well. Sometimes, it is difficult to maintain secrecy and loyalty in a multi-polar network for an extended period. This may result in a narrow-based repressive regime, the kind of small oligarchy of political and business elite depicted in Shleifer and Vishny (1993). Alternatively, such attempts may end up in alienation and political instability.
	The situation described above also carries the seeds for systemic abuse of power that may in the words of Cartier-Bresson (2000) 'enable a symbiosis between organised crime and politicians' (p. 18).
	Unforeseen consequences of attempts to 're-engineer' can be even worse.

Table 9.1 (continued)

Benign view	Malignant view
	Corruption diverts resources from productivity-enhancing public infrastructure to conspicuous private consumption by politicians (Bardhan, 1997).
Organized corruption is superior to disorganized corruption.	Shleifer and Vishny (1993) examine different networking arrangements for corruption. They conclude that compared to organized, disciplined, centralized, and predictable corruption wherein agents abide by established rules of the game (strong state: for example, monarchical and pre-Communist USSR arrangements), disorganized, decentralized, and anarchic corruption (weak state: for example, post-Communist Russia and many developing countries) is more devastating for growth and investment. The difference between different arrangements is that of the intensity rather than the direction of impact. Jean Cartier-Bresson (1997) demonstrates a similar point by examining transaction security in different networking arrangements wherein relative powers of the demand (public officials) and the supply (private agents) sides differ.
B. Macroeconomic performance	
Corruption 'oils the economic mechanism'. Bribes lower the business costs of taxes, customs duties, and regulations (Rose-Ackerman, 1999).	Both theoretical and empirical studies point to a strong negative correlation between the perception of corruption in a country and economic indicators such as the ratio of investment to GDP, the rate of economic growth, and total revenue to GDP ratio (Tanzi and Davoodi, 2000). Some of the channels through which adverse economic impact is galvanized are mentioned below.
Since governments generally allocate goods to individuals and firms on a basis other than the 'willingness to pay' principle, bribes indirectly introduce this criteria thereby clearing the market. In	First, given illegal contracts cannot be enforced, bribery increases uncertainty and transaction risk (Cartier-Bresson, 2000). Second, corruption increases the influence of criminal organizations as they guarantee enforcement of illegal transactions and assist in laundering money. This impairs the state's capacity to implement law and order, a prerequisite for economic progress (Carlson, 2000). Third, it can be argued that in developing countries, lower revenue collection owing to corruption impairs a state's capacity to adequately fund maintenance of law and

Table 9.1 (continued)

Benign view	Malignant view
particular, in a distortion-free economic environment, a Coasean bargain may result in the awarding of a contract to the firm that offers the highest bribe. Given only the low-cost firm will afford to offer the highest, bribes will not induce allocative inefficiency. 'In the second-best world of pre-existing policy-induced distortions, additional distortions in the form of black marketeering, smuggling and so on may actually improve welfare even when some resources have to be spent in such activities' (Bardhan, 1997, p. 16).	order and enforcement of contracts, thereby jeopardizing preconditions for economic growth. Fourth, corruption diverts resources from productivity enhancing investments in human capital to wasteful 'grand' infrastructure or military projects easily amenable to corruption (Shleifer and Vishny, 1993). Fifth, empirical evidence suggests corruption costs (time, money) to small and medium-sized enterprises (SMEs) are higher *vis-à-vis* large firms stifling the inception, growth, and competitive capacity of SMEs. Since SMEs serve as the backbone of economy by being labour-intensive and innovative, bribery adversely affects overall economic performance (Tanzi and Davoodi, 2000). Sixth, secrecy requirement for bribes breeds capital flight retarding capital formation. It also encourages undocumented economy (Nye, 1967). Seventh, bribery impedes foreign direct investment by operating as tax (Tanzi, 1998). Insofar as corruption's capacity to mimic a Coasean bargain, it is impaired in more than one way, in real practice. In particular, favouritism or nepotism for a particular client or secrecy requirements introduce conditions other than size of the bribe in the decision-making process. Bribers may also substitute lower quality goods. Even in the second-best world, corruption's ability to increase efficiency is doubtful since factors causing distortions are quite often the same as those responsible for corruption (Bardhan, 1997). Secrecy requirements may favour 'trusted' rather than the highest bidder being allotted a contract.
Bribes facilitate maintaining a lower tax burden by alleviating the need to raise wages of government employees. Lower	Bribes are worse than taxes in terms of consequences for growth. Bribes are an *ex ante* tax on capital reducing all future returns while taxes are levied *ex post* on profit. Negative profits can even be offset against taxable income in many countries encouraging innovation (Bardhan, 1997).

Table 9.1 (continued)

Benign view	Malignant view
tax burden is pro growth (Becker and Stigler, 1974).	The 'greatest victims of petty corruption are usually the poor' (World Bank, 1997, p. 103). 'Corruption distorts the re-distributive role of the state' (Cartier-Bresson, 2000, p. 18). Money destined for 'public spending' is either not allocated for health and education but instead on wasteful projects or it lands in the pockets of private, often already wealthy individuals skewing wealth distribution in a society (see incentive structures below).
C. Incentive structures	
Corruption provides incentives for business friendly action (Leff, 1964). 'Speed money' that is offered to jump slow-moving queues is efficient because it saves time for those who value it most (Lui, 1985).	Rules and rigidities are not exogenous but instead the product of government machinery. 'When rules can be used to extract bribes, more rules will be created' (Tanzi, 1998, p. 582). Evidence suggests that 'speed money' induces systemic slowdown to attract more bribes (Myrdal, 1968). Taking inspiration from Baumol (1990) and Murphy *et al.* (1991), Tanzi (1998) asserts that given increasing returns to corruption and rent-seeking, most able individuals in the society divert away from entrepreneurship and socially productive activities to corruption and rent-seeking, adversely affecting social surplus and economic growth. Tanzi and Davoodi (2000) suggest that corrupt countries tend to have high ratio of lawyers to engineers. We may add that increased visibility of medical doctors rendering services of an administrative nature (customs, police) in Pakistan Central Superior Services (CSS) alludes, among other factors, to existence of a similar distorted incentive structure for talent.
	Secrecy requirement for bribes results in incentive for misallocation of resources. Budget expenditure is diverted away from activities conducive for development but less amenable to corruption – health and education – towards activities offering better opportunities for corruption: infrastructure projects, custom-built high-tech equipment, defence purchases. Operation and maintenance expenditure are also reduced for similar reasons (Shleifer and Vishny, 1993; Tanzi, 1998; Mauro, 1997).

Table 9.1 (continued)

Benign view	Malignant view
	Bribery spreads. On the supply side, its implications for low business cost structure suck in all industry participants willy nilly so as to maintain competition. On the demand side, corruption induces behaviour akin to an auction for the governmental posts: 'those who pay most for a job get it, . . . who do not collect bribes . . . cannot' (Shleifer and Vishny, 1993, p. 603). Police and customs outposts in the Asian sub-continent are an example.

The starting point for the benign view is Leff (1964). He argued that the notion that corruption is harmful is based on an idealized conception of government – the 'government is good' position. In reality, many governments can be indifferent, outright hostile, or lukewarm to the process of economic development owing to other priorities (military, ideological, political), and to fears of a challenge emerging to established centres of political and economic power in case of progress, in-expertise, and inefficiency. In these circumstances, corruption can act as an extra-legal institution to facilitate business, encourage government officials to business friendly action, and mitigate governmental policy errors. Huntington (1968, p. 63–71) saw corruption playing three roles. First, it could foster and strengthen political parties and political participation thereby reducing the threat of some groups being thoroughly alienated from society. He argued: 'The nineteenth century experience of England and the United States is one long lesson in the use of public funds and public office to build party organization' (p. 70). This is required because 'In a modernizing polity the weaker and less accepted the political parties, the greater the likelihood of corruption' (p. 71). Second, it may dilute resistance against policy reform coming from organized pressure groups. Third, it could potentially overcome 'traditional laws and bureaucratic regulations which hamper economic expansion' (p. 68). As Bardhan (1997, p. 21) reminds us, historically, in Europe and in the United States, 'a great deal of corruption in dispensing licences, loans or minion and land concessions' assisted in the emergence of an entrepreneurial class, restrained sectarian warfare, and facilitated economic growth.

On the alternative view, corruption sustains a vicious cycle of rule substitution by politicians, over-regulation and systemic procrastination by bureaucrats, and wasteful use of talents in rent-seeking. Thus Mancur Olson (1982) in his monumental study *The Rise and Decline of Nations* advanced the thesis that differences in macroeconomic performance within and across nations could be explained by the degree of prevalence and influence exerted by collusive, cartelistic and restrictive business, trade, and professional associations in creating or preserving favourable redistributive monopoly positions for their members. The higher the influence of interest groups, the more focused the political process is on redistributing existing income at the cost of efficiency losses and the less successful it is in promoting efficiency enhancing, pro-growth policies that benefit a wider spectrum of the citizenry. Mueller (1983) collates a number of cross-country studies substantiating Olson's thesis. In terms of specific impacts of direct corruption as distinct from rent-seeking, Nye argued that it reduced administrative capacity, exacerbated ethnic dissent, undermined government legitimacy, and induced political and social instability (Nye, 1967). Also, it provided incentives for distortion in public spending – obviously officials receiving payments to help an enterprise win a bid for a public investment project have a vested interest in inflating the scale of the project so that they get larger commissions. Gunnar Myrdal (1968, p. 953) using examples from South Asia, argued that 'speed money' caused intentional systemic slowdown to attract more bribes, while 'official misconduct among politicians and administrators, and the concomitant spread of unlawful practices among businessmen and the general public' had been the cause of frequent political instability. Myrdal also cites Mende (1955):

> Probably no other symptom of Pakistani public life has contributed more to the demoralization of the 'common man' than corruption. [Illicit practices had reached such proportions that] their effect is likely to wipe out whatever benefits new economic projects might have secured for him. (p. 937)

Researchers such as Becker and Stigler (1974), Banfield (1975), Rose-Ackerman (1975; 1978) and Klitgaard (1988, 1991) have employed principal–agent models to examine ways in which honesty can be induced through incentives or persuasion. Rose-Ackerman develops a series of models to demonstrate widespread opportunities for legislative and administrative corruption when politicians, bureaucrats and economic markets players come into contact. Shleifer and Vishny (1993) translate insights derived from the microeconomic theory on commodity taxation and market structure to demonstrate the harmful consequences of corruption on economic development under different network arrangements (structure of government institutions and political process).

In similar vein, Lambsdorff (2002) uses the tools of 'new institutional economics' to explore the social structures surrounding corruption.

Because of the need to camouflage corrupt deals and because participants end up with potentially damaging information about each other, they are 'locked in' to each other even after the exchange is finalized. This results in corrupt agreements often being arranged by brokers or middlemen to enhance secrecy, so raising transactions costs. Also, corrupt deals may emerge from market arrangements with limited participation. The notion that corruption might re-establish the efficiency of market exchange in the face of excessive bureaucracy and regulation has to be counterbalanced by the reality that corruption limits exchanges to insiders as part of a long-term relationship that restricts competition. Politically-related inefficiencies are replaced by inefficiencies associated with lack of competition. He concludes that fighting corruption should focus less on individual moral attitudes and penalties, and more on destabilizing the long-term relationships by reducing the role of middlemen and using corporate criminal liability to attack the firms rather than those individuals ensnared in the web through 'minor' misdemeanours.

Lambsdorff's emphasis on institutions and lack of competition overlaps with the study by Lederman *et al.* (2005). Their starting point is that corruption is a type of crime, but that the factors governing its incidence appears to be quite different from that of other crimes (burglaries, theft and other forms of 'common' crime). What distinguishes corruption from the other crimes is its connections to government activities and authority, which gives corruption its own special characteristics and determinants. Based on a statistical analysis, they find that the political system, balance of powers, and the electoral system determines the incentives for those in office to be honest, while corruption festers in an environment where there is a lack of competition and the existence of rents that can be extracted through the abuse of public power. Political institutions and the structure of public governance emerge as the critical factors in tackling corruption.

THE ISLAMIC PERSPECTIVE ON CORRUPTION

There is fairly general acceptance that societal values and concepts of social justice shape moral conduct (Hayllar, 1991; Turner and Hulme, 1997). For many people, religion is an important influence, but for Muslims it is an overriding consideration. They cannot compartmentalize their behaviour into religious and secular dimensions, and their actions are bound by an encompassing set of duties and practices including morals and behaviour in all facets of life, public and private. Islam thus defines a distinct community within the larger human brotherhood. What is the Islamic position on corruption?

In the Holy Qur'an and *sunnah* – the primary sources of Islamic law – corruption refers to a broad range of behavioural digressions that threaten the social, economic and ecological balance (see 11:85; 28:4,77,83; 29:28–30; 30:41; 89:12). Such acts are explained at various places in the Holy Qur'an in plain language, in terms of being just or unjust, with reference to their detrimental impact on social organization and universally respected standards of moral virtue. A distinct advantage of such articulation is that it strikes a harmony among all the various approaches to ethics and caters for people coming from a diverse knowledge base and inclinations.

In the limited sense of understanding corruption in terms of the abuse of public office for private gain, there is a family of closely related concepts to which *shari'ah* draws attention. Corruption is depicted to stem from the abuse of judicial power, administrative power of any kind, political authority, and financial prowess. For example, The Holy Qur'an (2:188) prohibits rulers, judges, decision-makers and parties to a conflict from facilitating the unjustified appropriation of the property of others or public property by obtaining a favourable ruling in exchange for bribery. It calls such behaviour as '*batil*' meaning 'false or deceptive' on the one hand and '*ithm*' meaning 'criminal or sinful or inappropriate' on the other hand. Condemned are those in authority who spread corruption and mischief (*fasad*) on land by conspiring (racial) divisions among people, bestowing benefits on some and oppressing others (28:4; 89:11–14). Also the rich are advised to seek with their wealth lawful bounties and not engage in actions that spread corruption (*fasad*) on land (28:77). The Arabic word '*fasad*', we should note, translates into rottenness, spoiledness, corruption, decay, decomposition, putrefaction, depravity, wickedness, viciousness, iniquity, and pervertedness (Cowan, 1976). In the English translations of the Holy Qur'an, Marmaduke Pickthall (1994) frequently uses the word 'corruption' in lieu of *fasad* and its derivatives while Allama Abdullah Yusuf Ali (see Holy Qur'an, 1992) frequently uses 'mischief'.

Muslims put considerable store on events that took place in the early years of Islam, during the life of the Prophet (pbuh) and the early rightly-guided Caliphs. These years provide illustrations of what is considered to be appropriate behaviour:

- The *sunnah* confirms the above prohibition through a general sanction that censures both the givers and the receivers of '*rashwa*', the Arabic word for bribery, corruption, dishonesty. To illustrate, 'Narrated Abdullah ibn Amr ibn al-'As: The Apostle of Allah (peace be upon him) cursed the one who offers bribe as well as one who accepts bribe' (Abu-Dawood (Hadith, 3573). Allama Yusuf al-Qardawi (1996 [1960]) brings the same *hadith* through Musnad

Ahmad, Trimdhi, and Ibn Habban adding the word *fil-hukme* that means in matters of governance, decision-making and rules. He brings another *hadith* through Musnad Al-Hakim that adds condemnation of the mediator between the briber and the bribed, thus anticipating Lambsdorff's emphasis on the role of the middleman or broker in corrupt deals. Other *ahadith* capture the concept of corruption through reproaching the abuse of trust placed in officials by the state through acts such as accepting gifts, outright theft of public funds, and undermining rules in exchange for bribes, on recommendation or due to family or tribal considerations. Finally, people in general are prohibited from making recommendations in exchange for gifts as such behaviour falls under '*rashwa*'.

- The Prophet (pbuh) declined many who sought a public appointment on the grounds that such positions are a trust and given only to those possessing appropriate attributes (that is, 'stewardship' credentials or merit). Disapproving a similar request, he said, 'authority is a trust, and on the Day of judgment it is a cause of humiliation and repentance except for one who fulfils its obligations and (properly) discharges the duties attendant thereon' (Sahih Muslim (Hadith, 4491)).
- The second Caliph, Umar-bin-Khattab used to record the possessions of his officials at the time of their appointment and confiscated partly or wholly whatsoever they added while in office on suspicion of benefiting from public appointment (Al-Baladhuri, 1968).
- Umar-bin-Khattab instructed one of his commanders to adjust the value of gifts offered to him – that he had dispatched to the central treasury – against the tax liability of the people because taking anything more than the stipulated *jizya* (poll tax) was unjust (Hasanuz Zaman, 1991, p. 108).
- The Caliph Umar-bin-Abdal Aziz ruled: 'I am of the view that the ruler should not trade. It is (also) not lawful for the officer to trade in the area of his office . . . because when he involves himself in trade he inadvertently misuses his office in his interest and to the detriment of others, even if he does not like to do so' (Hasanuz Zaman, 1991, p. 128).
- Any doubts that remain for the believer after such contextual elaboration are to be resolved at the personal level through conscientious reflection (*ijtihad*).

These examples suggest that corruption is understood in Islam in terms of the abuse of trust through the misuse of judicial powers, administrative powers, riches, and political authority. As compared to Western thought, there is probably less controversy in Islam as to the meanings of the concept. This is due to at least four reasons.

- First, the value basis in Islam is drawn not with reference to the existing realities on the ground – that may reflect compromises on many accounts – but from eternal principles given in *shari'ah*.
- Second, many forms of corruption are expounded in *shari'ah* with concrete examples leaving little room for ambiguity.
- Third, Islam perceives a harmony among different conceptions of ethics. For instance, the Law-Giver in Islam can be conceived of as performing functions akin to Adam Smith's ([1759] 1976) 'Impartial Spectator' having perfect foresight for whom the utilitarian, virtue-based, legal, and justice-based interpretations of ethics are not in conflict but in fundamental sympathy and coherence with each other. All corrupt acts undermine communal harmony (in effect, the maximum good for the highest number) in one way or other and are therefore undesirable from a utilitarian perspective, lacking in virtue from a moral perspective, unjust in relation to the principles that safeguard rendering to every one their due, and culpable from a legal standpoint. Insofar as matters requiring *ijtihad* are concerned, such coherence is expected to emerge with time as human knowledge grows.
- Fourth, much of the clarity stems from classical Islam's firm commitment to private property, rule-based governance, transparency, and somewhat limited role for the state.

Against this backdrop, the arguments and conclusions advanced by Philip (1997) insofar as their external form, are fully consistent with the spirit of the Islamic position on the issue. There is, however, one caveat. From an Islamic perspective, the body of rules itself has to be sourced from *shari'ah* or rationally derived from it (*ijtihad*); a denial of this premise is itself tantamount to a grave form of corruption. To understand why it is so, we need to appreciate the Islamic conception of human nature and historical interaction.

As far as human nature is concerned, Islam does not admit the doctrine of original sin. According to it, all human beings are created in the best mould (Holy Qur'an: 30:30; 76:2–3; 95:4), that is, inclined to truth, modesty and compassion, and fearful of ultimate accountability on the day of judgement (22:35; 42:18; 70:27). Over time, however, a person is led away from this cast owing to conditioning by parents and society, that is, from social interaction. This results in divisions in faith, racism, egoism, jealousy, miserliness and deceit. In brief, a state of mind can result that is fixated with realizing self- or group-interest interpreted within the limited context of here and now, and at the neglect of or without being cognizant of the full repercussions of one's actions that unfold over a much broader horizon of time and space. This is the sense in which people who are by nature inclined to truth when brought up and immersed in a situational or social context, are conceived to become weak (4:28) in rising above these constraints and discerning absolute truth and justice. Under these circumstances, they may support and promote social values and conceptions of justice based on conjecture alone (4:27; 6:115–16). Such notions have the potential to secure gains for a limited number of people and may gratify tastes, desires, and greed in a way that could be injurious in general to mankind. Such notions, it is argued, cannot become the basis for a social order that can deliver sustained peace. The role of a chain of Prophets culminating in Muhammad (pbuh) has been to convey, live, implement and leave behind a blueprint of social order that is divorced from such defects and within ready access to those willing from among mankind.

From the Qur'anic perspective, recognizing that human beings possess the intellect (2:31; 76:2; 91:7–9; 31:20), free will (6:107; 10:99; 18:29; 81:27–29), and minimum blueprint for a peaceful social order, means they are responsible for the conditions that they create on Earth (8:53, 13:11). A number of examples are given from history whereby collective behaviour digressing from the revealed path resulted in social, economic, and ecological imbalances and disasters (6:06, 65). From this standpoint, the change in the (recent) Western social sciences literature to viewing corruption, even in its limited manifestation, as a menace rather than a blessing and as a problem rather than a solution, matches well with the Islamic position.

THE ISLAMIC ATTACK ON CORRUPTION

How is such corrupt behaviour to be remedied? The longstanding Islamic intellectual heritage suggests that education, law and administrative reform are the three key pillars in the Islamic fight against corruption, and we consider each in turn.

Education

Arguably, moral conduct is a manifestation of societal values and concepts of social justice. By inference, the starting point for curing corruption lies in reforming social values, grounding them in appropriate concepts of social justice, and linking them with a broader worldview. This is the very basis of the Islamic moral education programme. The Islamic worldview aspires firm belief in the all powerful, all knowledgeable God. Human beings are created by Him with a purpose – to serve as His vicegerents on earth – and for an appointed term at the end of which they face full accountability in terms of the beliefs, values and actions that they undertake. The benchmarking is to be done with reference to standards revealed in the Holy Qur'an and personified in the Prophet Muhammad (pbuh), the *sunnah*. For sure, compliance pleases God but He, the Almighty, is beyond any intrinsic need for seeking such pleasures. Rather, it is human beings themselves who are in need of such standards (5:66). Revelation elaborates a path for human beings – a catalogue of *huquq al-ibad* (people's rights on each other) and a blueprint of socio-economic laws – so that individuals, communities, and nations can coexist harmoniously.

What does this path involve? Here we introduce a distinction – valuable for later reference – owing to Frankfurt (1971) between first-order preferences (that is, 'basic' desires) and second-order preferences (that is, desires directed at their desires), since people are distinguished by the criterion that they have higher-order attitudes, namely attitudes towards attitudes and, especially, attitudes towards their own attitudes. Moreover, desires can be evaluated not only from the viewpoint of their practical realizability, but according to standards that represent something other than simply desiring. Translating this conception into the Islamic framework, learning of such path in this sense means comprehending higher-order beliefs, values, virtues, and conceptions of justice that support true equality of and peace among human beings. It means practising freedom from the servitude of 'lower-order' (first-order) tastes, desires, passions, and enticements in most cases not by abject denial but by admittance to the extent and through the channels permitted by higher-order norms elaborated in *shari'ah*. It means developing consciousness of ends and means, rights and obligations, and externalities of individual or community action all defined as right or wrong with reference to the objectives of mankind's creation and being. It means seeking and strengthening faith not only in worship and reflection but also in every action undertaken in life. It means seeking God not in escape but by participating 'righteously' in every action that defines and constitutes our being. It means viewing all action through the lenses of an origin destiny framework in which human beings are unable to escape accountability. It means internalizing 'Behold, two (guardian angels) appointed to learn (a person's doings) learn (and note them), one sitting on the right and one on the left. Not a word does one utter but there is a sentinel by him, ready (to note it)' (Holy Qur'an, 50:17–18). Summing up, education in Islam is aimed at instilling in believers a broad agreement on and a clear second-order preference for a catalogue of virtues so as to arbitrate among raw instincts and competing first-order desires, and self-actualize obedience to *shari'ah*. However, while shortcomings and failures at the personal level are recognized and a hope for the infinite mercy of God is always within reach, actions that have a negative bearing on communal relationship are to be externally regulated through the law of *shari'ah*.

Law and Incentive

The core law in Islam is God-given. As Khurshid Ahmad (2000) states, it focuses on making vicegerency of human beings a practical proposal by protecting the building blocks of social life, viz. faith, intellect, life, family, and property. There is a revealed obligatory punishment (*hadd*) for crimes undermining each of these foundation stones. Such punishment is consonant with the model of human nature depicted in the Qur'an. For punishment of all crimes other than *hudud* (plural of *hadd*), including corruption, *sunnah* provides guidance and there is scope for enacting discretionary punishment (*ta'zir*) by rulers, legislative assemblies, and judges. However, it is advised that, at maximum, punishment should be commensurate with the misdeed not exceed it (see El-Awa (1983) on this point). In this respect birth, rank, and ethnicity offer no protection. Islam teaches the equality of people, irrespective of race and tribes. The only criterion of merit is goodness and piety – colour, birth or rank do not matter. Bernard Lewis (1997) agrees that central to the classical Islamic teaching on the state is the principle that the ruler is not above the law, but subject to the law no less than the humblest of his servants. More succinctly, in Islam, 'the relationship between the Caliph and his subjects is contractual. The word *bay'ah* denoting . . . a contract by which the subjects undertook to obey and the Caliph in return undertook to perform certain duties specified by the jurists. If a Caliph failed in those duties – and Islamic history shows that this was by no means a purely abstract point – he could, subject to certain conditions, be removed from office' (Lewis, 1993, p. 97). Pointing to a distinct feature of the Islamic law, Gellner (1992) contends, 'A socially and politically transcendent standard of rectitude was ever accessible, beyond the reach of manipulation by political authority . . . if it sinned against it' (p.7).

In a way, external restraint (law in Islam) could be considered as a mechanism to actualize at least partially the second-order norms discussed above. Thus, in a society where law is based on *shari'ah*, to the extent that certain goods and services are prohibited by law, these will not be openly available in the market. Within this framework, many day-to-day dealing in goods and services will reflect first-order preferences as modified by budget constraints. However, it will be a depiction of only a partial truth if external deterrence is taken as the only incentive mechanism in Islam. To the contrary, there is a complementary and powerful 'spiritual' incentive structure that focuses on risks and rewards both here and in the hereafter. In the here, the corrupt will feel dissatisfaction and chaos amidst aplenty and the virtuous will experience an inner peace (*salam*) that transcends material acquisitions. In the hereafter there is the rendering of accountability and justice, and the *shari'ah* asserts that the most excellent trade is that a believer gives himself to the commandments of God in the here in return for blessings in the hereafter.

Administration

Gellner (1992) observes, 'a certain kind of separation of powers was built into Muslim society from the very start, or very nearly from the start' (p. 7). While Gellner is talking about a separation of executive and legislature, another distinction between executive and judicial also evolved quite early in the history of the Islamic nation. By rooting legislation in a handful of transcendent rules that can be expanded only through analogy (*qiyas*), the very structure of Islamic law has throughout history, nourished a class of jurists who were not necessarily under the control of the state. In fact, the relationship throughout the years has been a very difficult one to manage. Gellner notes that the political history of Islam displays a periodic emergence of an alliance between jurists and commoners against the authority, if the latter 'sinned' against law. Babeair (1993) illustrates the other side of the coin by elucidating the role that traditional jurists have played in learning and spreading moral education, and by acting as a force of moderation through mediating between rulers and masses.

In summary, the following inferences can be drawn about corruption and bribery on the basis of Islamic doctrine:

- From an Islamic perspective, 'lying' and 'corruption' are as clearly understood as 'truth' and 'honesty'. They are part of a universally comprehended parcel of vice and virtue ingrained in human conscience, linguistic differences notwithstanding.
- The terms used for corruption, '*fasad*', '*batil*', '*rashwa*', are powerfully negative ones, indicating severe approbation.
- There is a helpful distinction between corruption (*fasad*) as a broad concept encompassing unfaithfulness, dishonesty, betrayal of trust, misuse, iniquity and deceit in private and public dealings and bribery (*rashwa*) as private gain from public office or seeking recompense for rendering duties ordinarily considered as non-compensatory. These duties reflect on our being and existence as a citizen and as a part

of a community such as providing character recommendations on demand. Gifts for public officials are treated as *rashwa* and are also prohibited.

- At the moral plane, there is 'zero tolerance' for bribery in Islam; and Islam rejects any idea that bribery serves as 'the grease that oils the economic wheels'.
- There is no scope for legalizing corruption in the name of commissions, gifts, donations, advances, soft loans, loan write-offs and whatsoever. The touchstone of differentiation is if these flows would accrue had the suspect stayed at home, that is, had no public position or profile.
- Corruption is to be tackled by moral education designed to inculcate in believers a clear 'second-order' preference for virtuous behaviour, reinforced by legal structures and administrative systems reflecting and supporting this stance.

THE ISLAMIC SITUATION TODAY

In early Islamic society, egalitarianism and a high degree of transparency in the early Caliphate saw public funds handled with great caution and care, with military expeditions in particular scrutinized for potential corruption. The following report is indicative. Citing *Al-Tabari, Tarikh ar-Rusul wa'l-Mulk*, Bernard Lewis (1950) records, Umar the second Caliph asked Salman: '"Am I a king or a Caliph?" and Salman answered: "If you have levied from the lands of the Muslims one *dirham*, or more, or less, and applied it unlawfully, you are a king, not a Caliph." And Umar wept (p. 64).'

What is the position today? A wide variety of cross-country indicators are used by the World Bank to shed light on the various dimensions of governance. Several hundred such indicators are aggregated for many countries in a yearly survey (see Kaufman *et al.* (1999a and 1999b) for details). Primarily measured in qualitative units, these indicators are produced by a range of organizations (commercial-risk-rating agencies, multilateral organizations, think tanks, and other non-governmental organizations). They include the perspectives of diverse observers (experts, businesses and private citizens) and cover a wide range of topics (political stability and the business climate, the efficacy of public service provision, experiences with corruption, and so on).

Table 9.2 summarizes the World Bank database statistics for 2006 for Muslim countries (OIC member countries) *vis-à-vis* the total sample in terms of the number of countries falling into different quartiles, for a

Table 9.2 Performance indicators of governance for OIC member countries,[a] 2006

Quartile	Control of corruption	Accountability and voice	Rule of law	Government effectiveness	Regulatory framework
First	25[b] (52)[c]	29[b] (53)[c]	25[b] (53)[c]	25[b] (53)[c]	22[b] (52)[c]
Second	18 (52)	24 (52)	17 (53)	17 (53)	21 (51)
Third	11 (51)	3 (52)	13 (52)	12 (53)	12 (51)
Fourth	2 (52)	0 (52)	1 (53)	2 (53)	1 (52)
Total	56 (207)	56 (209)	56 (211)	56 (212)	56 (206)

Notes:
a. Member countries of the Organization of Islamic Countries. There are 56 OIC Member States. (For the full list of OIC members, see http://www.oic-oci.org.)
b. Number of OIC members in each quartile.
c. No. of countries in the total sample, and falling into each quartile, shown in parentheses.

Source: Extracted from World Bank Data Set of Aggregate Governance Indicator (http://info.worldbank.org/governance/wgi2007/resources.htm)

number of governance measures. The measures chosen relate to control of corruption, voice and accountability, rule of law, government effectiveness and the regulatory framework. While some OIC countries such as Qatar and UAE fall into the highest quartile on the corruption index (indicative of a strong control of corruption), a large number fall into the first and second quartiles (indicating poor control). Much the same is the case with the other measures. Do these statistics suggest a failure of the Islamic approach to corruption?

The first thing to be said is that while countries are called OIC members, we would prefer to call them 'Muslim' rather than 'Islamic', in the sense that they differ in the extent to which the government is committed to Islamic values. Lip service to religion is by no means confined to the West (Friday Muslims and Sunday Christians respectively).[4] Also, in some cases the commercial code and business practices are carried over from colonial days or are largely imported. It would not be appropriate to lay corruption in Muslim countries at the door of Islam any more than one would attribute to Christianity the murder and violence in the United States, car thefts in Britain or housebreaking in Australia.

Second, the data used for measuring governance are largely qualitative and for some indices, for example those related to corruption, only qualitative data are generally available. It can be argued that perceptions of the quality of governance – as reflected in these qualitative ratings – matter at least as much as objective data (from official statistics) and sometimes more accurately reflect actual outcomes. For instance, property rights are legally guaranteed in virtually all countries. Yet effective enforcement of those rights by the courts varies widely. When enterprises perceive that courts do not enforce these rights, they will look for other, less efficient and perhaps extra-legal, ways of enforcing contracts. Nevertheless, acceptance of what constitutes corrupt behaviour is culture-specific and does vary from country to country. Let us consider again Tanzi's (2000) definition of corruption. 'Here we shall simply define it as the intentional non-compliance with an arm's-length relationship' (p. 94), which requires that 'personal relationships should play no part in economic decisions involving more than one party' (p. 88). This principle underpins the efficient functioning of markets.

Nonetheless, to many, the notion that one should treat kith and kin in the same way as strangers would seem not just bizarre but a denial of self. Some scrupulous individuals in the West might 'bend over backwards' to avoid any suspicion of nepotism. To do so in some other societies would bring shame and dishonour. In them, it is a duty to assist a relative. Not so in Islam, however, a believer may point out. In particular, the Holy *Qur'an* (4:135; 5:8) cautions precisely against the twin extremes of refraining from just decisions because of blood relations or hatred. In response, a Westerner may pick some leaves from history and ask how long after Muhammad (pbuh) did it take for Islamic societies to relapse, on matters of governance, to the conditions depicted by the Arab adage: 'Me against my brother, my brother and I against our cousin, the family against the world'. Did pre-Islamic Arab cultural values overtake the universal values taught by Islam or did the failure result from an inability of Muslims to actualize their preferred set of values through rationally designed institutions, lately even for such simple tasks as education in Islamic ethics. No one would expect a religion to cast governmental institutions in stone for all times to come, if only because material conditions of human existence are continuously in a state of flux notwithstanding that the temptations for wealth, power, fame and sex have remained unchanged and therefore there is a need for steady principles. But that does not negate the conclusion that in societies where existing moral and social codes impel one to keep family and fraternal members, the idea that the arm's-length principle will be applied in the face of strong kinship ties is simply wanting.

These differences in values carry over into remedial policies. In some domains, corruption can be reduced by increasing penalties on those who engage in it or by increasing the openness of the rules, regulations, and laws, and by strengthening controls on civil servants. However, in other contexts, such as more traditional family-oriented cultures, these options are not likely, by themselves, to lead to enduring results. The values of the

Western 'nuclear family' are not universal ones, nor should they necessarily be so (Kottack, 1999). In other areas of social policy (suicide, personal crime, homelessness, and so on) the absence of 'family values' in modern states is often seen as a matter of regret. The reality is that all individuals live personal lives in families, kin groups, or territorial communities that, to varying degrees, define their boundaries through ethnicity, religion or spiritual commitments, and these situations condition ethical standards and moral norms (World Bank, 1999).

This leads us to the third, and most important, point. Islam and the West differ markedly in their underlying approaches to remedying corruption. Most Western researchers consider that corruption, at its core, is a problem of bad governance. Therefore, suggestions for remedial action focus on ways and means to improve governance. Among the factors considered important are political systems (parliamentary systems allow for strong monitoring of the executive by the legislature), separation of powers (checks and balances across different branches of government help prevent abuses of power), transparency (freedom of the press and expression increases accountability) and competition (having different agencies compete for provision of public services can reduce corruption). Implementing such an agenda requires action on multiple fronts: the broadest classification may entail an agenda for international reform and a programme for domestic reforms espoused for example, in World Bank (1997), Turner and Hulme (1997), Rose-Ackerman (1999) and OECD (2000).

Broadly speaking, recommendations for domestic reforms can be categorized under four heads: limit concentration of powers, curtail discretionary powers, build and strengthen institutions, and reinforce monitoring and accountability. For further discussion on these points the reader is referred to p. 207–10 above and the summary of mechanisms for facilitating given in Box 6.2.

By contrast, in Islam, corruption is seen in its core as a moral problem, and as such one which involves second-order preferences that are at risk of being modified over time. As Nerlich (1989) argues:

> It is a necessary, though not a sufficient condition of any moral self-appraisal that one have second-order desires, and of one's moral effectiveness that one can carry through some course of second-order action. (p. 113)

Interpreted in terms of the Islamic agenda, if there can be a moral regeneration, and a commitment to social justice and the public interest, all else should follow. If it does not, the outcome may reflect one or more of two things: (1) weakness of internal restraint: internalization of Islamic values and cognizance of strict accountability – due to a falling apart of the traditional education system; (2) weakness of external restraints due to sticking neither with *shari'ah* nor with developments in secular law and institutions. What is then needed is to rediscover the faith, values, egalitarianism and transparency of the early Islamic state and the early Caliphate.

ISLAM AND THE WEST: ASSESSING THE DIFFERENCES

There would thus appear to be some basic philosophical differences between the Islamic and Western approaches to corruption in terms of the moral dimension, and we now seek to explore some of the differences and offer some perspective on them.

To Western eyes, a moral regeneration which features so prominently (if not exclusively) in the Islamic agenda is a necessary first step, but certainly not a sufficient condition for an attack on corruption. The moral dimension, they would say, has been tried and found wanting. By and large it corresponds most closely to what is now called the first of three stages of anti-corruption measures (Klitgaard *et al.*, 2000). Fighting corruption, it is argued, is like fighting a contagious disease. The first stage is the raising of public awareness, the second is to prevent its spread by promoting preventive measures, and the third is to attack the disease by inoculation or surgery. Applied to corruption, in the first stage consciousness is raised about the existence and harms of corruption. Corruption is attributed to bad attitudes to authority and probity, and a pernicious political culture, and a cure sought in terms of a moral renovation and a cultural change. Such was the remedy sought by Leys back in 1965 when he argued the need for a nucleus of 'puritans' applying pressure for a code of ethics.

That puritanical approach did not work then and the implication in the Western literature is that it will not work now. As Klitgaard (2000) observes:

> the problem with this device is practical. We know little about how to engineer a moral renovation, so we must also work at other levels. (p. 4)

Following the medical analogy, the second stage looks to prevention and adds systems analysis to consciousness-raising. Civil service reforms emphasize information, incentives, and competition, and examine where in government and markets lie the vulnerabilities to corruption. The third stage attacks the disease itself, using undercover agents, infiltrators and key witnesses to root out and prosecute the offenders – in effect, cutting out the cancerous cells.

From a Western social sciences perspective, any Islamic approach that relies solely on seeking a moral rebirth from within the individual is seriously deficient. While consciousness-raising is needed, reliance upon self-restraint is considered to be not enough. A call for abstinence will not cure an AIDS epidemic. In terms of corruption, it would be considered more useful to move on to the external environment altering incentives to reduce temptation and impose constraints upon behaviour. Without such supporting stratagems to reform governance, the agenda may remain unfulfilled.

From an Islamic standpoint, the Western approach lacks a moral core. While agreeing with the need for incentives and institutional constraints (albeit in different guise), nevertheless the Western agenda is seen to downplay what it might be possible to achieve from a moral revival. 'Consciousness raising', after all, is not quite the same as 'moral disapprobation', reflecting perhaps to some degree a lack of agreement on a fully satisfactory definition of what is moral. According to writers such as Veatch (1971), the problem is that mainstream Western philosophy does not distinguish between values (in which there is a 'right' and 'wrong' and therefore a second-order preference exists) and tastes (in which there is no 'right' or 'wrong'). In contrast to the Platonic concept of the Good and the Kantian focus on the Ought and its justification, modern analytic philosophy has sought to develop against the backdrop of a value-neutral world. In the words of Joas (2000):

> In analytic philosophy, substantive clarifications of ethical questions were temporarily replaced by the attempt to construct a neutral metaethics, that is to say, a discipline that sets itself the goal of clarifying ethical statements, but is itself at the same time governed by the norm of value-freedom. (p. 125)

Not all agree with this value-free emphasis. One of the most significant exceptions in recent decades to the neglect in Western philosophy of the question of the genesis of values is Taylor (1989), for whom moral feelings necessarily reveal our value standards and would simply not be moral feelings if they were not related to our conception of the 'good'. He argues that an individual's moral and religious experience can call for an interpretation rooted in the cultural repertoire of interpretative patterns in which God, in the sense of the traditional faith of a particular culture, is indispensable. Thus, for him, a return to something like a metaphysical theory of the good is conceivable, even though he accepts that it is not possible for a philosophy which seemingly now has little interest in the realm of values, and which endeavours to find a neutral meta-position when dealing with ethical matters.

It can be noted in passing that this neglect of the realm of values and the implicit equation of values and tastes in mainstream philosophy carries through to Neoclassical economics, although it would take us too far afield to do justice to the point. Briefly, the standard continuous mono-utility function is an aggregate with no qualitatively different parts. It cannot readily accommodate second-order preferences. Writers such as Lutz and Lux (1979), and Etzioni (1988), thus argue that the neoclassical paradigm downplays the role of values, or sees them as one source of tastes, and ignores the moral dimension in the theory of choice.

To those schooled in the Islamic tradition, the criticism goes deeper. If economics can be seen as an imperialistic science concerned in essence with building a social system (see Casson (1995, p. 27)) and reflective of all the philosophical movements aimed at divorcing such an exercise from metaphysical concepts of the good, its focus on the 'external' rather than the 'internal' constraints is understandable albeit not altogether convincing. Without metaphysics, the very essence and narrative of being, for example, the purpose of life and successively unfolding accountability within and beyond it are sent to the realm of doubt and oblivion (Holy *Qur'an*, 45:22–24). Thus the context within which 'right' and 'wrong', 'good' and 'evil', 'virtues' and 'vices', and 'first-' and 'second-order' preferences attain their meaning is diminished and ultimately degraded thereby opening the way for the promotion of social arrangements that are based on parochial worldviews and egoistical conceptions of justice. It is precisely to keep metaphysics at the forefront of human beings' endeavours that Islam admits the right of the 'people of the book' to administer their 'personal laws' within jurisdictions otherwise ruled by *shari'ah*.

This mode of thinking has an immediate relevance for the topic at hand. A failure to explore in full, the ethical and moral dimensions to curing corruption is limiting since there may be many circumstances where the external factors constraining corruption are weak, leaving self-restraint as the only effective discipline. It is simply not possible to provide enough law enforcement officers, accountants and inspectors to verify more than a small portion of all transactions that take place in an economy, so that societies require that most transactions be based on voluntary compliance. In such a context, ethical norms are paramount, and society's attitudes and institutions can give further force to them or cause them to be weakened. For example, the same democratic apparatus which we consider as the pride of modern civilization, when operated by agents exhibiting self-interested behaviour, has been shown by the public choice school analysts to become a tool in the hands of special interest groups. There is also a perception in some quarters that corruption in Europe has increased in recent times (Porta and Meny, 1997). In some eyes, a contributing factor is the decline in the social democratic philosophy and a rise in the 'greed is good' syndrome in which the individual is elevated above the group or organization, and in which the ends in terms of the 'bottom line' are seen to be more important than the means. Such an ideological climate of selfishness, it is said, seems likely to be conducive to corruption (Holmes, 1999).

Reinforcing this concern with ethical standards, there has been some revision among some philosophers (for example, Goodin (1992)) about what a concern with ethics can be expected to achieve. It has long been recognized that ethical standards can make one 'good', irrespective of whether they are a matter of inner virtue (Aristotle) or external duty (Kant) (see Thomson (1953) and Kant (1940)). But modern social science points to other ways in which ethics can be good and can do one good. Obviously, in a Hobbesian sense, ethics are pragmatically sound in allowing one to benefit from the constraints that ethics imposes on others. That much is known and is familiar territory. But it is not just the case that, net of the costs to oneself, one benefits from the fact that others are bound by ethical considerations.[5] The suggestion now is that ethics can be empowering as well as constraining. Ethical norms, and the institutions underwriting them and giving force to them, can widen horizons and choices, enabling individuals to do more things than would have been possible in their absence. Trust and certainty in the integrity of market exchanges and inter-personal dealings are an important social lubricant, as Arrow (1974) observed many years ago. In this respect, ethics might be thought of as a pure 'public good'.

The corollary of this new thinking about ethics is that corruption is corrosive not only because it enables some in society to secure an unfair advantage over others; those engaging in corruption are harming us all by eroding norms and institutions which benefit us all. Declining morality in public life can set in train a cycle of decline. An insistence upon the maintenance of high standards in all facets of life – private and public – rightfully becomes a cornerstone of good governance.

In this emphasis upon the empowering effects of ethics, modern social science and strands of classical Islam would seem to have drawn closer together. Although many scholars and jurists, such as al-Ghazali (1058–1111 CE) (1356 AH) clearly recognize the importance of incentives and 'external' institutional constraints without diluting the role of ethics, there is also an important tradition in Islamic political philosophy which emphasizes the role of second-order preferences in fighting corruption. Consider, as one leading example, the views of Ibn Khaldun (1332 – 1406 CE) (1967), and the significance that he attaches to 'internal' forces as opposed to 'external' law enforcement.

> When laws are (enforced) by means of punishment, they completely destroy fortitude, because the use of punishment against someone who cannot defend himself generates in that person a feeling of humiliation. (p. 96)

> It is no argument that the men around Muhammad (pbuh) observed the religious laws, and yet did not experience any diminution of their fortitude, but possessed the greatest possible fortitude. When the Muslims got their religion from Muhammad (pbuh), the restraining influence came from themselves, as a result of the encouragement and discouragement he gave them in the Qur'an. . . . Umar said, 'Those who are not (disciplined) by the religious law are not educated by God.' Umar's desire was that everyone should have his restraining influence in himself. His certainty was that Muhammad (pbuh) knew best what is good for mankind. (p. 96).

> [The influence of] religion, then, decreased among men, and they came to use restraining laws. . . This led to a decrease in their fortitude. Clearly, then, governmental and education laws destroy fortitude, because their restraining influence is something that comes from outside. The religious laws, on the other hand, do not destroy fortitude, because their restraining influence is something inherent. (pp. 96–7)

CONCLUSION

Corruption is a problem that has been largely overlooked in Islamic economics. The principal objective of this chapter has been to analyse and elucidate the Islamic position on corruption and compare it with the Western social scientific tradition. That tradition, we showed, has undergone a marked transformation over recent decades. The view that corruption may act like much-needed 'grease for the squeaking wheels of a rigid administration' or 'oil for the economic mechanism' by removing or relaxing cumbersome regulations and obstructionist bureaucratic behaviour that stifle efficient investment and economic growth has given way to the view that the economic and social costs of corruption are enormous and that it is one of the most severe impediments to development and growth. This change has brought the Western literature much closer to Islam, for Islamic law (the *shari'ah*), we discovered, condemns corruption as a severe threat to the social, economic, and ecological balance.

Nevertheless, despite their apparent agreement, the two systems differ in how to cure corruption. Islam, although not exclusively so, looks to a significant degree to a moral renovation within the individual designed to stiffen resolve and foster self-restraint. The focus is upon shaping higher-order preferences, elaborated in the Holy Qur'an and *sunnah*, externally regulated through the law of *shari'ah* and reinforced by a powerful spiritual incentive system. The Western strategy has largely moved beyond an ethical approach and now aims to tackle corruption, at one level, by altering the individual's cost–benefit balance through incentives and punishment and, at another level, by infiltrating and rooting out those engaged in corrupt activities. In the Western approach the restraining influence comes from outside. In Islam, the restraining influence comes significantly from within. To Western eyes, such self-restraint will not work.

Our conclusion is that both approaches can learn from each other. Islamic societies can benefit from the practical stratagems and administrative and civil reforms now emphasized in the Western approach – in short, from better governance. They can also benefit from an open press and public debate, factors which exert a pressure of their own for accountability and help to curb arbitrary use of power and privilege – options all too often absent in Muslim countries. Equally, however, the significant ethical and moral dimensions to reducing corruption cannot be downplayed either, if only because there are situations where the external constraints confronting officials are weak and self-restraint is needed. Some social scientific thinking lends some support to this reasoning. Ethics can be empowering, as well as making good practical sense, since ultimately everyone benefits from the behavioural boundaries that ethics dictate. There is room for both lines of attack upon corruption.

NOTES

1. This chapter draws extensively on the earlier research of the authors (Iqbal and Lewis, 2002).
2. The value of the above definitions is in making clear that monetary gains may not be involved. In one major case of fraud, which led to the collapse of the Bank of Credit and Commerce International (BCCI) in 1991, the executives responsible for the deceptions did not appear to have enriched themselves enormously. Rather the motivation was retention of power, prestige and influence (M.K. Lewis, 1997).
3. Another dimension to corruption not explicitly mentioned above is the buying of sexual favours. This aspect featured in a corruption case in Wollongong, Australia involving local government in 2007.
4. The old aphorism about 'the businessman who prays on Sunday and then preys on his neighbours for the rest of the week' doubtless has its parallel for Muslims.
5 Moreover, according to the latest scientific thinking, moral judgements about what feels fair or not, or good or not, draw importantly on the social nature of moral intuition. Thus at a 2009 discussion on ethics sponsored by the Templeton Foundation, the view was expressed that we don't just care about our individual rights, or even the rights of other individuals. We also care about loyalty, respect, traditions, and significantly, religions. People link themselves together into communities and networks of mutual influence and seek goodness, not as a means, but as an end in itself (*International Herald Tribune*, April 10, 2009, p.7).

10. Conclusion

OUR APPROACH

The aim of this book has been to analyse, from an Islamic perspective, some of the major issues involved in public governance, economic governance, and corporate governance. In doing so, we have found it challenging that in spite of years of optimistic rhetoric, the achievements of Islamic economics have been disappointing in at least two major respects. At one level, 'Islamic economics' has not advanced far beyond explicating and sanctifying the *fiqhi* solutions and institutional structures of early Muslim polities. At another level, Islamic economics has presided over the re-invention of a replica of the contemporary conventional financial architecture under a different nomenclature, devoid of the social underpinnings and principles of justice that inspired creation of an Islamic financial system.

This volume departs from these prevalent approaches by taking the historical Islamic body of thought and institutional repertoire that constituted classical Islam not as sacrosanct in itself but as a prism through which one can reflect on the time-bound application of the normative framework of Islam (which consists of a set of basic axioms about the place, origin and destiny of humans in the universe and ethical parameters, values and goals that ought to guide one in choice of action and thus provide a means for ordering the collective affairs of the Muslim community). Once a set of such guiding principles is identified, it can be used to reformulate the overarching Islamic theory of governance and then elaborate the theoretical substructure of public, economic and corporate governance in Islam in the context of contemporary research, political realities and economic problems. The approach has been informed by three major inputs. These are, first, Islam, second, economic theory, and third, public choice analysis. Below, we summarize the key insights provided by each of these disciplines.

Islam

The question that lies at the core of Islam is: what kind of life ought one live to achieve success (*falah*) in the here and the hereafter? The answer is found in reflecting on the fundamental metaphysical problems of existence and the purpose of life. That is, why are we here? What does it mean to be a human being? What is the scope and role of authority in regulating the collective affairs of mankind? Where does the state fit into the lives of people and community? Which rules ought to be followed? What is right and wrong and just and unjust while interacting with others? In seeking to reach the truth about these matters, Islam sees rationality facing many challenges. For instance, people's conception of the just and unjust is influenced by envy, desire, interests of the immediate group with which one identifies, broader power relationships in the society and the information that they feed, norms inherited from the past, and disposition to groups 'other' than that with which one identifies. Also, humans have bounded rationality and a limited appreciation of all the known and unknown entities that respond to its action and create the conditions that confront its being. In the wake of these limitations, there is a risk in the eyes of believers that an exclusive reliance on reason may lead people astray from the source and purpose of life. Muslims believe that Allah – the Almighty God and the Creator of the universe – has throughout history revealed the truth about the Divine and the profane via a chain of Messengers and invited people to reconcile it with impartial reason and historical evidence veiled in the rise and fall of human civilization. Such Divine revelation consists of a code of conduct for organizing human affairs and a standard of values that guides actions most consistent with preserving justice and balance.

This philosophical backdrop provides some basic principles on which the Islamic theory of governance is based. These are, first, that sovereignty (*hakimiyya*) belongs to Allah alone. Second, human beings are the vicegerents of Allah on earth. Third, the will of the Sovereign is revealed to the vicegerents through the institution of Prophets. Fourth, the political authority is to be exercised either by the successor of the Prophet (Caliph or *imam*) or by the *umma* (popular vicegerency). Fifth, popular vicegerency is to be channelled through mutual consultation (*shura*). Sixth, implementation of *shari'ah* is the ultimate object of political authority in Islam. Seventh, temporal authority (*ulil-amr*) is owed obedience (*ita'aa*) so long as it admits *shari'ah* as the basis for legitimate exercise of political authority. Following this line of thought, we have sourced the normative principles of justice for ordering the secular affairs of the Muslim community from the Holy Qur'an and the *sunnah*. This blueprint has been used as the criterion in selecting among competing economic theories on government fiscal organization. Finally, by relating, modifying or building further upon these theories, we have evolved a contemporary Islamic perspective on governance.

Economic Theory

Conventional economic analysis focuses on how to organize economic relationships so that maximum wealth can be generated from scarce resources. Logic and sense perception alone are the basis of elucidating the order which achieves this objective. This means that man – *homo economicus* – is conceived as a collection of preferences that adjust to pecuniary incentives. Exhibited spontaneously and voluntarily in the market, these preferences create a Pareto-efficient transacting order that is taken for granted as 'natural'. The scope for government and its fiscal organization rests in the possibility of sustaining and extending this natural order, and addressing some of its failures. In this paradigm, governance is about the 'use of political authority and exercise of control in a society in relation to the management of its resources for social and economic development' (OECD, 1993).

Such exercise of authority essentially involves decision-making and raises the next series of questions: decision-making 'for whom', 'by whom', and with what resources ('to whom'). These three dimensions of decision-making apply irrespective of whether we are considering governing a nation, a government organization or a business enterprise. 'For whom' decisions are made is stipulated by the underlying charter or constitution. 'By whom' decisions are made depends on the decision-making structure developed. 'With what resources' determines 'to whom' accountability is due for the usage made of them. A governance agenda for decision-making correspondingly focuses on the following issues: the distribution of decision-making responsibilities among different participants in the organization; rules and procedures for making decisions; the degree of involvement in decisions; the structure through which the goals and objectives are set; the means of attaining those objectives; and the review and monitoring of performance.

The focal point of understanding governance in this manner is on developing internal and external supports for better decision-making. However, it evades dialogue on the set of normative principles that ought to guide decision-making. Here, in the absence of consideration of fundamental ethical questions and denial of absolute values in modern economics, the discussion boils down to the processes through which a government that reflects preferences of a given people – a nation – is selected. Correspondingly, the methodological dilemma faced in analysis of a given situation is that there could be more than one theory explaining the same economic phenomenon based on logic and/or empirical testing, and, there could be more than one structural arrangement – governance and economic systems – each with its own unique set of goals or preferences and a theoretical basis to achieve these goals through a unique set of means. How then to choose among various alternatives? When formulating, for this manuscript, an Islamic perspective on governance, we have sought to find a solution to this problem by replacing the standard methodological criteria of 'generality' and 'peer group acceptance' with principles extracted from *shari'ah.* In brief, we have filtered mainstream economic theories on the topics chosen for analysis using the standard of values – that is, theory-choice criteria – sourced from the Holy Qur'an and *sunnah.*

Public Choice

Inquiry into issues relating to political economy following standard economic methodology has been criticized for being too reductive in terms of the axioms of individual choice and too naive in not extending the self-seeking model of individual behaviour to political and bureaucratic action. In seeking to fill this gap, the public choice discipline highlights opportunistic and rent-seeking behaviour of those in whom authority for decision-making is vested. It then seeks to rectify such behaviour through an emphasis on norms, application of fiscal rules, reform of constitutions, and examination of voting procedures. For the purpose of this volume, the public choice analysis provides us with the missing dimension in traditional economic analysis, completing the picture about government behaviour and delivering useful insights on public and economic governance.

Other Inputs

Since traditional economic theory uses a model of human behaviour in markets (that is, pecuniary incentives) and is developed within a mould of logical positivism, there are limitations to the viewpoint that it offers. Islamic economics itself widens the concept of utility in three ways: to encompass the spiritual as well as the material; to extend utility from this life to the hereafter; and to recognize communal obligations and welfare. To these insights have been added views from other disciplines along with data to relate theory to practice for taxation and budget deficits.

OUR CONCLUSIONS

Having sketched the approach that was taken in the book, we now outline some conclusions.

The Centrality of Justice

Justice, the objective of *shari'ah* and what Islam seeks for human relations, provided our starting point, for justice is the inner core of governance in Islam. It was found that there are five key constituents of the Islamic theory of justice. These are: first, bringing both the state as well as markets under the umbrella of justice; second, providing a firm basis for the establishment of a welfare state by specifying the charge rate as well as expenditure categories for redistribution; third, defining justice in exchange (that is, prohibition of interest, *gharar* and gambling); fourth, sanctifying contracts and property rights subject to the previous reforms; and fifth, elaborating and specifying fairness in inheritance.

Justice in Exchange

In comparing the old and the contemporary Western views of justice with Islam, we note that Islam's search for justice in exchange in the form of prohibitions of usury and gambling were also a part of the Greek and Biblical teachings. Where Islam differs from them is on the value of commerce and trade. Islam not only permits and encourages trade but requires that it be free from restrictions and tariffs. In doing so, it pre-empts modern economics and the libertarian philosophy. On another account, however, the reluctance in certain strands of the libertarian tradition to admit a need for minimum welfare transfers falls far short of the Islamic egalitarian spirit. In fact, on this point, the Rawlsian welfare liberal enterprise of reconciling the apparently contradictory dimensions of justice (that is, the morally arbitrary distribution of wealth with the legal protection of property rights) through the principle of maxi-min comes very close to Islam. Lastly, there are three issues on which Islam stands out *vis-à-vis* contemporary visions of justice. First, it continues to emphasize justice in exchange. Second, it prohibits withdrawing wealth from circulation (that is, hoarding). Third, there are clear precedents in early Islamic history (albeit not always realized in practice) of discouraging feudalism and absentee landlords.

Normative Theories of Taxation

In terms of normative theories of taxation, both the ability-to-pay and the benefit principles are admitted in Islam. However, in the case of the sacrifice principle, the most likely interpretation in Islam would be that the incidence of general taxation (in aggregate) – excluding *zakah* – ought not be regressive. It was also concluded that the Equitable Taxation

(ET) approach of treating all income *pari passu* regardless of source is in harmony with Islam, given the income base, although Islam admits wealth as well as income in terms of the ability-to-pay criteria. The Fiscal Exchange (FE) position on the importance of rules and constitutions in preventing a tax system from becoming an attractive tool for political rent-seeking resonates with the spirit of Islam. However, the accommodation in Optimal Taxation (OT) of tastes, leisure and social welfare functions produces a wide range of results some of which appear quite arbitrary and contravening basic notions of justice.

Three Alternative Islamic Models of Taxation

In the wake of the above analysis, three alternative models of taxation acceptable in Islam were proposed. The first is the *zakah* model that calls for financing both the redistributive and general public expenditure through a tax on net worth and a tax on earned income. The second is the *fay* model that applies to general taxation only and presumes that the *zakah* system is in place. This model facilitates levying any economically feasible tax on the condition that, in aggregate, the incidence of general taxation not be regressive. To the extent that any one of these two models is approximated in reality, inheritance taxes will not be admissible, given that the *zakah* charge on net worth (along with Islamic laws on inheritance) takes care of uneven distribution. Finally there is a third solution applicable to both redistributive and general taxation. This 'integrated' model is based on the presumption either that it is difficult to unite all Muslim sects around one model of *zakah* or that it is politically or operationally infeasible to tax net worth. In other words, for one reason or another, there is a compulsion to go with the global trends in taxation. In that case, we call for the entire basis for taxation to be secularized but with five caveats: (a) overall tax incidence ought not be regressive; (b) a percentage of total tax dues collected must be (constitutionally) allocated for welfare payments; (c) taxpayers ought to be given a choice to pay part assessment of direct taxes in lieu of *zakah* (whether they use this option or how they assess personal *zakah* liability is left to personal choice); (d) *zakah* so tendered is credited to a separate account; (e) if voluntary *zakah* payments exceed the constitutional limit on welfare transfers, then funds are transferred from the *zakah* to the general account and vice versa.

While the *zakah* model appears closest to the spirit of Islam, on the basis of contemporary trends in economic management, one can understand that the third ('integrated') model above will be most appreciated, albeit on the basis of (OT-derived) theoretical articulations open to criticism on many counts. However, there are dissenting strains of thought in economics that continue to consider exemption of wealth from taxation as contrary to the principles of fairness in taxation. Introduction of wealth taxes in these analyses makes sense on a number of grounds such as reducing inequality, placing incentives for efficient utilization of wealth, lesser distortion to incentives compared to other tax alternatives, and the facilitation of administrative cross-checking in order to reduce evasion, especially of taxes on income from capital.

Taxation in Practice

Moving from the normative to the positive, the principles of fairness in fiscal management have been compromised by a wide margin in the Muslim countries. In some Muslim countries, there has been a dependency on income from a single mineral resource (for example, oil) while in others, tax policy has become the unfair art of the politically possible rather than equitable (although others are in the process of reforming their tax systems). In explaining such behaviour, we found common grounds with public choice theory. The importance that this theory places on the use of well-defined rules and constitutions to constrain such behaviour was found to be close to Islam at least insofar as a cure is sought in the apparatus 'external' to man.

Budget Deficits

It was argued that the focus of some classical economists on the potential for misuse of public debt can be seen to be consistent with the Islamic prohibition of fixed interest contracts. So too is Buchanan's argument that public debt transfers the burden of present consumption to future generations (through higher taxes). In contrast, the Barro–Ricardo hypothesis of the irrelevance of public debt is less in harmony with and less explanatory of the Islamic prohibition of fixed interest debt. In fact, the history of developing country debt provides some cogent reasons for the reluctance on the part of both the Islamic and the public choice literature to approve of the use of such debt for financing public expenditure.

Preferred Islamic Financing Modes

By allowing either interest-free debt or profit-and-loss sharing (PLS) arrangements to finance public sector needs beyond taxation, Islam imposes simultaneously moral discipline (that is, prohibiting the potential exploitation implicit in financing basic needs through fixed interest finance) and also commercial discipline on government activities. Public sector financing through either interest-free or PLS instruments has the potential to avoid the pitfalls highlighted both by the economic as well as public choice theory.

Debt Financing

The *ijtihadi* Islamic debt instruments are useful in tying debt to real assets and, in this respect, have advantages over conventional fixed interest finance. However, relative to PLS contracts, these instruments are inadequate for imposing a commercial discipline on government. The reason is that a PLS partner joins hands with government based on his own subjective assessment of project feasibility while any other form of lender does not have to do that. There is a dependence instead on government guarantees (and implicit contingent liabilities imposed upon taxpayers) to settle debts. This feature means that *ijtihadi* contracts offer little protection against the politics of special interest groups in carrying substandard investments through the political process. A public choice recommendation to put a constitutional limit on deficits and debt could be useful to constrain such behaviour.

Financial Contracting

In our view the microeconomic optimality of fixed interest debt can be overstated. Some research work has made assumptions that virtually guarantee such optimality while others have focused on conflicts of the type that conceivably could be resolved alternatively by changing managerial compensation schemes. Also, at the macroeconomic level, one only need look at the sub-prime crisis of 2008 to recognize that debt and the leverage it allows can play a significant role in accentuating business cycles. Having said that, the problems of moral hazard and adverse selection in the preferred Islamic PLS contracting modes cannot be wished away. Institutional and contractual solutions have to be found to alleviate these problems at least cost. It is in this context that we synthesized some of the insights derived from research on financial contracting with the principles of *shari'ah* to offer a holistic solution to designing the capital structure for commercial public sector ventures.

Islamic Governance Principles

The principles of Islamic governance that we have identified are quite general and are potentially applicable to a wide range of political, social and economic organizational structures. In particular, *shura, hisba* and the *shari'ah* supervisory and auditing process establish the basic building blocks needed for the governance of corporations in conformity with Islamic principles. Under *shura*, corporate activities and strategies ought to be fully discussed among shareholders, employees, suppliers and other interested parties, with a consensus-seeking consultative process applied to major decisions. *Hisba* offers a framework of social ethics to encourage ethical behaviour by the corporation, while providing a platform for social action by individual Muslims acting as 'private prosecutors' in the cause of better governance. Finally, religious supervision is a mechanism for jurists to monitor corporate compliance with Islamic precepts (although some questions have been raised by some authors about how impartial is the religious supervision of certain Islamic financial activities).

Governance and Corruption

The shift in social scientific thought in viewing corruption as 'grease that oils the economic wheel' to a 'menace that undermines economic growth' has brought rational understanding of the phenomenon closer to the Islamic position as revealed by our examination of the Holy Qur'an and traditions. Where the two conceptions differ is with respect to remedial action. The Western approach focuses on reforming public governance and designing appropriate detection systems and institutions that gear information and incentives towards minimizing opportunities and enticement for corruption. In short, it emphasizes constraints external to the individual. By comparison, Islam seeks to go beyond such constraints, and ideally instil in believers a clear 'second-order' preference for non-corrupt behaviour. It recommends developing a firm belief in transcendent accountability and stresses character building through practising moral virtues and shunning vices. In essence, much of the restraint comes from within through a moral renovation. It is our contention that both emphases are important in eliminating corruption and that the West and followers of Islam can learn from one another.

Rethinking Governance in Muslim Countries

Finally, integrating the above findings with the scorecard of Muslim countries on governance and managing fiscal affairs, we conclude that there is considerable scope for improvement on multiple fronts. There is a pressing need for rethinking governance, re-establishing supremacy of law (that is, of a constitution), reconfiguring education systems, reforming taxation in line with the domestic income and wealth profile, promoting savings in the general community, encouraging an appropriate investment climate, and reconsidering expenditure priorities. General policy recommendations on these issues are contained in Chapters 5 to 9.

SOME FURTHER ISSUES

In the process of synthesizing various themes in this volume, we have suggestions on a number of issues that we believe would benefit from further study.

An Alternative Macroeconomic Policy?

In examining the similarities and differences between the Islamic and the standard economic approaches to taxation and budget deficits, we found that the repeated castigation of hoarding behaviour in the Holy Qur'an and the persistent call for generosity (in charity) implied that there was no presumption that *laissez-faire* in itself was adequate despite the strong advocacy of trade and commerce. On both scores, Islam would presumably sit more comfortably with the possibility of a Keynesian less-than-full-employment outcome due to a combination of low marginal propensity to consume and instability in investment expenditure, although we note Kuran's (1993) observation of 'the futility of trying to place Islamic economics in the pro- or anti-market camps' (p. 294). In terms of resolving any such underemployment problems, however, Islam would part ways with Keynesianism. Consider, for example, the issue of a savings–investment gap in the light of the Islamic ban on fixed interest lending and borrowing. This prohibition effectively removes the Keynesian solution of public debt issuance from the realm of possibilities. On this basis, a government cannot alleviate 'hoarding' by reinforcing the very mentality that produces it, that is, offering fixed-interest return to savers so that they bring out wealth into economic circulation. Nor can government transfer the 'real risk' of investment to itself, that is, burden taxpayers (with hidden contingent liabilities) through the contrivance of a 'risk-free' reward to savers. To the contrary, a levy is imposed on wealth (*zakah*). Assuming tax authorities can reach most savings, one may ask what option is left with savers to protect their savings from diminishing (through *zakah*)? An obvious solution is for them to invest. Given no fixed-interest outlet, investment in any project (irrespective of location) having net positive expected rate of return thus becomes feasible.

Note also that the levy on wealth (*zakah)* if properly charged, could, in addition to the above role, address the problem of low consumption.

The conventional economic concern on this solution would be that the savings ratio will drop owing to *zakah*. Again, such is the confidence of Islam on the 'natural' propensity of people to save that, on balance, there is no excessive worry about this activity apart from an important moral injunction to prohibit extravagance. A question may be asked as to how to reconcile this position with inadequate savings rates in developing countries. As we saw in Chapters 4 and 5, a major problem in these countries has been stark inequality that shows in savings being concentrated at one end of the distribution spectrum, and often either hoarded or the wealth invested in industrialized countries. Some studies indicate excess production capacity in many developed nations while many developing countries are starved of capital. However, the real problem may not be the scarcity of capital but its sparse distribution. Parallelling Amartya Sen's (1982) theory of 'food' famines may be a theory of 'investment' famine – both in their origin being problems of distribution, the latter that of circulating savings. To that end, the Islamic emphasis on justice in exchange and its financing of redistribution through a charge on net worth offers a solution that is found neither in the books of *laissez-faire* nor in Keynesianism.

Need to Re-examine Distributive Theory?

The above discussion reminds us that a major preoccupation of many economists of past centuries was of investigating how the fruits of economic activity were distributed among different factors of production. For instance, in a letter written to Malthus on 9 October, 1820, Ricardo observed:

> Political economy you think is an enquiry into the nature and causes of wealth – I think it should rather be called an enquiry into the laws which determine the division of the produce of industry among the classes who concur in its formation. No law can be laid down respecting quantity, but a tolerably correct one can be laid down respecting proportions. Every day I am more satisfied that the former enquiry is vain and delusive, and the latter only the true objects of the science.

However, a lot of the interest of economists in distribution theory was lost due to the more or less unchanging historical relationship between the wage and non-wage shares of national income in the industrialized countries. For example, labour's share of output, investigated by Lawrence Klein (1962) as one of the five 'great ratios of economics' (p. 183) was found by him to exhibit statistically 'near constancy' over the period 1900–53 for the United States (p. 199).

From a development economics perspective, it may be interesting to reflect on the underlying causes – governance issues, institutional structure, taxation, contractual mechanisms, etc. – for this 'constancy' and map such studies over developing economies with different institutional structures. Pakistan, for instance, could offer one case study given its predominantly feudal agrarian economy with those in control of large landholdings permeating the 'governance' hierarchy and blocking tax reforms and efforts for mass education and development. Also, in view of the Islamic emphasis on participatory business arrangements and a net worth levy, there may be some merit in revisiting the question of distribution and examining the implications of the Islamic stance for factor shares in an economy.

PLS or Interest-free Debt?

Another area for study relates to the issue of financial contracting. It is hard to disagree with the notion that there has been an over-emphasis in Islamically motivated research on finding 'interest-free' debt alternatives to conventional fixed interest obligations and that many practitioners in the Islamic finance industry appear to have lost their way in the sense that replication of conventional loan structures has become the driving force for market growth. As El-Gamal notes in his (2005) review of Kuran's, *Islam and Mammon: The Economic Predicaments of Islamism* (2004), that the applications of Islamic economics to finance 'bear little resemblance to the economic theory of profit and loss sharing upon which they were built. Instead, a fast-growing industry is built on medieval ruses, with which contemporary financial practices are reproduced at a higher cost – to be borne by the industry's captive market of Muslim clients' (El-Gamal, 2005, p. 90). How close to conventional fixed interest debt does an Islamic financial product need to be before it is labelled (and hopefully eschewed) as a *hiyal* or legal fiction? It may now be time for the emphasis to be shifted toward finding institutional and transactional arrangements that make a wider use of PLS contracts possible by alleviating moral hazard and adverse selection.

Sustainability or Survival of the Fittest?

One final thought concerns viewing fiscal reality *vis-à-vis* theory as an important dimension of the struggle among different participants in the global system. Many institutions, originally conceived to render justice and liberate man, have become tools in the hands of special interest groups. One can observe tax systems removed from fairness, the export of ill-gained capital from locations where it is most needed, mercantilist tax and subsidy policies, trade in armaments, ill-used developing country debt, poor governance, and satisfaction of economic interests by repressing reform. A second look at these symptoms reveals that they appear in their most chronic form in jurisdictions with weak institutions. Thus there are two challenges faced by the contemporary world. First, insofar as the Muslim world is concerned, there is need to define, clarify and uphold constitutions and strengthen institutions at the expense of 'loyalties' to specific persons and their ruling styles. Deepak Lal (1998) offers the view that 'it is not Islamic beliefs in themselves that have hindered development [in Muslim countries] but dysfunctional étatism and dirigisme', along with 'family-based processes of socialization' (pp. 66–7). Second, there is a need at the global level to focus on the universality of man, and one way that this can happen is if international institutions can somehow be reshaped to address and resolve externalities outside national borders in a meaningful way. But who is going to bell the cat? Ibn Khaldun (1967) saw that centuries ago when he declared the following:

> This is what Muhammad actually had in mind when he forbade injustice. He meant the resulting destruction and ruin of civilisation, which ultimately permits the eradication of the human species. (p. 240)
>
> However, injustice can be committed only by persons who cannot be touched, only by persons who have power and authority. Therefore, injustice has been very much censured, and repeated threats against it have been expressed in the hope that perhaps the persons who are able to commit injustice will find a restraining influence in themselves. (p. 241)

Perhaps another way to say much the same thing is to recognize that Islam and Christianity can play a major role in this endeavour. As Karabell (2007) in his study *People of the Book. The Forgotten History of Islam and the West* points out:

> More people throughout the world believe that Muslim and Western societies are destined to clash and that they will always clash until one or the other triumphs. That belief is poisonous, and one antidote is the rich historical tradition that says other paths are not only possible but have been taken time and time again.
>
> . . . That is reason enough to take a look back and recognize that while the relationship between Islam and the West can be fratricidal, it can also be fraternal. Retrieving the forgotten history of relations between Islam and the West isn't a panacea, but it is a vital ingredient to a more stable, secure world. (p. 9)

References

Accounting and Auditing Organization for Islamic Financial Institutions (AAOIFI) (2003), *Sharia Standard No. 17*, Bahrain: AAOIFI.

Abed, G.T. (2003), 'Unfulfilled promise', *Finance & Development*, **40** (1), 10–14.

Abu-Rabi, Ibrahim M. (ed.) (1995), *Islamic Resurgence: Challenges, Directions and Future Perspectives (A Roundtable with Professor Khurshid Ahmad)*, Islamabad: Institute of Policy Studies.

Abu Yusuf Ibrahim (1392), *Kitab al-Kharaj*, Cairo: Dar al-Matba'ah al-Salafiyyah, English translation (1969) by A. Ben Shemesh, as *Kitab al-Kharaj: Taxation in Islam*, vol. iii, London: Luzac.

Acocella, Nicola (1998), *The Foundations of Economic Policy: Values and Techniques*, Cambridge: Cambridge University Press.

Adam, Nathif J. and Abdulkader Thomas (eds) (2004), *Islamic Bonds: Your Guide to Issuing, Structuring and Investing in Sukuk*, London: Euromoney Books.

Ades, Alberto and Rafael Di Tella (1997), 'The new economics of corruption: a survey and some new results', *Political Studies*, **45** (3) (special issue), 417–35.

Aggarwal, Rajesh K. and Tarik Yousef (2000), 'Islamic banks and investment financing', *Journal of Money, Credit, and Banking*, **32** (1), 93–120.

Aghion, Phillipe and Patrick Bolton (1992), 'An "incomplete contracts" approach to financial contracting', *Review of Economic Studies*, **59**, 473–94.

Aghnides, Nicolas P. (1969), *Mohammedan Theories of Finance*, originally published 1916 by Princeton University Press, New York: AMS Press.

Ahmad, Dallal (1993), 'The origins and objectives of Islamic revivalist thought', 1750–1850', *Journal of the American Oriental Society*, **113** (3), 341–60.

Ahmad, E. (1984), 'Islam and politics', in Y. Haddam, B. Haines and E. Findley (eds), *The Islamic Impact*, New York: Syracuse University Press, pp. 7–26.

Ahmad, Israr (1998), 'Islam ka nizam-e-muhasil', in *Islam ka mu'ashi nizam*, Lahore, Pakistan: Maktaba Markazi Anjuman-e-Khuddam-ul-Qur'an.

Ahmad, Khurshid (1976), 'Islam: basic principles and characteristics', in K. Ahmad and S. Azzam (eds), *Islam – its Meaning and Message*, Leicester: Islamic Foundation, accessed 8 January 2008 at www.witness–pioneer.org/vil/Articles/aqeedah/bpsc.html.

Ahmad, Khurshid (1994a), 'Elimination of riba: concept and problems', in K. Ahmad (ed.) *Elimination of Riba from the Economy*, Islamabad: Institute of Policy Studies, pp. 33–63.

Ahmad, Khurshid (1994b), *Islamic Approach to Development: Some Policy Implications*, Islamabad: Institute of Policy Studies.

Ahmad, Khurshid (2000), Islamic economics lecture to MIHE students, accessed 10 October 2000 at www.islamicfoundation.com/audio/khurshid_mihelecture3.ram.

Ahmad, Mahfooz (1995), 'Distributive justice and fiscal and monetary economics in Islam', in Mahmoud A. Guliad and Mohamed Aden Abdullah (eds), *Readings in Public Finance in Islam*, Jeddah, Saudi Arabia: Islamic Research and Training Institute, IDB, pp. 229–49.

Ahmad, Mufti Rasheed (2000), 'Maujuda nizam-e-muhasil ka shar'ee jaa'iza', *Mahnama Sahil*, September, 15–19.

Ahmad, Mumtaz (ed.) (1986), *State, Politics and Islam*, Indianapolis, IN: American Trust Publications.

Ahmad, S.M. (1952), *Economics of Islam*, Lahore, Pakistan: Institute of Islamic Culture.

Ahmad, Ziauddin (1991), *Islam, Poverty and Income Distribution*, Leicester: Islamic Foundation.

Ahmed, Manzooruddin (1991), *Islamic Political System in the Modern Age*, first printed 1983, Karachi, Pakistan: Royal Book Company.

Ahmed, Ziauddin, Munawar Iqbal and M. Fahim Khan (eds) (1983), *Money and Banking in Islam*, Islamabad: Institute of Policy Studies for International Centre for Research in Islamic Economics, King Abdul Aziz University, Jeddah.

Alatas, Syed Hussein (1990), *Corruption: its Nature, Causes and Consequences*, Avebury: Aldershot.

Algaoud, L.M. and M.K. Lewis (1999). 'Corporate governance in Islamic banking: the case of Bahrain', *International Journal of Business Studies*, **7** (I), 56–86.

Algaoud, L.M., and M.K. Lewis (2007), 'Islamic critique of conventional financing', in M. Kabir Hassan and M.K. Lewis (eds), *Handbook of Islamic Banking*, Cheltenham, UK and Northampton, MA, USA: Edward Elgar, pp. 38–48.

Ali, A.J. (2005), *Islamic Perspectives on Management and Organization*, Cheltenham, UK and Northampton, MA, USA: Edward Elgar.

Ali, Muhammad Mohar (1997), *Sirat Al-Nabi and the Orientalists*, vol.

1A, Madinah, Saudi Arabia: King Fahad Complex for the Printing of the Holy Qur'an.
Allen, F. and D. Gale (1992), 'Measurement distortion and missing contingencies in optimal contracts', *Economic Theory*, (2), 1–26.
Allen, Franklin and Andrew Winton (1995), 'Corporate financial structure, incentives and optimal contracting', in R.A. Jarrow, V. Maksimovic and W.T. Ziemba (eds) *Handbook in Operation Research and Management Science*, Amsterdam: Elsevier, pp. 693–721.
Amis, Martin (2008), *The Second Plane*. London: Jonathan Cape.
Anwar, Muhammad (1995), 'Financing socio-economic development with zakat funds', *Journal of Islamic Economics*, **4** (1 and 2), 15–32.
APP (2001), 'Reckless governance cause of huge debt, says Sattar', *Dawn*, 16 June 2001, front page, accessed 16 June 2001 at www.dawn.com.
Apreda, Rodolfo (2003), 'The semantics of governance', University of Cema working paper series, no. 245, September.
Arrow, K.J. (1963), *Social Choice and Individual Values*, 2nd edn, first published 1951, New York: John Wiley.
Arrow, K.J. (1964), 'The role of securities in the optimal allocation of risk bearing', *Review of Economic Studies*, **31**, 91–6. (Reprinted in K.J. Arrow (1983), *Collected Papers of Kenneth J. Arrow – General Equilibrium*, Oxford: Basil Blackwell, pp. 46–57.)
Arrow, K.J. (1974), *The Limits of Organization*, New York: Norton.
Ashtor, E. (1976), *A Social and Economic History of the Near East in the Middle Ages*, London: Collins.
Askari, H. and R. Taghavi (2005), 'The principle foundations of an Islamic economy', *Banca Nazionale del Lavoro Quarterly Review*, **58**, (235), 187–205.
Askary, S. and F. Clarke (1997), 'Accounting in the Koranic verses', *Proceedings of International Conference, The Vehicle for Exploring and Implementing Shariah Islami'iah in Accounting, Commerce and Finance*, Macarthur, NSW: University of Western Sydney.
Atiyah, E. (1955), *The Arabs*, Harmondsworth: Penguin Books.
Atkinson, Anthony B. and Joseph E. Stiglitz (1976), 'The design of tax structure: direct versus indirect taxation', *Journal of Public Economics*, **6** (1, 2), 55–75.
Atkinson, Anthony B. and Joseph E. Stiglitz (1980), *Lectures on Public Economics*, London: McGraw-Hill.
Auerbach, Alan J. and Laurence J. Kotlikoff (1987), *Dynamic Fiscal Policy*, Cambridge: Cambridge University Press.
Babeair, Abdulwahab Saleh (1993), 'The role of the Ulama in modern Islamic society: an historical perspective', *Islamic Quarterly*, **37** (2), 80–94.

Bahlul, Raja (2000), 'People vs God: the logic of 'divine sovereignty', in Islamic democratic discourse', *Islam and Christian Muslim Relations*, **11** (3), 287–97.

Al-Baladhuri (d. 892 CE), Ahmad ibn Yahya ibn Jabir (1968), *The Origins of the Islamic State* [*Kitab Futuh Al-Buldan*], translated by Philip Khuri Hitti, 2 vols, New York: AMS Press, vv. 125–126, 344–345.

Ball, Laurence and N. Gregory Mankiw (1995), 'What do budget deficits do?', NBER working paper no. W5263, Cambridge, MA: National Bureau of Economic Research.

Banfield, Edward C. (1975), 'Corruption as a feature of government organization', *Journal of Law and Economics*, **18** (3), 587–605.

Banks, J. and J. Sobel (1987), 'Equilibrium selection in signaling games', *Econometrica*, **55**, 647–62.

Bardhan, P. (1997), *The Role of Governance in Economic Development: A Political Economy Approach*, Paris: OECD.

Barro, Robert J. (1974), 'Are government bonds net wealth?', *Journal of Political Economy*, **82** (6), 1095–117.

Baumol, William J. (1990), 'Entrepreneurship: productive, unproductive, and destructive', *Journal of Political Economy*, **98** (5) part 1, 893–921.

Baydoun, N. and R. Willett (2000). 'Islamic corporate reports', *ABACUS*, **36** (1), 71–89.

Baydoun, N., A. Mamman and A. Mohmand (1999), 'The religious context of management practices: the case of the Islamic religion', *Accounting, Commerce & Finance. The Islamic Perspective Journal*, **3** (1 and 2), 52–79.

Becker, Gary S. (1968), 'Crime and punishment: an economic approach', *Journal of Political Economy*, **76** (2), 169–217.

Becker, Gary S. and George J. Stigler (1974), 'Law enforcement, malfeasance, and compensation of enforcers', *Journal of Legal Studies*, **3** (1), 1–19.

Bell, Stephen (2002), 'Economic governance and institutional dynamics: the market, the state, and networks', in Stephen Bell (ed.), *Economic Governance & Institutional Dynamics*, South Melbourne: Oxford University Press, pp. 1–33.

Bennett, Adam (2003), 'Failed legacies', *Finance & Development*, **40** (1), 22–5.

Bennett, Clinton (1998), *In Search of Muhammad*, London and New York: Cassell.

Bennett, James T. and Thomas J. DiLorenzo (1984), 'Political entrepreneurship and reform of the rent-seeking society', in David C. Colander (ed.), *Neoclassical Political Economy: the Analysis of Rent-seeking and DUP Activities*, Cambridge, MA: Ballinger.

Ben Shemesh, A. (1967), *Taxation in Islam*, vol. 1, translation of Abu Zakariyya Yahya b. Adam, *Kitab al Kharaj*, Leiden, the Netherlands: E.J. Brill.
Ben Shemesh, A. (1969), 'Introduction', in *Kitab al-Kharaj: Taxation in Islam*, London: Luzac.
Bentham, Jeremy (1789), 'Principles of morals and legislation', in J. Bowring (ed.), *The Internet Encyclopedia of Philosophy*, 22 January 2002 at www.utm.edu:80/research/iep/text/bentham/ benthpri.htm.
Berger, P.L. and T. Luckmann (1966), *The Social Construction of Reality: A Treatise in the Sociology of Knowledge*, New York: Doubleday.
Berlin, Isaiah (2002), *Liberty: Incorporating Four Essays on Liberty*, edited by Henry Hardy, New York: Oxford University Press.
Bernanke, Ben, Mark Gertler and Simon Gilchrist (1996), 'The financial accelerator and the flight to quality', *Review of Economics and Statistics*, **78** (1), 1–15.
Bernheim, Douglas (1989), 'A neoclassical perspective on budget deficits', *Journal of Economic Perspectives*, **3** (2) (Spring), 55–72.
Bhutto, Zulfikar Ali (1976), 'World Muslim unity: address to the Islamic summit held in Lahore, 22 February 1974', in *Thoughts on Some Aspects of Islam*, Lahore, Pakistan: Sh. Muhammad Ashraf.
Bird, Richard M. (1978), 'Perspectives on wealth taxation', *Bulletin for International Fiscal Documentation*, **32** (November), 479–88.
Bird, Richard M. (1987), 'Tax reform in developing countries', National Centre for Development Studies, working paper no. 87/3, Canberra: ANU.
Blair, M.M. (1995), *Ownership and Control: Rethinking Corporate Governance for the Twenty-first Century*, Washington, DC: Brookings Institution.
Blatt, J.M. (1983), *Dynamic Economic Systems*, New York: Sharpe.
Blaug, Mark. (1980), *The Methodology of Economics*, Cambridge: Cambridge University Press.
Blum, W.J. and H. Kalven Jr (1963), *The Uneasy Case for Progressive Taxation*, Phoenix edn, Chicago, IL: University of Chicago Press.
Blum, John M., Bruce Catton, E.S. Morgan, A.M. Schlesinger Jr, K.M. Stampp and C. Vann Woodward (1963), *The American Experience: A History of the United States*, London: Rupert Hart-Davis.
Boadway, R., and M. Keen (1993), 'Public goods, self-selection and optimal income taxation', *International Economic Review*, **34**, 463–78.
Bodin, Jean (1576), *Les Six Livres de la Republique*, abridged edn translated by M.J. Tooley in 1955 as *Six Books of the Commonwealth*, Oxford: Basil Blackwell, accessed at www.constitution.org/bodin/ bodin-6.txt.

Boettke, Peter J. (1999), 'Ludwig von Mises', NYU Working Papers, accessed 12 July 1999 at www.gmu.edu/departments/economics/pboettke/mises.htm.

Boland, Lawrence A. (1998), *The Foundations of Economic Method*, internet release, first published 1982, London: George Allen & Unwin.

Bonner, William and Addison Wiggin (2006), *Empire of Debt. The Rise of an Epic Financial Crisis*, Hoboken, NJ: John Wiley & Sons.

Bowle, John (1961), *Western Political Thought*, London: Methuen.

Brancato, C.K. (1997), *Institutional Investors and Corporate Governance: Best Practices for Increasing Corporate Value*, Chicago, IL: Irwin.

Brennan, G. and J.M. Buchanan (1980), *The Power to Tax: Analytical Foundations of Fiscal Constitution*, Cambridge: Cambridge University Press.

Brennan, Geoffrey, and James M. Buchanan (1987), 'The logic of the Ricardian Equivalence Theorem', in J.M. Buchanan, C.K. Rowley and R.D. Tollison (eds), *Deficits*, Oxford: Basil Blackwell.

Brown, N.J. (1997), *The Rule of Law in the Arab World*, Cambridge: Cambridge University Press.

Brown R. (ed.) (1905), *A History of Accounting and Accountants*, Edinburgh: T.C. and E.C. Jack.

Brown R.G. (1962), 'Changing audit objectives and techniques', *Accounting Review*, October, 696–703.

Brunner, Johann K. (1989), *Theory of Equitable Taxation*, Berlin: Springer-Verlag.

Buchanan, J.M. (1958), *Public Principles of Public Debt*, Homewood, IL: Irwin.

Buchanan, J.M. (1967), *Public Finance in Democratic Process*, Chapel Hill, NC: University of North Carolina Press.

Buchanan, J.M. (1980), 'Rent seeking and profit seeking', in J.M. Buchanan, R.D. Tollison and G. Tullock (eds), *Towards a Theory of the Rent Seeking Society,* College Station, TX: Texas A & M University Press.

Buchanan, J.M. (1992), 'Public debt' in P. Newman, M. Milgate and J. Eatwell (eds), *The New Palgrave Dictionary of Money and Finance*, vol. 3, London: Macmillan, pp. 228–32.

Buchanan, James M. and Marilyn R. Flowers (1980), *The Public Finances: An Introductory Textbook*, 5th edn, Homewood, IL: Richard D. Irwin.

Buchanan, James M., Richard E. Wagner and John Burton (1978), *The Consequences of Mr Keynes*, London: Institute of Economic Affairs.

Buchanan, J.M., R.D. Tollison and G. Tullock (eds.) (1980), *Towards a Theory of the Rent Seeking Society*, College Station, TX: Texas A & M University Press.

Buiter, Willem H. (1990), *Principles of Budgetary and Financial Policy*, New York and London: Harvester Wheatsheaf.

Buiter, Willem H. (2001), 'Notes on "A code for fiscal stability"', *Oxford Economic Papers*, **53**, 1–19.

Buiter, W., R. Largo and N. Stern (1997), 'Enterprise performance and macroeconomic control', *Banca Nazionale del Lavoro Quarterly Review*, **50** (200), 1–22.

Burgess, Robin and Nicholas Stern (1993), 'Taxation and development', *Journal of Economic Literature*, **31** (2), 762–830.

Burgess-Limerick, R., B. Abernethy and B. Limerick (1994), 'Identifying underlying assumptions is an integral part of research: an example from motor control', *Theory & Psychology*, **4**, 139–46.

Cadbury, A. (2002), *Corporate Governance and Chairmanship*, Oxford: Oxford University Press.

Cadbury Committee Report (1992), *The Financial Aspects of Corporate Governance*, London: Gee & Co.

Calder, N. (2002), 'Law', in S.H. Nasr (ed.), *Encylopedia of Islamic Philosophy*, part I, Lahore, Pakistan: Suhail Academy.

Camerer, C. (1988), 'Gifts as economic signals and social symbols', *American Journal of Sociology*, **94** (supplement), 180–214.

Canella, A.A., Jr (1995), 'Executives and shareholders: a shift in the relationship', *Human Resource Management*, **34** (2), 165–84.

Carlson, John (2000), 'Money laundering and corruption: two sides of the same coin', in *No Longer Business as Usual: Fighting Bribery and Corruption*, Paris: OECD, pp. 127–36.

Cartier-Bresson, Jean (1997), 'Corruption networks, transaction security and illegal social exchange', *Political Studies*, **45** (3) (special issue), 463–76.

Cartier-Bresson, Jean (2000), 'The causes and consequences of corruption: analyses and lessons learnt', in *No Longer Business as Usual: Fighting Bribery and Corruption*, Paris: OECD, pp. 11–27.

Casson, Mark (1995), *Entrepreneurship and Business Culture: Studies in the Economics of Trust*, Aldershot, UK and Brookfield, US: Edward Elgar.

Chapra, M. Umer (1985), *Towards a Just Monetary System*, Leicester: Islamic Foundation.

Chapra, M Umer (1992), *Islam and the Economic Challenge*, Leicester: Islamic Foundation.

Chapra, M. Umer (2000), *The Future of Economics: An Islamic Perspective*, Leicester: Islamic Foundation.

Chapra, M. Umer (2007), 'The case against interest: is it compelling?', *Thunderbird International Business Review*, **49** (2), 161–86.

Chaudhry, Muhammad Aslam (1996), *Muslim Political Thought*, Lahore, Pakistan: Publishers Emporium.

Child, J. (1976), 'Participation, organization, and social cohesion', *Human Relations*, **29** (5), 429–51.

Chiu, Becky and Mervyn K. Lewis (2006), *Reforming China's State Owned Enterprises and Banks*, Cheltenham UK and Northampon, MA, USA: Edward Elgar.

Clark, Barry (1998), *Political Economy: A Comparative Approach*, Westport, CT: Praeger Publishers.

Clark, Colin (1977), 'The scope for, and limits of, taxation', in Institute of Economic Affairs (ed.), *The State of Taxation*, London: Institute of Economic Affairs, pp. 19–28.

Creane, S., Rishi Goyal, A. Mushfiq Mobarak and Randa Sab (2003), 'Banking on development', *Finance and Development*, **40** (1), 26–30.

Commons, John R. (1932), 'The problem of correlating law, economics and ethics', *Wisconsin Law Review*, **8**, 3–26.

Conard, J.W. (1959), *Introduction to the Theory of Interest*, Berkeley, CA: University of California Press.

Cosgel, Metin M. (2004), 'Efficiency and continuity in public finance: the Ottoman system of taxation', University of Connecticut Department of Economics working paper 2004–02R.

Cowan, J.M. (ed.) (1976), *The Hans Wehr Dictionary of Modern Written Arabic*, 3rd edn, New York: Spoken Language Services.

Crone, P. (1996), 'The rise of Islam in the world', in F. Robinson (ed.), *Islamic World*, Cambridge: Cambridge University Press, pp. 2–31.

Cullis, John, and Philip Jones (1992), *Public Finance and Public Choice*, Singapore: McGraw-Hill.

Cunningham, Andrew (1990), *Islamic Banking and Finance*, London: Middle East Economic Digest.

Dale, Stephen F. (1996), 'The Islamic world in the age of European expansion: 1500–1800', in F. Robinson (ed.), *Islamic World*, Cambridge: Cambridge University Press, pp. 62–89.

Davis, J.H., F.D. Schoorman and L. Donaldson (1997), 'Towards a stewardship theory of management', *Academy of Management Review*, **22** (I), 20–47.

Davis, K.T. and M.K. Lewis (1980), *Monetary Policy in Australia*, Melbourne, VIC: Longman Cheshire.

Al-Dawudi, Abu Ja'far Ahmad ibn Nasr [d. 1012 CE] (1995), *Kitab al-Amwal*, translated by Abu'l Muhsin Muhammad Sharfuddin, Islamabad: Islamic Research Institute.

DeLorenzo, Y.T. and A.S. Ed. Al Shaikh-Ali (1990), *Usul Al Fiqh Al Islami: Source Methodology in Islamic Jurisprudence: Methodology for Research and Knowledge*, Virginia: The International Institute of Islamic Thought internet edition at www.usc.edu/dept/MSA/law/alalwani_usulalfiqh/.

Dhonte, Pierre and Ishan Kapur (1997), 'Towards a market economy: structures of governance', IMF working paper WP/97/11.

Diamond, Peter A. (1965), 'National debt in a neoclassical growth model', *American Economic Review*, **55** (December), 1126–50.

Doi, Abdur Rahman i (1989), *Shari'ah: The Islamic Law,* Kuala Lumpur: A.S. Nordeen.

Dowd, Kevin (1992), 'Optimal financial contracts', *Oxford Economic Papers*, **44**, 672–93.

Dowd, K. and M.K. Lewis (eds) (1992), *Current Issues in Financial and Monetary Economics*, London: Macmillan.

Dworkin, Ronald (1981), 'What is equality? Part 2: equality of resources', *Philosophy and Public Affairs*, **10** (4), 283–345.

Dybvig, P.H. and J.F. Zender (1991), 'Capital structure and dividend irrelevance with asymmetric information', *Review of Financial Studies*, **4**, 201–19.

Ebrahim, Muhammed-Shahid and Akram Safadi (1995), 'Behavioral norms in the Islamic doctrine of economics: a comment', *Journal of Economic Behavior and Organization*, **27**, 151–7.

Edgeworth, F.Y. (1925), *Papers Relating to Political Economy*, 3 vols, London: Macmillan for the Royal Economic Society.

El-Awa, Mohamed S. (1983), *Punishment in Islamic Law: A Comparative Study*, Delhi: Markazi Maktaba Islami.

El-Gamal, Mahmoud A. (2005), 'Review of Kuran, Timur (2004). *Islamic and Mammon: The Economic Predicaments of Islamism*', Princeton, NJ: Princeton University Press, *Review of Islamic Economics*, **9** (1), 89–92.

El-Gamal, Mahmoud A. (2007), 'Mutuality as an antidote to rent-seeking shari'a-arbitrage in Islamic finance', *Thunderbird International Business Review*, **49** (2), 187–202.

Elmendorf, Douglas W. and N. Gregory Mankiw (1998), 'Government debt', NBER working paper 6470.

El-Qorchi, Mohammed (2005), 'Islamic finance gears up', *Finance and Development*, **42** (4), 46–9.

Emmons, William R. and Frank A. Schmid (1998), 'Universal banking, control rights, and corporate finance in Germany', *Federal Reserve Bank of Saint Louis Review*, **80** (4), 19–44.

Esposito, John L. (1987), 'Islam in Asia: an introduction', in *Islam in Asia:*

Religion, Politics, and Society, New York, Oxford: Oxford University Press.
Esposito, John L. (1995), *The Islamic Threat: Myth or Reality*?, New York, Oxford: Oxford University Press.
Etzioni, Amitai (1988), *The Moral Dimension*, New York: Free Press.
Feldstein, Martin (1976), 'On the theory of tax reform', *Journal of Public Economics*, **6** (1,2), 77–104.
Fender, I. and J. Mitchell (2005), 'Structured finance: complexity, risk and the use of ratings', *BIS Quarterly Review*, June, 67–79.
Feyerabend, P.K. (1965), 'Problems of empiricism', in R.G. Colodny (ed.) *Beyond the Edge of Certainty: Essays in Contemporary Science and Philosophy*, Englewood Cliffs, NJ: Prentice-Hall, pp. 145–260.
Fischer, Stanley, and William Easterly (1990), 'The economics of the government budget constraint', *World Bank Research Observer*, **5** (2), 127–42.
Fisher, Irving (1930), *The Theory of Interest*, New York: Macmillan.
Frankfurt, Harry G. (1971), 'Freedom of the will and the concept of a person', *Journal of Philosophy*, **68** (1), 5–20.
Fremond, O. and M. Capaul (2002), 'The state of corporate governance: experience from country assessments', World Bank policy research working paper no. 2858, accessed 8 January, 2008 at www.worldbank.org.
Friedman, Benjamin M. (1989), *Day of Reckoning*, New York: Vintage Books.
Friedman, Milton (1953), 'The methodology of positive economics' in *Essays in Positive Economics*, Chicago, IL: University of Chicago Press, pp. 3–43.
Friedman, Milton (1962), *Capitalism and Freedom*, Chicago, IL: Chicago University Press.
Friedman, M. (1963), *Inflation: Causes and Consequences*, Bombay, India: Asia Publishing House.
Friedman, Milton (1968), 'The role of monetary policy', *American Economic Review*, March, 1–17.
Friedman, Milton (1970), 'The social responsibility of business is to increase its profits', *New York Times Magazine*, 13 September, pp. 32–33, 122, 124, 126.
Friedman, Milton (1975), 'Unemployment versus inflation? an evaluation of the Phillips Curve', Institute of Economic Affairs occasional paper 44, London.
Friedman, Milton (1977), *Tax Limitation, Inflation and the Role of Government*, Dallas, TX: Fisher Institute.

Friedrich, Carl J. (1966), 'Political pathology', *Political Quarterly*, **37**, 70–85.

Frischtak, L. and I. Atiyas (eds) (1996), *Governance, Leadership and Communication*, Washington, DC: World Bank.

Fusfeld, Daniel R. (1999), *The Age of the Economist*, 8th edn, Reading, MA: Addison-Wesley.

Gelauff, G.M.M. and C. den Broeder (1997), *Governance of Stakeholder Relationships: The German and Dutch Experience*, SUERF Société Universitaire Européenne de Recherches Financières studies no I, Amsterdam: SUERF.

Gellner, Ernest (1981), *Muslim Society*, Cambridge: Cambridge University Press.

Gellner, Ernest (1992), *Postmodernism, Reason and Religion*, London, New York: Routledge.

George, Henry (1930), *Progress and Poverty: An Enquiry into the Cause of Industrial Depressions and of Increase of Want with Increase of Wealth*, 50th anniversary edn of *The Modern Library*, New York: Random House.

Gerber, Haim (1981), 'The Muslim law of partnerships in Ottoman court records', *Studia Islamica*, **53**, 109–19.

Gertler, Mark and R. Glenn Hubbard (1993), 'Corporate financial policy, taxation, and macroeconomic risk', *Rand Journal of Economics*, **24** (2), 286–303.

Gertler, Mark and Simon Gilchrist (1993), 'The role of credit market imperfections in the monetary transmission mechanism: arguments and evidence', *Scandinavian Journal of Economics*, **95** (1), 43–64.

Ghaffari, Maulana Nur Muhammad (1989), *Islam ka Qanun-e-Muhasil*, 2nd edn, Lahore, Pakistan: Markaz-e-Tehqiq Diyal Singh Trust Library.

Al-Ghazali, Abu Hamid (1356 AH/1937 CE), *al-Mustasfa min Ilm al-Usul*, 2 vols, Cairo: al-Maktabah al-Tijariyyah.

Al-Ghazali, Abu Hamid (1958), *Tahafut Al-Falasifah*, translated into English by Sabih A. Kamali, *Incoherence of Philosophers*, Lahore, Pakistan: Pakistan Philosophical Congress.

Al-Ghazali, Abu Hamid (1964), *Counsel for Kings*, translated by F.R.C. Bagley, London: Oxford University Press.

Al-Ghazali, Abu Hamid (n.d.), *Ihya Ulum al Din*, 4 vols, Beirut: Dal Nadwah.

Ghazanfar, S.M. and A.A. Islahi (1990), 'Economic thought of an Arab scholastic: Abu Hamid al-Ghazali', *History of Political Economy*, **22** (2), 381–403.

Ghazanfar, S.M. and A.A. Islahi (1997), *Economic Thought of Al-Ghazali*,

Islamic economic research series, King Abdulaziz University -2, Jeddah, Saudi Arabia: Scientific Publishing Centre.

Ghazanfar, S.M. and A.A. Islahi (1997), 'Explorations in medieval Arab-Islamic thought: some aspects of Ibn Qayyim's economics' (691–751 AH/AD 1292–1350), *History of Economic Ideas*, **1**, 7–25.

Gilani, Manazar (2000), 'Aik Islami mua'she nazriyah ibn-e-Hazm kee nazar main: Islami riyasat zakat kay sawa bhee jabrun maal wasool ker sakti hai', *Mahnama Sahil*, September, 47–53.

Gilibert, P.L. and A. Steinherr (1994), 'Private finance for public infrastructures: in search of a new framework', *EIB Papers*, 23, 77–90.

Goode, Richard (1977), 'The economic definition of income', in J.A. Pechman (ed.), *Comprehensive Income Taxation*, Washington, DC: Brookings Institution, pp. 1–36.

Gooden, S. (2001), 'Participation of stakeholders in the corporate governance of Islamic financial institutions', *New Horizon*, **114**, November, 12–15.

Goodin, Robert E. (1992), *Motivating Political Morality*, Oxford: Blackwell.

Gopal, M.H. (1935), *Mauryan Public Finance*, London: George Allen & Unwin.

Greenspan, Alan (1966), 'Gold and economic freedom', *Objectivist*, (July), 96–101.

Greenspan, Alan (1981), 'Can the US return to a gold standard?', *Wall Street Journal*, 1 September, accessed 11 December, 2008 at www.2yhgold.com/news-gold-silver-Can-the-US-return-to-a-Gold-Standard-Alan-Greenspan-1981-.zspx?langue=endarticleid=159048_Gold_Standard.

Grimsey, D. and M.K. Lewis (2004), *Public Private Partnerships: the Worldwide Revolution in Infrastructure Provision and Project Finance*, Cheltenham, UK and Northampton, MA, USA: Edward Elgar.

Grimsey, D. and M.K. Lewis (eds) (2005), *The Economics of Public Private Partnerships*, The International Library of Critical Writings in Economics, Cheltenham, UK and Northampton, MA, USA: Edward Elgar.

Grout, P. (1997), 'The economics of the private finance initiative', *Oxford Review of Economic Policy*, **13** (4), 53–66.

Hakim, Sam (2007), 'Islamic money market instruments', in M. Kabir Hassan and M.K. Lewis (eds), *The Handbook of Islamic Banking*, Cheltenham, UK and Northampton, MA, USA: Edward Elgar, pp. 161–71.

Hamidullah, Muhammad (1988), Ehd-e-Nabawi Mein Nizame Maliyaa wa Taqweem, in *Khutabat-e-Bahawalpur*, Islamabad: Idara-e-tehqiqat Islami, Al Jamia Al Alamiya Al Islamiya.

Hamoudi, H.A. (2006), *Muhammad's Social Justice or Muslim Cant?: Langdellianism and the Failures of Islamic Finance*, Columbia Law School Public Law and Legal working paper group no. 06–116, New York: Columbia Law School.

Handy, C. (1999), *The Hungry Spirit*, New York: Broadway Books.

Haniffa, R. and M.A. Hudaib (2002), 'A theoretical framework for the development of the Islamic perspective of accounting', *Accounting, Commerce & Finance: The Islamic Perspective Journal*, **6** (1 and 2), 1–74.

Hansen, A.H. (1949), *Monetary Theory and Fiscal Policy*, New York: McGraw Hill.

Harberger, Arnold C. (1998), 'Monetary and fiscal policy for equitable economic growth', in V. Tanzi and K. Chu (eds), *Income Distribution and High-quality Growth*, Cambridge, MA: MIT, pp. 203–41.

Harding, Karen (1993), 'Causality then and now: Al Ghazali and quantum theory', *American Journal of Islamic Social Sciences*, **10** (2), 165–77.

Harmon, M. Judd (1964), *Political Thought from Pluto to the Present*, New York: McGraw-Hill.

Hart, Oliver (2001), 'Financial contracting', National Bureau of Economic Research working paper, accessed 20 January 2003 at www.nber.org/papers/w8285.

Hasan, Samiul (2007), *Philanthropy and Social Justice in Islam: Principles, Prospects and Practices*, Kuala Lumpur: A.S. Noordeen.

Hasanuz Zaman, S.M. (1991), *Economic Functions of an Islamic State (The Early Experience)*, revised edn, Leicester: Islamic Foundation.

Hasanuz Zaman, S.M. (1993), 'Islamic criteria for the distribution of tax burden', *Journal of Islamic Economics*, **3** (1), 17–32.

Hasanuz Zaman, S.M. (1994), 'Practical options for central and commercial banking', in K. Ahmad (ed.), *Elimination of Riba from the Economy*, Islamabad: Institute of Policy Studies, pp. 197–216.

Haslett, David W. (1994), *Capitalism with Morality*, New York: Oxford University Press.

Hassan, M. Kabir and M.K. Lewis (eds) (2007a), *The Handbook of Islamic Banking*, Cheltenham, UK and Northampton, MA, USA: Edward Elgar.

Hassan, M. Kabir and M.K. Lewis (2007b), 'Islamic finance: a system at the Crossroads?', *Thunderbird International Business Review*, **49** (2), 151–60.

Hausman, Daniel M. and Michael S. McPherson (1996), *Economic Analysis and Moral Philosophy*, Cambridge: Cambridge University Press.

Hawkins, J.A. (1997), 'Why investors push for strong corporate boards', *McKinsey Quarterly*, **3**, 144–8.

Hayek, F.A. (1944), *The Road to Serfdom*, London: Routledge & Kegan Paul.

Hayllar, M R. (1991), 'Accountability: ends, means and resources', *Asian Review of Public Administration*, **3** (2), 10–22.

Head, John G. (1997), 'Prolegomena to fundamental tax reform', in R. Krever (ed.), *Tax Conversations*, London: Kluwer Law International.

Head, John G. and Richard Krever (eds) (1997), 'Taxation towards 2000', Australian Tax Research Foundation conference series no. 19, Australian Tax Research Foundation.

Heidenheimer, Arnold J. (ed.) (1970), 'Introduction', in *Political Corruption: Readings in Comparative Analysis*, New York: Holt, Rinehart and Winston, pp. 3–28.

Heilbroner, Robert L. (1967), *The Worldly Philosophers*, 3rd revised edn, New York: Simon and Schuster.

Heller, R. (2000), *Peter Drucker: The Great Pioneer of Management Theory and Practice*, London: Dorling Kindersley.

Hettich, Walter (1979), 'Henry Simons on taxation and the economic system', *National Tax Journal*, **32** (1), 1–9.

Hettich, Walter and Stanley L. Winer (1985), 'Blueprints and pathways: the shifting foundations of tax reform', *National Tax Journal*, **38** (4), 423–45.

Hettich, Walter and Stanley L. Winer (1999), *Democratic Choice and Taxation: A Theoretical and Empirical Analysis*, Cambridge: Cambridge University Press.

Hirschman, A. O. (1970), *Exit, Voice and Loyalty*, Cambridge, MA: Harvard University Press.

Hitti, Philip K. (1986), *History of the Arabs*, 11th reprint of 1970 edn, London: Macmillan Education, Macmillan International College Editions.

Holcombe, Randall G. and Jeffrey A. Mills (1995), 'Politics and deficit finance', *Public Finance Quarterly*, **23** (4), 448–66.

Holmes, L. (1999), 'Corruption in Europe', *Dialogue*, **18** (2), 19–25.

The Holy Qur'an (1992), English Translation of the Meanings and Commentary, translated by Allama Abdullah Yusuf Ali, The Presidency of Islamic Researches, Ifta, Call and Guidance (ed.), Al-Madinah Al-Munawarah, Saudi Arabia: King Fahd Holy Qur'an Printing Complex.

Human Rights Watch (2001), 'Afghanistan: crisis of impunity', *Human Rights Watch*, 13 (3 C/July), page 1: summary and recommendations, accessed 8 February 2008 at www.hrw.org/reports/2001/afghan2/Afghan0701.htm.

Huntington, Samuel P. (1968), *Political Order in Changing Societies*, New Haven, CT and London: Yale University Press.

Hupe, Peter L. and Michael J. Hill (2006), 'The three action levels of governance: reforming the policy process beyond the stages model', in Guy Peters and Jon Pierre, *Handbook of Public Policy*, London: Sage Publications, pp. 13–30.
Hussain, Jamila (1999), *Islamic Law and Society. An Introduction*, Sydney: Federation Press.
Ibn al-Ukhuwwah, Muhammad b. Muhammad (1976), *Ma'alim al'qurbah fi ahkam al-hisbah*, edited by M. Mahmud Sha'ban, Cairo: S.A. 'Isa al-Muti'i.
Ibn Kathir (1988), *Al-Bidayah wa'l Nihayah*, vol. 4, Cairo: Dar al-Rayyanb lil'Turath.
Ibn Khaldun (1332–1406 CE), Abd-ar-Rahman Abu Zayd ibn Muhammad (1967), *An Introduction to History: The Muqaddimah*, translated from the Arabic by Franz Rosenthal, abridged and edited by N.J. Dawood, London: Routledge and Kegan Paul.
Ibn Manzur, Jamal al-din Muhammad b. Mukurrum (1300–1308 AH), *Lisan al-Arab*, 20 vols, Cairo: Bulaq.
Ibn Taymiyyah (1976), *al-Hisbah fi'l-Islam*, Cairo: Dar al-Sha'b, English translation by Muhtar Holland (1982), *Public Duties in Islam: The Institution of the Hisbah*, Leicester: Islamic Foundation.
Iley, Richard A. and M.K. Lewis (2007), *Untangling the US Deficit. Evaluating Causes, Cures and Global Imbalances*, Cheltenham, UK and Northampton, MA, USA: Edward Elgar.
Iqbal, Justice Javid (1986), 'The concept of state in Islam', in M. Ahmad (ed.) *State, Politics, and Islam*, Indianapolis, IN: American Trust Publications.
Iqbal, Muhammad (1996), *The Reconstruction of Religious Thought in Islam*, edited by M.S. Sheikh, 3rd edn, first printed 1928, Lahore, Pakistan: Institute of Islamic Culture.
Iqbal, Munawar (1993), *Fiscal Reform in Muslim Countries with Special Reference to Pakistan*, Jeddah, Saudi Arabia: IRTI, Islamic Development Bank.
Iqbal, Munawar, (ed.) (n.d.) *Distributive Justice and Need Fulfilment in an Islamic Economy*, Islamabad: IIIE, International Islamic University.
Iqbal, Munawar and Khan, Tariqullah (2004), 'Financing public expenditure: an Islamic perspective', IRTI occasional paper no. 7, Jeddah, Saudi Arabia: IRTI, Islamic Development Bank.
Iqbal, Zafar (2000), 'Economic rationale for the state collection of zakah', *International Journal of Islamic Financial Services*, **2** (1).
Iqbal, Zafar and Mervyn K. Lewis (2002), 'Governance and corruption: can Islamic societies and the West learn from each other?', *American Journal of Islamic Social Sciences*, **19** (2), 1–33.

Islahi, A.A. (1988), *Economic Concepts of Ibn Taimiyah*, Leicester: The Islamic Foundation.

Islahi, A.A. (2005), *Contributions of Muslim Scholars to Economic Thought and Analysis* (11–905 AH/AD 632–1500), Jeddah, Saudi Arabia: Scientific Publishing Centre, King Abdulaziz University.

Iwai, K. (2002), 'The nature of the business corporation: its legal structure and economic functions', *Japanese Economic Review*, **53** (3), 1–31.

Jackson, John, Ron McIver and Campbell McConnell (1994), *Economics*, 4th edn, Sydney, NSW: McGraw-Hill.

Jaimovich, Dany and Ugo G. Panizza (2006), 'Public debt around the world: a new dataset of central government debt', Inter-American Development Bank working paper no. 561, March.

James, Simon and Christopher Nobes (1983), *The Economics of Taxation*, 2nd edn, Oxford: Philip Allan.

Jensen, Michael C. (1986), 'Agency costs of free cashflow, corporate finance and takeovers', *American Economic Review*, **76**, 323–39.

Jensen, Michael C. (1998), *Foundations of Organizational Strategy*, Cambridge, MA: Harvard University Press.

Jensen, Michael C. and William H. Meckling (1976), 'Theory of the firm: managerial behavior, agency costs and ownership structure', *Journal of Financial Economics*, **3** (4), 305–60.

Joas, Hans (2000), *The Genesis of Values*, translated by Gregory Moore, Oxford: Polity Press and Blackwell Publishers.

Johnson, Harry, G. (1969), 'Inside money, outside money, income, wealth and welfare in monetary theory', *Journal of Money Credit and Banking*, **I** (1), 30–45.

Kahf, Monzer (1989), 'Zakat: unresolved issues in the contemporary fiqh', *Journal of Islamic Economics*, **2** (1), 1–22.

Kahf, Monzer (1995), 'Taxation policy in an Islamic economy', in *Readings in Public Finance in Islam*, Jeddah, Saudi Arabia: Islamic Research and Training Institute, Islamic Development Bank, pp. 105–127.

Kahf, Monzer (1997), 'Potential effects of zakat on government budget', *IIUM Journal of Economics & Management*, **5** (1), 67–85.

Kahn, C. Harry (1973), 'Consumption and net-worth taxes', in R.A. Musgrave (ed.), *Broad-Based Taxes: New Options and Sources*, Baltimore, MD and London: Johns Hopkins University Press, pp. 133–54.

Kaldor, N. (1955), *An Expenditure Tax*, London: George Allen and Unwin.

Kaldor, N. (1956), 'Alternative theories of income distribution', *Review of Economic Studies*, 23 (2), reprinted in N.J. Kaldor (1980), *Essays on Value and Distribution*, London: Duckworth, pp. 209–236.

Kamali, Mohammad Hashim (1998), *Principles of Islamic Jurisprudence*, 2nd revised edn, Kuala Lumpur: Ilmiah Publishers.

Kamali, Mohammad Hisham (2007), 'Commodity futures: an Islamic legal analysis', *Thunderbird International Business Review*, **49** (3), 309–39.

Kant, I. (1940), *Fundamental Principles of the Metaphysics of Morals*, edited by T.K. Abbott, London: Longmans Green.

Karabell, Zachary (2007), *People of the Book. The Forgotten History of Islam and the West*, London: John Murray.

Karim, Maulana Fazlul (1969), *Al-Hadis – An English Translation and Commentary of Mishkat-ul-Masabih*, 3rd edn, Dacca, East Pakistan: F.K. Islam Mission Trust.

Kaufmann, D., A. Krayy and P. Zoido-Lobaton (1999a), 'Aggregating governance indicators', World Bank policy research working paper 2195, Washington, DC: World Bank.

Kaufmann, D., A Krayy and P Zoido-Lobaton (1999b), 'Governance matters', World Bank policy research working paper 2196, Washington, DC: World Bank.

Kay, J. (1993), 'Efficiency and private capital in the provision of infrastructure', in *Infrastructure Policies for the 1990s*, Paris: Organisation for Economic Co-operation and Development, pp. 55–73.

Kay, J. and A. Silbertson (1995), 'Corporate governance', *National Institute Economic Review*, August, 84–96.

Kazmi, Aqdas Ali (2001), 'Tax policy and resource mobilization in Pakistan', a paper read at the Sixteenth Annual General Meeting of the Pakistan Society of Development Economists, Islamabad: 22–24 January 2001.

Keynes, J.M. (1936), *The General Theory of Employment, Money and Interest*, London: Macmillan.

Khaliffa, A.S. (2003), 'The multidimensional nature and purpose of business in Islam', *Accounting, Commerce & Finance: The Islamic Perspective Journal*, **7** (1 and 2), 1–25.

Khan, Mahmood, H. and Mohsin S. Khan (1998), 'Taxing agriculture in Pakistan', PPAA/98/3 paper on policy analysis and assessment of the International Monetary Fund, accessed 4 April 2002, at www.imf.org/external/pubs/ft/ppaa/ppaa9803.pdf.

Khan, Muhammad Akram (1982), 'Al-Hisbah and the Islamic economy', in Khurshid Ahmad (ed.), *Public Duties in Islam*, Leicester: Islamic Foundation, pp. 135–48.

Khan, Muhammad Akram, (ed.) (n.d.), *Economic Teachings of Prophet Muhammad (pbuh): A Select Anthology of Hadith Literature on Economics*, new and revised edn, Karachi, Pakistan: Darul-Ishaat.

Khan, M. Fahim (2007), 'Islamic methods for government borrowing and

monetary management', in M. Kabir Hassan and M.K. Lewis, (eds), *The Handbook of Islamic Banking*, Cheltenham, UK and Northampton, MA, USA: Edward Elgar, pp. 285–301.
Khan, W.M. (1985), *Towards an Interest-Free Islamic Economic System*, Leicester: Islamic Foundation.
Kiesling, Herbert (1992), *Taxation and Public Goods*, Ann Arbor, MI: University of Michigan Press.
Klein, L.R. (1962), *An Introduction to Econometrics,* Englewood Cliffs, NJ: Prentice-Hall.
Klein, M. (1997), 'The risk premium for evaluating public projects', *Oxford Review of Economic Policy*, **13** (4), 29–42.
Klitgaard, R. (1988), *Controlling Corruption*, Berkeley, CA: University of California Press.
Klitgaard, R. (1991), 'Gifts and bribes', in R. Zeckhauser (ed.), *Strategy and Choice*, Cambridge, MA: MIT Press.
Klitgaard, R. (2000), 'Subverting corruption', *Finance and Development*, **37** (2), 2–5.
Klitgaard, R., Robert MacLean-Abaroa and H. Lindsey Parris Jr. (2000), *Corrupt Cities: A Practical Guide to Cure and Prevention*, Oakland, CA: ICS Press and World Bank Institute.
Kolm, Serge-Christophe (1996), *Modern Theories of Justice*, Cambridge, MA: MIT Press.
Kopits, George, and Steven Symansky (1998), *Fiscal Policy Rules*, Washington, DC: IMF.
Kottack, C.P. (1999), *Mirror for Humanity*, New York: McGraw Hill.
Kuhn, T.S. (1962), *The Structure of Scientific Revolutions*, Chicago, IL: University of Chicago Press.
Kuhn, T.S. (1974)',Second thoughts on paradigms', in F. Suppe (ed.), *The Structure of Scientific Theories*, Urbana, IL: University of Illinois Press, pp. 459–82.
Kuran, Timur (1993), 'The economic impact of Islamic fundamentalism', in M.E. Marty and R. Scott Appleby (eds), *Fundamentalisms and the State: Remaking Politics, Economies, and Militance*, Chicago, IL: University of Chicago Press, pp. 302–41.
Kuran, Timur (1995), 'Islamic economics and the Islamic subeconomy', *Journal of Economic Perspectives*, **9** (4), 155–73.
Kuran, Timur (1996), 'The discontents of Islamic economic morality', *American Economic Review*, **86** (2), 438–42.
Kuran, Timur (1997), 'The genesis of Islamic economics; a chapter in the politics of Muslim identity', *Social Research*, **64** (1), 301–38.
Kuran, Timur (1998), 'Over-stating the Arab state: politics and society in the Middle East', *Independent Review*, **3** (1), 111–13.

Kuran, Timur (2004), *Islam and Mammon: The Economic Predicaments of Islamism*, Princeton, NJ: Princeton University Press.

Kzrak, M. and A. Schubert (1997), 'The present state of monetary governance in Central and Eastern Europe', *Focus on Transition*, **1**, 28–56.

Lairson, Thomas D. and David Skidmore (1993), *International Political Economy: The Struggle for Power and Wealth*, Orlando, FL: Harcourt Brace College Publishers.

Lal, Deepak (1999), *Unintended Consequences*, 2nd edn, first published 1998, Cambridge, MA: MIT Press.

Lambsdorff, J.G. (2002), 'Making corrupt deals: contracting in the shadow of the law', *Journal of Economic Behavior and Organization*, **48**, 221–41.

Lambton, Ann K.S. (1968), 'The internal structure of the Saljuk Empire', in Bayne Fisher, John Andrew Boyle and Ilya Gershevitch (eds), *The Cambridge History of Iran: The Saljuk and Mongol Periods*, vol. 5, Cambridge: Cambridge University Press, pp. 203–82.

Lambton, Ann K.S. (1981), *State and Government in Medieval Islam*, London Oriental Series, volume 36, Oxford: Oxford University Press.

Lannoo, K. (1995), *Corporate Governance in Europe*, CEPS working party report no 12. Brussels: Centre for European Policy Studies.

Lawson, M.K. (1984), 'The collection of danegeld and heregeld in the reigns of Aethelred II and Cnut', *English Historical Review*, **99**, 721–38.

Lawson, Tony (1997), *Economics and Reality*, London and New York: Routledge.

Lederman, D., N. Loayza and R.R. Soares (2005), 'Accountability and corruption: political institutions matter', *Economics & Politics*, **17** (1), 1–35.

Leff, Nathaniel H. (1964), 'Economic development through bureaucratic corruption', *American Behavioral Scientist*, **8** (3), 8–14.

Leming, Michael R. (2002), Chapter 1, 'Religion and world-construction' in *Peter Berger's Sacred Canopy*, accessed 6 Novemer, 2002 at www.stolaf.edu/people/leming/soc265rel/questions/chBerger1.html.

Lerner, A.P. (1943), 'Functional finance and the federal debt', *Social Research*, (February), 38–51.

Lerner, A.P. (1948), 'The burden of the national debt', in L.A. Metzler, *et al.* (eds), *Income, Employment and Public Policy: Essays in Honor of Alvin H Hansen*, New York: Norton, pp. 255–75, excerpts reprinted in R.W. Houghton (ed.) (1970), *Public Finance*, Harmondsworth: Penguin, pp. 299–304.

Levy, Reuben (1979), *The Social Structure of Islam*, reprint of 1957 edn, Cambridge: Cambridge University Press.

Lewer, Joshua J. (2007), 'Estimating the institutional and network effects of religious cultures on international trade', *Kyklos*, **60** (2), 255–77.

Lewis, Bernard (1950), *The Arabs in History*, London: Hutchinson's University Library.

Lewis, Bernard (1993), 'Islam and liberal democracy', *Atlantic*, **271** (2), 89–98.

Lewis, Bernard (1997), 'The West and the Middle East', *Foreign Affairs*, **76** (1), 114–30.

Lewis, C.S. (1947), *The Abolition of Man*, New York: Macmillan.

Lewis, M.K. (1997), 'Counteracting fraud: the case of BCCI revisited', *Review of Policy Issues*, **3** (2), 3–35.

Lewis, M.K. (1999), 'Corporate governance and corporate financing in different cultures', in Zeljko Sevic (ed.), *Banking Reform in South East European Transitional Economies*, London: University of Greenwich Business School, Balkan Center for Public Policy and Related Studies Humanities Research Centre, pp. 33–66.

Lewis, M.K. (2001), 'Islam and accounting', *Accounting Forum*, **25** (2), 103–27.

Lewis, M.K. (2002), 'Islamic banking from the Western perspective', presentation to Reshaping Global Financial Architecture Through the Islamic System, The 1st International Conference on Islamic Banking, Finance and Insurance, Labuan, Malaysia, January.

Lewis, M.K. (2003), 'Globalisation and corporate governance' in M. Shanahan and G. Treuren (eds), *Globalisation: Australian Regional Perspectives*, Adelaide, SA: Wakefield Press, pp. 66–94.

Lewis, M.K. (2005), 'Islamic corporate governance', *Review of Islamic Economics*, **9** (1), May, 5–29.

Lewis, M.K. (2007), 'Comparing Islamic and Christian attitudes to usury', in M. Kabir Hassan and M.K. Lewis (eds), *The Handbook of Islamic Banking*, Cheltenham, UK and Northampton, MA, USA: Edward Elgar, pp. 64–81.

Lewis, M.K. and L.M. Algaoud (2001), *Islamic Banking*, Cheltenham, UK and Northampton, MA, USA: Edward Elgar Publishing, Inc.

Lewis, M.K. and K.T. Davis (1987), *Domestic and International Banking*, Oxford: Philip Allan and Cambridge MA: MIT Press.

Lewis, M.K. and P.D. Mizen (2000), *Monetary Economics*, Oxford and New York: Oxford University Press.

Lewis, M.K. and R.H. Wallace (eds.) (1997), *The Australian Financial System: Evolution, Policy and Practice*, Melbourne, VIC: Addison Wesley Longman.

Leys, Colin (1965), 'What is the problem about corruption?', *Journal of Modern African Studies*, **3** (2), 215–24.

Leys, Simon (1997), *The Analects of Confucius*, translation, New York: W.W. Norton.

Lietaer, Bernard (2001), *The Future of Money*, London: Century, Random House.

Lindahl, Erik (1919), 'Just taxation – a positive solution', translated by Elizabeth Henderson in R.A. Musgrave and A.T. Peacock (1958), *Classics in the Theory of Public Finance*, London: Macmillan, pp. 168–76.

Lindert, Peter H. (1991), *International Economics*, 9th ed., Boston, MA: Irwin.

Lindholm, C. (1996), *The Islamic Middle East. An Historical Anthropology*, Oxford: Blackwell.

Locke, John (1690), *Two Treatises of Government*, London: Awnsham & John Churchill.

Lui, Francis T. (1985), 'An equilibrium queuing model of bribery', *Journal of Political Economy*, **93** (August), 760–81.

Lutz, Mark A. (2001), 'On the norm of equality', *International Journal of Social Economics*, **28** (10,11,12), 782–99.

Lutz, Mark A. and Kenneth Lux (1979), *The Challenge of Humanistic Economics*, Menlo Park, CA: Benjamin/Cummings Publishing.

Lybeck, Johan A. (1988), 'Comparing government growth rates: the non-institutional vs. the institutional approach', in J.A. Lybeck and M. Henrekson (eds), *Explaining the Growth of Government*, Amsterdam: North-Holland, pp. 29–47.

Macklem, Tiff (1994/95), 'Some macoeconomic implications of rising levels of governmernt debt', *Bank of Canada Review*, **94/95** (Winter), 41–60.

Mankiw, Gregory (2000), 'The savers-spenders theory of fiscal policy', AEA papers and proceedings, *American Economic Review*, **90** (2), 120–25.

Al-Mawardi, Abu al-Hasan 'Ali b. Muhammad (1985), *Al-Ahkam al-sultaniyah*, first published 1405, Beirut.

Mawdudi, S.A.A. (1974), *Tafhim al-Qur'an: An Understanding of Qur'an*, Lahore, Pakistan: Urdu Digest Printers.

Mawdudi, S.A.A. (1975), *The Economic Problem of Man and Its Islamic Solution*, Lahore, Pakistan: Islamic Publications, (original Urdu edition published 1947).

Mawdudi, S.A.A. (1994), *Economic System of Islam*, translated into English by Riaz Husain, edited by K. Ahmad, 2nd edn, Lahore, Pakistan: Islamic Publications.

Mawdudi, S.A.A. (1998), *Islami Riyasat*, original Urdu edition published 1967, Lahore, Pakistan: Islamic Publications.

Mawdudi, S.A.A. (2002), *Rasa'il-o Masa'il*, 4 vols., Lahore, Pakistan: Islamic Publications, v.1, 251.
Mauro, P. (1997), 'Why worry about corruption', *IMF Economic Issues No. 6*, Washington, DC: IMF.
McMillen, Michael J.T. (2007), ' Islamic project finance', in M. Kabir Hassan and M.K. Lewis (eds), *The Handbook of Islamic Banking*, Cheltenham, UK and Northampton, MA, USA: Edward Elgar, pp. 200–39.
Meltzer, A.H. (1988), *Carnegie-Rochester Conference Series on Public Policy*, **29**, 3–10, Amsterdam: North-Holland.
Mende, Tibor (1955), *South-East Asia between Two Worlds*, London: Turnstile Press.
Milgrom, Paul, and John Roberts (1992), *Economics, Organization and Management*, Englewood Cliffs, NJ: Prentice Hall.
Mill, J.S. (1848), *The Principles of Political Economy: With Some of Their Applications to Social Philosophy*, London: Parker.
Mill, J.S. (1869), *On Liberty,* London: Longman, Roberts and Green, accessed at Bartteby.com, 1999.
Miller, David (ed.) (1991), 'Justice', *The Blackwell Encyclopaedia of Political Thought*, Oxford: Blackwell Publishers, p. 260–63.
Mirrlees, James A. (1971), 'An exploration in the theory of optimum income taxation', *Review of Economic Studies*, **38** (2), 175–208.
Mises, Ludwig von (1949), *Human Action: A Treatise on Economics*, 4th revised edn, (1996) San Francisco, CA: Fox & Wilkes.
Mishan, E.J. (1969), *Welfare Economics: An Assessment, Professor Dr F. De Vries Lectures*, Amsterdam: North-Holland Publishing Company.
Modigliani, Franco, and Merton H. Miller (1958), 'The cost of capital, corporate finance, and the theory of investment', *American Economic Review*, **48** (3), 261–97.
Modigliani, Franco and Merton H. Miller (1963), 'Corporate income taxes and the cost of capital: correction', *American Economic Review*, **53** (3), 433–43.
Monks, R.A.G. and N. Minow (1995), *Corporate Governance*, Cambridge, MA: Oxford and Blackwell Business.
Mookherjee, Dilip and Ivan Png (1989), 'Optimal auditing, insurance, and redistribution', *Quarterly Journal of Economics*, **104**, 399–415.
Moore, M.P. (2007), 'How does taxation affect the quality of governance?', IDS working paper 280, Brighton: IDS, accessed 22 May, 2008 at www.ids.ac.uk/ids/bookshop/wp/wp280.pdf.
Morais, Richard C. (2007), 'Don't call it interest', *Forbes Asia*, July 23, 104–6.

Al-Mubarak, Muhammad (1973), *Ara' Ibn Taymiyyah fi'l-Dawlah*, Beirut: Dar al-Fikr.
Mueller, Dennis C. (1983), *The Political Economy of Growth*, New Haven, CT and London: Yale University Press.
Muller, Jerry Z. (1993), *Adam Smith in his Time and Ours: Designing the Decent Society*, New York: Free Press.
Muna, F.A. (1980), *The Arab Executive*, London: Macmillan.
Murphy, Kevin M., Andrei Shleifer and Robert W. Vishny (1991), 'The allocation of talent: implication for growth', *Quarterly Journal of Economics*, **106** (2), 503–30.
Murtuza, A. and W. Abdallah (2007), 'Islamic Muhtasib and American CPAs: a comparative study of institutions meant to protect public interest', *Journal of Accounting, Business & Management*, **14**, 41–52.
Musgrave, R.A. (1959), *The Theory of Public Finance*, New York: McGraw Hill.
Musgrave, R.A. (1976), 'ET, OT and SBT', *Journal of Public Economics*, **6** (1,2), 3–16.
Musgrave, R.A. (1981), *Fiscal Functions: Order and Politics*, Memphis, TN: P.K. Seidman Foundation.
Musgrave, Richard A. (1985), 'Public finance and distributive justice', in D. Greenaway and G.K. Shaw (eds), *Public Choice, Public Finance and Public Policy*, Oxford: Basil Blackwell.
Muslim (n.d.), *Sahih*, vol. 5, Cairo: Maktabah M. Ali Sabih.
Myers, Stewart and N.S. Majluf (1984), 'Corporate financing and investment decisions when firms have information that investors do not have', *Journal of Financial Economics*, **13** (2), 187–221.
Myles, Gareth D. (1995), *Public Economics*, Cambridge: Cambridge University Press.
Myrdal, Gunnar (1968), *Asian Drama: An Enquiry into the Poverty of Nations*, New York: Twentieth Century Fund.
Nasr, S.H. (1984), 'Islamic work ethics', *Hamdard Islamicus*, **7** (4), 25–35.
Nasr, S.H. (2002), 'The Qur'an and *Hadith* as a source and inspiration of Islamic philosophy', in S.H. Nasr (ed.), *Encyclopedia of Islamic Philosophy*, Part I, Lahore: Suhail Academy.
Nasr, S.V.R. (1994), *The Vanguard of the Islamic Revolution: The Jama at-i-Islami of Pakistan*, Berkeley, CA: University of California Press.
Nerlich, Graham (1989), *Values and Valuing: Speculations on the Ethical Life of Persons*, Oxford: Clarendon Press.
Nienhaus, Volker (2007), 'Governance of Islamic banks', in M. Kabir Hassan and M.K. Lewis (eds), *The Handbook of Islamic Banking*, Cheltenham, UK and Northampton, MA, USA: Edward Elgar, pp. 128–43.

Niskanen, W.A. (1992), 'The case for a new fiscal constitution', *Journal of Economic Perspectives*, **6** (2), 13–24.

Noonan, John T. Jr. (1993), 'Development in moral doctrine', *Theological Studies*, **54** (4), 662–77.

Nozick, R. (1974), *Anarchy, State and Utopia*, New York: Basic Books.

Nyazee, Imran Ahsan Khan (1999), *Islamic Law of Business Organisation: Partnerships*, New Delhi: Kitab Bhamn.

Nye, J S. (1967), 'Corruption and political development: a cost-benefit analysis', *American Political Science Review* **61** (2), 417–427, reprinted in Arnold J. Heidenheimer (ed.) (1970), *Political Corruption: Readings in Comparative Analysis*, New York: Holt, Rinehart and Winston, pp. 564–78.

Obaidullah, Mohammed (2007), 'Securitization in Islam', in M. Kabir Hassan and M.K. Lewis (eds), *The Handbook of Islamic Banking*, Cheltenham, UK and Northampton, MA, USA: Edward Elgar, pp. 191–9.

O'Brien, D.P. (1975), *The Classical Economists*, London: Oxford University Press.

OECD (Development Assistance Committee) (1993), *DAC Orientations on Participatory Development and Good Governance*, Paris: OECD.

OECD (1999), *OECD Principles of Corporate Governance*, Paris: OECD.

OECD (2000), *No Longer Business as Usual: Fighting Bribery and Corruption*, Paris: OECD.

Olson, Mancur (1982), *The Rise and Decline of Nations: Economic Growth, Stagflation and Social Rigidities*, New Haven, CT: Yale University Press.

Orr, Adrian, Malcolm Edey and Michael Kennedy (1995), 'Real long-term interest rates: the evidence from pooled time series', *OECD Economic Studies* 25, 1995/II, Paris: OECD, 76–107.

Osman, Nuhannad Fathi M. (1976), 'The juristic rules of conquered land and land taxation: Fay' and Kharaj, their origins and development in medieval Islam', PhD thesis, Near Eastern Studies, Princeton University.

Ostrom, E. (1999), 'Institutional rational choice: an assessment of the institutional analysis and development framework', in P.A. Sabatier (ed.), *Theories of the Policy Process*, Boulder, CA: Westview Press, pp. 35–71.

Palley, T. (2005), 'The questionable legacy of Alan Greenspan', *Challenge*, **48** (6), (November/December).

Pardy, R. (1992), 'Institutional reform in emerging securities markets', World Bank policy research working paper WPS 907, Washington, DC: World Bank.

Parker, R.H. and G.C. Harcourt (eds) (1969), *Readings in the Concept and Measurement of Income*, Cambridge: Cambridge University Press.
Peacock, A.T. and J. Wiseman (1961), *The Growth of Public Expenditure in the United Kingdom*, Oxford: Oxford University Press.
Pesek, B. and T.R. Saving (1967), *Money, Wealth and Economic Theory*, New York: Macmillan.
Phelps, Edmund S. (1968), 'Money–wage dynamics and labour-market equilibrium', *Journal of Political Economy*, **76** (August), 678–711.
Philip, Mark (1997), 'Defining political corruption', *Political Studies*, **45** (3) (special issue), 436–62.
Phillips, A.W. (1958), 'The relationship between unemployment and the rate of change of money wage rates in the United Kingdom, 1861–1957', *Economica*, **25**, 283–99.
Phillips, J.B. (1958), *The New Testament in Modern English, A Translation*, London: Collins.
Pickthall, Mohammed Marmaduke (translator) (1994), *The Meaning of the Glorious Qur'an*, New Delhi: Idara Isha'at-e-Diniyat.
Pigou, A.C. (1928), *Public Finance*, London: Macmillan.
Pigou, A.C. (1951), *A Study in Public Finance*, 3rd ed, London: Macmillan.
Popper, Karl R. (1959), *The Logic of Scientific Discovery*, London: Hutchinson.
Porta, D. Della and Y. Meny (1997), *Democracy and Corruption in Europe*, London: Pinter.
Pound, J. (1995), 'The promise of the governed corporation', *Harvard Business Review*, March-April, reprinted in *Corporate Governance* (2000), Cambridge, MA: Harvard Business School Press, pp. 79–103.
Qadir, Ghulam (1994), 'Interest-free banking: a proposal', in K. Ahmad (ed.), *Elimination of Riba from the Economy*, Islamabad: Institute of Policy Studies, 105–116.
Al-Qardawi, Allama Yusuf (1996), *Islam mayn Halalo Haram*, translated into Urdu by Shams Pirzada, first published 1960, Lahore, Pakistan: Islamic Publications.
Al-Qardawi, Allama Yusuf (1981), *Economic Security in Islam*, translated into English by Muhammad Iqbal Siddiqi. Lahore, Pakistan: Kazi Publications.
Al-Qardawi, Allama Yusuf (1983), *Fiqhuz Zakah*, vol. 1, translated into Urdu by Sajidur Rahman Siddiqi, 2nd edn, Lahore, Pakistan: Albadar Publications.
Al-Qardawi, Allama Yusuf (1984), *Fiqhuz Zakah*, vol. 2, translated into Urdu by Sajidur Rahman Siddiqi, 2nd edn, Lahore, Pakistan: Albadar Publications.
Al-Qardawi, Allama Yusuf (2003), *The Lawful and Prohibited in*

Islam, accessed 24 January 2003 at www.masmn.org/Books/Yusuf_Al_Qaradawi/The_Lawful_and_Prohibited_in_Islam.

Qureshi, Anwar Iqbal (1978), *Fiscal System of Islam*, Lahore: Institute of Islamic Culture, initial study sponsored by the Harvard Law School, International Program in Taxation.

Ra'ana, Irfan Mahmud (1991), *Economic System Under Umar The Great*, Lahore, Pakistan: Sh. Muhammad Ashraf.

Rahman, Abdul (1998), 'Issues in corporate accountability and governance: an Islamic perspective', *American Journal of Islamic Social Sciences*, **15** (1), 55–69.

Rahman, Fazlur G. (1964), 'Riba and interest', *Islamic Studies*, **3** (1), 1–43.

Rahman, Y.A. (1994), *Interest Free Islamic Banking*, Kuala Lumpur: Al-Hilal Publishing.

Ramsey, Frank P. (1927), 'A contribution to the theory of taxation', *Economic Journal*, **37** (145), 47–61.

Rangaswami, K. (1927), *Aspects of Ancient Indian Economic Thought*, Mylapore, India: Madras Law Journal Press.

Rawls, John (1971), *A Theory of Justice*, Cambridge, MA: Harvard University Press.

Redman, Deborah A. (1991), *Economics and the Philosophy of Science*, New York: Oxford University Press.

Ricardo, David (1820), letter to T.R. Malthus, dated 9 October, reproduced in David Ricardo, Piero Sraffra and Maurice Dobb (1952), *The Works and Correspondence of David Ricardo: Volume 8, Letters 1819–June 1821*, Cambridge: Cambridge University Press, pp. 278–9.

Ricardo, David (1888), *The Works of David Ricardo, with a Notice of the Life and Writings of the Author*, J.R. McCulloch (ed), London: John Murray.

Robbins, L. (1935), *An Essay on the Nature and Significance of Economic Science*, 2nd edn, London: Macmillan, accessed 11 December 2008 at http://mises.org/books/robbinsessay2.pdf.

Robertson, D.H. (1966), 'Some notes on the theory of interest', in *Essays in Money and Interest*, selected with a memoir by Sir John Hicks, London: Collins (The Fontana Library) pp. 202–22.

Robinson, Joan (1970), *Freedom and Necessity: An Introduction to the Study of Society*, New York: Pantheon of Random House.

Robinson, Joan (1978), *Contributions to Modern Economics*, New York: Academic Press.

Rogow, Arnold A. and Harold D. Lasswell (1963), *Power, Corruption and Rectitude*, Englewood Cliffs, NJ: Prentice Hall, pp. 132–4.

Rose-Ackerman, Susan (1975), 'The economics of corruption', *Journal of Public Economics*, **4** (2), 187–203.

Rose-Ackerman, Susan (1978), *Corruption: A Study of Political Economy*, New York: Academic Press.

Rose-Ackerman, Susan (1999), *Corruption and Government: Causes, Consequences, and Reform*, Cambridge: Cambridge University Press.

Rosen, Harvey S. (1995), *Public Finance*, 4th edn, Boston, MA: Irwin/ McGraw-Hill.

Rosly, Saiful Azhar, and Mahmood M. Sanusi (1999), 'The application of Bai-al-Inah and Bai-al-Dayn in Malaysian Islamic bonds: an Islamic analysis', *International Journal of Islamic Financial Services*, **1** (2), accessed 10 April, 2002 at http://islamic-finance.net/journal.html.

Rowbotham, Michael (2000), *Goodbye America! Globalisation, Debt and the Dollar Empire*, Annandale, NSW: Environook.

Russell, Bertrand (1961), *History of Western Philosophy*, new edn, London: George Allen & Unwin.

Saeed, A. (1996), *Islamic Banking and Interest: A Study of the Prohibition of Riba and its Contemporary Interpretation*, Leiden, Netherlands: E.J. Brill.

Salama, Abidin Ahmad (1995), 'Fiscal analysis of zakah with special reference to Saudi Arabia's experience in zakah', in *Readings in Public Finance in Islam*, Jeddah, Saudi Arabia: IRTI, IDB.

Samuelson, Paul A. (1954), 'The pure theory of public expenditure', *Review of Economics and Statistics*, **xxxvi** (4), November, 387–9.

Samuelson, Paul A. (1955), 'A diagrammatic exposition of a theory of public expenditure', *Review of Economics and Statistics*, **37**, 350–6.

Samuelson, P. (1997), *Where do the European and American Models Differ?*, temi di discussione, no. 320, November, Rome: Banca d'Italia.

Sandford, C.T. (1971), *Taxing Personal Wealth*, London: George Allen & Unwin.

Sandford, C.T. (2000), *Why Do Tax Systems Differ?*, Bath: Fiscal Publications.

Sandford, C.T., J.R.M Willis and D.J. Ironside (1975), *An Annual Wealth Tax*, London: Heinemann for the Institute of Fiscal Studies.

Al-Sayed, Abdul Malik A. (1982), *Social Ethics of Islam: Classical Islamic-Arabic Political Theory and Practice*, New York: Vantage Press.

Schacht, J. (1964), *An Introduction to Islamic Law*, Oxford: Oxford University Press.

Schamell, E.H. (1962), *Lindley on the Law of Partnership*, 12th edn, London: Sweet and Maxwell.

Schmoller, Gustav (1893), 'The idea of justice in political economy', *Annals of the American Academy of Political and Social Science*, vol. 4 (1893–4), German edition, *Jahrbuch fur Gesetzebung Vewallung, und Volkswirtschaft*, translated by Ernest Halle and Carl Schutz.

Schneider-Lenne, E.R. (1992), 'Corporate control in Germany', *Oxford Review of Economic Policy*, **8**, 13–35.
Schumpeter, J.A. (1934), *The Theory of Economic Development*, Cambridge, MA: Harvard University Press.
Schumpeter, J.A. (1954), *History of Economic Analysis*, London: George Allen & Unwin.
Seligman, Edwin R.A. (1931), *Essays in Taxation*, 10th edn, 1969 reprint, New York: Augustus M. Kelley.
Sen, A.K. (1982), *Poverty and Famines*, Oxford: Clarendon Press.
Sen, Amartya (1999), *Development as Freedom*, New York: Knopf.
Shahab, Rafiullah (1998), 'Ushri aur kharaji arazi: Pakistan main ushri nahin sirf kharaji zameen hai', in *Islam ka mu'ashi nizam*, Lahore, Pakistan: Maktaba Markazi Anjuman-e-Khuddam-ul-Qur'an, pp. 77–9.
Shaikh, M.A. (1988), 'Ethics of decision making in Islamic and Western environments', *American Journal of Islamic Social Sciences*, **5** (1), 115–28.
Shakow, David J., and Reed Shuldiner (2000), 'A comprehensive wealth tax', *Tax Law Review*, **53** (4), 499–584.
Sharfuddin, Abu'l Muhsin Muhammad (1995), 'Introduction', in *Kitab Al-Amwal*, Islamabad: Islamic Research Institute.
Al-Shatibi, Abu Ishaq Ibrahim (n.d.), *Al-Muwafiqat fi usul ak-Sharia'ah,* vol. II, Cairo: Maktabah al-Tijariah al-Kubra.
Sheehan, P.J. (1995), 'Reason, values and public policy', Centre for Strategic Economic Studies working paper, Victoria University of Technology, Melbourne.
Shirazi, I.M. (2001), *War, Peace and Non-Violence: An Islamic Perspective*, London: Fountain Books.
Shirazi, Nasim Shah (1996), *System of Zakat in Pakistan*, Islamabad: International Institute of Islamic Economics.
Shleifer, A. and R.W. Vishny (1993), 'Corruption', *Quarterly Journal of Economics*, **108** (August), 599–617.
Shleifer, A. and R.W. Vishny (1997), 'A survey of corporate governance', *Journal of Finance*, **52** (2), 737–83.
Siddiqi, M.N. (1980), 'Muslim economic thinking: a survey of contemporary literature'. in K. Ahmad (ed.), *Studies in Islamic Economics,* Leicester: Islamic Foundation, pp. 191–315.
Siddiqi, M.N. (1982), 'Islamic laws on riba and their economic implication', *International Journal of Middle East Studies*, **14** (11), 3–16.
Siddiqi, M.N. (1983), *Banking Without Interest*, Leicester: Islamic Foundation.
Siddiqi, M.N. (1996), *Role of the State in the Economy*, Leicester: Islamic Foundation.

Siddiqi, M.N. (2006), 'Freedom', entry prepared for *Encyclopedia of Islamic Economics*, Markfield: Islamic Foundation.

Simons, H.C. (1938), *Personal Income Taxation*, Chicago, IL: Chicago University Press.

Simon, M.C. (1998), 'The rise and fall of bank control in the United States: 1890–1939', *American Economic Review*, **88** (5), 1077–93.

Smirnov, A. (1996), 'Understanding justice in an Islamic context: some points of contrast with Western theories', *Philosophy East and West*, **46** (3), 337–50.

Smith, Adam (1759), *The Theory of Moral Sentiments*, eds. D.D. Raphael and A.L. Macfie, Glasgow edn (1976), Oxford: Oxford University Press.

Smith, Adam (1776), *The Wealth of Nations*, edited by E.A. Seligman (1966), (2 vols), Vol. 2. London: J.M. Dent & Sons, Everyman's Library.

Smith, Roger S. (1993), *Personal Wealth Taxation: Canadian Tax Policy in a Historical and International Setting*, Toronto, ON: Canadian Tax Foundation.

Sourial, M.S. (2004), 'Corporate governance in the Middle East and North Africa: an overview', mimeo, Cairo: Ministry of Foreign Trade.

Spengler, J. (1964), 'Economic thought of Islam: Ibn Khaldun', *Comparative Studies in Society and History*, **6** (3), 268–306.

Sterba, James P. (1992), 'Introduction', in *Justice: Alternative Political Perspectives*, Belmont, CA: Wadsworth Publications.

Stern, Nicholas (1976), 'On the specification of models of optimum income taxation', *Journal of Public Economics*, **6** (1,2), 123–62.

Stern, Nicholas (1987), 'The theory of optimal commodity and income taxation: an introduction', in D. Newbery and N. Stern (eds), *The Theory of Taxation for Developing Countries*, Oxford: Oxford University Press, pp. 22–59.

Stigler, G.J. (1971), 'The theory of economic regulation', *Bell Journal of Economics and Management*, **2** (1), 1–21.

Stiglitz, Joseph E. (1987), 'Pareto-efficient and optimal taxation and the new new welfare economics', in A.J. Auerbach and M. Feldstein (eds), *Handbook of Public Economics*, vol. 2, Amsterdam: Elsevier Science Publishers, pp. 991–1042.

Stiglitz, Joseph E. (1988), *Economics of the Public Sector*, 2nd edn, New York: W.W. Norton.

Stiglitz, Joseph E. (1994), *Whither Socialism?*, 2nd printing, MA, Cambridge: MIT Press.

Stiglitz, J.E. and A. Weiss (1981), 'Credit rationing in markets with imperfect information', *American Economic Review*, **71** (3), 393–410.

Stiglitz, J.E. and A. Weiss (1992), 'Asymmetric information in credit markets and its implications for macro-economics', *Oxford Economic Papers*, **44**, 694–724.

Stone W.E. (1969), 'Antecedents of the accounting profession', *Accounting Review*, April, 284–91.

Stork, M. (1999), *Guide to the Qur'an*, Singapore: Times Books International.

Sugden, Robert (1992), 'Social Justice', Chapter 18 in Shaun Hargreaves Heap, Martin Hollis, Bruce Lyons, Robert Sugden and Albert Weale (eds), *The Theory of Choice: A Critical Guide*, Oxford: Blackwell.

Suud, M. Abu (1980), 'The economic order within the general conception of the Islamic way of life', *Islamic Review*, **55** (2), 2426 & (3), 1114.

Al-Suyuti (1968), *Husn al-Muhadarah fi Muluk Misr wa'l Qahirah*, vol. 2, Cairo: Dar Ilhya'al-Kutub al-Arabiyyah.

Tag el-Din, S.I. (2006), 'Political background of the Islamic economic system', entry prepared for *Encyclopedia of Islamic Economics*, Markfield: Islamic Foundation.

Tag El-Din, Seif El-Din and N. Irwani Abdullah (2007), 'Issues of implementing Islamic hire-purchase in dual banking system: Malaysian experience', *Thunderbird International Business Review*, **49** (2), 225–49.

Tahir, Sayyid (1995), 'Fiscal implications of the elimination of riba', *Hikmat-e-Qur'an*, **14** (4) English section, 1–6.

Tahir, Sayyid *et al.* (1999), *IIIE's Blueprint of Islamic Financial System including Strategy for Elimination of Riba*, Islamabad: International Institute of Islamic Economics.

Tahir-ul-Qadri, Muhammad (1995), *Islamic Philosophy of Human Life*, Lahore, Pakistan: Minhaj-ul-Quran Publications.

Tanzi, Vito (1998), 'Corruption around the world: causes, consequences, scope, and cures', *IMF Staff Papers*, **45** (4), 559–94.

Tanzi, Vito (2000), *Policies, Institutions and the Dark Side of Economics*, Cheltenham, UK and Northampton, MA, USA: Edward Elgar.

Tanzi, Vito and Hamid R Davoodi (2000), 'Corruption, growth, and public finances', IMF working paper WP/00/182, November, Washington DC.

Tanzi, Vito and Howell H. Zee (2000), 'Tax policy for emerging markets: developing countries', *National Tax Journal*, **53** (2), 299–322.

Tariq, Arsalan and Humayon Dar (2007), 'Risks of *sukuk* structures: implications for resource mobilization', *Thunderbird International Business Review*, **49** (2), 203–23.

Tawney, R.H. (1926), *Religion and the Rise of Capitalism*, London and New York: Harcourt Brace.

Tawney, R.H. (1931), *Equality*, London: George Allen & Unwin.

Tawney, R.H. (1961), *Religion and the Rise of Capitalism*, originally published 1937, Harmondsworth: Penguin.

Taylor, Arthur J. (1972), *Laissez-faire and State Intervention in Nineeteenth-century Britain*, Macmillan: Economic History Society.

Taylor, Charles (1989), *Sources of the Self: The Making of the Modern Identity*, Cambridge, MA: Harvard University Press.

Thomson, J.A.K. (1953), *The Ethics of Aristotle*, translation, Harmondsworth: Penguin.

Tilman, Robert O. (1968), 'Emergence of black-market bureaucracy: administration, development, and corruption in the new states', *Public Administration Review*, **28** (5): 440–2.

Timmerman, Kenneth R. (1991), *The Death Lobby: How the West Armed Iraq*, Boston, MA: Houghton Mifflin.

Tinder, Glenn (1989), 'Can we be Good without God?' *Atlantic Monthly*, **264** (6), 69–85.

Toulmin, S. (1961), *Foresight and Understanding*, London: Hutchinson.

Toussaint, Eric (1999), *Your Money or Your Life! The Tyranny of Global Finance*, translated by Raghu Krishnan and Vicki Briault Manus, London, Dar-es-Salam: Pluto Press, Mkuki na Nyota Publishers.

Townsend, Robert M. (1979), 'Optimal contracts and competitive markets with costly state verification', *Journal of Economic Theory*, **21**, 265–93.

Toynbee, A.J. (1956), *A Study of History, vol. III, The Growth of Civilizations*, Oxford: Oxford University Press.

Tullock, G. (1965), *The Politics of Bureaucracy*, Washington, DC: Public Affairs Press.

Tullock, G. (1980), 'Rent seeking as a negative sum game', in J.M. Buchanan, R.D. Tollison and G. Tullock (eds) *Towards a Theory of the Rent Seeking Society*, College Station, TX: Texas A & M University Press, pp. 16–26.

Turner, Mark and David Hulme (1997), *Governance, Administration and Development*, London: Macmillan.

Udovitch, Abraham L. (1970), *Partnership and Profit in Medieval Islam*, Princeton, NJ: Princeton University Press.

Uhr, John (2006), 'Constitutions and rights', in B.G. Peters and J. Pierre (eds), *Handbook of Public Policy*, London: Sage Publications, pp. 169–85.

Ul Haq, I. (1995), *Economic Doctrines of Islam*, Islamabad: International Institute of Islamic Thought.

Usher, Dan (1992), *The Welfare Economics of Markets, Voting and Predation*, Manchester: Manchester University Press.

Usmani, Muhammad Taqi (2000), *An Introduction to Islamic Finance*, Karachi, Pakistan: Idaratul Maʾarif.

Veatch, Henry B. (1971), *For an Ontology of Morals: A Critique of Contemporary Ethical Theory*, Evanston, IL: Northwestern University Press.

Versi, Anver (1998), 'The new slavery', *African Business*, **233** (June), 7.

Vogel, F.E. and S.L. Hayes II (1998), *Islamic Law and Finance: Religion, Risk and Return*, The Hague: Kluwer Law International.

Wagner, Richard E. (1987), 'Liability rules, fiscal institutions, and the debt', in J.M. Buchanan, C.K. Rowley and R.D. Tollison (eds), *Deficits*, Oxford: Basil Blackwell, pp. 374–90.

Warde, Ibrahim (2000), *Islamic Finance in the Global Economy*, Edinburgh: Edinburgh University Press.

Watt, W.M. (1996), *A Short History of Islam*, Oxford: One World.

Weber, Max (1930), *The Protestant Ethic and the Spirit of Capitalism*, translated by Talcott Parsons (1996), Los Angeles, CA: Roxburg Publishing Co.

Wells, H.G. (1961), *The Outline of History*, London: Cassell.

Whittington G. (1992), 'Accounting and finance', in *The New Palgrave Dictionary of Money and Finance*, vol. 1, edited by P. Newman, M. Milgate and J. Eatwell, London: Macmillan, pp. 6–10.

Wicksell, Knut (1896), 'A new principle of just taxation', in R.A. Musgrave and A.T. Peacock (eds), *Classics in the Theory of Public Finance*, London: Macmillan, pp. 72–118.

Williamson, O.E. (1996), *The Mechanisms of Governance*, New York: Oxford University Press.

Wilson, R. (1983), *Banking and Finance in the Arab Middle East*, London: Macmillan.

Wilson, R. (2003), 'Islam and business ethics', *New Horizon*, **132**, (August/September), 15–16.

Winrich, J. Steven (1984), Self reference and the incomplete structure of neoclassical economics', *Journal of Economic Issues*, **18** (4) (December), 987–1005.

Wohlers-Scharf, T. (1983), *Arab and Islamic Banks: New Business Partners for Developing Countries*, Paris: OECD.

Wolf, T. and E. Gurgen (2000), 'Improving governance and fighting corruption in the Baltic and CIS countries: the role of the IMF', IMF working paper April (00/1), Washington, DC.

Wolfson, Dirk J. (1979), *Public Finance and Development Strategy*, Baltimore, MD: Johns Hopkins University Press.

World Bank (1997), *World Development Report (1997): The State in a Changing World*, New York: Oxford University Press.

World Bank (1999), *Culture in Sustainable Development. Investing in Cultural and Natural Endowments*, Washington, DC: IBRD.

World Development Report (2002), *Building Institutions for Markets*, New York: Oxford University Press.

Wueller, P.H. (1938), 'Concepts of taxable income: the German contribution', *Political Science Quarterly*, **LIII**, 1938, 83–110, reprinted in R.H. Parker and G.C. Harcourt (eds) (1969), *Readings in the Concept and Measurement of Income*, Cambridge: Cambridge University Press.

Yusuf, S.M. (1988), *Economic Justice in Islam*, New Delhi: Kitab Bhavan.

Zarqa, Muhammad Anas (1995), 'Islamic distributive schemes', in *Readings in Public Finance in Islam*, Jeddah, Saudi Arabia: Islamic Research and Training Institute, IDB, pp. 181–227.

Zarqa, Muhammad Anas (1980), 'Islamic economics: an approach to human welfare', in K. Ahmad (ed.), *Studies in Islamic Economics*, Leicester: Islamic Foundation.

Zee, Howell H. (1998), 'Taxation of financial capital in a globalised environment: the role of withholding taxes', *National Tax Journal*, **51** (3), 587–99.

Ziadeh, Nicola (1963), *al-Hisbah wa'l-Muhtasib fi'l Islam*, Beirut: Catholic Press.

Zweigert, K. and H. Kotz (1998), *An Introduction to Comparative Law*, 3rd edn, Oxford: Clarendon Press.

Index